Lecture Notes in Computer Science 6407

Commenced Publication in 1973
Founding and Former Series Editors:
Gerhard Goos, Juris Hartmanis, and Jan van Leeuwen

Bing Xie   Juergen Branke
S. Masoud Sadjadi   Daqing Zhang
Xingshe Zhou (Eds.)

Autonomic and Trusted Computing

7th International Conference, ATC 2010
Xi'an, China, October 26-29, 2010
Proceedings

 Springer

Volume Editors

Bing Xie
Peking University, Software Institute
YiHe Yuan Road 5, Haidian District, Beijing, 100871, P.R. China
E-mail: xiebing@sei.pku.edu.cn

Juergen Branke
University of Warwick, Warwick Business School
Coventry CV4 7AL, UK
E-mail: juergen.branke@wbs.ac.uk

S. Masoud Sadjadi
Florida International University, School of Computing and Information Sciences
11200 SW 8th St., Miami, FL 33199, USA
E-mail: sadjadi@cs.fiu.edu

Daqing Zhang
Institute TELECOM SudParis, Telecommunication Network and Services Dept.
9 rue Charles Fourier, 91011 Evry Cedex, France
E-mail: Daqing.Zhang@it-sudparis.eu

Xingshe Zhou
Northwestern Polytechnical University, School of Computer Science
Xi'an 710072, China
E-mail: zhouxs@nwpu.edu.cn

Library of Congress Control Number: 2010936709

CR Subject Classification (1998): D.2, C.2, D.4, H.3-4, K.6

LNCS Sublibrary: SL 2 – Programming and Software Engineering

ISSN	0302-9743
ISBN-10	3-642-16575-3 Springer Berlin Heidelberg New York
ISBN-13	978-3-642-16575-7 Springer Berlin Heidelberg New York

springer.com

© Springer-Verlag Berlin Heidelberg 2010
Printed in Germany

Typesetting: Camera-ready by author, data conversion by Scientific Publishing Services, Chennai, India
Printed on acid-free paper   06/3180

Preface

Computing systems including hardware, software, communication, and networks are becoming increasingly large and heterogeneous. In short, they have become increasingly complex. Such complexity is getting even more critical with the ubiquitous permeation of embedded devices and other pervasive systems. To cope with the growing and ubiquitous complexity, autonomic computing (AC) focuses on self-manageable computing and communication systems that exhibit self-awareness, self-configuration, self-optimization, self-healing, self-protection and other self-* properties to the maximum extent possible without human intervention or guidance. Organic computing (OC) additionally addresses adaptability, robustness, and controlled emergence as well as nature-inspired concepts for self-organization.

Any autonomic or organic system must be trustworthy to avoid the risk of losing control and retain confidence that the system will not fail. Trust and/or distrust relationships in the Internet and in pervasive infrastructures are key factors to enable dynamic interaction and cooperation of various users, systems, and services. Trusted/ trustworthy computing (TC) aims at making computing and communication systems—as well as services—available, predictable, traceable, controllable, assessable, sustainable, dependable, persistent, security/privacy protectable, etc.

A series of grand challenges exists to achieve practical autonomic or organic systems with truly trustworthy services. Started in 2005, ATC conferences have been held at Nagasaki (Japan), Vienna (Austria), Three Gorges (China), Hong Kong (China), Oslo (Norway) and Brisbane (Australia). The 2010 proceedings contain the papers presented at the 7th International Conference on Autonomic and Trusted Computing (ATC 2010), held in Xi'an, China, October 26–29, 2010.

This year, we received 68 submissions representing 20 countries and regions, from Asia, Europe, North America and the Pacific. All submissions were reviewed by at least three members of the Technical Program Committee. We accepted 20 submissions, corresponding to an acceptance rate of 29%. Besides the 20 regular and thoroughly reviewed papers, the proceedings includes three invited papers and two keynote abstracts. The first keynote was by Liu Zhen (Nokia Research Center, China) entitled "What Would Come After Location-Based Services?"; and the second keynote was by Huaimin Wang (National University of Defense Technology, China) entitled "Evaluation and Evolution of Trustworthy Software Based on Evidence of Software Lifecycle: A Practice Supported by Trustie in China."

We would like to thank all the researchers and practitioners who submitted their work to ATC 2010, organized a workshop, or helped in any other way to make the conference a success. Special thanks go to the 46 PC members for all their work evaluating the papers, which was highly appreciated and absolutely vital to ensure the high quality of the conference. We offer our sincere thanks to the Steering Committee, the Workshops Chairs and the Publicity Chairs for their strong support and active work. We also thank the Local Chairs Yuying Wang and Haipeng Wang from Northwestern Polytechnical University of China for all the miscellaneous work.

The conference is technically co-sponsored by Nokia and the Aviation Industry Corporation of China (AVIC). Last but not least, we would like to thank the Northwestern Polytechnical University for hosting the conference.

October 2010

Bing Xie
Juergen Branke
S. Masoud Sadjadi
Daqing Zhang
Xingshe Zhou

Organization

Honorary Chairs

Zhen Liu   Nokia Research Center, China
Christian Muller-Schloer   Leibniz University Hannover, Germany
Huaimin Wang   National University of Defense Technology, China

General Chairs

Raouf Boutaba   University of Waterloo, Canada
Daqing Zhang   Institut Télécom SudParis, France
Xingshe Zhou   Northwestern Polytechnic University, China

Program Chairs

Bing Xie   Peking University, China
Juergen Branke   University of Warwick, UK
S. Masoud Sadjadi   Florida International University, USA

Advisory Committee Chairs

Jean Camp   Indiana University, USA
Tharam Dillon   Curtin University of Technology, Australia
Hartmut Schmeck   Karlsruhe Institute of Technology, Germany

Workshops Chairs

Noura Limam   Pohang University of Science and Technology,
                               South Korea
Chunming Rong   University of Stavanger, Norway
Peidong Zhu   National University of Defense Technology, China

Program Vice Chairs

Yunwei Dong   Northwestern Polytechnic University, China
Xiaolin (Andy) Li   Oklahoma State University, USA
Xiaoguang Mao   National University of Defense Technology, China

Publicity Chairs

Carlos Becker Westphall   Federal University of Santa Catarina, Brazil
Onyeka Ezenwoye   South Dakota State University, USA
Qianxiang Wang   Peking University, China
Yan Wang   Macquarie University, Australia
Naixue Xiong   Georgia State University, USA

Panel Chair

Wolfgang Reif   University of Augsburg, Germany

Demo/Exhibition Chair

Alvin Chin   Nokia Research Center, Beijing China
Ming Zhao   Florida International University, USA

Award Chairs

Zhong Chen   Peking University, China
Juan Gonzalez Nieto   Queensland University of Technology, Australia

International Liaison Chairs

Hui-Huang Hsu   Tamkang University, Taiwan
Sajid Hussain   Acadia University, Canada
Junzhou Luo   Southeast University, China
Roy Sterritt   University of Ulster at Jordanstown, UK
Bin Xiao   Hong Kong Polytechnic University, HK

Industrial Liaison Chair

Martin Gilje Jaatun   SINTEF, Norway
Wensheng Niu   China Aeronautical Computing Institute, China

Financial and Local Arrangement Chair

Yuying Wang   Northwestern Polytechnic University, China

Web Administration Chair

Haipeng Wang   Northwestern Polytechnic University, China

Steering Committee

Jianhua Ma (Chair)	Hosei University, Japan
Laurence T. Yang (Chair)	St. Francis Xavier University, Canada
Jadwiga Indulska	University of Queensland, Australia
Hai Jin	Huazhong University of Science & Technology, China
Jeffrey J.P. Tsai	University of Illinois at Chicago, USA
Theo Ungerer	University of Augsburg, Germany

Program Committee

Lawrie Brown	Australian Defence Force Academy, Australia
Liqun Chen	HP Labs, UK
Alva L. Couch	Tufts University, USA
Dengguo Feng	Institute of Software, Chinese Academy of Sciences, China
Christopher Gill	Washington University, St. Louis, USA
Christophe Guéret	VU University Amsterdam, The Netherlands
Jinhua Guo	University of Michigan at Dearborn, USA
Peter Gutman	University of Auckland, New Zealand
Joerg Haehner	University of Hanover, Germany
Mike Hinchey	Irish Software Engineering Research Centre, Ireland
Ray Hunt	University of Canterbury, New Zealand
Xiaolong Jin	University of Bradford, UK
Audun Jøsang	University of Oslo, Norway
Sy-Yen Kuo	National Taiwan University, Taiwan
Miroslaw Kutylowski	Wroclaw University of Technology, Poland
Bo Lang	BeiHang University, China
Xiaolin (Andy) Li	Oklahoma State University, USA
Javier Lopez	University of Malaga, Spain
Antonio Maña Gomez	University of Malaga, Spain
Gregorio Martinez	University of Murcia, Spain
Daniel Merkle	University of Southern Denmark, Denmark
Martin Middendorf	University of Leipzig, Germany
Chris Mitchell	Royal Holloway, University of London, UK
Jan Newmarch	Monash University, Australia
Frank Ortmeier	Otto-von-Guericke-University, Germany
Guenther Pernul	University of Regensburg, Germany
Jason Reid	Queensland University of Technology, Australia
Martin Serrano	Waterford Institute of Technology, Ireland
Kuei-Ping Shih	Tamkang University, Taiwan
Kenichi Takahashi	Institute of Systems & Information Technologies, Japan
Juergen Teich	University of Erlangen-Nürnberg, Germany
Theo Ungerer	University of Augsburg, Germany
Guilin Wang	University of Birmingham, UK
Huaxiong Wang	Nanyang Technological University, Singapore
Yan Wang	Macquarie Unversity, Australia

Keynotes

What Would Come After Location-Based Services?

Zhen Liu

Nokia Research Center, Beijing, China
zhen.38.liu@nokia.com

Location-based services have become the most popular mobile services in recent years. A variety of mobile applications were developed and used which take advantage of users' location information. Compared to online services, location-based services have the advantage of allowing users to obtain information or services that are specific to their whereabouts.

In this talk, we discuss what would be the next wave of popular mobile services. We look at different possible directions of where mobile services will go, and provide arguments why some services which are for now still in their infancy will become the next most popular mobile services.

Evaluation and Evolution of Trustworthy Software Based on Evidence of Software Lifecycle: A Practice Supported by Trustie in China

Huaimin Wang

School of Computer Science
National University of Defense Technology, China
whm_w@163.com

The Internet era brings new challenges as well as opportunities to software technologies and again makes trustworthy software a hot topic. This talk probes into the concept of software trustworthiness by focusing on its objectivity and subjectivity, and clarifies two points: (1) trustworthy software is usually derived from the evolution processes in collaboration environments with a social-network foundation; (2) evidence of software lifecycle is fundamental for increasing the trustworthiness of software as well as for the evaluation of such trustworthiness.

This talk will thus introduce a conceptual architecture of an evidence-based software trustworthy evolution environment, together with its design challenges and principles. A practice in China toward such a promising environment called Trustie will be presented. Trustie is an online practical service environment for the large-scale collaborative production of trustworthy software on the Internet, which is composed of various key technologies and software production elements including a software collaboration platform, software resource repository, a software trustworthiness classification model and evidence framework, a software production line framework, and multiple spectrums of software tools and production lines.

Table of Contents

Autonomic and Organic Computing

AC/OC Network and Protocol

Trust Models and Application

Trustworthy Computing

Trust-Related Security

Invited Session

Self-organizing Computer Vision for Robust Object Tracking in Smart Cameras

Stefan Wildermann[1], Andreas Oetken[1], Jürgen Teich[1], and Zoran Salcic[2]

[1] University Erlangen-Nuremberg, Germany
{stefan.wildermann,andreas.oetken,juergen.teich}@cs.fau.de
[2] The University of Auckland, New Zealand
z.salcic@auckland.ac.nz

Abstract. Computer vision is one of the key research topics of modern computer science and finds application in manufacturing, surveillance, automotive, robotics, and sophisticated human-machine-interfaces. These applications require small and efficient solutions which are commonly provided as embedded systems. This means that there exist resource constraints, but also the need for increasing adaptivity and robustness. This paper proposes an autonomic computing framework for robust object tracking. A probabilistic tracking algorithm is combined with the use of multi-filter fusion of redundant image filters. The system can react on unpredictable changes in the environment through self-adaptation. Due to resource constraints, the number of filters actively used for tracking is limited. By means of self-organization, the system structure is re-organized to activate filters adequate for the current context. The proposed framework is designed for, but not limited to, embedded computer vision. Experimental evaluations demonstrate the benefit of the approach.

1 Introduction

The importance of computer vision systems has rapidly grown in recent years. As a motivational example, note that there are over 1,700 cameras installed in a typical Las Vegas casino, as stated in [1]. Keeping track of events is not possible without being supported by computer vision systems. Further fields of application are pose estimation of parts on an assembly line as well as automatic quality tests in industrial production, or performing vision tasks of a service robot. Computer vision also finds its way in our everyday life. Sophisticated human-machine-interfaces for game control [2] or virtual reality rely on such image processing techniques as face detection and object tracking. Moreover, camera-based approaches are of increasing importance in the automotive area, for example in advanced driver assistance systems.

The integration of advanced image sensor technology, processing units, and communication interfaces in an embedded system facilitates *smart cameras* [3] which are not only able to capture video sequences, but also to perform computer vision tasks and provide the extracted information via a network. There exists a

B. Xie et al. (Eds.): ATC 2010, LNCS 6407, pp. 1–16, 2010.

variety of different processing units used to build smart cameras, ranging from CPUs [4], over DSPs [5] and customizable processors [6] to FPGA platforms [1], [7], [8].

A challenge is that the cameras are operating in dynamic environments and thus facing unpredictable conditions. This means that illumination conditions may significantly differ due to night, bad weather, shadows, etc. Moreover, it cannot be guaranteed that cameras are always calibrated and installed with the same angles and orientation. Robustness and adaptivity become objectives in embedded computer vision as a consequence. One approach to increase robustness is to use not only one but several redundant image filter algorithms on the same input image. Embedded camera systems are, however, required to be small, cheap, and power efficient which induces resource, computational, and non-functional (example power) constraints. This means that not all available filters may be active at the same time due to these limitations.

This paper proposes a methodology to implement autonomic smart cameras for object tracking. The system designer provides a set of filter algorithms suitable for the object tracking task. The system then decides autonomically which filters to apply during operation depending on the environmental conditions and their performance in the current context. This autonomy also simplifies customizability of embedded computer vision systems, which is necessary to reduce time-to-market by re-using and extending pre-existing solutions: The system design can be changed, even during operation. The framework then organizes itself to integrate the new filter algorithms.

The paper is organized as follows. Section 2 presents related work in adaptive computer vision. Section 3 introduces the probabilistic tracking framework. Concepts for self-adaptivity and self-organization for the object tracking based on video input are presented in Section 4. The experimental evaluation of the proposed concept is provided in Section 5. Section 6 concludes this paper.

2   Related Work

A self-adaptive smart camera concept based on an FPGA platform is presented in [9]. However, no run-time reconfiguration is done in the architecture presented there. An architecture that uses hardware reconfiguration for image processing applications is presented in the AutoVision project [10] where image filters can be dynamically exchanged. However, reconfiguration is steered by predefined control events without using self-organizing properties.

[11] provides the *democratic integration* algorithm which is used to adapt weights in multi-cue fusion. In [12], this idea is adopted in combination with probabilistic tracking but does not apply the self-adapting behavior. In [13], this approach is modified by using a feedback loop to adapt the weights of the cues depending on their performance. The algorithm is only tested for a static system setup comprised of two image cues.

In this paper, we present a more flexible approach which combines probabilistic tracking with multi-cue fusion and self-adaptive and -organizing properties.

The approach results in an autonomic tracking framework which is designed for, but not limited to, embedded computer vision with resource constraints.

3 Tracking Using Multi-filter Fusion

This section gives an overview of the proposed system framework. It describes the probabilistic tracking algorithm and the multi-filter fusion approach. Self-adaptation and -organization are presented in more detail in the next section.

3.1 Overview

An overview of the proposed framework is given in Fig. 1. The framework combines several methods to achieve an autonomic computer vision system for object tracking. First, *multi-filter fusion* is applied which means to use not only a single, but several image filter algorithms on the same input frame. The set of all available filters provided by the designer is denoted as F. Due to resource constraints, only a subset of these filters can actively run at instant of time t, denoted as $F_{active,t} \subseteq F$. The *system* component illustrated in Fig. 1 contains each active filter $f_i \in F_{active,t}$ to process the input frame. This can be done

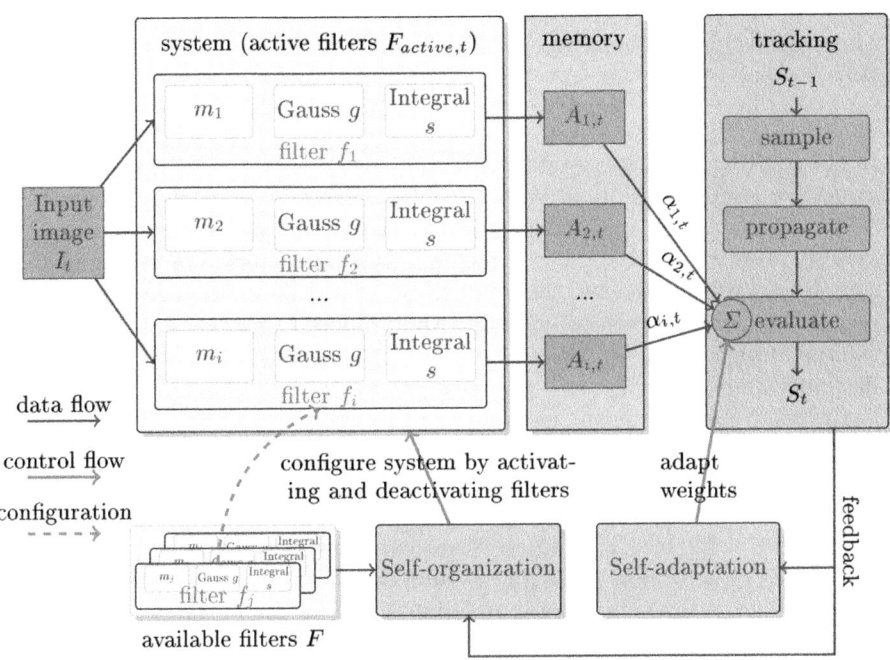

Fig. 1. Schematic overview of framework for robust tracking. Several filters are calculated on the same input image. Tracking is done by particle filtering which combines the filter results for evaluating the particles, illustrated by Σ. Self-adaptation dynamically updates the filter weights $\alpha_{i,t}$. Self-organization replaces image processing filters.

sequentially on a single processor, or in parallel on a multi-processor system or field-programmable platform. Our current research focuses on implementing this part on an FPGA-based system where hardware modules are dynamically reconfigured. Independent of this design decision, resource constraints exist, which allow to run only the subset of filters. The purpose of the *self-organization* component is therefore to reconfigure the system by deciding which filters should actively run in the system depending on their performance in the current context and the environmental conditions.

The filter results are combined by the *tracking* component. A probabilistic approach is chosen which has the advantage that tracking is always aware of the uncertainty of its own perception and can not only handle ambiguities and noisy sensor data, but also recover from errors.

Self-adaptation is introduced to deal with unpredictable changes in the environment. The purpose is to compensate if some of the filters show bad results by relying on the remaining ones instead. It evaluates the performance of the image filters and uses this to weight how much each filter should contribute to the tracking result, as already evaluated for a static embedded system in [9].

3.2   Particle Filtering

This section gives a brief introduction to Bayesian tracking and particle filtering. More details can be found in [14]. The *system model* describes how the system state x_t evolves over time:

$$x_t = g(x_{t-1}, \mathcal{N}_g). \tag{1}$$

In our tracking scenario, the state $x_t = (p_t, v_t, r_t)^T$ is the object's position p_t, its velocity v_t, and its size r_t at each instant of time t. $\mathcal{N}_g$ is a multivariate Gaussian random variable that models the system dynamics. The algorithm does not directly observe the object but percepts it by measurements y_t from image sensors. Both, sensor noise and the imprecision of applied image algorithms, induce uncertainty into this measurement. In the proposed framework, the feature extraction does not generate discrete object locations, but rather the non-Gaussian likelihood function $p(y_t|x_t)$.

Bayesian tracking means to build the posterior probability density function $p(x_t|y_{1:t})$ which represents the belief of the object state taking different possible values. It is built using the sequence of measurements from time 1 to t. Assume that we have tracked an object up until time instant $t-1$, when a measurement y_t becomes available. The object state can now be updated using the prior probability distribution $p(x_{t-1}|y_{t-1})$ and the measurement likelihood $p(y_t|x_t)$ by applying the theorem of total probability in Equ. 2 and Bayes rule in Equ. 3:

$$p(x_t|y_{1:t-1}) = \int p(x_t|x_{t-1})p(x_{t-1}|y_{1:t-1})\mathrm{d}x_{t-1} \tag{2}$$

$$p(x_t|y_{1:t}) = \eta \cdot p(y_t|x_t) \cdot p(x_t|y_{1:t-1}) \tag{3}$$

where η is a normalizing constant which can be ignored.

Particle filtering is a recursive filtering approach for Bayesian tracking. The measurements are processed sequentially without having to store the complete data from time 1 to t. The basic algorithmic framework that is also applied in our work is proposed in [15]. The posterior probability distribution is approximated by a set of N state samples with corresponding weights $S_t = \{\langle x_{j,t}, w_{j,t} \rangle\}$, where $j = 1, ..., N$ is used to identify different samples.

The filtering mechanism basically consists of three steps.

- In the *sampling* step, a set of hypothesis about possible object positions is generated by drawing samples from the particle set S_{t-1} according to their weights.
- The *propagation* step applies the system model of Equ. 1 to predict the new state of each drawn particle, corresponding to Equ. 2.
- The *evaluation* step evaluates each propagated sample based on measurements performed on the input image. The weight of each sample is set to the corresponding value of the measurement probability distribution $p(y_t|x_t)$ This step corresponds to Equ. 3.

3.3   Multi-cue Tracking Framework

As depicted in the schematic overview of the system architecture given in Fig. 1, the system consists of a set of active filters. Each filter $f_i \in F_{active,t}$ processes the input image I_t to produce an output image $A_{i,t}$. When performing the particle filtering, the results of these image filters are combined to evaluate the particles.

In our implementation, each image $A_{i,t}$ is generated by applying three filters, see Fig. 1:

$$A_{i,t} = (s \circ g \circ m_i)(I_t) \tag{4}$$

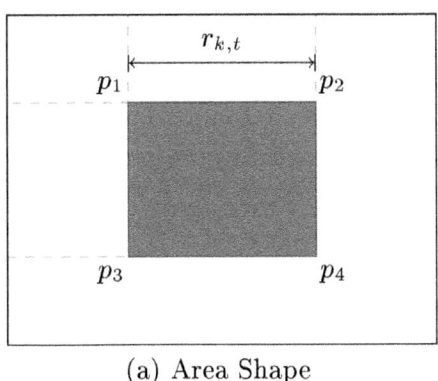

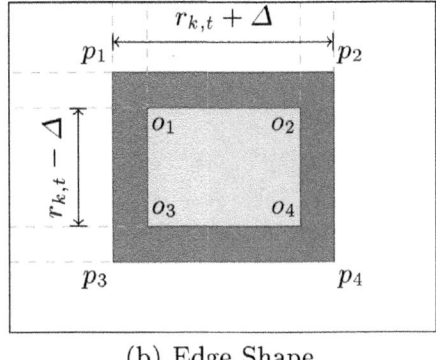

(a) Area Shape   (b) Edge Shape

Fig. 2. Integral images are used to (a) efficiently calculate the sum of pixel values within an rectangular area by just considering the values of the four corner points. Further shapes can be evaluated. (b) The edge shape is calculated by subtracting area p_1, p_2, p_3, p_4 from area o_1, o_2, o_3, o_4.

where m_i is the actual *classification filter* which extracts certain features from the image, g is a *Gaussian convolution* filter to smooth the image and reduce noise, and s generates the *integral image* which is described below. Each resulting image is stored in memory. Examples of possible image filters are given in the case study of Section 5.

The filter result $A_{i,t}$ of each active filter f_i is stored as an integral image. The integral image holds the sum of all pixel values in the rectangular area above and to the left of (x, y) in each pixel (x, y). The purpose of this image representation is to quickly calculate the accumulated pixel values in an arbitrary rectangular area. This is illustrated in Fig. 2(a): The sum of pixel values within the area comprised of corner points p_1, p_2, p_3, and p_4 in an integral image A is calculated as

$$pixel\_sum_A(p_1, p_2, p_3, p_4) = A(p_4) - A(p_2) - A(p_3) + A(p_1). \qquad (5)$$

This can be used to obtain sums within more complex shapes, as given in Fig. 2(b) for the edge shape.

Algorithm 1. Tracking Algorithm. Generates new particle set by sampling, propagation, and evaluation.

Require: filter results $A_{i,t}, \forall f_i \in F_{setup,t}$
Require: particle set S_{t-1}
1: $S_t = \emptyset$;
2: **for** $k = 1$ to $|S_{t-1}|$ **do**
3:        $\langle x_{j,t-1}, w_{j,t-1} \rangle = \text{sample}(S_{t-1});$ // Sample
4:        $x_{k,t} = g(x_{j,t-1} + \mathcal{N}_g);$ // Propagate
5:        **for each** filter $f_i \in F_{setup,t}$ **do** // Evaluate the new particle
6:                **Calculate** area or edge shape around position $p_{k,t}$ with size $r_{k,t}$:

$$pixel\_sum_i = eval(A_{i,t}, x_{k,t}) \qquad (6)$$

7:        **end for**
8:        $w_{k,t} = \eta \sum\limits_{f_i \in F_{setup,t}} \alpha_{i,t} \cdot pixel\_sum_i;$
9:        $S_t = S_t \cup \{\langle x_{k,t}, w_{k,t} \rangle\};$
10: **end for**

The outline of the tracking algorithm illustrated in Fig. 1 is shown in Algorithm 1. The new set of particles S_t is generated by first drawing samples from the previous set S_{t-1} according to their weights (line 3). Second, each drawn particle $s_{j,t}$ is propagated by a linear motion model together with a Gaussian diffusion to generate a new particle hypothesis $x_{k,t}$ (line 4) according to

$$x_{k,t} = \begin{pmatrix} 1 & 1 & 0 \\ 0 & 1 & 0 \\ 0 & 0 & 1 \end{pmatrix} \cdot x_{j,t-1} + \mathcal{N}_g. \qquad (7)$$

The new particle is then evaluated (line 6) by applying one of the shape patterns illustrated in Fig. 2. The filter designer provides which shape to choose for a filter.

The particle radius $r_{k,t}$ is used to determine the shape sizes. The values of the image filters are combined using a weighted sum (line 8) where $\alpha_{i,t}$ is the weight associated with image filter f_i. The index t is used because self-adaptation can change these weights during operation.

4   Self-Adaptation and Self-Organization

Section 3 described the basic components of the proposed framework for tracking. Further robustness is introduced by two additional concepts: self-adaptation and self-organization. There are various definitions of both concepts, e.g, [16], [17]. We use the following.

Definition 1. Self-adaptation *(SA) is the ability of a system to evolve a set of system parameters to adapt to changes of the system requirements and/or environment without being controlled or managed by an outside source.*

Self-adaption is performed to update the filter weights $\alpha_{i,t}$. There are three major reasons for this: First, the system is able to autonomously adapt to environmental changes. Second, it is possible to compensate failures of image filters by suppressing their contribution to the tracking result. Finally, this concept is necessary for self-organization where the system structure is altered which, as a consequence, requires an adaptation of the system parameters.

Definition 2. Self-organization *(SO) is the ability of a system to change its structure and/or behavior to become more organized in solving a task over time without being controlled or managed by an outside source.*

This follows the definition of [16]. In contrast to the definition of Mühl et al. [17], we do not require a decentralized control. Above definition is equivalent to their definition of *structure-adaptive systems*. In our work, *self-organization* is applied to determine the system configuration by means of selecting suitable image filters. The reason for this is that one set of filters may perform better than another set. It is possible not only to suppress erroneous filters, as done by adaptation, but also to take them out of the system and replace them with more adequate filters. The tracking result is obtained as feedback which indicates how the overall system performs, as well as how the individual active filters perform. This feedback is then used by to perform SA and SO.

4.1   Self-Adaptation

Self-adaptation is based on the performance of each filter, i.e., on each filter's contribution to the overall tracking result. The metric to measure this contribution is called *quality*. We propose the particle $\langle \hat{x}, \hat{w} \rangle \in S_t$ with the maximal particle weight as the feedback of the tracking component with the property

$$\forall \langle x_j, w_j \rangle \in S_t : w_j \leq \hat{w}. \tag{8}$$

Algorithm 2. Weight Adaptation Algorithm. Evolves the filter weights.

Require: filter results $A_{i,t}, \forall f_i \in F_{active,t}$
Require: max. particle $< \hat{x}, \hat{w} >$
 1: **if** $\hat{w} > \theta_{min}$ **then**
 2:    **calculate** $q_{i,t}^*$ according to Equ 9;
 3:    **normalize** by Equ. 11 $\forall f_i \in F_{active,t}$;
 4: **else**
 5:    $q_{i,t} = \frac{1}{|F_{active,t}|}, \forall f_i \in F_{active,t}$;
 6: **end if**
 7: $\alpha_{i,t+1} = \alpha_{i,t} + \lambda \cdot (q_{i,t} - \alpha_{i,t}), \forall f_i \in F_{active,t}$; // learn new values based on democratic integration

---

The adaptation is then performed as shown in Algorithm 2. The quality calculation is done in lines 1-6. If the tracking result $\hat{w}$ exceeds a predefined threshold θ_{min}, the tracking is assumed to have found a valid object. The quality is calculated for each filter (line 2) and then normalized (line 3). If $\hat{w}$, however, does not exceed that threshold, the system is steered towards re-initialization by setting all qualities to an equal value (line 5).

The quality calculation for a filter $f_i \in F_{active,t}$ is done according to

$$q_{i,t}^* = \max\{0, eval(A_{i,t}, \hat{x}) - avg(A_{i,t})\} \tag{9}$$

where the *max*-function ensures a non-negative result, *eval* evaluates the filter at the given position according to one of the shape patterns of Fig. 2, and *avg* calculates the average filter value[1]. Parameter update is done in line 7 by applying the democratic integration concept [11] using the normalized weights

$$q_{i,t} = \frac{q_{i,t}^*}{\sum\limits_{f_{j'} \in F_{active,t}} q_{j',t}^*}. \tag{11}$$

4.2   Self-Organization

Self-organization changes the system setup by replacing image filters. There are $\binom{n}{k}$ possible setups where n is the total number of possible filters and k is a number of filters that can operate at the same time. Tracking is a (soft) real time application, so we do not want to evaluate all of these possible setups during operation. We propose instead to individually determine how each module performs based on measuring its quality as well as the tracking results of setups it is part of. To do this, the system keeps track of the following properties for each module:

---

[1] Note that *avg* can be calculated efficiently using the integral image: Consider an image of size w × h. Since the last pixel of the integral image $A_{c,t}$ contains the sum of all pixel values, *avg* is calculated as

$$avg(A_{c,t}) = A_{c,t}(w - 1, h - 1)/(w \cdot h). \tag{10}$$

- $Q_{quality,i}$ is learned by the system by observing the qualities the filter f_i had during operation.
- $Q_{result,i}$ is learned by the system by observing the tracking results of system setups the filter f_i is part of.

Both values are initially set to 1. If f_i is part of the current system setup $F_{active,t}$ at time instant t, the module properties are updated according to

$$Q_{quality,i} = (1 - \beta) \cdot Q_{quality,i} + \beta \cdot q_{i,t} \tag{12}$$
$$Q_{result,i} = (1 - \beta) \cdot Q_{result,i} + \beta \cdot \hat{w} \tag{13}$$

where β is a *discount factor* that steers the learning process.

The overall performance of an image filter is represented by the *fitness* which combines both metrics:

$$fitness_c = Q_{quality,c} \cdot Q_{result,c}. \tag{14}$$

The proposed self-organization mechanism relies on exploration and exploitation, which are basic principles for unsupervised learning.

Exploration means to perform trial and error. Filters are randomly switched by activated and deactivating them. They are than evaluated to achieve new knowledge about their performance. This approach covers concepts like variation, risk taking, experimentation, and discovery [18].

Exploitation means to apply the knowledge achieved beforehand. The goal is to make active the most efficient filters, which have performed best so far. It includes such concepts as refinement, efficiency, and selection [18].

Of course, both concepts have a tradeoff. Adaptive systems which only perform exploration can never benefit from the information gathered by experiments. On the other hand, systems solely engaging in exploitation are likely to be trapped in a suboptimal equilibrium. As a result, it is necessary to include both concepts into learning frameworks for self-organization. Moreover, the additional inclusion of self-adaptation and multi-filter fusion mechanisms in the proposed framework may help in reducing the risks of exploration by compensating decisions when flawed or inefficient modules are included. The ratio between exploration and exploitation is steered by $p_{exploit}$ which defines the probability of choosing exploitation in a system re-organization step.

Algorithm 3 outlines the basic self-organization process. A system re-organization is possible at the earliest $\theta_{changed}$ time steps after having performed the previous modification at time step t_{mod}. This is required to give the system some time to evaluate the quality of the new filters in the current context.

No modification is required if the system efficiently manages to track an object. The measure of efficiency, denoted N_{eff}, depends on the number of image filters effectively contributing to the tracking result and is defined as

$$N_{eff} = \frac{1}{\sum\limits_{f_i \in F_{active,t}} (q_{i,t})^2}. \tag{15}$$

Algorithm 3. Self-organization Algorithm. Exchange image filters if necessary.

Require: normalized filter qualities $q_{i,t}$, $1 \leq i \leq N$
Require: particle set S_{t-1}
1: **if** $t - t_{mod} > \theta_{mod}$ **then**
2:      **calculate** effective number of active image filters N_{eff}.
3:      **if** $\hat{w} < \theta_{min}$ **or** $N_{eff} < \theta_{eff}$ **then**
4:          **generate** random number $rnd \in [0, 1]$;
5:          **if** $rnd \leq p_{exploit}$ **then**
6:              doExploitation();
7:          **else**
8:              doExploration();
9:          **end if**
10:         $t_{mod} = t$;
11:     **end if**
12: **end if**

It is based on the normalized quality measures. System re-organization is performed if N_{eff} or the tracking result $\hat{w}$ are below predefined thresholds (line 3).

The basic behavior of both approaches is similar: First, the active filter $f_{rem} \in F_{active,t}$ with the lowest weight α_{rem} is selected. Then, an inactive module $f_{add} \in F \setminus F_{active,t}$ is determined which replaces f_{rem}. Exploration selects one of the modules with uniform probability. Exploitation selects the modules with probabilities proportional to their fitnesses.

Replacement works by removing the filter module of f_{rem} from the setup and add the module of f_{add}. The same weight as the one of the removed module is taken for the new one $\alpha_{add,t+1} = \alpha_{rem,t}$. This is possible since self-adaptation finds the new setting of the weights.

5   Experimental Results

We want to illustrate the idea of the proposed framework by applying it to *human motion tracking* in which we use the following image filters:

- *Skin color classification* classifies each pixel as either skin color or non-skin color [19]. We use classification in RGB and YCbCr color spaces. The area shape is used for particle evaluation.
- *Background subtraction* learns a background model which is subtracted from the current image to obtain foreground objects. The area shape is used for particle evaluation.
- *Motion detection* subtracts the previous frame from the current input image to detect moving object. Since motion is commonly detected on the edges of the object, the edge shape is applied for particle evaluation.
- *Edge detection* identifies edges in the image by applying the Canny edge detector. The edge shape is used for particle evaluation.

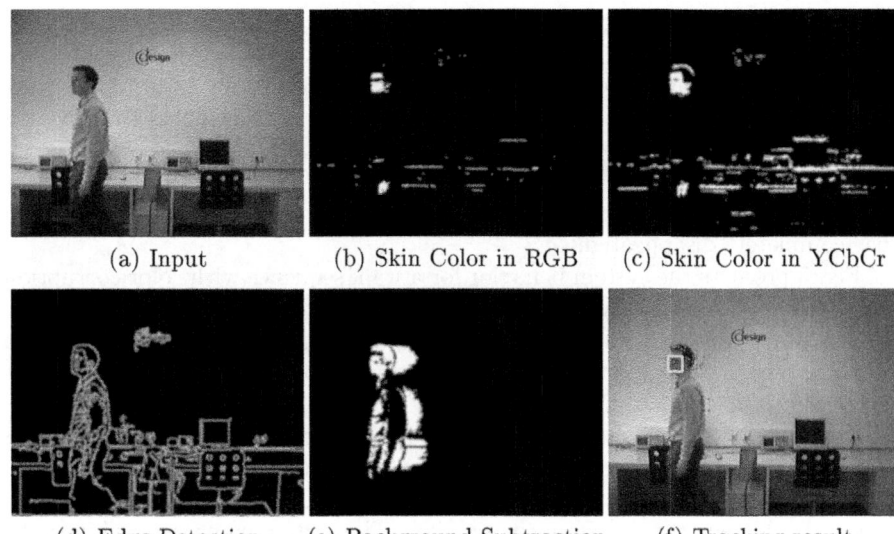

(a) Input	(b) Skin Color in RGB	(c) Skin Color in YCbCr
(d) Edge Detection	(e) Background Subtraction	(f) Tracking result

Fig. 3. Examples of a tracking result. Four filters are combined which where selected online by the self-organizing component. The particles radius and color depends on their weight. The position and size of the particle with maximal weight is indicated by the rectangle.

- *Sobel filters* calculating the horizontal and the vertical derivative approximations are included, using the edge shape for particle evaluation.

Examples of the use of some of the above image filters are shown in Fig. 3.

The presented methodology is tailored for FPGA-based smart cameras. We have developed a prototype. Due to space limitations, we only provide a brief overview of this prototype. It is based on an FPGA using the *ReCoBus* technology [20]. It consists of a CPU sub-system managing the control flow and running parts of the tracking framework. The system also consists of a dynamic hardware part which supports partial reconfiguration. This makes it possible to replace hardware modules at run-time. Modules for above filters were developed. The reconfiguration times of the modules on the proposed FPGA-based system-on-chip are 13.5 ms, leaving sufficient time for one module reconfiguration per image frame. Moreover, the platform uses four ReCoBus bus macros allowing to run four filters concurrently.

To test the proposed methodology independent of the embedded platform, the tracking system has been implemented in software. It is applied to several walking sequences which can be classified into four scenarios:

(A) Person continuously walking through the scene.
(B) Person walking through the scene, but stops walking for a while.
(C) Color corruption of the input video stream.
(D) A combination of the three above scenarios.

We implemented the system with $N = 200$, $\theta_{min} = 60$, $\lambda = 0.2$, $\theta_{mod} = 20$, $p_{exploit} = 0.80$, and $\beta = 0.2$. The qualities of the filters as well as their fitnesses are measured for each time instant. Fig. 4 shows the results for a continuous walk sequence. The person enters around frame 200. The system notices the person when the tracking result exceeds the threshold θ_{min}. The skin color filters are loaded into the system and have the highest contribution until the person reaches the edge of the frame. Here, the background subtraction works until the person has completely disappeared.

Fig. 5 presents the system behavior for a walk sequence with color corruption appearing at frame 170 where it is switched to gray scale. as can be seen, the system starts to re-organize when the corruption happens. This re-organization is performed until the color filters are removed from the system and a more adequate setup is determined.

Fig. 6 shows the results for a walk sequence where the person stops walking around frame 230, waits, and then proceeds walking again around frame 330. The skin color filters work together with background subtraction until the person stops. At this point, the system re-organizes. The system manages tracking with the skin color and the edge detection filters.

Finally, Fig. 7 shows the results of a sequence where three persons cross the scene. The person enters around frame 150 and crosses the scene. Skin color and background subtraction perform best. As in test-case (A), the color filters have a problem when the person reaches the border of the frame. Background subtraction performs best at this point and gets the highest fitness shown in Fig. 7(c). A person enters a second time between frames 500 and 700. Here, a

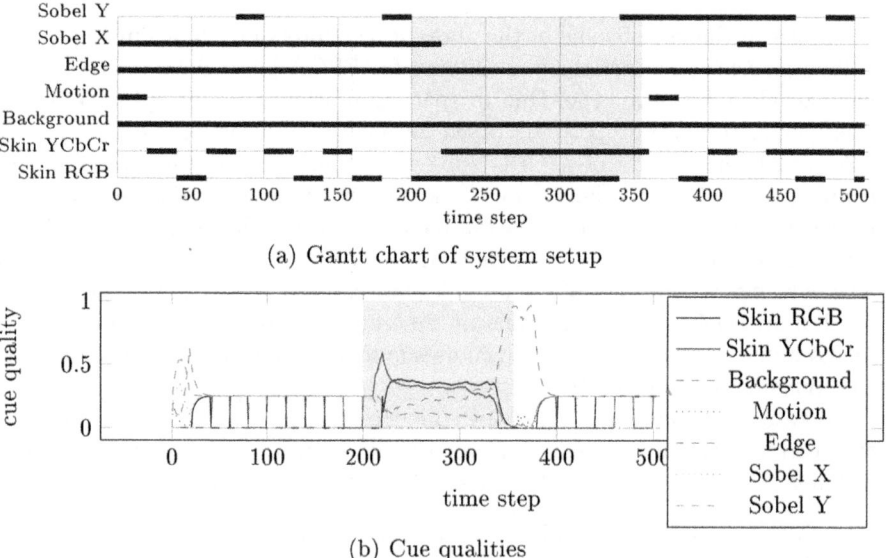

(a) Gantt chart of system setup

(b) Cue qualities

Fig. 4. Gantt chart and cue qualities for test case (A)

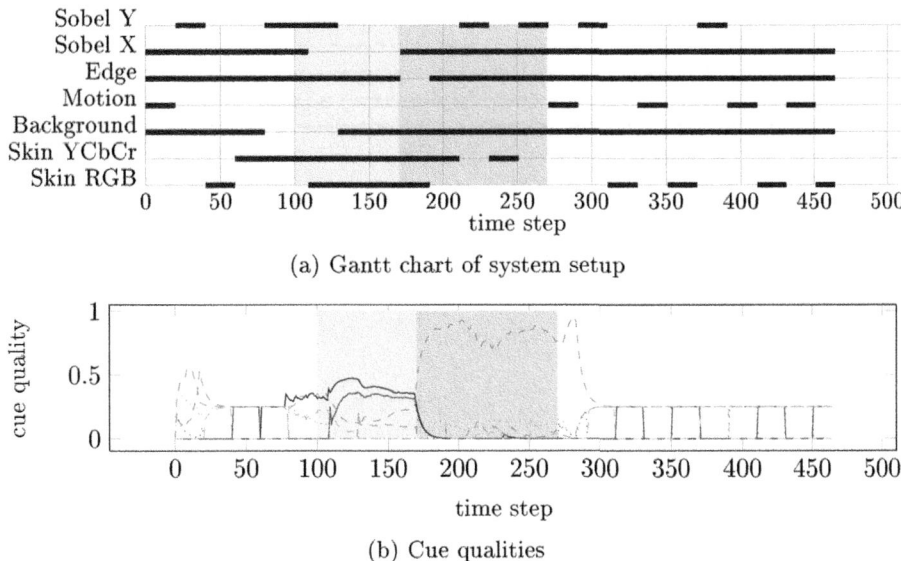

(a) Gantt chart of system setup

(b) Cue qualities

Fig. 5. Gantt chart and cue qualities for test case (B) (legend see Fig. 4)

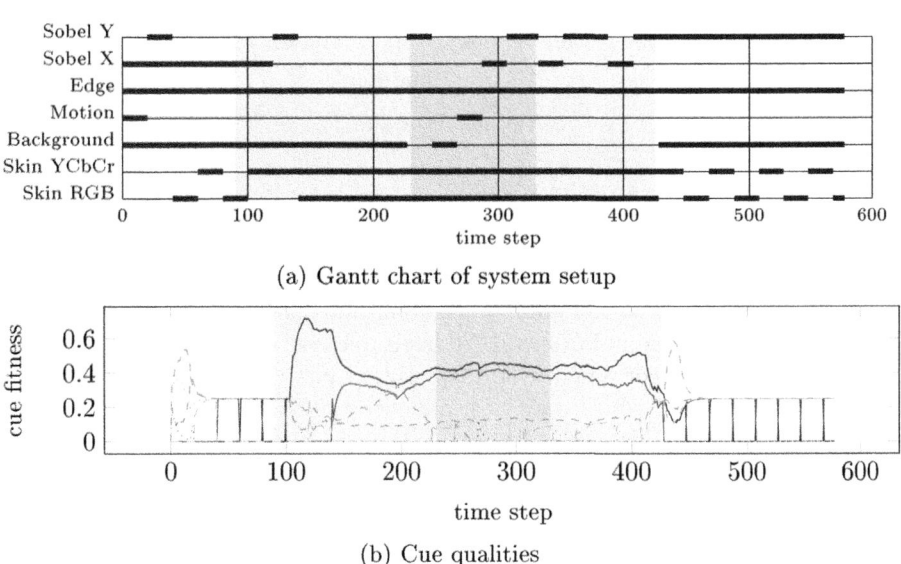

(a) Gantt chart of system setup

(b) Cue qualities

Fig. 6. Gantt chart and cue qualities for test case (C) (legend see Fig. 4)

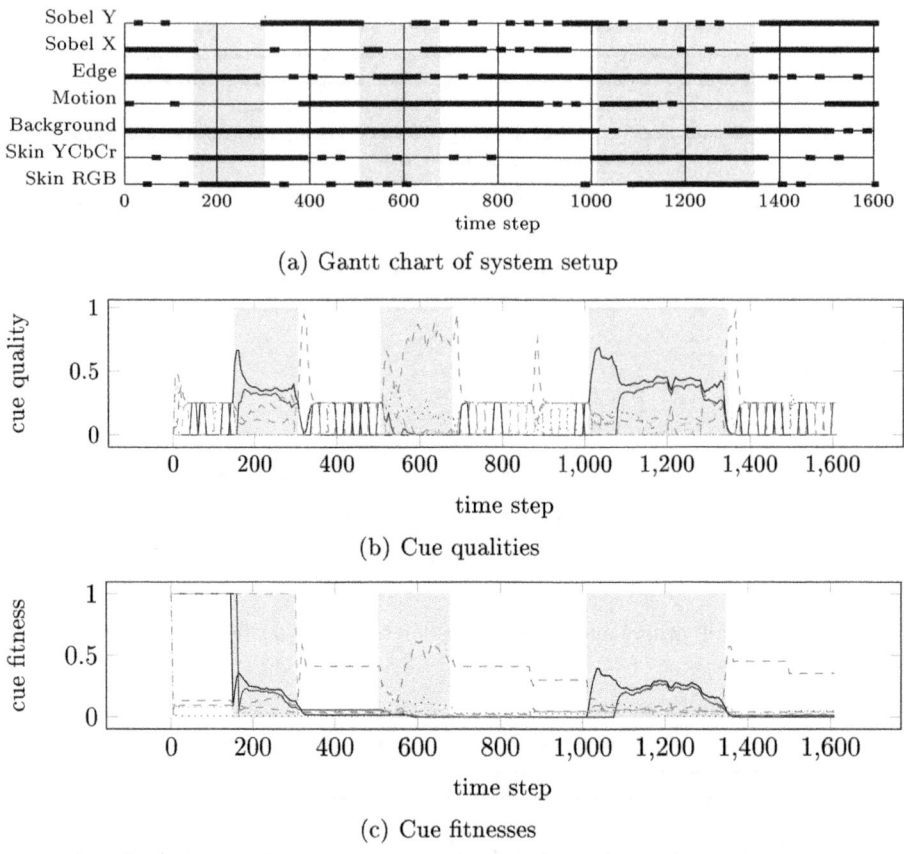

(a) Gantt chart of system setup

(b) Cue qualities

(c) Cue fitnesses

Fig. 7. Gantt chart, cue qualities and fitnesses for test case (D) (legend see Fig. 4)

temporal color corruption occurs. This does not have an effect on tracking since the system relies on background subtraction and motion detection. A person enters a third time around frame 950. This is detected at frame 1,000 where the system loads skin color again in an exploration phase. The person temporally stops at frame 1,200 which does not influence the tracking result because the color filters have the highest weight.

6   Conclusion

This paper proposed an autonomic computing framework for robust object tracking as a part of smart camera system. This is achieved by using a Bayesian tracking approach and combining it with multi-filter fusion. Self-adaption reacts on environmental conditions by changing the contribution of each filter. An additional self-organization component is included which is necessary to satisfy resource constraints. Experimental results demonstrate that the mechanism chooses a set of image filters which meet the requirements of the current environmental conditions.

In future work, we want to add adaptable classifiers in the system which can be trained online during tracking. We furthermore intend to investigate various computer architectures for building such autonomic computer vision systems and meet specific design requirements, especially targeting embedded real-time operation.

Acknowledgment

This research was supported in part by FuE-Programm "Informations- und Kommunikationstechnik" IUK-0706-0003 in Bavaria, Germany.

References

1. Fleck, S., Busch, F., Straßer, W.: Adaptive probabilistic tracking embedded in smart cameras for distributed surveillance in a 3d model. Embedded Systems 2007(1), 24–24 (2007)
2. Microsoft's Project Natal-Homepage,
   http://www.xbox.com/en-US/live/projectnatal/
3. Wolf, W., Ozer, B., Lv, T.: Smart cameras as embedded systems. Computer 35(9), 48–53 (2002)
4. Rowe, A., Goode, A.G., Goel, D., Nourbakhsh, I.: CMUcam3: An open programmable embedded vision sensor. Technical Report CMU-RI-TR-07-13, Robotics Institute, Pittsburgh, PA (May 2007)
5. Bramberger, M., Brunner, J., Rinner, B., Schwabach, H.: Real-time video analysis on an embedded smart camera for traffic surveillance. In: Proceedings of RTAS 2004, p. 174. IEEE Computer Society Press, Los Alamitos (2004)
6. Wang, G., Salcic, Z., Biglari-Abhari, M.: Customizing multiprocessor implementation of an automated video surveillance system. EURASIP J. Embedded Syst. 2006(1), 1–12 (2006)
7. Johnston, C.T., Gribbon, K.T., Bailey, D.G.: FPGA based remote object tracking for real-time control. In: International Conference on Sensing Technology, pp. 66–72 (2005)
8. Schlessman, J., Chen, C.Y., Wolf, W., Ozer, B., Fujino, K., Itoh, K.: Hardware software co-design of an FPGA-based embedded tracking system. In: Proceedings of CVPRW 2006, p. 123. IEEE Computer Society Press, Los Alamitos (2006)
9. Wildermann, S., Walla, G., Ziermann, T., Teich, J.: Self-organizing multi-cue fusion for FPGA-based embedded imaging. In: Proceedings of FPL 2009, Prague, Czech Republic, pp. 132–137 (2009)
10. Alt, N., Claus, C., Stechele, W.: Hardware software architecture of an algorithm for vision-based real-time vehicle detection in dark environments. In: Proceedings of DATE 2008, pp. 176–181. ACM, New York (2008)
11. Triesch, J., Malsburg, C.V.D.: Democratic integration: Self-organized integration of adaptive cues. Neural Computing 13(9), 2049–2074 (2001)
12. Spengler, M., Schiele, B.: Towards robust multi-cue integration for visual tracking. In: Proceedings of ICVS 2001, pp. 93–106. Springer, Heidelberg (2001)

13. Shen, C., Hengel, A.V.D., Dick, A.: Probabilistic multiple cue integration for particle filter based tracking. In: Proceedings of Digital Image Computing: Techniques and Applications, pp. 10–12 (2003)
14. Arulampalam, S., Maskell, S., Gordon, N., Clapp, T.: A tutorial on particle filters for online nonlinear non-gaussian bayesian tracking. IEEE Transactions on Signal Processing 50, 174–188 (2002)
15. Isard, M., Blake, A.: Condensation—conditional density propagation for visual tracking. Journal on Computer Vision 29(1), 5–28 (1998)
16. Cakar, E., Mnif, M., Müller-Schloer, C., Richter, U., Schmeck, H.: Towards a quantitative notion of self-organisation. In: IEEE Congress on Evolutionary Computation, pp. 4222–4229 (2007)
17. Mühl, G., Werner, M., Jaeger, M.A., Herrmann, K., Parzyjegla, H.: On the definitions of self-managing and self-organizing systems. In: KiVS 2007 Workshop: Selbstorganisierende, Adaptive, Kontextsensitive verteilte Systeme (SAKS 2007), pp. 291–301. VDE Verlag (March 2007)
18. March, J.G.: Exploration and exploitation in organizational learning. Organization Science 2(1), 71–87 (1991)
19. Vezhnevets, V., Sazonov, V., Andreeva, A.: A survey on pixel-based skin color detection techniques. In: Proceedings of Graphicon, pp. 85–92 (2003)
20. Koch, D., Beckhoff, C., Teich, J.: Recobus-builder a novel tool and technique to build statically and dynamically reconfigurable systems for FPGAs. In: Proceedings of FPL 2008, pp. 119–124 (September 2008)

A Formal Framework for Compositional Verification of Organic Computing Systems*

Florian Nafz, Hella Seebach, Jan-Philipp Steghöfer,
Simon Bäumler, and Wolfgang Reif

Department of Software Engineering and Programming Languages,
University of Augsburg, 86135 Augsburg, Germany
{nafz,seebach,steghoefer,baeumler,reif}@informatik.uni-augsburg.de

Abstract. Because of their self-x properties Organic Computing systems are hard to verify. Nevertheless in safety critical domains one may want to give behavioral guarantees. One technique to reduce complexity of the overall verification task is applying composition theorem. In this paper we present a technique for formal specification and compositional verification of Organic Computing systems. Separation of self-x and functional behavior has amongst others, advantages for the formal specification. We present how the specification of self-x behavior can be integrated into an approach for compositional verification of concurrent systems, based on Interval Temporal Logic. The presented approach has full tool support with the KIV interactive theorem prover.

Keywords: Organic Computing, Formal Methods, Compositional Reasoning.

1 Introduction

In Organic Computing (OC) systems [24], a potentially vast number of components interact with each other and make local decisions in order to fulfill global goals. Such systems are highly desirable as they exhibit characteristics of self-organization and are therefore highly resilient, adaptive and robust. Therefore, they should be ideally suited for environments in which safety is a critical concern and those characteristics are requirements of the domain.

However, such domains usually require a rigorous process of analysis and verification in order to get a system approved for deployment. In automotive and aviation systems, certification authorities require proof that a system behaves safely under all circumstances. Such a proof is more often than not provided by formal analysis and verification. But due to the dynamic, complex, and highly-parallel nature of Organic Computing systems, such an analysis is extremely hard to perform and many tools and techniques (e.g., model checking) are not suitable for sufficiently large examples.

This paper introduces a different approach: "conventional" complex systems have been analyzed with compositional methods in which parts of the system are regarded separately before the analyses are combined to make statements for the entire system.

---

* This work is partly sponsored by the German Research Foundation (DFG) in the special priority program SPP 1183 "Organic Computing".

B. Xie et al. (Eds.): ATC 2010, LNCS 6407, pp. 17–31, 2010.

This compositional and local reasoning is now applied to OC-systems whose correct behavior can be expressed by rely/guarantees [18,22,7]. These systems can be modularized in a natural way as they usually consist of several components (e.g. agents).

For this purpose, self-organization behavior and functional behavior are regarded separately. The functional behavior can then be expressed as rely/guarantees and be verified with a compositional technique. Especially one wants to guarantee that after a reconfiguration the system again works as intended. This property is a safety property [2]. In this paper we present an approach for verification of this kind of properties. The specification of functional behavior with rely/guarantees for systems and the integration of the self-x behavior into the environment is shown. The approach is applied to self-organizing resource-flow systems, a system class in which self-x principles are beneficial.

Previous work included formal analysis of failure modes for OC-systems which only applied to specific instances of a system and was therefore limited [15]. Further, separation of self-organization and functional behavior was not considered. The general approach to formally specify a system with invariants which express correct system behavior has been detailed in [14] and a way to use these invariants for a reconfiguration mechanism has been proposed in [25]. The present paper builds on these foundations and provides the formal framework which is necessary to thoroughly and rigorously analyze and verify such OC-systems.

The paper is structured as follows: Section 2 describes the formal framework as the foundation of the verification approach which is introduced in Section 3. The technique is then applied to self-organizing resource-flow systems in Section 4 where a formal model is given and the necessary specification and verification steps are sketched. Section 5 compares the approach with related work before the paper closes with a discussion of the benefits and limitations of the proposed framework and an outlook to future work.

2   Formal Framework

In this section we provide an overview of the formal framework we use for modeling and verification of Organic Computing systems. We will start by giving an introduction into the logic framework and its semantics. Afterwards we show how to define behavioral corridors on the system model to exclude unwanted behavior. This technique also allows to separate functional behavior from self-x behavior of the system, which has several advantages for system verification.

2.1   Temporal Logic Framework

In the following, an informal overview over the temporal logic calculus used is given, which is also integrated in the interactive theorem prover KIV [5]. A formal semantics and a detailed description can be found in [6,4].

The used temporal logic (ITL$^+$) is a variant of interval temporal logic (ITL) [23,9] that is extended by explicitly including the behavior of the environment into each step. Further ITL$^+$ combines temporal formulas and program constructs within the same formalism. The basis for ITL$^+$ are infinite sequences[1] π of states, which are called *traces* or *intervals*. A state σ is defined by one evaluation $e \in eval(v_1,...,v_n)$, where $eval(V)$ is the set of all possible evaluation of the variables $v_i \in V$.

In our setting we introduce an additional intermediate state σ'_i to distinguish between system and environment transitions. Therefore besides variables v there are also *primed* v' and *double primed* v'' variables. For each variable v *in* V there is a corresponding primed and double primed variable. The sets of all primed/double primed variables is denoted accordingly by V' and V''. The relation between v and v' is called *system transition*, whereas the relation between v' and v'' *environment transition*. The value of v'' in a state must be equal to the value of v in the next successive state ($\sigma''_0 = \sigma_1$). Thereby the system and the environment transition alternate. For an intuition this is depicted in Figure 1.

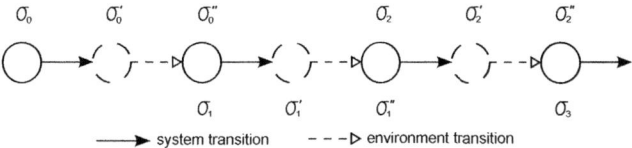

Fig. 1. A trace as sequence of states

The explicit inclusion of the environment allows for a separation of system and environment. Further, an arbitrary environment is considered without stipulating syntactic restrictions for the formula describing the system behavior. Especially in the case of OC-systems which interact with their environment, an explicit model of the behavior of the environment is advantageous [30]. It allows a detailed modeling of the environments properties and the interaction between system and its environment.

The logic contains the standard predicate logic operators $\neg$ (not), $\wedge$ (and), $\vee$ (or), $\rightarrow$ (implies), $\leftrightarrow$ (equivalence) and quantifiers $\forall, \exists$. Predicate logic formulas however are only evaluated over a triple of states σ_i, σ'_i and σ''_i. For example $p(V, V')$ denotes a predicate which is evaluated over the unprimed and primed state. To express properties over intervals the following operators – which are also standard operators in linear temporal logic (LTL) – can be used.

$\square\ \varphi$	φ holds now and *always* in the future
$\Diamond\ \varphi$	φ holds now or *eventually* in the future
φ **until** ψ	ψ eventually holds and φ holds *until* ψ holds
φ **unless** ψ	always if φ does not hold, then ψ holds or ψ held earlier
$\circ\ \varphi$	there is a next step which satisfies φ (*strong next*)
last	the current state is the *last*
$\varphi_1 \parallel \varphi_2$	*interleaving*

Further, the formulation of programs in SPL (Simple Programming Language) [21], a program like syntax is supported. The semantics of both formulas and programs can be

---

[1] For simplicity we assume that the systems have no terminal states as it does not impose any serious restrictions. Therefore all traces we consider are infinite.

expressed as a set of traces. In ITL$^+$ programs and temporal formulas can be mixed. This can be used for the parallel composition of programs with the interleaving operator [4]. The calculus supports symbolic execution of parallel programs, which is a successful technique for interactive verification (e.g. Dynamic Logic [16,17]). It is a very intuitive strategy for programs as the proof advances step by step similar most humans do it when trying to understand a program [20]. Furthermore, it can be automated to a large extend.

2.2 Organic Computing Systems

In self-x systems - just like in traditional systems - failures and environmental disturbances can not be prohibited. Disturbances and failures force the system into a state where it can not provide its functionality. Therefore we can distinguish the state space of a system into two sets.

- A set S_{func} of *functional* states, in which the system can provide the desired functionality,
- A set S_{reconf} of *erroneous* or *reconfiguration* states in which the system can't provide the functionality and a reconfiguration has to take place to get back to a state within S_{func}.

For those sets $S := S_{func} \cup S_{reconf}$, with $S_{func} \cap S_{reconf} = \emptyset$ holds. In opposition to most traditional systems self-x systems are characterized by their ability to compensate disturbances. Traditional systems without self-x properties and any degree of freedom have traces in which the system switches to an error state s_{err}, for example caused by component failures or other environmental influences. In that state the traditional system can't provide its functionality anymore and without restarting it will never return to a functional state. The OC-system, however, has the ability to compensate the failure (e.g. by self-reconfiguration) and get back into a functional state, where it can again meet its requirements.

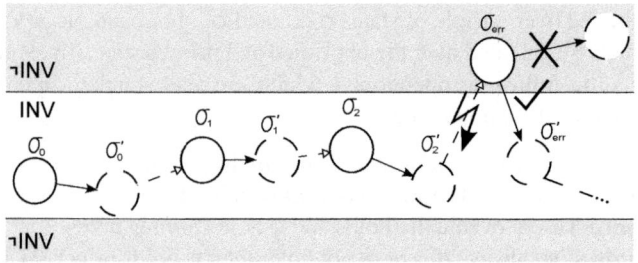

Fig. 2. Behavioral Corridors and Traces

In Figure 2 a possible trace of a self-x system is shown. In this example the set of functional states is $S_{func} = \{\sigma_0, \sigma'_0, \sigma_1, \sigma'_1, \sigma_2, \sigma'_2, \sigma'_{err}, ...\}$ and there is one error state in $S_{reconf} = \{\sigma_{err}\}$. The system switches via an environment transition (e.g. a component failure) into an error state σ_{err}. The self-x system then starts a self-organization and reaches a state σ'_{err} in which functional correctness can be assured again.

2.3 Specification of Functional Corridors

The last example leaves some open questions. For example, it is unclear how to distinguish functional states from erroneous states in which reconfiguration has to occur. Further, we want to restrict the system transitions in such a way that it always stays in functional states and tries to get back into a functional state, if not in one. The proposed technique is called *restore invariant approach* and is described informally in [14]. The idea is to define behavioral corridors, by defining a predicate $INV(V)$ which holds in all functional states and does not hold otherwise. The predicate can in some sense be seen as an invariant, as the systems goal is that this invariant holds on the entire trace.

In the above OC-system the set of functional states is then defined by $S_{func} := \{\sigma \in S | INV(\sigma)\}$. As long as INV holds the system is in a state within the corridor, whenever it is false the system has left the corridor and needs to get back. Traces only consisting of states out of S_{func} are in some sense "good" traces within the corridor. It is desired that an OC-system has only traces that consist of states out of S_{func} or whenever a failure occurs and it enters a state out of $S_{reconf} := S \setminus S_{func}$ there will eventually be some state $s \in S_{func}$ later in the trace. This property can be expressed as a temporal logic formula $\Box INV \vee \Box(\neg INV \rightarrow \Diamond INV)$. This formula can also be used to specify the self-organization (SO) mechanism of the system, as it describes what the effect of the self-organization is. Usually self-organization after a component failure decreases redundancy, as hardware components that broke can't be recreated, but the systems functionality can still be provided as another component can take over, for example. This also means that there is some point where restoration of the invariant is not possible anymore. For a realistic (non-perfect) self-organization we need to modify the specification of the SO-mechanism by adding a predicate Θ stating that no solution is possible anymore or weaker, no solution was found. With some simplifications the specification of the reconfiguration then looks as follows:

$$\Box(\neg INV \rightarrow \Diamond(INV \vee \Theta))$$

Θ can be seen as some kind of quality predicate as depending on how it is formulated some algorithms can fulfill the specification or not. For example, the weakest Θ is stating "Algorithm result is, 'found no solution'" whereas the strongest is $\Theta = false$ ("Reconfiguration is always possible and successful"). Of course, one wants to have something in between like "As long as enough redundancy is available" or "As long as a functional state is reachable". An example is given in the case study.

The idea of the *restore invariant approach* is reflected in a two-layered architecture (see [14]). One layer is the observer/controller (o/c) layer, which is responsible for the self-x intelligence of the system and incorporates the self-organisation mechanism, for instance. It further observes the invariant and starts a self-organization phase whenever it is violated. This o/c can be either implemented as a central o/c agent or as several o/c agents on top of each component of the functional system. For an implementation o/c_{impl} the self-organisation property for a defined Θ must hold and be proven.

$$o/c_{impl} \models \Box(\neg INV(V) \rightarrow \Diamond(INV(V') \vee \Theta)) \tag{1}$$

The second layer is the functional layer, which contains the functional part of the system. The functional layer does not necessarily consist of one monolithic component.

Especially in a self-x system it will be composed out of several components (one may say "agents") providing the functionality. The presented approach will show how component specifications can be composed to one global system.

3   Formal System Specification and Verification

In this section first we will briefly describe the rely/guarantee view on systems, which is common in compositional reasoning. This allows us to reason about individual components and derive global system properties by doing so. Therefore we present the used compositional theorem. Afterwards we describe the idea of the formal approach and how the separation is advantageous for the compositional specification.

3.1   Rely/Guarantee Specifications

The behavior of a system is specified as a transition system described by the formula $G(V, V')$. This expresses the guarantee the system gives. To be able to guarantee its specified behavior the system relies on a certain, but not necessarily completely fixed or predefined behavior of its environment. In an arbitrary environment a system will not be able to give any guarantees. The environment is specified by a transition formula $R(V', V'')$. A typical property of the environment R is that the local variables of the particular system are not changed $R(V', V'') :\Leftrightarrow V' = V''$. The system behavior is then formulated using the "sustain"-operator $\overset{+}{\rightarrow}$, which is used in most rely/guarantee based compositional proof techniques.

$$R(V', V'') \overset{+}{\rightarrow} G(V, V')$$

Informally the formula means, that if rely R holds up to step i, then guarantee G must hold up to step $i + 1$. It allows to formulate that a system or component violates its guarantee G only after its assumption R is violated. This is needed to break circularity when applying compositional reasoning. Guarantees are formulated as propositional predicates over unprimed and primed variables, while for relies predicates over primed and double primed variables are used. In this way it can be formalized which steps are allowed for the system and which for the environment. The $\overset{+}{\rightarrow}$ operator therefore can be derived using the standard TL **unless** operator:

$$R \overset{+}{\rightarrow} G := G \textbf{ unless } (G \wedge \neg R)$$

3.2   Modularization

Usually systems consist of several components running in parallel. A component Ag_i is specified in the same way by a local rely R_i and a local guarantee G_i. Hence, from a point of view of each component, the other components are in its environment. The local rely can therefore also contain some properties assuming "good" or also "bad" behavior of the other components in the system. To be able to give global guarantees by local reasoning we use a compositional theorem. Details and proofs can be found in [6].

Theorem 1. *If:*

   i. for all $i = 1, \ldots, n$: $G_i(V, V') \vdash G(V, V') \wedge \bigwedge_{j \in \{1..n\} \wedge j \neq i} R_j(V, V')$
   ii. for all $i = 1, \ldots, n$: $R_i(V, V') \wedge R_i(V', V'') \vdash R_i(V, V'')$
   iii. $R(V, V') \vdash \bigwedge_{i \in \{1..n\}} R_i(V, V')$

then: $R_1(V', V'') \overset{+}{\dashrightarrow} G_1(V, V') \parallel \ldots \parallel R_n(V', V'') \overset{+}{\dashrightarrow} G_n(V, V') \vdash R(V', V'') \overset{+}{\dashrightarrow} G(V, V')$

Premises *i* - *iii* contain only predicate logic formulas, which are considerably easier to be proven, than interleaved temporal logic formulas. These three proof obligations have the following informal meaning:

i. The guarantee of each component preserves the global guarantee and does not violate the assumptions of all other components.
ii. The assumptions of all components are transitive. With this property, the components assumption is preserved even if other components make several steps.
iii. All component assumptions hold if the global assumption holds. Therefore, no component assumption is violated in the environment step.

The use of this theorem enables the proof of a global rely/guarantee (r/g) property by reasoning over local r/g properties for the individual components. If the system consists of identical components of the same type only the premises for one of this components have to be proven. The theorem allows then to reason about a system with an arbitrary number of these components. The theorem was proven with KIV and can therefore be applied directly during a proof.

3.3   Organic Computing System – Specification and Verification

The global behavior of an OC-system is formulated by a global r/g property $R_{ocsys} \overset{+}{\dashrightarrow} G_{ocsys}$. One big advantage of the separation (Sect. 2.3) of the complete system into an observer/controller (o/c) and a functional system (sys) is, that from the point of view of the functional system, the o/c is contained in the environment, and vice versa. Using the compositional approach we consider both parts as abstract components which run in parallel, specified by local r/g properties. The according proof obligation for the separation then looks like:

$$R_{o/c}(V', V'') \overset{+}{\dashrightarrow} G_{o/c}(V, V') \parallel R_{sys}(V', V'') \overset{+}{\dashrightarrow} G_{sys}(V, V') \tag{2}$$
$$\vdash R_{ocsys}(V', V'') \overset{+}{\dashrightarrow} G_{ocsys}(V, V')$$

The behavior of the functional system is specified as a transition system described by the formula $G_{sys}(V, V')$. This expresses the guarantee the functional system gives. Hence, for the system verification, the specification of the self-organization mechanism can be integrated into the environment, which can be assumed by the functional system.

$$R_{sys}(V', V'') :\Leftrightarrow (V' = V'') \vee SO(V', V'')$$

This formula states that either no changes are made to the system variables V (no self-organization takes place) or in case a self-organization takes place the variables are changed according to $SO(V',V'')$. Here the effect of a reorganization is assumed to occur in one transition. This does not mean that the self-organization takes one step, just that the effect is seen by the agent in one point of time. An o/c implementation needs to reflect this, which is expressed by refining formula (1).

$$o/c_{impl} \models \quad (\neg INV(V) \rightarrow (V = V') \text{ until } \Diamond(INV(V') \vee \Theta)$$
$$\wedge (\, INV(V) \rightarrow (V = V'))$$

For the verification of safety properties [2] it is sufficient to use the safety closure here, and leave the liveness part of the formula beside[2]. Based on this $SO(V',V'')$ can be specified as

$$SO(V',V'') :\Leftrightarrow \quad (\neg INV(V') \rightarrow (V' = V'' \vee INV(V'') \vee \Theta)$$
$$\wedge (INV(V') \rightarrow (V' = V''))$$

Informally the specification of the functional system states that under the assumption of a correct self-organization algorithm and environment R_{sys}, the system will guarantee G_{sys}. This specification can later be replaced by an actual implementation, for example given as a pseudo program $Prog_{sys}$, whose syntax is supported in ITL^+. This leads to the following proof obligation for the implementation.

$$Prog_{sys} \vdash R_{sys}(V',V'') \xrightarrow{+} G_{sys}(V,V') \tag{3}$$

The o/c layer is defined similar. It needs to guarantee the assumed self-organization for the functional system $SO(V,V')$. Further it relies on the global environment to not change its local variables.

$$o/c_{impl} \vdash R_{o/c}(V',V'') \xrightarrow{+} G_{o/c}(V,V') \tag{4}$$

For a particular system usually some more concrete assumptions and guarantees are made, like the particular effect of the o/c layer on the functional system. Further, the global environment usually is allowed to change some of the variables, in order to model failures. We will have a closer look on this in the next section when applying the approach to a case study.

Verification: Besides the verification of (3) and (4), the derived proof obligations when applying the compositional theorem to (2) need to be verified. As both parts of an OC-system usually consist of several components again, the strategy is to also use modularity for verification of the local relies of o/c and sys.

4   Self-organizing Resource Flow Systems

In the previous section the general approach was described. In this section we want to focus on the class of self-organizing resource-flow systems to demonstrate the

---

[2] For each formula φ exists formulas s and l, where s is a safety and l is a liveness formula, so that following equation holds: $\varphi \leftrightarrow s \wedge l$. The safety closure of φ is the strongest formula s that satisfies this equation [1].

application of the presented approach. For the sake of brevity, we will present the compositional verification of the functional part of the system. But as the relies of the functional systems are the guarantees of the o/c layer, all interesting issues should be tackled.

4.1 Design of Self-organizing Resource-Flow Systems

The components of resource-flow systems can be described by a pattern called Organic Design Pattern (ODP-RFS) as seen in Fig. 3.

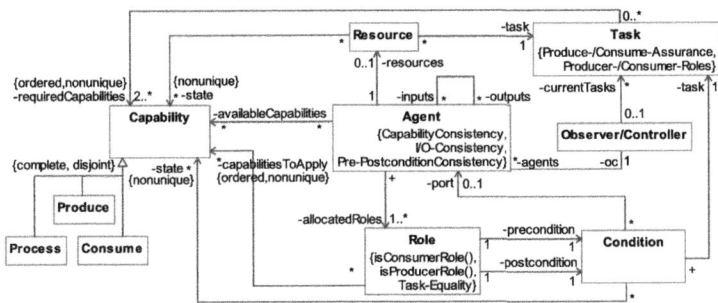

Fig. 3. Components of Resource-Flow Systems

Agents are the main components in these systems, processing the *resources* according to a given *task*. Every *agent* has several *capabilities*, divided into producing, processing, and consuming *capabilities* (*produce*, *process*, and *consume*). Consequently, the *task* is a sequence of *capabilities* beginning with a producing *capability* and ending with a consuming *capability*. Furthermore, the agent knows a couple of agents he can interact with and hand over *resources*. This is encapsulated in the *inputs* and *outputs* relation. The *role* concept is introduced to define correct resource-flows through the system. This means an *agent* has *roles* allocated telling him from which *agent* he receives the *resource* (*precondition/port*), which *capabilities* to apply, and then to which *agent* to hand over the *resource* (*postcondition/port*). Thus, the *roles* establish the connections between the *agents* and the combination of all *roles* forms the resource-flow. The OCL-constraints in Fig. 3 specify correct allocations of *roles* to *agents* and are used in the formal model of the resource-flow systems to specify the self-organization mechanism, as described in the next section. For more details on the SE process and modeling of self-organizing resource-flow systems see [26]. In this case study, self-organziation is done by role allocation. In case of a failure the system calculates a new valid role allocation, to be able to fulfill the task again.

4.2 Formal Model and Verification

The functional part of the system model described above, is formally represented as an abstract resource-flow system by defining data types for all the concepts and their relations. For instance, the static part of an agent is represented as a tuple

$$agent := (\quad .id : Nat \times .availableCapabilties : list(capability) \times .inputs : list(agent)$$
$$\times .outputs : list(agent) \times .allocatedRoles : set(role))$$

".identifier : type" splits into a selector *identifier* and the type of this element of the tuple. E.g. for an agent *Ag*, *Ag.availableCapabilties* selects the list of capabilities the agent *Ag* has. The agent is a five-tuple consisting of a natural number as identifier, a list of the capabilities it can perform, two lists of agents for possible inputs and outputs and a set of roles which are currently assigned to this agent. To express the location of the individual resources we use a so called *store*, which is a data structure (associative array) mapping agent identifiers to resources *locST : Nat ⇒ Resource*. The resource at agent *id* is selected by *locST[id]*. If there is no resource a special resource value ⊥ is returned. A role is represented as a tuple:

$$role := (\quad .precondition : condition \times .capabilitiesToApply : list(capability)$$
$$\times .postcondition : condition)$$
$$condition := (.port : agent \times .state : list(capability) \times .task : Task)$$

Task, Resource are defined in the same way. Capabilities are defined abstractly as sorts. The set *Agents* contains one variable of type *agent* for each agent in the system. *#Agents* is then the amount of agents in system. In this case study we verified a system with one simultaneous task in the system. As described in Section 2.3 we strictly separate the self-x from the functional behavior. For the verification of the functional system only the specification of the self-organisation is used and its implementation is verified separately.

Global system behavior: In the example one global guarantee the system should give is that resources are always processed according to their task. Formally speaking for every key *m* of the location store holds that the state of the associated resource is a prefix of the task.

$$G(V, V') :\Leftrightarrow \forall\ m : (m \in locST) \rightarrow$$
$$locST[m].state \sqsubseteq locST[m].task \rightarrow locST'[m].state' \sqsubseteq locST'[m].task'$$

The behavioral corridor for that class of system is specified as *INV(V)*. It expresses a valid role allocation. For instance one part of *INV* is stating that only capabilities can be assigned that are available.

$$INV_i(V) :\Leftrightarrow \forall ag \in Agents, \forall r \in ag.allocatedRoles :$$
$$r.capabilitiesToApply \subseteq ag.availableCapabilties$$

The complete invariant is a conjunction of several predicate logic formulas like this one. They can also be derived from the ODP-RFS, by translating the OCL constraints into the equivalent predicate logic formula. [25] provides more details about defining corridors for self-organizing resource-flow systems and how the constraints look like. Further a possible realization via a constraint solver is presented. On part of Θ in this example is defined as:

$$\Theta :\Leftrightarrow \exists c \in Task, \neg \exists ag \in Agent : c \in ag.availableCapabilities$$

This states that for at least one needed capability, there is no agent that can perform it. $SO(V,V')$ is derived by substitution of (1). Besides the specification of the self-organization we assume that the environment does not change internal system variables, except *availableCapabilities*. This is done by specifying a conjunction $\bigwedge_{w \in V \setminus L} w' = w''$ of all variables, except the variables in L, which in this case consist of all *available-Capabilities* of *Agents*. The environment is allowed to arbitrarily take or even give capabilities to the agents. Together with $SO(V',V'')$ this forms the rely for the complete system.

Local behavior: Next we define the r/g specification for a single agent. Besides the global rely, a single agent also relies on good behavior of the other agents. That means e.g. it assumes that another agent is not taking its resource away or changing it. Only during a reconfiguration this is allowed. For technical reasons we introduce a variable *reconfCnt* which is counting the reconfigurations, indicating if there was a reconfiguration or not. The rely R_i for an agent i is below. For better readability of the formulas we use a special formatting and the following abbreviations: *allocR := allocatedRoles*, *prec := precondition* and *postc := postcondition. capToApp := capabilitiesToApply*.

$$
\begin{aligned}
R_i := \quad & (\neg\, isEmpty(locST'[allocR.prec.port']) \\
& \wedge\, reconfCnt' = reconfCnt'') \\
& \rightarrow locST'[allocR.prec.port'] = locST''[allocR.prec.port'']\,) \\
\wedge\quad & (isEmpty(locST'[allocR.postc.port']) \\
& \rightarrow isEmpty(locST''[allocR.postc.port''])) \\
\wedge\, & (reconfCnt' \le reconfCnt'') \\
\wedge\, & (SO(V,V'))
\end{aligned}
$$

Note that only a part of the global rely is included as from a local point of view, more variables are allowed to change (e.g. location store). Under this assumption an agent guarantees that it will process the resource correctly.

$$
\begin{aligned}
G_i := (\quad & \neg\, isEmpty(locST[allocR.prec.port]) \\
& \wedge\, isEmpty(locST[allocR.postc.port]) \\
\rightarrow\quad & locST = locST' && (1) \\
\vee(\quad & locST[allocR.prec.port].state = allocR.prec.state && (2) \\
& \wedge\, locST[allocR.prec.port].task = allocR.prec.task \\
& \wedge\, locST'[allocR.prec.port].state := \\
& \qquad\qquad locST'[allocR.prec.port].state + allocR.capToApp\,) \\
\vee(\quad & locST[allocR.prec.port].state = allocR.postc.state && (3) \\
& \wedge\, locST[allocR.prec.port].task = allocR.postc.task \\
& \wedge\, locST'[allocR.postc.port] := locST[allocR.prec.port] \\
& \wedge\, locST'[allocR.prec.port] := \perp\,)
\end{aligned}
$$

Formula G_i describes the behavior of an agent i. If there is a resource in its input port waiting to be process and the outgoing port is free the agent can ...

(1) ... do nothing.
(2) ... process it according to the role, if the resource has a state and task that fits to its assigned role.
(3) ... give it to the next agent if the workpiece is already processed.

$R_i \xrightarrow{+} G_i$ describes the guaranteed behavior of a particular agent i. In this case study we have nearly homogeneous agents, therefore most agents have the same behavior. The only slight difference in agent behavior is that some agents have a producer or consumer role. That means they create or remove resources from the system. Here the rely/guarantee looks analogous except that a producer agent doesn't have to wait for an incoming resource and a consumer agent doesn't have to forward the resource.

A system with one producer, one consumer and n-process agents can than be specified by interleaving their local rely-guarantee formulas.

$$SYS_{RFS} := R_{producer} \xrightarrow{+} G_{producer} \parallel R_1 \xrightarrow{+} G_1 \parallel ... \parallel R_n \xrightarrow{+} G_n \parallel R_{consumer} \xrightarrow{+} G_{consumer}$$

The resulting sequence we want to prove is then given by:

$$SYS_{RFS} \vdash R(V',V'') \xrightarrow{+} G(V,V')$$

Applying Theorem 1, we get a total of seven proof obligations. For premise (i) and (ii) we get one proof obligation for each type of agent (producer, consumer, process). Further we get one proof obligation for premise (iii).

Verification: All proof obligations were formally proven with the interactive theorem prover KIV, which fully supports higher order logic, concurrency and the presented temporal logic. As the resulting proof obligations are all predicate logic and the agents are no more interleaved after modularization, the proofs are straightforward. They start with a case distinction of the conjunctions on the right-hand side of the sequence. Most premises can then be closed by the simplifier of KIV automatically. Only some interaction for reasoning over the location store was needed.

5   Related Work

There is a lot of work done in the area for compositional reasoning for concurrent systems in general. Cau and Collette [10], use a similar technique for defining relies and guarantees but without the focus on a calculus and tool support. Solanki et. al. [28] use compositional reasoning together with ITL. They use a rely/guarantee variant that allows guarantees to be formulated in ITL. The tool they use (ana)Tempura [9,23]. This technique is applied to a semantic web service description. Both do not consider self-x properties, like self-reconfiguration of the system.

Formal verification of self-x systems is a young research area [11]. But there is already some interesting work done on this topic. In [30] Wooldridge states that for the verification of agents the environment is essential. He presents a formal model where the behavior of an agent within an environment is described as a sequence of interleaved environment states and agent actions. This is similar to the idea of ITL$^+$ and also allows for explicit modeling of the environment. We further show the integration of this idea into a modular approach for compositional reasoning.

In [13] a Temporal Belief Logic (TBL), was introduce to define semantics and formalize and verify properties of systems specified in the *Concurrent METATEM* language. Here modal operators are used to distinguish knowledge of different agents. The main difference to our approach is that we utilize compositionality and can do local reasoning. In [3] a policy-based modeling approach based on PobSAM is presented, which also proposes a separation of the self-x part from the functional part of the system. Further an operational semantics based process algebras is presented, but they do not consider compositionality. In [29] the specification language ASSL and a tier-based framework for specification of autonomic systems is presented. Formal verification is not considered.

In the area of compositional verification of multi-agent systems [12] presents a formalization using Temporal Multi-Epistemic Logic (TMEL). Here the system structure is exploited for compositional verification and their proofs were constructed by hand. In [8,19], Jonker et al. present a compositional approach for one-to-many negotiation protocols of agents. They verify one abstraction level against another level until they reach a so called primitive component, where they can apply standard verification techniques. For specification of dynamic properties they use different variants of temporal logic, depending on the type of properties.

Smith and Sanders present an incremental top-down approach for the formal development of self-organizing systems in [27]. The verification of the global system is done by verifying all refinement steps down to component level. Their work provides good strategies for the refinement between different abstraction layers, which also could be used for further refinement on the component level in this paper. While in this paper a strict separation of self-x and functional behavior is assumed, they make no explicit distinction.

6 Summary and Outlook

In summary, we have presented a method for formal specification and compositional verification of systems with self-x properties. We first presented how the separation of the self-x mechanism and the functional system can be used to split the verification task into a verification of the particular self-x algorithm and a verification of the functional system by using only the specification of the self-x algorithm. Furthermore a technique for compositional verification of such systems is presented. As basis for this work an ITL variant [4] that provides a compositional interleaving operator and a rely-guarantee theorem for modularization is used. The logic is fully integrated into the interactive theorem prover KIV and all proofs where done within this tool. The advantage of the use of an interactive theorem prover is, that it can deal with infinite datatypes, because it provides powerful techniques for abtraction.

The approach is applied to a resource-flow system as case study. This case study was chosen as therefore already a software engineering process and design framework was developed and a continuous approach including verification was desired. Nevertheless the approach is applicable to all kind of sytems fitting into the two layered architecture. The main advantage of these technique is that it is independent of the number of agents. Only one rely-guarantee for each agent type is needed. Further for a particular implementation only local reasoning is needed.

Next steps are to extend this approach to liveness properties. So, we can prove properties like, "eventually the system will produce some output", so it shows some progress. This mainly depends on the behavior of the environment, as it can interfere with every progress by breaking enough of the system. Here, the environment needs to be adapted to allow expressions like "if long enough nothing breakes". First experiments in this direction were very promising.

References

1. Abadi, M., Lamport, L.: Conjoining specifications. ACM Trans. Program. Lang. Syst. 17(3), 507–535 (1995)
2. Alpern, B., Schneider, F.B.: Recognizing safety and liveness. Distributed Computing 2(3) (1987)
3. MohammadReza, M.: PobSAM: Policy-based managing of actors in self-adaptive systems. ENTCS. Elsevier Science B.V., Eindhoven (2009)
4. Balser, M.: Verifying Concurrent System with Symbolic Execution – Temporal Reasoning is Symbolic Execution with a Little Induction. PhD thesis, University of Augsburg, Germany (2005)
5. Balser, M., Reif, W., Schellhorn, G., Stenzel, K.: KIV 3.0 for Provably Correct Systems. In: Hutter, D., Traverso, P. (eds.) FM-Trends 1998. LNCS, vol. 1641, pp. 330–337. Springer, Heidelberg (1999)
6. Bäumler, S., Balser, M., Nafz, F., Reif, W., Schellhorn, G.: Interactive verification of concurrent systems using symbolic execution. AI Communications 23(2-3), 285–307 (2010)
7. Bäumler, S., Nafz, F., Balser, M., Reif, W.: Compositional proofs with symbolic execution. Ceur Workshop Proceedings, vol. 372 (2008)
8. Brazier, F.M.T., Cornelissen, F., Gustavsson, R., Jonker, C.M., Lindeberg, O., Polak, B., Treur, J.: Compositional verification of a multi-agent system for one-to-many negotiation. Applied Intelligence 20(2), 95–117 (2004)
9. Cau, A., Moszkowski, B., Zedan, H.: ITL – Interval Temporal Logic. Software Technology Research Laboratory, SERCentre, De Montfort University, The Gateway, Leicester LE1 9BH, UK (2002), http://www.cse.dmu.ac.uk/STRL/ITL/
10. Cau, A., Collette, P.: Parallel composition of assumption-commitment specifications: A unifying approach for shared variable and distributed message passing concurrency. Acta Inf. 33(2), 153–176 (1996)
11. Cheng, B.H.C., Giese, H., Inverardi, P., Magee, J., de Lemos, R.: 08031 – software engineering for self-adaptive systems: A research road map. In: Software Engineering for Self-Adaptive Systems (2008)
12. Engelfriet, J., Jonker, C.M., Treur, J.: Compositional verification of multi-agent systems in temporal multi-epistemic logic. In: Rao, A.S., Singh, M.P., Müller, J.P. (eds.) ATAL 1998. LNCS (LNAI), vol. 1555, pp. 177–193. Springer, Heidelberg (1999)
13. Fisher, M., Wooldridge, M.: On the formal specification and verification of multi-agent systems. Int. J. Cooperative Inf. Syst. 6(1), 37–66 (1997)
14. Güdemann, M., Nafz, F., Ortmeier, F., Seebach, H., Reif, W.: A specification and construction paradigm for Organic Computing systems, pp. 233–242. IEEE Computer Society Press, Los Alamitos (2008)

15. Güdemann, M., Ortmeier, F., Reif, W.: Formal modeling and verification of systems with self-x properties. In: Yang, L.T., et al. (eds.) ATC 2006. LNCS, vol. 4158, pp. 38–47. Springer, Heidelberg (2006)
16. Harel, D.: Dynamic logic. In: Gabbay, D., Guenther, F. (eds.) Handbook of Philosophical Logic, vol. 2, pp. 496–604. Reidel, Dordrechtz (1984)
17. Heisel, M., Reif, W., Stephan, W.: A Dynamic Logic for Program Verification. In: Meyer, A.R., Taitslin, M.A. (eds.) Logic at Botik 1989. LNCS, vol. 363, pp. 134–145. Springer, Heidelberg (1989)
18. Jones, C.B.: Tentative steps toward a development method for interfering programs. ACM Trans. Program. Lang. Syst. 5(4), 596–619 (1983)
19. Jonker, C.M., Treur, J.: Compositional verification of multi-agent systems: a formal analysis of pro-activeness and reactiveness. In: International Journal of Cooperative Information Systems, pp. 51–92. Springer, Heidelberg (1998)
20. King, J.C.: Symbolic execution and program testing. Commun. ACM 19(7), 385–394 (1976)
21. Manna, Z., Pnueli, A.: Temporal verification diagrams. In: Hagiya, M., Mitchell, J.C. (eds.) TACS 1994. LNCS, vol. 789, pp. 726–765. Springer, Heidelberg (1994)
22. Misra, J., Mani Chandi, K.: Proofs of networks of processes. IEEE Transactions of Software Engineering (1981)
23. Moszkowski, B.: Executing Temporal Logic Programs. Cambridge University Press, Cambridge (1986)
24. Müller-Schloer, C., von der Malsburg, C., Würtz, R.P.: Organic computing. Informatik Spektrum 27(4), 332–336 (2004)
25. Nafz, F., Ortmeier, F., Seebach, H., Steghöfer, J.-P., Reif, W.: A Universal Self-Organization Mechanism for Role-Based Organic Computing Systems. In: González Nieto, J., Reif, W., Wang, G., Indulska, J. (eds.) ATC 2009. LNCS, vol. 5586, pp. 17–31. Springer, Heidelberg (2009)
26. Seebach, H., Nafz, F., Steghöfer, J.-P., Reif, W.: A software engineering guideline for self-organizing resource-flow systems. In: Proceedings of IEEE SASO 2010, IEEE Computer Society Press, Los Alamitos (2010)
27. Smith, G., Sanders, J.W.: Formal development of self-organising systems, pp. 90–104. Springer, Heidelberg (2009)
28. Solanki, M., Cau, A., Zedan, H.: Augmenting semantic web service descriptions with compositional specification. In: Feldman, S.I., Uretsky, M., Najork, M., Wills, C.E. (eds.) Proc. of 13th int. conference on World Wide Web, pp. 544–552. ACM, New York (2004)
29. Vassev, E., Paquet, J.: Assl - autonomic system specification language. In: Software Engineering Workshop, Annual IEEE/NASA Goddard, pp. 300–309 (2007)
30. Wooldridge, M., Dunne, P.E.: The computational complexity of agent verification (2001)

On-Line Adaptive Algorithms in Autonomic Restart Control

Hiroyuki Okamura[1], Tadashi Dohi[1], and Kishor S. Trivedi[2]

[1] Department of Information Engineering, Graduate School of Engineering
Hiroshima University, Higashi-Hiroshima, 739–8527, Japan
{okamu,dohi}@rel.hiroshima-u.ac.jp
[2] Department of Electrical and Computer Engineering,
Duke University, Durham, NC 27708-0291, USA
kst@ee.duke.edu

Abstract. Restarts or retries are typical control schemes to meet a deadline in real-time systems, and are regarded as significant environmental diversity techniques in dependable computing. This paper reconsiders a restart control studied by van Moorsel and Wolter (2006), and refines their result from theoretical and statistical points of views. Based on the optimality principle, we show that the time-fixed restart time is best even in non-stationary control setting under the assumption of unbounded restart opportunities. Next we study statistical inference for the restart time interval and develop on-line adaptive algorithms for estimating the optimal restart time interval via non-parametric estimation and reinforcement learning. Finally, these algorithms are compared in a simulation study.

Keywords: autonomic restart, on-line adaptive control, non-parametric statistics, job completion time, Q-learning.

1 Introduction

Since many software systems executed continuously for long periods of time, it is quite important to diversify their operating environments by monitoring/controlling them at judiciuosly chosen time epochs. For instance, some faults may cause the software to age due to error conditions that accrue with time and/or load. This phenomenon is called *software aging* which affects the performance of applications and eventually cause them to fail [26], and has been observed in widely-used communication software like Internet Explorer, Netscape and xrn as well as commercial operating systems and middleware. A complementary approach to handle software aging and its related transient failures, called *software rejuvenation*, has already become much popular as a typical and low cost environment diversity technique of operational software [10]. In general, software rejuvenation is a preventive and proactive solution that is particularly useful for counteracting the phenomenon of software aging. It involves stopping the running software occasionally, cleaning its internal state and restarting it.

B. Xie et al. (Eds.): ATC 2010, LNCS 6407, pp. 32–46, 2010.

Cleaning the internal state of a software may involve garbage collection, flushing operating system kernel tables, reinitializing internal data structures, restaring application or hardware reboot.

Huang *et al.* [10] and Garg *et al.* [7] represented degradation phenomena of a telecommunication billing application by a continuous-time Markov chain and a Markov regenerative stochastic Petri net with two-step failure mode, and derived the steady-state system availability. Garg *et al.* [8] considered a transaction-based software system, which involves arrival and queueing of jobs, and analyzed both effects of aging; hard failures that result in an unavailability and soft failures that result in performance degradation. The workload-based models of aging and rejuvenation were considered by Bao *et al.* [3] and Wang *et al.* [25], where the reliability and performability analyses of clustered systems with rejuvenation were presented under varying workload. Vaidyanathan and Trivedi [21] developed a comprehensive approach to bridge the gap between the measurement-based approach and the analytical modeling approach, named measurement-based semi-Markov workload model. Avritzer *et al.* [1] proposed three algorithms for detecting the need for preventive rejuvenation by monitoring the changing values of a customer-effecting performance metric such as response time. The underlying model there is a multi-server Markovian queue and the resulting algorithms are based on simple parametric statistics.

This paper considers a novel restart scheme in real-time software systems. Restarts or retries are typical control schemes to meet a deadline especially in real-time systems, and are regarded as significant environment diversity techniques in dependable computing. For software systems aging in time, restart is one of the most popular rejuvenation strategies. The main concern of this paper is to develop an autonomic restart mechanism in restart control.

In general, one of the most significant requirements in autonomic/autonomous systems is a *self-adaptability* to varying external environments. Ideally, the software system in operation should autonomously estimate environment parameters and using this feedback tune configurable system parameters to maintain the required levles of performance/availability. Naturally, such an autonomic/autonomous function is composed of two subfunctions: the observer (estimator) and the controller (optimizer). Since environment parameters such as degradation rate of processing will generally vary with time, an observer in the autonomic system needs to perform an on-line estimation. On the other hand, a controller generally affects the system behavior and hence the on-line samples according to its control rule, it may often prevent an accurate estimation of system parameters by the observer.

Significant challenges of the autonomic system are (i) an accurate on-line estimation of the current environment parameters, (ii) control of system parameters so as to reduce system costs as much as possible, (iii) control of system parameters so as to ensure if the on-line estimation is sufficiently accurate. It is worth noting that (ii) is incompatible with (iii) because they are in a trade-off relationship. That is, in autonomic systems, the problem of control activity is more difficult than that of estimation. At the same time, it is known that the above challenges may give rise to the following mathematical problems: statistical estimation of the current environment parameters using incomplete samples observed in on-line environment and derivation of the nearly optimal solution toward the trade-off between estimation accuracy and cost reduction by using the estimated environment parameters.

Reinecke, van Moorsel and Wolter [14,15] tried to control restart timing based on a a simple stochastic model [11, 22, 23, 24]. Strictly speaking, their algorithm does not treat an autonomic/autonomous control with self-adaption. More precisely, in [14, 15], the authors assumed to collect the processing time data of jobs with the aim of statistical estimation from the on-line experience beforehand, and to control the restart timing using them. Unfortunately, they did not mention clearly how to use the obtained samples for estimating environment parameters, and did not refer to an autonomic/autonomous control by taking account of the trade-off between estimation and control.

In this paper, we utilize a framework of reinforcement learning [9, 18] to develop an autonomic/autonomous restart control in software systems. The reinforcement learning is a methodology that agents adapt to their environments by learning and experiencing interaction. In the mathematical sense, reinforcement learning is identical to a simulation-based method to solve Markov decision processes (MDPs) and aims at implementing a self-adaptivity for an agent through simulated on-line samples. In other words, the framework of reinforcement learning may be attractive to realize an autonomic restart control.

The commonly-used reinforcement learning technique is *Q-learning* [9]. Although the theoretical validation of the Q-learning is based on MDPs to describe activities by agents, it should be noted that the Q-learning does not always need the detailed model description in computation. Conversely this may be regarded as an advantage for controlling complex systems whose activities could not be represented explicitly. A few examples of the use of Q-learning algorithms in dependable computing can be found in the literature. Okamura, Nishimura and Dohi [12] applied this technique to a checkpoint placement problem. Zhu and Yuan [27] designed an automatic error recovery scheme by the Q-learning algorithm. Recently Eto, Dohi and Ma [6] also gave a Q-learning algorithm to control the software rejuvenation timing for a software system with multiple degradation states [5]. It is worth mentioning that the Q-learning algorithms in the above examples are all conventional/standard algorithms without any improvement which can be seen in the literature [9]. However, as mentioned later in this paper, the standard Q-learning algorithm does not function well in our autonomic restart control. To overcome this problem as well as to address the weakness found in [14,15], we propose a hybrid method based on the conventional Q-learning and MDPs.

The remainder of this paper is organized as follows. In Section 2, the related work on the restart control and its statistical estimation scheme are summarized. In Section 3 we describe the basic restart model following [11, 14, 15, 22, 23, 24] and give some preliminary results to characterize the underlying control problem. Next, we define an MDP for the restart control problem in a discrete setting, that is somewhat different from the earlier results. By casting the restart control problem as a dynamic programming problem, we describe the underlying control problem more clearly. On-line adaptive algorithms are developed in Section 4, where two algorithms are presented. The first algorithm is a model-free algorithm based on the conventional Q-learning. The second algorithm is a hybrid algorithm combining Q-learning and dynamic programming, that is also based on the traditional non-parametric statistics with censoring [20]. In particular, the exploration strategies to ensure the accurate parameter estimation of the environment are based on reinforcement learning scheme. Simulation experiments are used to quantitatively compare the two proposed algorithms in Section 5. Finally, the paper concludes with remarks and future directions in Section 6.

2   Related Work

Here we summarize the related contributions presented in past to distinguish the present paper in terms of statistical estimation techniques. The statistical aspect for estimating the rejuvenation policy was focused by some authors. Dohi *et al.* [4] and Suzuki *et al.* [19] derived non-parametric estimators of the optimal software rejuvenation schedules by means of the total time on test statistics of the underlying system failure time data. The advantage of non-parametric estimation is not to need any parametric form of the system failure time distribution, because the probability law which governs the system failure or degradation is rarely known in advance. Rinsaka and Dohi [16] improved non-parametric estimators in [4, 19] by using kernel density estimators in terms of the convergence speed of algorithms.

In this way, the non-parametric estimation is consistent with our autonomic concept used in the restart control. However, since their approaches are based on the *complete samples* of system failure time without censoring and the associated estimate of the optimal solution found from the samples, they can be validated only for the case where a sufficient number of past observations are available. In that sense, the non-parametric estimation algorithms mentioned above are regarded as an *off-line algorithms* for non-parametric estimation. In other words, the above approaches failed to handle the future prediction of system failure time and did not provide the prediction-based rejuvenation scheduling based on on-line observations. Recently, Rinsaka and Dohi [17] proposed a non-parametric predictive inference algorithm of preventive rejuvenation schedule, where the optimal solution could be characterized by upper and lower bounds. Strictly speaking, this is not also an adaptive on-line algorithm, because it is based on the complete sample of failure time data. In general, it is not so easy to collect the complete sample of system failure times in the situation where the rejuvenation of software should be triggered.

An adaptive scheme without the assumption of complete samples was proposed by Bao *et al.* [2]. However, their approach could not guarantee any statistically valid property such as strong consistency in [4, 19, 16, 17], *i.e.* the resulting estimator does not asymptotically converge to the real (but unknown) optimal solution as the number of system failure time data increases monotonically. Consequently, the practical problem is how to determine the software rejuvenation schedule autonomously under the assumption that no prior knowledge and data on the system failure time are available.

Apart from the software rejuvenation policy with the presence of system failure, we consider an optimal restart control which minimizes the expected total completion time of a job under the assumption that the completion time distribution of each job is not known. This technology is quite useful to realize high performance and dependable computing in real-time software systems if it is implemented as a self-healing function for job processing. Reinecke, van Moorsel and Wolter [14, 15] presented a sample-based algorithm by collecting processing data by a maximum restart time interval limit or a deadline from the on-line experience beforehand and using the empirical histogram. But this algorithm with separate phases of data collection and restart control may not function well in on-line fashion when the completion of jobs frequently succeeds, because almost all data are censored and the collection of a sufficient number of samples is impossible. As described in Section 1, the autonomic restart control consists of two phases: estimation phase of the operational circumstance and control phase of optimal restart time. If the control is separately performed just after estimation phase with the complete data, the validation of the resulting restart control based on any criterion of optimality depends on the accuracy of estimation. However, we have a trade-off relation between control and estimation in the on-line fashion, *i.e.*, if the restart (control) was not triggered, the complete data of job completion time can be obtained, and the accuracy in estimation can be improved. Again the present work proposes new on-line adaptive algorithms in autonomic restart control with the aim of overcoming weaknesses of existing algorithm [14, 15].

3   Model Description

3.1   Preliminary Results

First of all we describe the basic restart model in [22, 23, 24]. Let T denote a completion time of a task or transaction without restarting and be a nonnegative random variable having a cumulative distribution function (c.d.f.) $F(t)$ and probability density function (p.d.f.) $f(t)$. Suppose that a software system starts operating at time $t = 0$. Let $\tau_1, \tau_2, \ldots, \tau_k, \ldots$ be scheduled restart time intervals. If the task is not completed at τ_{i+1} from the beginning of the i-th restart, the system issues again a restart command for the current processing task, where a time overhead c (> 0) is needed for each restart command. Define the completion time after the $(i - 1)$-st restart, provided that it is triggered, by the random variable $\tilde{T}_{\pi_i}$, where $\pi_i = \{\tau_i, \ldots\}$ is a set of restart time intervals after the i-th restart (see Fig. 1). Let $\pi_i^* = \{\tau_i^*, \ldots\}$ denote the optimal restart time intervals minimizing the expected total completion time $\mathrm{E}[\tilde{T}_\pi]$. From the principle of optimality [13], it is seen that the optimal restart time interval must satisfy:

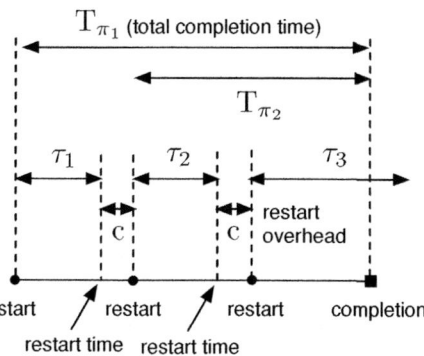

Fig. 1. Possible behavior of restart control

$$E[\tilde{T}_{\pi_i^*}] = \min_{\tau_i} \left\{ \int_0^{\tau_i} \overline{F}(t)dt + \overline{F}(\tau_i)\left(c + E[\tilde{T}_{\pi_{i+1}^*}]\right) \right\}, \tag{1}$$

for $i = 1, 2, \ldots$, where $\overline{F}(\cdot) = 1 - F(\cdot)$. Based on the optimality equations above, we have the following fundamental result:

Proposition 1. *Suppose that an infinite number of restarts can be allowed. The periodic (time-fixed) restart policy is the best in the class of non-stationary restart policy.*

Proof: If an infinite number of restarts are allowed, from the renewal nature of restarts, it is seen that each system condition at the beginning of restart is identical and that all the minimum expected completion times are also identical under the optimal restart time intervals, i.e. $E[\tilde{T}_{\pi_1^*}] = E[\tilde{T}_{\pi_2^*}] = \cdots$. From Eq. (1), the optimal restart time intervals $\tau_1^*, \ldots$ must satisfy the following optimality equations:

$$v^* = \min_{\tau_i} \left\{ \int_0^{\tau_i} \overline{F}(t)dt + \overline{F}(\tau_i)(c + v^*) \right\}, \tag{2}$$

where $v^* = E[\tilde{T}_{\pi_1^*}] = E[\tilde{T}_{\pi_2^*}] = \cdots$. Since v^* is constant, the optimal time intervals $\tau_1^*, \ldots$ can be given by a fixed time satisfying Eq. (2). □

Let T_τ be a total completion time under the periodic restart policy with restart time interval τ. From Proposition 1, it is immediate to see that the periodic restart time τ^* minimizing

$$E[T_\tau] = \frac{\int_0^\tau \overline{F}(t)dt + c\overline{F}(\tau)}{F(\tau)} \tag{3}$$

is always optimal under the unbounded restart condition. van Moorsel and Wolter [22, 24] gave only a necessary condition of the optimal (periodic) restart time interval based on Eq. (3), although they did not refer to sufficient conditions for existence of finite optimal periodic restart interval.

3.2   Formulation

Dissimilar to van Moorsel and Walter [22,23,24], we formulate a different restart control problem in discrete time with a constant interval h as an MDP. Let T denote a discritized completion time of a task with the probability mass function (p.m.f.) p_i, $i = 1, 2, \ldots$, where $p_i \in [0, 1]$ indicates a probability that a task is completed for the duration of $[(i - 1)h, ih)$. A restart manager (RM) controls the restart operation and can issue a restart command to the system at every time slot $0, h, 2h, \ldots$. At each time slot, RM makes a decision whether the restart command is issued or not. When the system receives a restart command, it stops processing the current task, initializes the processing condition and restarts the task. The overhead time required by the restart operation is given by ch, where c is positive integer. From the practical point of view, we suppose a deadline for a single task, which is denoted by T_d. Also, without any loss of generality, the deadline is given by a scale of the time slot, i.e., $T_d = Hh$ is satisfied. Under the above assumptions, the state space of system operation is defined by the elapsed time of processing from the initial condition (or the number of time slots experienced) and the remaining time to the deadline (or the remaining number of time slots), i.e.,

$$S := S^E \otimes S^R, \tag{4}$$

$$S^E := \{0, 1, \ldots, H - 1\}, \quad S^R := \{H, \ldots, 1\}, \tag{5}$$

where S, S^E and S^R are the whole state space, states of elapsed time and remaining time, respectively. For each system state $(i, j) \in S$, RM has an action space consisting two actions: $A_{i,j} := \{\text{restart}, \text{continue}\}$.

In this paper we consider minimization of the expected total completion time. Let T_π be the total completion time for a task under a restart control π. van Moorsel and Walter [22,23,24] treated a simple optimization problem minimizing $\mathrm{E}[T_\pi]$. However, since the existence of a deadline is assumed in this paper, we solve the minimization problem $\mathrm{E}[\min(T_\pi, T_d)]$ instead. Let $Q_r(i, j)$ and $Q_c(i, j)$ be the expected net completion time when RM takes respective actions; 'restart' and 'continue' at the system state $(i, j) \in S$. Based on the principle of optimality, we have the following optimality equations in which the optimal restart sequence must minimize $\mathrm{E}[\min(T_\pi, T_d)]$:

$$V(i, j) = \min\{Q_r(i, j), Q_c(i, j)\}, \tag{6}$$

$$Q_r(i, j) = \begin{cases} ch + V(0, j - c), & (j > c) \\ jh, & (j \leq c), \end{cases} \tag{7}$$

$$Q_c(i, j) = h + (1 - \kappa_{i+1})V(i + 1, j - 1), \tag{8}$$

$$Q_r(i, 1) = h, \tag{9}$$

$$Q_c(i, 1) = h, \tag{10}$$

where κ_i is the probability that a task is completed when the elapsed time from the initial condition is in $[(i - 1)h, ih)$, provided that the task is not completed until the elapsed time $(i - 1)h$. It corresponds to a discrete hazard rate, i.e.,

$$\kappa_i = \frac{p_i}{1 - \sum_{j=1}^{i-1} p_j}. \tag{11}$$

For convenience, let $\kappa_1 = p_1$. The above equation can be solved backwardly from the system state $(i, 1)$, $i = 0, \ldots, H - 1$.

4 On-Line Adaptive Restart Controls

4.1 Model-Free Algorithm

Reinforcement learning is a methodology that agents adapt to their environments by learning and experiencing interaction. Dissimilar to usual supervised learning, there is no supervisor in the reinforcement learning. The agents can get any reward from the external environment by taking their actions, and can learn in order to survive by try and error, taking account of the amount of rewards received. In general, the environment in the reinforcement learning has the following features [18]: (i) Agents before learning have no sufficient knowledge to survive in the environment. (ii) Environment is basically uncertain and can be changed probabilistically by the agent's actions. (iii) Reward is also probabilistic and is caused by the change of environment.

The reinforcement leaning is regarded as a simulation-based dynamic programming to solve MDPs and can be naturally implemented in the restart control problem. In fact, the reinforcement learning contains a number of learning algorithms within its framework to solve the underlying MDPs via non-parametric approaches. In this paper we focus on the Q-learning [9, 18]. The optimality equations in Eqs. (6)–(10) are constructed by $Q_r(i, j)$ and $Q_c(i, j)$ which are derived when the first action is selected as 'restart' or 'continue' at the state (i, j) and the later actions are selected based on the principle of optimality. In general, $Q_r(i, j)$ and $Q_c(i, j)$ are called *Q-factors* and play a central role in the Q-learning. In other words, the Q-learning can be viewed as an algorithm to estimate the Q-factors by try and error of agents.

The restart control scheme based on the Q-learning is developed as follows.

Model-Free Algorithm (Q-Learning-Based Restarting Algorithm)

Step 1: RM observes the system state (i, j) where i is the elapsed time slot from the last restart and j is the remaining time slot to the deadline.
Step 2: RM chooses an action of 'restart' or 'continue'.
Step 3: After taking place the action chosen, RM observes the next system state (i', j') and the cost R in the transition from (i, j) to (i', j').
Step 4: Update the Q-factor using the following equation:

$$\begin{aligned} Q_a(i, j) :=\ & (1 - \beta) Q_a(i, j) \\ & + \beta\left[R + (1 - \mathcal{X}) \min\{Q_r(i', j'), Q_c(i', j')\}\right], \end{aligned} \tag{12}$$

where $0 < \beta \le 1$ is a learning rate, $Q_a(i, j)$ indicates the Q-factor corresponding to the action chosen in **Step 2**, and $\mathcal{X}$ is an indicator variable for the task completion.

Step 5: If the task is not completed, go to **Step 1** with $i := i'$ and $j := j'$. Otherwise, if the task is completed, set $i := 0$ and $j := H$ and wait for the next task in **Step 1**.

The cost R depends on the criterion for the optimal restart time sequence. In the case of expected total completion time, the cost becomes

$$R = j - j'. \tag{13}$$

As seen in the above algorithm, the Q-learning is a model-free algorithm since it does not depend on the transition probabilities in the update formula. Therefore it can be negatively pointed out that the Q-leaning is often less accurate than the model-based algorithms.

One of the most significant problems is how to choose an action in **Step 2** in an adaptive restart control based on the Q-leaning, by taking account of a trade-off between estimation and optimization. The difficulty of adaptive controls is to execute both estimation and optimization in one algorithm. To obtain accurate estimation, we need a large number of samples based on a variety of environments, and the agent in the reinforcement learning widely explores system environments to ensure the estimation accuracy. However, it is easily seen that such a wide exploring range causes increase of costs wasted by the agent. Therefore the exploration strategy affects the performance of the control directly. In this paper, we propose the following selection rules for an action taken in **Step 2**.

Random strategy: Select the action 'restart' with probability $1/(H - j + 2)$, or 'continue' with probability $(H - j + 1)/(H - j + 2)$. This strategy maximizes the entropy of the system state provided that the task is not completed.

Greedy strategy: Select the action with the lowest Q-factor. At each step, the action is selected so as to satisfy

$$a := \underset{a \in \{r,c\}}{\mathrm{argmin}} . Q_a(i, j) \tag{14}$$

ε-greedy strategy: RM selects the action based on the random strategy with probability ε. Otherwise, the selection rule is same as the greedy strategy.

4.2   Model-Based Algorithm

The drawback of model-free algorithm is clearly to degrade the accuracy of Q-factors. Since there is no information on the model structure, the model-free algorithm has a limitation to minimize the cost. Therefore we alternatively consider a model-based algorithm and apply a plug-in estimation to the processing time distribution. The idea behind the plug-in estimation is the use of the empirical distribution from observed samples instead of parametric distributions, though Reinecke, van Moorsel and Wolter [14, 15] also used the empirical histogram. In the restart control problems over a discretized time horizon, we need only the information on the hazard rate function κ_i. Therefore, the plug-in estimation seems to be an effective method to obtain the optimal restart time sequence without the assumption on the processing time distribution.

Let N_i and C_i be bins for each discritized time duration $i = 1, \ldots, H$, where N_i and C_i represent the number of completed tasks during $[(i-1)h, ih)$ and the number of restarted or truncated processes at time ih. Then the hazard rate function is estimated by using both N_i and C_i:

$$\hat{\kappa}_i = \frac{N_i}{\sum_{j=i}^{H} N_j + \sum_{j=i}^{H} C_j}, \tag{15}$$

where for convenience we define $0/0 = 0$.

From the estimator in Eq. (15), we develop an update procedure for Q-factors based on the optimality equations. For example, in the case of expected total completion time criterion, the updated Q-factors are given by the following backward algorithm:

Step 1: For $i = 0 : H - 1$,

$$Q_r(i, 1) := h, \quad Q_c(i, 1) := h.$$

Step 2: For $j = 2 : c$ and $i = 0 : H - j$,

$$
\begin{aligned}
Q_r(i, j) &:= jh, \\
Q_c(i, j) &:= h + (1 - \hat{\kappa}_{i+1}) \\
&\quad \times \min(Q_r(i+1, j-1), Q_c(i+1, j-1))
\end{aligned}
$$

Step 3: For $j = c + 1 : H$ and $i = 0 : H - j$,

$$
\begin{aligned}
Q_r(i, j) &:= ch + \min(Q_r(0, j-c), Q_c(0, j-c)), \\
Q_c(i, j) &:= h + (1 - \hat{\kappa}_{i+1}) \\
&\quad \times \min(Q_r(i+1, j-1), Q_c(i+1, j-1)).
\end{aligned}
$$

The exploration rule is also important to realize an efficient adoptive control in this scheme. Similar to the model-free algorithm, we can consider three strategies: random, greedy and ε-greedy strategies, in the same way, based on the Q-factors and the system state.

5   Simulation Experiments

In this section, we compare the model-free algorithm and the model-based algorithm by using three exploration strategies in a simulation study. Throughout the simulation, the processing time p.d.f. of a task is a hyper/hypo exponential distribution used in [22, 23, 24], i.e.,

$$f(t) = \sum_{i=1}^{m} p_i \frac{\lambda_i^{\alpha_i} t^{\alpha_i - 1}}{(\alpha_i - 1)!} e^{-\lambda_i t}, \tag{16}$$

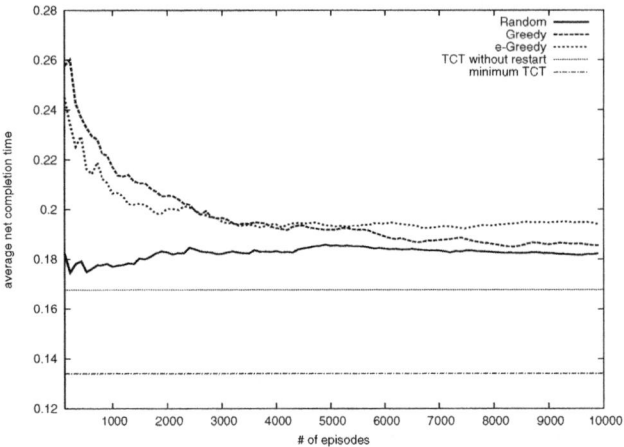

Fig. 2. Behavior of average processes of total completion times (model-free algorithms)

where $m = 2$, $\alpha_1 = 2$, $\lambda_1 = 20$, $\alpha_2 = 1$, $\lambda_2 = 2$. The deadline is $T_d = 1$ and the number of time slots is $H = 100$. Thus the time length of one time slot is given $h = 0.01$. The overhead time of a restart is $ch = 0.01$ with $c = 1$.

The optimal restart time sequence based on the optimality equations consists of three restart times (but not intervals) $t_1^* = 0.21$, $t_2^* = 0.43$ and $t_3^* = 0.66$. Then the minimum expected total completion time (TCT) is 0.134. On the other hand, if no restart is applied, the corresponding expected total completion time becomes 0.208. In the simulation, we define one episode as a life of one task, namely it gives all the events from the beginning of processing to the completion or truncation by the deadline. At every 100 episodes, we compute the average of total completion time for all the episodes (mean total completion time per episode).

Figure 2 illustrates the average total completion time over 10000 episodes under the model-free algorithms with random (Random), greedy (Greedy) and ε-greedy (e-Greedy) strategies. The exploration probability of ε-greedy is fixed as $\varepsilon = 0.1$. Also, the learning rate is 0.5. Two upper and lower horizontal lines in the figure indicate the expected total completion times with no restart control and optimal restart control, respectively. If the average of completion time is less than the upper horizontal line, it means that the corresponding algorithm is effective to reduce total completion time. On the other hand, if the average behavior is greater than the upper line, the algorithm does poorly function.

From the result in Fig. 2, it can be shown that the graphs for all the model-free algorithms are positioned over the upper horizontal line. On the other, Fig. 3 depicts the average behavior of total completion times under the model-based algorithms with three exploration strategies. Although both Random and Greedy could not provide good results for autonomic restart control in this case, e-Greedy was successful to reduce the total completion time.

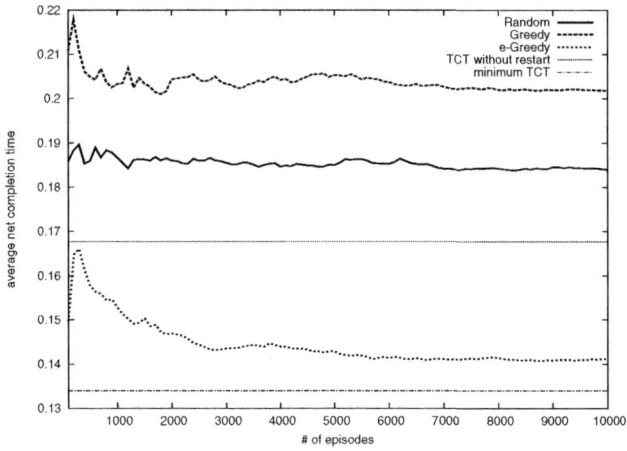

Fig. 3. Behavior of average processes of total completion times (model-based algorithms)

Table 1. Estimated restart times under TCT criterion

algo.	min NCT	Restart ($\times h$)
optimal	0.133998	21, 43, 66
MF RN	0.108323	0, 2, 3, 5, 12, 13, 14, 17–71
MF GR	0.159047	2–5, 9, 40, 41, 45, 62, 69, 79–81, 86, 93, 98
MF EG	0.140954	9, 11, 14, 44, 53, 58, 69, 71, 80, 83, 92, 98, 99
MB RN	0.134584	20, 41, 62, 86
MB GR	0.201684	6, 13, 20, 27, 34, 41, 48, 55, 62, 69, 76, 83, 90, 97
MB EG	0.135305	19, 39, 59, 79

Table 1 presents estimated minimum total completion time and its associated restart times in each algorithm, where MF and MB indicate the model-free and model-based algorithms, and RN, GR and EG denote random, greedy and ε-greedy strategies on the selection rule. Also, the optimal restart sequence is given by the top row in the table. From these results, the model-free algorithm shows rather different aspect on restart times from the optimal ones. On the other hand, MB-RN and MB-EG can estimate nearly optimal solution which are close to the optimal restart times. It can be checked that the estimated values of minimum total completion time are also close to the analytical minimum total completion time. Although MB-RN gives good estimates for the restart policy, one finds that it does not affect the determination of restart control policy because the control is randomly selected. From the observation here it is concluded that MB-EG can select the restart policy based on the current Q-factors, and that MB-EG can reduce the total completion time (see Figure 3).

6   Concluding Remarks

This paper has developed an autonomic/autonomous restart control with the on-line adaptive algorithm. An essential difficulty of developing autonomic/ autonomous system is that one must select both of the control policy to ensure the near optimal solution and the action selection strategy to explore the overall system and action space. For this challenging problem, we have developed a control scheme based on the reinforcement learning. Since the reinforcement learning is defined on MDPs, we have refined a conventional restart model as an MDP in discrete setting, and proposed two estimation algorithms for environment parameters by using the conventional Q-learning and a hybrid method. On the action selection, we have applied three commonly-used strategies in the learning theory.

In simulation experiments, we have investigated effectiveness of the proposed algorithms. As a result, it has been shown that the performance of the model-free algorithm was inferior to the model-based approach. In particular, the model-free method has not been useful for all the cases of total completion time. This is because the minimization problem with total completion time is severe to a penalty in executing a restart operation. While, it has been shown that the model-based approach proposed in this paper functioned well in the minimization of total completion time. For the exploration strategy, the simulation result has told us that the greedy method did not always provide the optimal restart control and that a sophisticated exploration strategy such as ε-greedy method was needed to realize an autonomic/autonomous mechanism.

In the future, we will test the usefulness for the adaptive on-line algorithms proposed here in the cases with sudden change of environment which is governed by a different probability law. In fact, the conventional Q-learning originally has focused on such a situation. To do so in our on-line adaptive algorithm, it may be possible to use weighted samples of processing time instead of the original sample data in order to learn the past history of software operations.

References

1. Avritzer, A., Bondi, A., Grottke, M., Weyuker, E.J., Trivedi, K.S.: Performance assurance via software rejuvenation: monitoring, statistics and algorithms. In: Proceedings of 36th Annual IEEE/IFIP International Conference on Dependable Systems and Networks (DSN 2006), pp. 435–444. IEEE CS Press, Los Alamitos (2006)
2. Bao, Y., Sun, X., Trivedi, K.S.: Adaptive software rejuvenation: degradation model and rejuvenation scheme. In: Proceedings of 33rd Annual IEEE/IFIP International Conference on Dependable Systems and Networks (DSN-2003), pp. 241–248. IEEE CS Press, Los Alamitos (2003)
3. Bao, Y., Sun, X., Trivedi, K.S.: A workload-based analysis of software aging, and rejuvenation. IEEE Transactions on Reliability 54(3), 541–548 (2005)

4. Dohi, T., Goševa-Popstojanova, K., Trivedi, K.S.: Estimating software rejuvenation schedule in high assurance systems. Computer Journal 44(6), 473–485 (2001)

5. Eto, H., Dohi, T.: Analysis of a service degradation model with preventive rejuvenation. In: Penkler, D., Reitenspiess, M., Tam, F. (eds.) ISAS 2006. LNCS, vol. 4328, pp. 17–29. Springer, Heidelberg (2006)

6. Eto, H., Dohi, T., Ma, J.: Simulation-based optimization approach for software cost model with rejuvenation. In: Rong, C., Jaatun, M.G., Sandnes, F.E., Yang, L.T., Ma, J. (eds.) ATC 2008. LNCS, vol. 5060, pp. 206–218. Springer, Heidelberg (2008)

7. Garg, S., Telek, M., Puliafito, A., Trivedi, K.S.: Analysis of software rejuvenation using Markov regenerative stochastic Petri net. In: Proceedings of 6th International Symposium on Software Reliability Engineering (ISSRE 1995), pp. 24–27. IEEE CS Press, Los Alamitos (1995)

8. Garg, S., Pfening, S., Puliafito, A., Telek, M., Trivedi, K.S.: Analysis of preventive maintenance in transactions based software systems. IEEE Transactions on Computers 47, 96–107 (1998)

9. Gosavi, A.: Simulation-Based Optimization: Parametric Optimization Techniques and Reinforcement Learning. Kluwer Academic Publishers, Dordrecht (2003)

10. Huang, Y., Kintala, C., Kolettis, N., Fulton, N.D.: Software rejuvenation: analysis, module and applications. In: Proceedings of 25th International Symposium on Fault Tolerant Computing (FTC 1995), pp. 381–390. IEEE CS Press, Los Alamitos (1995)

11. Maurer, S.M., Huberman, B.A.: Restart strategies and Internet congestion. Journal of Economic Dynamics and Control 25, 641–654 (2001)

12. Okamura, H., Nishimura, Y., Dohi, T.: A dynamic checkpointing scheme based on reinforcement learning. In: Proceedings of The 10th International Symposium on Pacific Rim Dependable Computing (PRDC 2004), pp. 151–158. IEEE CS Press, Los Alamitos (2004)

13. Puterman, M.: Markov Decision Processes. John Wiley & Sons, New York (1994)

14. Reinecke, P., van Moorsel, A., Wolter, K.: A measurement study of the interplay between application level restart and transport protocol. In: Malek, M., Reitenspiess, M., Kaiser, J. (eds.) ISAS 2004. LNCS, vol. 3335, pp. 86–100. Springer, Heidelberg (2004)

15. Reinecke, P., van Moorsel, A., Wolter, K.: The fast and the fair: a fault-injection-driven comparison of restart oracles for reliable web. In: Proceedings of 3rd International Conference on the Quantitative Evaluation of Systems (QEST 2006), pp. 375–384. IEEE CS Press, Los Alamitos (2006)

16. Rinsaka, K., Dohi, T.: A faster estimation algorithm for periodic preventive rejuvenation schedule maximizing system availability. In: Malek, M., Reitenspieß, M., van Moorsel, A. (eds.) ISAS 2007. LNCS, vol. 4526, pp. 94–104. Springer, Heidelberg (2007a)

17. Rinsaka, K., Dohi, T.: Non-parametric predictive inference of preventive rejuvenation schedule in operational software systems. In: Proceedings of The 18th International Symposium on Software Reliability Engineering (ISSRE 2007), pp. 247–256. IEEE CS Press, Los Alamitos (2007b)

18. Sutton, R.S., Barto, A.: Reinforcement Learning. MIT Press, Cambridge (1998)

19. Suzuki, H., Dohi, T., Goševa-Popstojanova, K., Trivedi, K.S.: Analysis of multi step failure models with periodic software rejuvenation. In: Artalejo, J.R., Krishnamoorthy, A. (eds.) Advances in Stochastic Modelling, pp. 85–108 (2002), Notable Publications

20. Tsai, W.-Y., Jewell, N.P., Wang, M.-C.: A note on the product-limit estimator under right censoring and left truncation. Biometrika 74(4), 883–886 (1987)
21. Vaidyanathan, K.V., Trivedi, K.S.: A comprehensive model for software rejuvenation. IEEE Transactions on Dependable and Secure Computing 2(2), 124–137 (2005)
22. van Moorsel, A., Wolter, K.: Analysis and algorithms for restart. In: Proceedings of 1st International Conference on the Quantitative Evaluation of Systems (QEST 2004), pp. 195–204. IEEE CS Press, Los Alamitos (2004)
23. van Moorsel, A., Wolter, K.: Optimal restart times for moments of completion time. IEE Proceedings of Software Engineering 151(5), 219–223 (2004)
24. van Moorsel, A., Wolter, K.: Analysis of restart mechanisms in software systems. IEEE Transactions on Software Engineering 32(8), 547–558 (2006)
25. Wang, D., Xie, W., Trivedi, K.S.: Performability analysis of clustered systems with rejuvenation under varying workload. Performance Evaluation 64(3), 247–265 (2007)
26. Yurcik, W., Doss, D.: Achieving fault-tolerant software with rejuvenation and reconfiguration. IEEE Software 18(4), 48–52 (2001)
27. Zhu, Q., Yuan, C.: A reinforcement learning approach to automatic error recovery. In: Proceedings of 37th Annual IEEE/IFIP International Conference on Dependable Systems and Networks (DSN 2007), pp. 729–738. IEEE CS Press, Los Alamitos (2007)

Designing Self-healing in Automotive Systems

Hella Seebach[1], Florian Nafz[1], Jörg Holtmann[2], Jan Meyer[2], Matthias Tichy[2],
Wolfgang Reif[1], and Wilhelm Schäfer[2]

[1] Department of Software Engineering and Programming Languages,
University of Augsburg, 86135 Augsburg, Germany
{seebach,nafz,reif}@informatik.uni-augsburg.de
[2] Software Engineering Group, University of Paderborn, Paderborn, Germany
{jholtmann,jmeyer,mtichy}@s-lab.upb.de, wilhelm@upb.de

Abstract. Self-healing promises to improve the dependability of systems. In particular safety-critical systems like automotive systems are well suited application, since safe operation is required in these systems even in case of failures. Prerequisite for the improved dependability is the correct realization of the self-healing techniques. Consequently, self-healing activities should be rigorously specified and appropriately integrated with the rest of the system. In this paper, we present an approach for designing self-healing mechanisms in automotive systems. The approach contains a construction model which consist of a structural description as well as an extensive set of constraints. The constraints specify a correct system structure and are also used in the self-healing activities. We exemplify the self-healing approach using the adaptive cruise control system of modern cars.

Keywords: Organic Computing, Automotive Systems, Self-Organization.

1 Introduction

Self-x operations are increasingly utilized in today's systems in order to satisfy the functional requirements even in case of failures, unexpected environmental changes, etc. without any manual interventions. Self-healing deals with the detection and correction of partial system failures. Building a self-healing system is very challenging as it must address most of the possible failure scenarios and has to handle all repairable ones. Consequently, the self-healing part of the system should not be build in an ad-hoc fashion but rather be specified in a formal way based on proven platforms and best practices.

In previous works, a design pattern (Organic Design Pattern (ODP)) for self-organizing resource-flow systems has been developed [11,14,16] and evaluated in the context of production automation systems. In this work, self-organization is the basis for self-healing and other self-x properties. The design pattern formally specifies all relevant parts of the system and defines constraints, which have to be maintained in operable system states. Thus, a corridor (set of valid systems states) is defined. Whenever the constraints are violated, the system reconfigures

B. Xie et al. (Eds.): ATC 2010, LNCS 6407, pp. 47–61, 2010.

to return into this corridor to repair the system. This is called the Restore Invariant Approach.

Self-healing is also applicable to other domains. This especially holds for safety-relevant systems, for example avionics and automotive systems, which must operate continuously. In avionics, redundancy is the standard for fly-by-wire systems [8] to ensure a continuous and thus safe operation. However, redundancy is typically not employed for automotive systems due to the prohibitive costs and the tight integration of hardware and software which are typically sold as a single product by the automotive suppliers. Due to the increasing amount of software in automotive systems [10] and the resulting reliance on the safe operation of the software and electronics as well as the adoption of software standards like AUTOSAR [1], the usage of self-healing in automotive systems becomes feasible. There are already some projects [21], [2] working on the requirements needed for self-healing in the automotive domain. They establish concepts for the possibility of redundancy and how software components can be relocated on runtime. But these approaches do not specify how correct system states can be defined and thus, how guarantees about a correct system behavior can be given which is absolutely required for self-healing safety-relevant systems.

Automotive systems consist of a number of software components that are deployed on independent computing units in the car. Data is exchanged between these components over different buses, examples of data are sensor data, status reports, or commands. In order to describe the valid system states of such "data-flow systems", we adapted the ODP and the restore invariant approach. The techniques were then applied to the adaptive cruise control system of a car.

In the next section, we present the adaptive cruise control system which is used as a running example. Section 3 contains a presentation of the ODP as well as its adaptation to data-flow systems including the constraints defined for this domain. Thereafter, we present the application of the adapted ODP to the adaptive cruise control including self-healing scenarios in Section 4. After a discussion of related work in Section 5, we close with a conclusion and an outlook on future work.

2   Adaptive Cruise Control

In a modern car more and more functions are realized with software [9]. This includes safety-relevant functions like driver assistance or in the future X-by-wire systems. These functions need special techniques like redundancy to guarantee correct behavior. Examples for safety-relevant systems are advanced driver assistant systems. These systems assist the driver to avoid accidents. They use sensors to identify dangerous situations. If such a situation is detected the driver is warned visually or auditory. It is even possible that the assistance systems can regulate the car, to prevent dangerous situations. Therefore, the system has to interact with other subsystems in the car.

As a typical example for a safety-relevant driver assistance system, we use an adaptive cruise control (ACC) in this paper [22]. It is an extended speed

control. The functionality is that if no obstacle is detected it accelerates the car
to the speed which was entered by the driver. If an obstacle is detected the car
is decelerated, so that there is an adequate gap between the car and the obstacle
(mainly another car).

The structure of the ACC system is presented in Fig. 1. The figure shows
the system structure by means of electronic control units (ECUs) with software
components (...-SW) deployed to it. The ECUs are connected to each other
by bus systems enabling message exchange. Different bus systems have to be
connected by a gateway, which translates between the different bus protocols
and handles throughput differences.

The ACC system normally consists of a speed sensor, an object detection
system, and a control unit. The object detection system is either a radar (radio
detection and ranging) or lidar (light detection and ranging). Using either device,
the ACC detects if there are obstacles in front of the car. If one is detected, the
car's speed is adapted. This is first done with the engine brake. If this is not
enough then the brakes are activated, too. Thus, the ACC is in contact with
the *BrakeControl-ECU* and the *EngineControl-ECU* and additionally with the
LightControl-ECU to show the braking situation to other traffic participants.

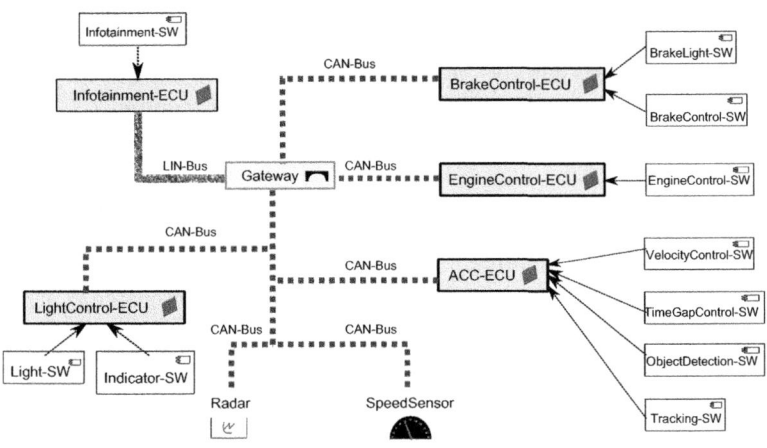

Fig. 1. Overview of the ACC system structure

In this example we use some abstractions for the ACC system. We assume
that every control unit is connected to a communication bus. Furthermore, the
sensors are directly connected to the bus, so they are called intelligent sensors
in the automotive domain. We also assume that it is possible to reconfigure
the software at runtime. This is currently not possible since the automotive
manufacturers configure the ECUs' functions statically at design time. But in
the future online reconfiguration will become more and more interesting and will
be realized. During the reconfiguration process the ACC system is deactivated
and then restarted. This is currently a common procedure to handle software

errors. When the system is deactivated the driver is informed that he has to drive manually without any help. But in the future it is a possible scenario that redundancy enables the continuous operation even during the reconfiguration process. The AUTOSAR standard [1] with its standardized interfaces and its run-time environment (RTE) is the first step towards a system that can be reconfigured.

We have chosen an example from the automotive industry because it is a typical representative of a data-flow system. The characteristics of such systems are that data are produced (e.g., by a sensor) and sent to other systems in a next step. These can be actuators or other software subsystems. There, the incoming data are used to execute an action or to calculate new commands. Thus, in data-flow systems the data are sent from one system to another, so data chains are established. This is very similar to resource-flow systems where resources are sent from one agent to another but there are some differences like the possibility to use data parallel on different agents. This is formulated in the next section.

3   The Organic Design Pattern for Data-Flow Systems

The organic design pattern (ODP) has been developed to design and construct self-organizing systems in a top-down manner. This section describes shortly the ODP for resource-flow systems (RFS) and then maps to data-flow systems like automotive systems. In particular the constraints required to describe this domain are discussed.

3.1   ODP for Resource-Flow Systems

As the complexity of modern software systems increases steadily, the administration and maintenance becomes more and more time intensive. Therefore the ODP has been defined to develop such systems in a top-down manner and to specify guarantees for these systems which are maintained by the system itself without external control. Previously, the ODP was defined for self-organizing resource-flow systems. One major contribution of this paper is the adaptation of the ODP-RFS to data-flow systems. But first the ODP-RFS and its concepts, goals, and mechanisms are described.

The ODP-RFS combines a top-down engineering approach [17] with self-organizing concepts which allow, for example, self-healing behavior. The pattern defines the main concepts of resource-flow systems with self-x behavior and constraints which are modeled to define correct system states. Based on these concepts the respective engineer is able to define additional domain specific constraints. Fig. 2 shows the main concepts the ODP-RFS also includes, so for a better understanding of the following explanations please refer to this figure.

Self-healing requires some kind of redundancy in the system. In systems designed with the help of the ODP-RFS the redundancy is achieved by redundant *capabilities* the system components called *agents* have. Additional redundancy comes into the system by variable resource-flow possibilities or communication possibilities respectively. The agents have *roles* specifying from which agent they receive *resources*, which capabilities to apply to the resource and to which agent then to hand over the processed resource.

The agent is restricted in its behavior by constraints and is able to permanently monitor these constraints. In case of a violation of at least one of the constraints, the agent needs to heal the system. This means the agent starts a reconfiguration process which in the context of the ODP-RFS is a reallocation of roles to the agents. The constraints specified on system class level define what a correct role allocation looks like and thus define a correct resource-flow within the system. One aspect of correctness here means that every resource entering the system leaves the system processed by all capabilities the resource needs (specified in the *task*). The role allocation can be calculated by several mechanisms, for example a constraint solver or distributed algorithms, tailored to restore the constraints. More details to the ODP-RFS can be found in [11].

How the concepts of the ODP-RFS and the constraints mentioned can be used in the class of data-flow systems, especially automotive systems, is described in the following section.

3.2   Adapting the ODP to Data-Flow Systems

Considering data as resources, data-flow systems (DFS) as they occur for example in automotive systems are in several points very similar to resource-flow systems. They only pass data instead of resources to other *agents*. Therefore the ODP-DFS inherits many concepts and constraints already defined in the ODP-RFS. Fig. 2 shows the adapted ODP. Similar to resource-flow systems, data-flow systems consist of agents. In the ODP-RFS the *agents* are, for example robots or autonomous vehicles while in ODP-DFS the *agents* are, for instance ECUs. Each *agent* has different *capabilities* which are used to work on the data or change the state of the data. In the ACC example data from the radar sensor is sent to different software components (represented by the capabilities) like *Tracking-SW* or the *ObjectDetection-SW* which calculates data dependent on the radar data.

In data-flow systems the *agents* have different types of properties they provide, for example a certain amount of memory or the clock speed of an ECU. The different properties are necessary to allow parallel processing of data, a common feature in data-flow systems. Accordingly the *capabilities*—mainly software components—an *agent* has, require several types of properties of the agent. This fact is encapsulated in three new concepts, the type of the property (*PropertyType*), the required property (*RequiredProperty*) and the provided property (*ProvidedProperty*). The properties are used to describe which capabilities can be allocated to which agent (e.g., which software can be deployed to which ECU).

In RFS the *task* has been considered as an ordered sequence of *capabilities*. For a consistent terminology the term is also used in the ODP-DFS. But the term task should not be mixed with the term task that is used in the automotive industry. There the term is used for an operating system resource. Here it is used for the specification of capabilities. In data-flow systems the *task* is more complex than in resource-flow systems because the data can be used in different software components simultaneously. For example the radar sensor data are used in the *Tracking-SW* as well as in the *ObjectDetection-SW*. As a new functionality of the ODP-DFS the data could easily be split up or merged. For that purpose every *capability* defines its *posts*, that means which *capabilities* follow in the processing order. Thus, the *task* is a graph of *capabilities* with a partial order.

Another new concept in the ODP-DFS is the *channel* concept. In resource-flow systems the *agents* are able to hand over their resources directly to other *agents*. In data-flow systems the agents are connected via communication buses like CAN or LIN which are used for example in the automotive industry. The *channel* in the ODP-DFS models these communication buses. An *agent* is able to communicate to all other *agents* connected to the same *channel*.

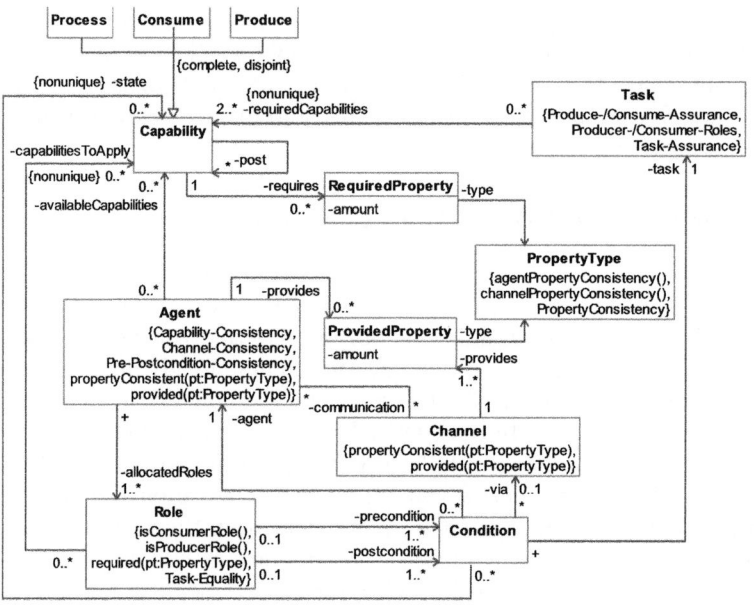

Fig. 2. Organic Design Pattern for Data-Flow Systems

The concept of *roles* in data-flow systems is very similar to the concept in the ODP-RFS. The *role* determines which *capabilities* an *agent* performs and from which *agent via* which *channel* it receives the data or to which *agent via* which *channel* the *agent* has to send the data. The difference here is only the *via* concept of the *pre- and postconditions* which is in addition to the *role* concept from the ODP-RFS.

In some of the classes of the ODP-DFS OCL-constraints[1] are defined to specify correct system states. For example in the class task, there are three constraints defining a correct task or role allocation to agents (*Producer-/Consumer-Assurance, Producer-/Consumer-Roles, Task-Assurance*). In the next section the

---

[1] Object Constraint Language, OMG Available Specification.

constraints are explained in detail and are represented in a formal notation (standard logic notation). In [7,14] the translation from OCL-constraints to a standard logic notation is presented.

3.3   Constraints

As mentioned above, a correct configuration of the system (which leads to correct behavior) is defined by constraining the system. This is done by annotation of OCL-constraints to the ODP-DFS. In case of a failure, one or more of the constraints are violated and the system needs to calculate a new configuration, such that the constraints hold again. This can be done by using a standard off-the-shelf constraint solver, like KodKod [19], Alloy [12], or Cassowary [5]. In [14] this specification approach with constraints is presented for ODP-RFS systems and non-numerical constraints. As described in Section 3.2, the major extensions besides some artifacts like the channel concept are much more complex tasks in form of graphs as well as quantitative restrictions, for example for bus load or RAM. In the following we describe some of the constraints for the ODP-DFS, especially the more complex ones resulting from the extensions of the ODP. For better readability constraints are written in standard logic notation not in OCL notation.

Basic Constraints: These constraints are a standard set for the role model proposed with the ODP. They just need to be adopted to the designation used in ODP-DFS and the additional associations. The values which can be assigned in a role must adhere to the agents situation. For example, only available capabilities can be assigned or channels which the agent is connected to. This is expressed in the two constraints *Capability-Consistency* and *Channel-Consistency.*

Capability-Consistency:
$$\forall a \in Agent \,, \forall r \in a.allocatedRoles:$$
$$r.capabilitiesToApply \subseteq a.availableCapabilities$$
Channel-Consistency:
$$\forall a \in Agent \,, \forall r \in a.allocatedRoles:$$
$$(\forall c \in r.precondition : c.via \subseteq a.communication)$$
$$\wedge(\forall c \in r.postcondition : c.via \subseteq a.communication)$$

A more complex constraint is ensuring that if one agent has a role which tells it to send data to another one via a specific channel, the other one must have a role assigned, with a precondition, telling him that he receives data via this channel. So they must be *connected* with respect to their role assignment.

Pre-Postcondition-Consistency:
$$\forall a \in Agent \,, \forall r \in a.allocatedRoles \,:$$
$$(\forall c \in r.postcondition \,, \exists a_{rec} \in c.agent : connected(a, a_{rec}))$$
$$\wedge(\forall c \in r.precondition \,, \exists a_{send} \in c.agent : connected(a_{send}, a))$$

$$connected(a_{send}, a_{rec}) :\Leftrightarrow$$
$$\exists r_{send} \in a_{send}.allocatedRoles \,, \exists r_{rec} \in a_{rec}.allocatedRoles,$$
$$\exists c_{send} \in r_{send}.postcondition \,, \exists c_{rec} \in r_{rec}.precondition :$$

$$c_{send}.agent = a_{rec} \wedge c_{rec}.agent = a_{send}$$
$$\wedge c_{send}.via = c_{rec}.via \wedge c_{send}.task = c_{rec}.task$$

Further basic constraints are for instance, that a producer role has an empty set of preconditions (*isProducer*) and analogously a consumer role an empty set of postconditions (*isConsumer*). *Produce-/Consume-Assurance* states that roles with produce or consume capabilities must apply the first or the last element of the task. Likewise, the first and the last element of a task has to be a produce and a consume capability, respectively (*Produce-/Consume-Assurance*), see for example Fig. 4.

Extension to graph like tasks: Further it must be assured that the state within a role always conforms to the actual task.

$$\forall c \in Condition : c.state \sqsubseteq c.task$$

Here "$\sqsubseteq$" formally denotes a prefix relationship between state and task. In [14] we just considered simple tasks in form of lists, with strongly sequential application of capabilities and no forks. Therefore the prefix relationship for lists was sufficient. In the domain of data-flow-systems we now have tasks which are graph like structures, describing the dependencies on the processing steps. Several successors mean that the result needs to be processed by each one and therefore for example transmitted to several agents which have the required capabilities assigned. For a task T described as a graph a state S is a subgraph describing the part which is already done. The prefix property over graphs is defined as follows:

Task-Assurance:
$$S \sqsubseteq T :\Leftrightarrow V(S) \subseteq V(T)$$
$$\wedge E(S) \subseteq E(T)$$
$$\wedge S = T - (V(T) \backslash V(\mathcal{C}_{T^{-1}}(V(S))))$$

where $T - (V(T) \backslash V(\mathcal{C}_{T^{-1}}(V(S)), V(S))))$ is the subgraph induced by building the transitive closure over T^{-1} (T with reverse edge relation) starting from the nodes in S.

Further we need a constraint describing the effect of the application of a capability. The state in the postcondition must be the result of the application of a capability to the state in the precondition. We formally express that with the function "$++$".

$$\forall r \in Role : \forall c_{post} \in r.postcondition :$$
$$c_{post}.state = r.precondition.state + +r.capabilityToApply$$

For lists and one precondition, $++$ is the standard list concatenation operator. Extending the definition to graph like structures and multiple conditions in roles leads to the following definition:

$$S + +c = \left(\bigcup_{s \in S} s \right) \cup \left(\bigcup_{v \in fin(S)} (v, c) \right)$$

where $fin(S)$ is the set of all sinks of all state graphs in S and S is a set of state graphs and c a capability.

Extension for parallel role execution: During reconfiguration a simple assignment of the capabilities to one agent that can perform them and ensuring that the data can be sent via a channel to the next one is not sufficient. Usually, capabilities require some amount of properties, like memory or processor power, which the agent needs to provide. As the roles are executed in parallel, an agent might not be able to perform a capability because it lacks memory as it is reserved to several other assigned capabilities. The following constraint makes a pessimistic assumption to assure that capabilities are only assigned if there is enough amount of needed properties available. Same holds for the channel, as it is not exclusive, it needs to be ensured that the load of the channels is not greater then the bandwidth provided[2].:

$Property$-$Consistency$:
$$\forall pt \in PropertyType :$$
$$\left(\quad (\forall a \in Agent :$$
$$\left(\sum_{r \in a.aRole} \sum_{c \in r.capToApp} c.requires(pt)\right) \leq a.provides(pt))$$
$$\vee \; (\forall ch \in Channel :$$
$$\left(\sum_{r \in aRole|_{r.pc.via==ch}} \sum_{c \in r.capToApp} c.requires(pt)\right) \leq ch.provides(pt)))$$

There are a few further constraints derived from the cardinalities of the pattern. A cardinality of one leads to a constraint that there must be exactly one element. For example,

$$\forall c \in Condition : \|c.task\| = 1$$

states that there is exactly one task connected to a condition.

Together these constraints express a valid configuration of the system (a valid role allocation) and whenever a failure occurs the system needs to reconfigure according to these constraints.

4   Application of the ODP to the Automotive Domain (ACC)

In Section 3 the ODP and the specific ODP-DFS for data-flow systems have been described. In this section a specific automotive system, the ACC, is modeled with the ODP-DFS. This is done in a simplified way while abstracting from technical issues. Thus, the functionality of the ODP-DFS is shown and can be understood without knowledge how the ACC system works in detail. The instantiation of the ODP-DFS yields to several diagrams which specify the structure of the ACC example. These diagrams are called domain models.

---

[2] aRole := allocatedRoles, capToApp := capabilityToApply, pc := postcondition.

Fig. 3 shows the domain model of a *16bitAgent* representing a 16-bit ECU. In the ACC scenario four types of agents exist: A 16-bit agent, a 32-bit agent, a gateway agent, and a sensor agent. These agent types represent ECU types (ECUs with word size of 16/32 bit) or other types of hardware devices (gateway/sensor). A domain model exists for every agent type which determines what kind of capabilities the agent type has in general (e.g., which software components can be deployed to a 16-bit ECU) and which properties the agent provides. Additionally the properties required by the capabilities are defined. In Fig. 3 the small annotation in the upper right corner indicates which general ODP-DFS concept the domain specific concept is derived from.

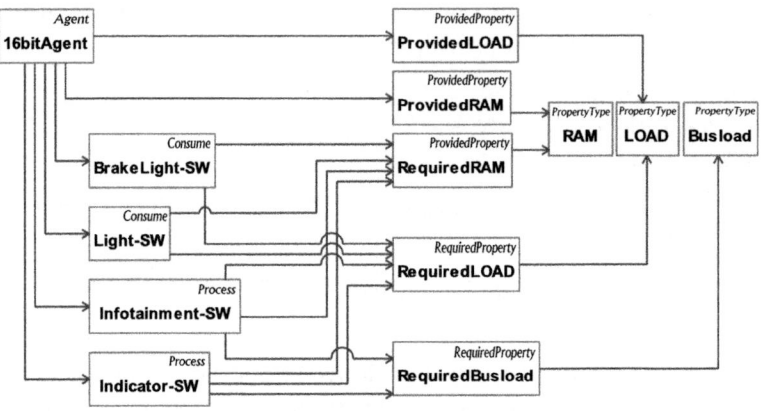

Fig. 3. Domain model for a 16-bitAgent

A *16bitAgent* has four capabilities, *BrakeLight-SW*, *Light-SW*, *Infotainment-SW*, and *Indicator-SW*. All these capabilities represent software components (SW) which can be deployed on any ECU with a 16-bit word size. For example in Fig. 1 the components *Light-SW* and *Indicator-SW* are running on *LightControl-ECU*. These components could also run on a different 16-bit ECU. In contrast, 32-bit ECUs can compute bigger values and can address more memory than a 16-bit ECU. Thus, they are able to deal with more time and resource consuming operations needed by software components like *ObjectDetection-SW*, *VelocityControl-SW*, *Tracking-SW*, *TimeGapControl-SW*, *EngineControl- SW*, and *BrakeControl-SW*. A 32-bit ECU can also handle software components which are designed for 16-bit ECUs.

The agent (ECU) provides *RAM* and a certain *LOAD* which is required by the capabilities running on the agent. Every capability (software component) that runs on it, decreases the provided load by a certain value. So the capabilities are categorized as *produce, consume* and *process* capabilities as shown in Fig. 2. This means that some capabilities produce (e.g., sensors) bus load if they send the data via channels to another agent or just process (*Indicator-SW*) the data (also producing bus load), while other capabilities consume the data (*BrakeLight-SW*) and thus do not require any bus load. The need for free bus load of the channel is encapsulated in the concept of the *RequiredBusload* which must accordingly be provided by the bus the 16-bit ECU is connected to. In Fig. 3 the missing links between *BrakeLight-SW/Light-SW* and *RequiredBusload* also indicate that these capabilities do not produce any bus load and thus are consuming capabilities.

After defining the agents in the scenario with all its capabilities and properties the next step is to define the task the system has to fulfill. As already mentioned, a task is a graph of capabilities with a partial order. Fig. 4 shows the task for our running example ACC. Every depicted capability fulfills a part of the ACC functionality and represents the corresponding software component in Fig. 1.

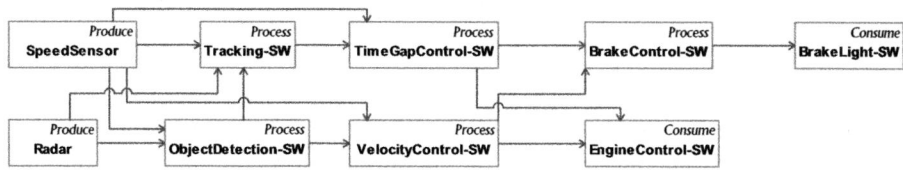

Fig. 4. A task for the ACC example

The task starts with the data producing capabilities *Radar* and *SpeedSensor*, which deliver sensor data to the dependent capabilities *ObjectDetection-SW* and *Tracking-SW*. *ObjectDetection-SW* keeps track of the current velocity and of objects within the driving direction of the vehicle. Based on this data and the stored desired speed, the software component decides whether the ACC has to apply velocity or time gap control. In velocity control mode the component *VelocityControl-SW* is active. In this case it adjusts the current velocity to the desired velocity by sending signals to *EngineControl-SW* and *BrakeControl-SW*. In time gap control mode, the components *Tracking-SW* and *TimeGapControl-SW* are active. The first one determines and filters relevant target objects from the complex radar data. Afterwards, *TimeGapControl-SW* compares the vehicle's current velocity with the velocity of the relevant target objects and operates engine and brakes via *EngineControl-SW* and *BrakeControl-SW*, respectively. When the brake is actuated, the brake lights are turned on by sending a signal to *BrakeLight-SW*.

When all agents and the task for the system are defined, it is possible to specify scenarios for self-healing. This is presented in the next paragraph.

Self-healing Scenarios. One possible instance of our domain model is already given by our ACC example in Fig. 1. The ECUs *BrakeControl-ECU*, *EngineControl-ECU*, and *ACC-ECU* have a word size of 32-bit, while *LightControl-ECU* and *Infotainment-ECU* have a word size of 16-bit. The only software component needing just 16-bit running on a 32-bit ECU is *BrakeLight-SW* (cf. Fig. 3). Furthermore, we have a *LIN-Bus* which delivers input and feedback to the user via the infotainment system. There is also a *CAN-Bus* with more throughput for a fast delivery of signals from the time critical systems ACC, engine control, and brake control. These two buses are connected by a gateway, which translates between the protocols and compensates the throughput differences. Since some software components also need a certain bus load, the possible throughput of these buses also influences the reconfiguration scenario.

One possible scenario is that the *ACC-ECU* crashes. In this case, we have to move the deployed software components *ObjectDetection-SW*, *VelocityControl-SW*, *Tracking-SW*, and *TimeGapControl-SW* to other ECUs. One condition for this reconfiguration is that every 32-bit component has to be deployed on a 32-bit ECU, and that 16-bit components can be deployed on 16-bit as well as 32-bit ECUs. The second condition is that these 32-bit ECUs have to be connected to the high-throughput *CAN-Bus*. The third and last condition in this case is that *Tracking-SW* and *TimeGapControl-SW* have to be deployed onto the same ECU, since the first one produces a lot of traffic for the second one such that even the high-throughput bus may not suffice.

After detecting the ACC-ECU's crash, the reconfiguration is started. The reconfiguration calculates a new possible and correct deployment for the software components on the ECUs. To realize this deployment different strategies are possible. One scenario is to use a planning algorithm to re-allocate the software components, similar to [13]. While the constraint solver is working (and the reconfiguration is done) the ACC functionality is deactivated and the driver is informed. After finishing the reconfiguration the system is started and the functionality is working again.

The reconfiguration has changed the system instance to the one depicted in Fig. 5. The software components *Tracking-SW* and *TimeGapControl-SW* are, as stated in the third condition, deployed together on *BrakeControl-ECU*. Since there were not enough resources on this ECU, the formerly deployed *BrakeLight-SW* requiring only a 16-bit ECU was moved to *Light-Control-ECU*. The remaining two components *VelocityControl-SW* and *ObjectDetection-SW* were moved to *Engine*

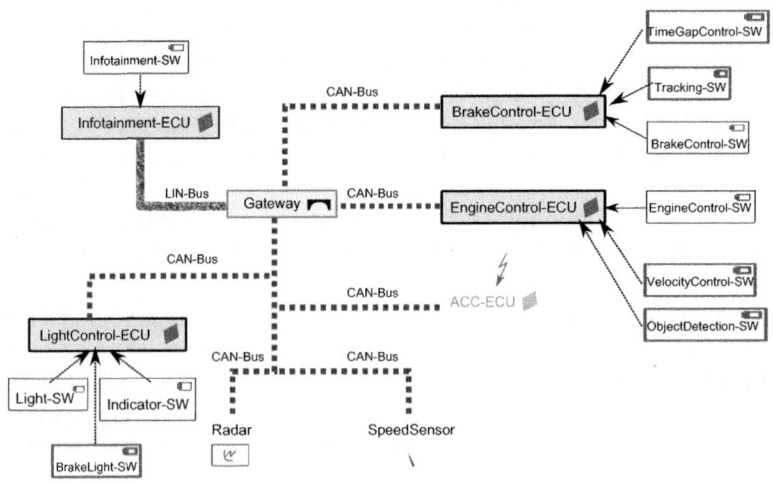

Fig. 5. The ACC system after the reconfiguration

Control-ECU. No component was moved to *Infotainment-ECU* because it is connected via the low-throughput *LIN-Bus.*

Further self-healing scenarios our approach could be applied to are the failures of sensors or software components. Newer versions of the ACC system use a combination of different sensor systems to retrieve more detailed data (e.g., camera and radar). If one part of such a sensor combination fails, the other part can resume its work with lower quality characteristics. This leads to a graceful degradation of the sensor system. In case of the failure of a software component the problem is more challenging, because backup components have to be provided on other ECUs. The current resource constraints in the automotive sector make it difficult to use redundancy, but there is a trend towards more powerful ECUs. This would support the self-healing ability of automotive systems to deal with failed software components, also.

5   Related Work

Other approaches also deal with the reconfiguration in automotive systems. The Dyscas project [4,3] specified a system architecture for automotive systems which also provides reconfiguration possibilities. These possibilities are mainly captured in the developed middleware. But the described reconfiguration is mainly used to recognize errors and to degrade the functionality, so that a minimal functionality is still there. In contrast our approach uses the reconfiguration to re-establish the entire functionality. By using the different constraints it is possible to calculate a new configuration for the whole system.

Another approach that deals with reconfiguration is described in [6]. There, a possibility is demonstrated how the AUTOSAR tool Systemdesk[3] can be extended to model reconfiguration possibilities. The system can then choose between the different reconfigurations at runtime. The problem with this approach is that every possible reconfiguration has to be modeled at design time and then be stored at the ECUs. The number of needed scenarios is exponential with the components and sensors in the system. To avoid that amount of data and the development work, we use the constraint solver to calculate a correct reconfiguration. Additionally we can also react to situations that nobody has thought about during the development phase.

In [20] an extension to the AUTOSAR standard is demonstrated that makes dynamical reconfiguration and self-healing possible. But this approach only takes some properties like memory into account. Other constraints like that two software components have to be deployed to the same node are missing. In our approach it is possible to specify such constraints. As already mentioned, we are currently working on a planner to rearrange the software components on the ECUs to attain the calculated correct system states. In [15] a PDDL planner for a robotic scenario is presented. It also uses constraints for defining the reconfiguration task. The tasks there are sequences of capabilities and it does not consider quantitative constraints like presented in this paper.

---

[3] www.dspace.de

[18] proposed a framework for self-healing and self-adaptive networks of hardware/software nodes was presented. It focuses on the restarting of jobs on other nodes in case of a failure. Properties like load balancing are addressed. In contrast to this work, they consider no dependencies between the particular jobs.

6   Conclusions and Future Work

We have shown that the ODP is applicable to data-flow systems and especially to automotive systems. With only minor adjustments and extensions the pattern was successfully applied to an adaptive cruise control system. Furthermore, we were able to show how to self-heal the system after an ECU failure simply by exploiting the constraints which are specified for the ODP-DFS.

The AUTOSAR standard supports the basic requirements for self-healing by propagating a component-based software design and appropriate interface definitions for decomposition. However, it currently does not support reconfiguration at runtime since all connections between components and hardware nodes are fixed prior to runtime. Nevertheless, there are ongoing efforts to extend AUTOSAR to support reconfiguration [20].

The application of the restore invariant approach to the constraints defined in this paper computes a new system configuration based on the response to failures. We did not address how to reconfigure the system from the old to the new configuration. Depending on the current system configuration, the desired system configuration and additional constraints, the reconfiguration maybe encompasses multiple and possibly concurrent steps. We are currently investigating whether planning as in [13] can be integrated into our approach for this purpose.

Finally, the presented ODP-DFS will be extensively evaluated to check whether all relevant characteristics of data-flow systems are contained in the pattern. This includes redundancy to support safety-critical systems and time to support real-time systems. In this area it is possible that extensions are necessary. The application to other domains than automotive systems is especially interesting.

References

1. Autosar specification (2009), www.autosar.org
2. Amor-Segan, M., McMurran, R., Dhadyalla, G., Jones, R.: Towards the Self Healing Vehicle. In: Automotive Electronics, 2007 3rd Institution of Engineering and Technology Conference on, pp. 1–7 (2007)
3. Anthony, R., Leonhardi, A., Ekelin, C., Chen, D., Trngren, M., de Boer, G., Jahnich, I., Burton, S., Redell, O., Weber, A., Vollmer, V.: A future dynamically reconfigurable automotive software system. In: Proceedings of the IESS (2007)
4. Anthony, R., Rettberg, A., Chen, D., Jahnich, I., de Boer, G., Enkelin, C.: Towards a dynamically reconfigurable automotive control system architecture. International Federation for Information Processing (IFIP) 231, 71–84 (2007)
5. Badros, G.J., Borning, A., Stuckey, P.J.: The cassowary linear arithmetic constraint solving algorithm. ACM Trans. Comput.-Hum. Interact. 8(4), 267–306 (2001)

6. Becker, B., Giese, H., Neumann, S., Schenck, M., Treffer, A.: Model-based extension of autosar for architectural online reconfiguration. In: Proceedings of the ACES-MB 2009, CEUR Workshop Proceedings, CEUR-WS.org, pp. 123–137 (2009)
7. Beckert, B., Keller, U., Schmitt, P.H.: Translating the object constraint language into first-order predicate logic. In: Proceedings, VERIFY, Workshop at Federated Logic Conferences (FLoC), pp. 113–123 (2002)
8. Brière, D., Favre, C., Traverse, P.: A family of fault-tolerant systems: electrical flight controls, from airbus a320/330/340 to future military transport aircraft. Microprocessors and Microsystems 19(2), 75 (1995)
9. Broy, M.: Challenges in automotive software engineering. In: International Conference on Software Engineering, ICSE (2006)
10. Grimm, K.: Software technology in an automotive company: major challenges. In: ICSE 2003: Proceedings of the 25th International Conference on Software Engineering, pp. 498–503. IEEE Computer Society, Washington (2003)
11. Güdemann, M., Nafz, F., Ortmeier, F., Seebach, H., Reif, W.: A specification and construction paradigm for organic computing systems. In: Brueckner, S.A., Robertson, P., Bellur, U. (eds.) SASO, pp. 233–242. IEEE Computer Society, Los Alamitos (2008)
12. Jackson, D.: Software Abstractions: Logic, Language, and Analysis. The MIT Press, Cambridge (2006)
13. Klöpper, B., Meyer, J., Tichy, M., Honiden, S.: Planning with utilities and state trajectories constraints for self-healing in automotive systems. In: Proc. of the Fourth IEEE International Conference on Self-Adaptive and Self-Organizing Systems Budapest, Hungary. LNCS, Springer, Heidelberg (2010)
14. Nafz, F., Ortmeier, F., Seebach, H., Steghöfer, J.P., Reif, W.: A universal self-organization mechanism for role-based organic computing systems. In: González Nieto, J., Reif, W., Wang, G., Indulska, J. (eds.) ATC 2009. LNCS, vol. 5586, pp. 17–31. Springer, Heidelberg (2009)
15. Satzger, B., Pietzowski, A., Trumler, W., Ungerer, T.: Using automated planning for trusted self-organising organic computing systems. In: Rong, C., Jaatun, M.G., Sandnes, F.E., Yang, L.T., Ma, J. (eds.) ATC 2008. LNCS, vol. 5060, pp. 60–72. Springer, Heidelberg (2008)
16. Seebach, H., Nafz, F., Steghöfer, J.P., Reif, W.: software engineering guideline for self-organizing resource-flow systems. In: Proceedings of the Fourth IEEE International Conference on Self-Adaptive and Self-Organizing Systems (2010)
17. Seebach, H., Ortmeier, F., Reif, W.: Design and Construction of Organic Computing Systems. In: Proceedings of the IEEE Congress on Evolutionary Computation 2007. IEEE Computer Society Press, Los Alamitos (2007)
18. Streichert, T., Haubelt, C., Koch, D., Teich, J.: Concepts for Self-Adaptive and Self-Healing Networked Embedded Systems. In: Organic Computing. Springer, Heidelberg (2008)
19. Torlak, E., Jackson, D.: Kodkod: A relational model finder. pp. 632–647 (2007), http://dx.doi.org/10.1007/978-3-540-71209-1_49
20. Trumler, W., Helbig, M., Pietzowski, A., Satzger, B., Ungerer, T.: Self-configuration and self-healing in autosar. In: APAC-14 (2007)
21. Weiss, G., Zeller, M., Eilers, D., Knorr, R.: Towards Self-organization in Automotive Embedded Systems. In: González Nieto, J., Reif, W., Wang, G., Indulska, J. (eds.) ATC 2009. LNCS, vol. 5586, pp. 32–46. Springer, Heidelberg (2009)
22. Winner, H., Hakuli, S., Wolf, G.: Handbuch Fahrerassistenzsysteme- Kapitel Adaptive Cruise Control. Vieweg Verlag (2009)

Trustworthy Organic Computing Systems: Challenges and Perspectives

Jan-Philipp Steghöfer[1], Rolf Kiefhaber[1], Karin Leichtenstern[1],
Yvonne Bernard[2], Lukas Klejnowski[2], Wolfgang Reif[1], Theo Ungerer[1],
Elisabeth André[1], Jörg Hähner[2], and Christian Müller-Schloer[2]

[1] Insitut für Informatik
Universität Augsburg, Universitätsstrasse 6a, D-86159 Augsburg
{steghoefer,kiefhaber,leichtenstern,reif,
ungerer,andre}@informatik.uni-augsburg.de
[2] Institut für Systems Engineering, FG System- und Rechnerarchitektur
Leibniz Universität Hannover, Appelstrasse 4, D-30167 Hannover
{bernard,klejnowski,haehner,cms}@sra.uni-hannover.de

Abstract. Organic Computing (OC) systems differ from classical software systems as the topology and the participating components of the system are not predefined and therefore are subject to unforeseeable change during the systems' runtime. Thus, completely new challenges to the verification and validation of such systems as well as for interactions between system components and, of course, between the system and the user arise. These challenges can be subsumed by the terms trustworthiness or trust.

This paper proposes – after exploring the notions and principles of trust in the literature – a definition of trust which encompasses all aspects that define the trustworthiness of an Organic Computing system. It then outlines the different research challenges that have to be tackled in order to provide an understanding of trust in OC-systems and gives perspectives on how this endeavour can be taken on. Current research initiatives in the area of trust in computing systems are reviewed and discussed.

Keywords: Organic Computing, Trust, Trustworthy Systems.

1 Introduction

Organic Computing (OC) systems [34] are highly dynamic, composed of a possibly vast number of adaptable components and are located in an ever changing environment. To cope with these circumstances, OC systems employ self-organisation mechanisms which yield a number of highly desirable properties, e.g. the ability to self-heal, to self-adapt, or to self-configure. However, classical techniques for analysis and design of software systems are no longer suitable for systems of such complex structure. Novel aspects that could not be observed in other systems, such as emergent properties, and the extreme dynamics of OC-systems require a new way to think about such systems as well as the development of new mechanisms to describe, measure and harness these properties.

B. Xie et al. (Eds.): ATC 2010, LNCS 6407, pp. 62–76, 2010.

An important aspect that becomes especially prominent in this kind of systems is *trust*. How can a system that changes all the time, that reacts autonomously and potentially in unforeseeable ways be trusted? One answer to this question is that a paradigm shift is needed. People will have to learn to give up some of the control they possess over a system at the moment. However, in many domains, such a shift will never fully occur. A nuclear reactor will never be controlled solely by a completely autonomous system. There will always be humans in the loop making the final decisions and able to intervene at critical points. Nonetheless, there are a lot of domains where autonomy and adaptivity can increase system performance and decrease the need for human intervention. An important prerequisite for the acceptance of OC-systems in such domains is trust. Trust is thus an enabling concept.

But trust is also important with regard to the entities that constitute such a complex system. They are expected to work together for a common aim in a highly dynamic and potentially hostile environment. As the size of autonomous systems and the number of constituting entities grows, the relationships and interdependencies between the entities become increasingly difficult to manage and maintain. The increasing complexity of modern computing systems leads to unexpected errors which can not be prevented with conventional software design methods only. In these situations, trust is a decisive factor: it has been linked with reduction of such complexity in large-scale systems [27]. As a societal mechanism it provides a framework for cooperation and a defence against malicious intruders. Again, trust acts as an enabling concept.

Furthermore, research in Organic Computing and other areas that deal with complex artificial systems (e.g. Autonomic Computing, bio-inspired self-organisation, and Distributed Artificial Intelligence, to name only a few), strives for the same end: make complex systems graspable and manageable. Trust is thus not only a concept that inevitably has to be regarded to make such systems accessible for human users, but one which – when investigated directly – contributes to the very purpose of the research in complex artificial systems.

In order to achieve these goals, different aspects of trust have to be regarded. We argue that trust is a multi-faceted concept that includes functional correctness, safety and security as well as reliability, credibility and finally usability. Among other things, it will be necessary to devise methods to describe and measure the trustworthy interaction of parts of the system, enable the observation of predefined policies at runtime, and the development of algorithms that take into account aspects of trust in self-organising systems. In particular, the user interface can no longer be implemented in a conventional fashion. Questions dealing with the transparency of self-organisation processes and adaptive representation of information on different kinds of displays have to be investigated.

In this paper, we propose a multi-faceted definition of trust and substantiate it with related definitions from the literature. There is a long tradition of research on trust and Section 2 points out the common principles that are evident in the different fields. In Section 3, we will then propose a definition suitable for self-organising systems that honours this tradition and incorporates the knowledge of the different facets. Section 4 points out the challenges associated with trust in Organic Computing systems. The paper concludes with an overview of related initiatives and a discussion of concepts proposed and existing ones in Section 5.

2   Trust and Trustworthiness in the Literature

> Trustworthiness, the capacity to commit oneself to fulfilling the legitimate expectations of others, is both the constitutive virtue of, and the key causal precondition for the existence of any society. [16]

Much of the original research on trust comes from the humanities. Psychologists and sociologists have tried for a very long time to get a grasp of the inner workings of trust in interpersonal and interorganisational relationships. Other fields, like economics and computer science, have benefitted significantly from those general findings and adapted them to the special requirements of their respective fields and the new context they are applied to.

An excellent overview of the research on trust conducted in the last 50 years in the humanities is given by Tschannen-Moran and Hoy [45]. Although the findings are applied to the American school system, they are usually general enough to be applicable to other forms of organisations and it is easy to transfer the examples involving principals, faculty and students to any hierarchically structured company or artificial system. Trust is seen as a multi-dimensional construct, deeply rooted in the interactions, behaviour and thinking of individuals and paramount to any form of cooperation within an organisation or society. It is the enabler of cooperation, a view that is shared by many researchers on the topic. It is sustained by sociologists [17] and also adapted in papers on trust in artificial systems, most prominently in multi-agent systems [38].

The multi-dimensionality of trust is a common concept. However, which dimensions contribute to trust is diverse. The differences can often be attributed to the concrete field of research the contributions stem from. The fact that the facets of trust depend on the context is however acknowledged [45]. Grandison and Sloman [19] identify reliability, dependability, honesty, truthfulness, security, competence, and timeliness for their definition of trust in the context of internet applications, Kini and Choobineh [24] in their paper on trust in e-commerce systems use "competence, dependability, and security of the system" as the relevant dimensions. The more sociologically inclined [45] define willing vulnerability, benevolence, reliability, competence, honesty, and openness as the constituting facets of trust.

An important aspect that is emphasized in much of the literature is the predictability that comes with trust. Mui et al. [33] even make this the core concept of their definition: "Trust: a subjective expectation an agent has about another's future behaviour based on the history of their encounters." Others make similar, explicit statements (e.g. the notion of *expectations* in the definition of Corritore et. al. [12]) while in some cases, the same meaning is conveyed in a more implicit fashion, by talking about *reliance* [23] or future *intentions* [40].

The definition of Mui et. al. hints at another commonality: Trust depends on experience and is subject to change over time. When two persons meet, their attitude towards each other is influenced by previous encounters in a similar context. They may have a positive or a negative default attitude towards their counterpart and may thus be more or less inclined to cooperate, a phenomenon coined *basic trust* [9] or *initial trust* [31]. This initial trust is then gradually replaced by experiential trust [30] that is accumulated from the evaluations of interactions with the new counterpart. If no interactions take place between two individuals for some time, the trust slowly deteriorates and has to be rebuilt [48]. Often, the initial trust can be supplemented by organisational measures such as reputation (see, e.g., [31,5,48,11]), where the lack of experience with a new interaction partner is replaced by the knowledge of other, more experienced members of the system.

But even if somebody has been deemed untrustworthy, there may be situations where cooperation might still be beneficial. Whenever a common goal has to be achieved, even enemies might decide to put their differences aside for a while and – although explicitly distrusting each other – cooperate to pursue a certain end with a presumed beneficial outcome for both parties. This shows how important it is to regard trust relative to a context [17]. This notion is also relevant in another regard: One trusts a doctor on a medical diagnosis but not for fixing a car [48]. Context, however, can not only be the role one finds itself in but also other environmental circumstances such as location, the time of day, or the presence of other entities [1].

Trust becomes relevant in situations that involve a risk on behalf of the trusting individual [28,40]. It is, however, debatable if individuals are more willing to trust when it is not a personal loss that can result from an interaction but an unfavourable outcome for an entire group [25]. This implies that trust is a concept that has to be regarded separately on different levels: it can be interpersonal [39], i.e. between single individuals, intraorganisational [47], i.e. between all the individuals in a group or interorganisational [44], i.e. between two distinct groups. The former has been studied intensively, e.g. by mixed-motive games such as the prisoner's dilemma (see, e.g., [13]). Within or between organisations, rules, norms, and compensation can play an important role in creating and sustaining trust and help create incentives for trustworthy behaviour [25,31].

Finally, there is a consensus that trust is a highly subjective property [14]. The relationship between trustor and trustee is unique and potentially the result of many interactions and experiences. Even if mechanisms like reputation or a normative framework are in place, each individual still has to decide on its own whether to trust an interaction partner. This fact is witnessed by the strong emphasis on relationships in the literature [45], but also made explicit in some definitions of trust [17]. Cultural differences can also heavily affect the disposition to trust or deceive [21]. As the final decision about whether or not to trust is an individual one and can be based on very different criteria, different general attitudes and different experiences, trust is also not a transitive property that is inherited or passed on. If A trusts B and C trusts A, C can still distrust B.

Of course, the definitions one finds in the literature are never all-encompassing. They usually focus on those parts of the trust concept that are relevant for the work the definition has to be applied to and leave out concepts that do not fit into the general framework of the field. As an example, the psychological treatment of trust relies heavily on the notions of moods, emotions and shared values. In an economic setting, researchers assume the "homo oeconomicus", a purely rational being, not driven by human shortcomings. Computer scientists take this to the extreme: their agents do not suffer from anything that is illogical, irrational or not based on fact.

As such, definitions from the field of Computer Science emphasise other properties of trust. Interactions of systems are still important, as are subjectivity, risk and context. But trust has to be measurable, has to be quantifiable, traceable, and be subject of calculations as well as intentional modification. Often, trust is modularized into concepts more familiar to experts of the field. Safety, reliability and performance are factors that play a role in such cases [20]. Likewise, the definition proposed in the next section is an adaptation of the principles of trust to the domain of life-like, self-organising systems.

3   A Definition of Trust in Organic Computing Systems

Trust is a multi-faceted concept that incorporates all constituting entities and users of a system and thus enables cooperation in systems of distributed entities. It allows the entities to gauge the confidence they place in their interaction partners in a given context and evolves with the experiences of the entities over time. It is comprised of the following facets:

Functional correctness: The quality of a system to adhere to its functional specification under the condition that no unexpected disturbances occur in the system's environment.

Safety: The quality of a system to be free of the possibility to enter a state or to create an output that may impose harm to its users, the system itself or parts of it, or to its environment.

Security: The absence of possibilities to defect the system in ways that disclose private information, change or delete data without authorization, or to unlawfully assume the authority to act on behalf of others in the system.

Reliability: The quality of a system to remain available even under disturbances or partial failure for a specified period of time as measured quantitatively by means of guaranteed availability, mean-time between failures, or stochastically defined performance guarantees.

Credibility: The belief in the ability and willingness of a cooperation partner to participate in an interaction in a desirable manner. Also, the ability of a system to communicate with a user consistently and transparently.

Usability: The quality of a system to provide an interface to the user that can be used efficiently, effectively and satisfactorily that in particular incorporates consideration of user control, transparency and privacy.

This definition adheres to the facets' description in the literature and is very well compatible to their intuitive, colloquial meaning. At the same time, it is precise and avoids ambiguities as best as possible. All the definitions speak about an abstract "system" to avoid focus on either hardware or software-systems and even the domain of Organic Computing. This allows explicitly to apply the definition to all aforementioned systems.

For some of the definitions, it is important to clearly define the system boundary. If, e.g., the system under consideration is a software program, then the boundary is defined in a way that other software, middleware, or hardware is excluded. In such a case, an error in the underlying hardware (like, e.g., the infamous Pentium-FDIV-Bug) can of course still manifest in the system but does not render the consideration of its functional correctness, safety, security, etc. void. This implicit reliance on the trustworthiness of the underlying system is defined as *infrastructure trust* [2].

The *functional correctness* of a system can be proved formally if a sufficiently abstract specification of the desired functionality is available [15]. Techniques such as model checking or logical deduction are used to show that the implementation adheres to the specification. This is in contrast to validation techniques such as testing and simulation that can not exhaustively show correct system behaviour. Of course, a proof of the correctness of a software system is bound to fail if there is no assumption about the correctness of the underlying platform.

A system's *safety* is compromised if it can reach a state where it causes damage (e.g., a nuclear reactor core that reaches the state "meltdown") or when the system's output causes damage (e.g., if a software that controls a robot arm commands the robot to move through the workspace in an uncontrolled fashion) [43]. The notion of system boundary is also important in this case: the control software can not be held responsible for errors in the robot's microcontroller that causes the same behaviour.

Security encompasses all aspects that have to do with the resilience of a system against attacks by a malicious party from the outside [37]. Here, again, it is important to define the system boundary and thus "outside". Typical aspects of security are authentication, authorization, and encryption. They guarantee that system users and components are who they claim they are, only authorized operations can be performed and that information is hidden from unauthorized system components or users. Security becomes especially relevant in open, dynamic systems where entities can enter and leave the system at any time [49], a condition that usually holds for self-organising systems.

The notion of *reliability* as defined above is close to the definition of the IEEE standard 610.12-1990 [22] and applies to systems consisting of several interdependent hardware or software components. Disturbances can be unexpected input values, performance-intensive computations, or failure of an external service. A system has to be robust with regards to such disturbances and maintain its functionality as long as possible. As it is an unreasonable demand to guarantee that the system will always be available, certain metrics are introduced that measure reliability and enable a practical definition of a reliable system, usually a statistical measure of the probability of failure or the time a system will probably be functional before failures can be expected [36].

Many of the aspects of the term trust as used in the literature on multi-agent systems and artificial societies are subsumed in *credibility*. Models and mechanisms are used to find malicious or selfish agents and to exclude them from interactions or to enact special measures when forced to interact with them (as, e.g., in [38]). This includes "liars", agents that claim to provide a certain quality of service and do not deliver or try to deceive other agents or the user in similar ways. Furthermore, credibility describes a property a system has with regard to its interactions with a user. The user has to be able to comprehend the actions of the system and intervene if these actions do not concur with his preferences.

In this way, credibility and usability are closely related. While the former states that the actions of the system have to be transparent for the user and still controllable, the latter deals with the way information and possible actions are presented to the user. This problem becomes accentuated if the user interface has to adapt to the display device. Large, distributed, organic systems will not be limited to a single device or even kind of device for user interaction, but will be available through standard PCs, PDAs, phones, public touchscreens, and other devices with different degrees of privacy and different modes of interactions. But still, efficiency, effectiveness and an overall satisfactory user experience as demanded by ISO 9241-11 [3] have to be guaranteed in OC-systems.

4   Challenges and Opportunities

The broad approach to trust in OC-systems outlined in the previous section brings about many interesting research questions. Some of the most pressing ones are described in the following.

4.1   Trust Models and Trust Metrics

Especially in multi-agent systems (MAS), trust models have been researched thoroughly (see, e.g., [50]). Most of them consider bilateral trust between two agents, some incorporating notions of reputation or trust values provided by the system. None of them, however, capture all the facets of our definition of trust. They are tailored to ensure agent credibility – the notion that an agent will do as it promised. Apart from this agent-to-agent point of view, trust will also have to be considered from other angles: trust between the user and a system and between the constituting agents and the system becomes important.

In many cases, Organic Computing systems will be composed of agents running on diverse hardware devices. These devices have different capabilities and differ, e.g., in the supported communications and security mechanisms available. Such circumstances will have to be incorporated into the trust metrics. They directly influence the ability of a device to contribute to the different facets such as security and reliability. The way a device behaves in an interaction can be analysed automatically and a trust value can be generated that represents the *device trust*.

In contrast to this automatic evaluation, *user trust*, the measure for the trust between two human users of a system – or the agents representing them respectively – can only be generated by the users themselves. The inherent subjectivity of this measure makes it necessary to devise methods with which users are able to enter the trust value after an interaction with another user in a consistent way and in a fashion that allows to compare trust values from different users.

Additionally, the effects of a highly dynamic system on the trust metrics need to be considered. A highly reconfigurable system changes the data basis of the trust models at runtime. The current trust models and trust metrics need to be adapted to consider this circumstance.

The newly established models and metrics will have to be incorporated in a *trust management* [19] system. This system will collect the information required, evaluate the model based on given criteria and metrics and will thus enable the evaluation of new and existing trust relationships. Especially in social settings, the trust management system will have to incorporate *reputation* [33] to allow trust relationships between agents that have not met yet.

4.2   Trusted Algorithms and Controlled Emergence

One of the ways to achieve life-like behaviour in Organic Computing systems is the deployment of self-organisation techniques. Self-organisation allows a system to automatically reconfigure and adapt to changing environmental circumstances by autonomously altering its structure. While this autonomy is inherently detrimental to trust, the problem is exacerbated by *emergent phenomena*, i.e. macroscopic behaviour that results from the microscopic interaction of entities [41]. The very nature of emergence contradicts a treatment of trust by combining the trust values of the parts of a self-organising system that contribute to the emergent phenomenon, as emergence "cannot be derived from the simple summation of properties of its constituent subsystems" [34].

Instead, there are two ways to establish trust in such systems. Firstly, algorithms have to incorporate the notion of trust directly. As trust is mainly important in the interactions of entities, the algorithms need to ensure that communication is safe and an exploitation or defection – either maliciously or unintentionally – is prevented. Secondly, mechanisms to control emergent misbehaviour are required. Emergence can have positive as well as negative effects on overall system performance and functionality. If the emergent behaviour is detrimental to a system, the term *emergent misbehaviour* is used. Such misbehaviour has to be detected and prevented or avoided completely to begin with.

Incorporating trust and mechanisms to achieve trustworthiness is a way to distributedly control emergent effects in complex systems and thus reach a system performance that is near the optimum. Self-organisation mechanisms can use trust models and metrics to form structures that adhere to the trust relationships within the system, thus reducing the need for costly communication protocols that involve a lot of mutual checks and negotiation between interaction partners. Undesired behaviour can also be avoided by observing the system and placing restrictions on the behaviour the entities in the system exhibit. If the system no longer works within the restrictions, a reconfiguration can restore correct behaviour.

In the context of OC, it is especially worthwhile to investigate mechanisms which lead to better system performance based on self-organised trust and reputation systems. So-called "Trusted Communities" consist of agents able to modify their behaviour between egoistic and altruistic extremes. A social feedback process punishes or rewards agents for their behaviour, which in turn leads to behavioural adjustment. Such an adaptive feedback loop has the advantage that agents can find the optimal level of egoism/altruism according to the current situation (rather than being preprogrammed to follow a fixed algorithm). It can, e.g., make perfect sense in a sparsely populated environment to act rather selfishly, while in a densely populated area cooperation is the better choice.

Moreover, Trusted Communities allow for individual and role-based trust assignment. This way, a single agent can be part of several Trusted Communities, playing different roles with different trust levels. Being a member of a Trusted Community is an advantage since it saves the agent from checking and rechecking the trustworthiness of its partners. Since trust is also a measure for predictability of an interaction partner, it makes sense to communicate preferably with members of a known group.

4.3   Formal Treatment of Trust in Highly Dynamic Systems

Formal methods come into play in several areas of the proposed holistic approach to trust. First of all, functional correctness, safety, security, and at least in part reliability can be shown with the help of formal analysis and verification. Furthermore, the inner workings of the trust models, their evaluation and their incorporation into algorithms for trustworthy Organic Computing systems will have to be treated formally to ensure that they adhere to their requirements, produce correct results and are not exploitable.

However, existing techniques for formal analysis and verification are unfit to deal with the dynamics of OC-systems. Classical formal methods either rely on system traces, i.e. exemplary executions of the system or a model thereof or on logical deductions about the system's behaviour. The former approach works as long as the number of variables and interactions are limited. If , however, there are many interactions and system behaviour becomes complex, the number of possible traces grows exponentially (state explosion [46]). The latter approach is semi-automatic symbolic execution of the specified system, usually performed with theorem provers such as KIV [7] which is more suitable for complex systems but requires input from an expert during the proof.

While the state explosion problem has been subject to intensive research over the last couple of years (see, e.g., [10]), there is still no feasible solution for systems that exhibit the dynamics and interactivity of self-organising systems. Recent developments in interactive verification by means of symbolic execution however, provide possibilities to verify systems of many concurrent, interacting processes [6]. These techniques will have to be adapted and extended to enable the formalisation, analysis and verification of trust, its models, and its interplay in agent interactions on a sound formal foundation.

4.4 Software Engineering for Trust

Classical software engineering methodologies have been enhanced to include safety and security in recent years [29,32]. This has become very important in embedded systems for safety-critical applications that are ubiquitous in many domains such as avionics and plant-control where human life is at stake and certification requires the application of rigorous standards as well as in security-sensitive domains where systems containing valuable private information are publicly accessible or allow transactions that can result in financial damage.

However, even these extended approaches do not take into consideration all facets of the holistic trust concept. To accommodate these additional aspects, existing software engineering processes will have to be amended with supplementary artefacts and new techniques, ranging from requirements analysis to testing and deployment of trustworthy Organic Computing system. These techniques have to be strongly correlated with the formal methods that will be used to analyse and verify the system. Such a relation allows to develop the formal system model along with the actual system and provide analysis and verification already very early on in the engineering process. The feedback will allow the software engineers to create a more robust and resilient system and help gain insights into the strength and weaknesses of the proposed architecture.

While a generic system architecture for Organic Computing systems is neither feasible nor particularly useful, there are strong indications for the usefulness of reference architectures for particular system classes. The architecture of a system class generically describes the constituting elements and in many cases, also the interactions between the elements. Such encompassing specifications allow a software engineer to make formal statements not about individual applications (i.e., instances of the reference architecture) but about the system class as a whole. These formal guarantees are then inherited by the applications as long as certain parts of the interaction dynamics remain the same. This again allows to build more robust systems and adds to the trustworthiness of a system.

4.5 Trustworthy User Interfaces

It is still unclear, how a user interface (UI) for a self-organising systems has to look and adapt in different contextual situations in order to establish or improve the trust relationship between a user and the system. Should the self-organising processes be conveyed to the user? If they should, how? If not, how can the user be informed about changes in the configuration of the system? These choices not only have a direct consequence for the amount of information that has to be conveyed and the kinds of controls that will be available to the user, but also influences the way a user will interact and perceive the system.

To create and automatically manage trustworthy user interfaces, the four steps of Yan et al.'s trust management model [51] have to be addressed.

1. The consideration of the *trust establishment* between the trustor and trustee is the first step. Trust (sub-)facets (e.g. privacy and transparency) can influence the trust relationship between the user (trustor) and the user interface (trustee). Thus, a first challenge is to reveal and investigate these trust factors and their interplay for user interfaces of OC-systems. Glass et al. [18] give an interesting starting point. They investigated some trust aspects for a user interface of an adaptive system and revealed some critical trust factors, such as the usability, transparency and the granularity of the feedback.

2. While interacting with the UI, *trust monitoring* is required to control the trust relationship between the user and the user interface. Thus, we see a need to continuously measure the relevant trust factors (e.g. the transparency) as well as the user trust in different contextual situations. A second challenge therefore is to investigate and find new evaluation methods to trace the trust factors and user trust. We are interested in finding and investigating monitoring methods that objectively enable the measurement of users' trust, possibly dependent on their physiological data (e.g. skin conductance).

3. Then, *trust assessment* uses the measured values of the trust factors and the measured user trust to analyse and interpret the current trust relationship.

4. The last factor of Yan and MacLaverty's trust management model is finally to *control* and *re-establish* the trust relationship between the trustor and trustee whenever its value has changed.

Another topic worthy of consideration in this context is the heterogeneity of interaction devices used to interact with an Organic Computing system. They will not only feature different capabilities regarding presentation and input but will also be used in very different contexts. From private home computers to cell phones with a numerical keyboard to public touchscreen devices – the user interface will have to be capable of conveying the right information and making the right controls available to the user depending on context. Especially with regard to privacy, the location and the publicity of a display is very important.

5   Related Initiatives and Discussion

It has been recognized by several researchers that trust is not only a crucial aspect of modern computing systems, but also a multi-dimensional concept (see, e.g., [42]) that has to be re-evaluated for different domains. The original *Trustworthy Computing* whitepaper [35] defined three perspectives on the trustworthiness of computing systems: the user's goals, the industry's means, and the operating organisation's execution. Each was divided into different aspects, many of which (security, safety, usability, transparency, to name just a few) can be found in our definition. An important driver of the aspect description is the interlink between a system and the company that operates or provides it. This stems from the industrial origin of the initiative where the relations between company and customer are of utmost importance for the successful operation of a system. In the domain of self-organising systems however, much more fundamental questions have to be asked before this link can be established. These foundational questions also necessitate the more formal definitions of trust and its aspect, that go beyond the informal descriptions of the original whitepaper.

The TrustSOFT project[1] also uses a multi-dimensional definition of trust [20]. It resembles the above definition as it recognizes the importance of functional correctness, security, safety, reliability and so forth, but neglects usability. As the systems regarded are component systems, the user interface is not a primary concern. It is provided by a GUI that merely uses the underlying trustworthy components and can be regarded separately.

Dependable computing addresses the issue of trust from another perspective. The main goal is to avoid faults and failures. If systems depend on one another and they accept that depencence, they are said to trust each other [4]. However, trust is not something that is acquired during runtime or changes while the system's run. Our definition of trust is more akin to the definition of dependability, although dependability too is something static that is achieved by construction, not by repeated interaction.

The Trustworthy Computing initiative, as well as TrustSOFT and the Dependable Computing community do not explicitly consider systems in which the entities composing a system are very dynamic. Self-Organisation and the dynamics of an execution environment are of none or minor concern. In the domain of multiagent systems, the *Normative Multiagent Systems* (NMAS) community (for a very good introduction to the current research questions in this area see [8]) is dealing with these problems more explicitly. In NMAS, norms control the agents' behaviour as well as the behaviour of entire organisations. Norms lead to the formation of organisations in which adherence to norms is observed and non-compliance is sanctioned. This enables cooperative behaviour and forms a legal and social reality within a system that is very similar to human forms of organisations. So far, however, norms are mainly concerned with the interactions of the agents and their behaviour towards each other and do not consider aspects like functional correctness, safety, or usability.

The definitions in this paper, as well as the challenges and opportunities outlined above are not conflicting with existing initiatives. Instead of a competing proposal, we see our work as complimentary. Each of the research communities mentioned here is focusing on specific classes of systems with different fundamental assumptions and different goals. We strive to position ourselves within this environment and contribute our unique view of self-organisation, emergence and user-centric Organic Computing systems.

6 Conclusion

In this paper, we surveyed the current literature on trust and elaborated a definition of trust that is applicable to self-organising systems. In our holistic approach, trust is composed of the facets functional correctness, safety, security, reliability, credibility and usability as defined in Section 3. We then identified challenges

---

[1] http://www.trustsoft.uni-oldenburg.de/en/index.html

and research questions that arise from the survey and positioned the initiative within the existing research framework in trustworthy computing systems.

The AgentLink Roadmap [26], published in 2005, claims that reputation mechanisms, norms, and social structures within agent systems have to be subject of research in the medium-term future which was defined to be about five years away. Trust mechanisms for coping with malicious agents were put into the long-term future, a period that falls into the middle of the current decade. As many self-adaptive and self-organising systems use MAS as a basis, research on trust in self-organising systems will always be tightly coupled to research on trust in MAS.

The challenges discussed in the last sections fit into the framework proposed in the roadmap, both with regard to timing and research questions. While they are by far not exhaustive, they hint at the research that will have to be conducted in the next years in order to make trustworthy Organic Computing systems available to the mainstream of software engineers and software developers. By achieving these goals, multiagent systems, self-organising systems and Organic Computing systems will hopefully finally make the step out of the research laboratories to innovative software companies and finally into the real world.

Acknowledgements

This research is partly sponsored by the research unit "OC-Trust" (FOR 1085) of the German Research Foundation (DFG).

References

1. Abdul-Rahman, A., Hailes, S.: Supporting trust in virtual communities. In: Proc. of the 33rd Hawaii International Conference on System Sciences, vol. 6, pp. 1–25 (2000)
2. Abrams, M.D., Joyce, M.V.: Trusted system concepts. Computers & Security 14(1), 45–56 (1995)
3. Abran, A., Khelifi, A., Suryn, W., Seffah, A.: Usability meanings and interpretations in ISO standards. Software Quality Journal 11(4), 325–338 (2003)
4. Avižienis, A., Laprie, J.C., Randell, B., Landwehr, C.: Basic concepts and taxonomy of dependable and secure computing. IEEE transactions on dependable and secure computing, 11–33 (2004)
5. Azzedin, F., Maheswaran, M.: Evolving and managing trust in grid computing systems. In: Proc. of the IEEE Canadian Conference on Electrical & Computer Engineering, pp. 1424–1429. IEEE, Los Alamitos (2002)
6. Balser, M., Reif, W.: Interactive verification of concurrent systems using symbolic execution. In: Proc. of 7th International Workshop of Implementation of Logics, IWIL 2008 (2008)
7. Balser, M., Reif, W., Schellhorn, G., Stenzel, K., Thums, A.: Formal system development with KIV. In: Maibaum, T. (ed.) FASE 2000. LNCS, vol. 1783, Springer, Heidelberg (2000)

8. Boella, G., Pigozzi, G., van der Torre, L.: Normative systems in computer science - ten guidelines for normative multiagent systems. In: Normative Multi-Agent Systems. Dagstuhl Seminar Proceedings, vol. (09121), Dagstuhl (2009)
9. Boon, S.D., Holmes, J.G.: The dynamics of interpersonal trust: Resolving uncertainty in the face of risk. Cooperation and Prosocial Behaviour, 190–211 (1991)
10. Clarke, E.M., Grumberg, O., Jha, S., Lu, Y., Veith, H.: Progress on the state explosion problem in model checking. In: Wilhelm, R. (ed.) Informatics: 10 Years Back, 10 Years Ahead. LNCS, vol. 2000, pp. 176–194. Springer, Heidelberg (2001)
11. Coleman, J.S.: Foundations of social theory. Belknap Press (1994)
12. Corritore, C.L., Kracher, B., Wiedenbeck, S.: On-line trust: concepts, evolving themes, a model. International Journal of Human-Computer Studies 58(6), 737–758 (2003)
13. Deutsch, M.: Trust and suspicion. The Journal of Conflict Resolution 2(4), 265–279 (1958)
14. Deutsch, M.: Cooperation and trust: Some theoretical notes. In: Nebraska Symposium on Motivation, vol. 10, pp. 275–319. University of Nebraska Press (1962)
15. Dunlop, D.D.: An investigation of functional correctness issues. PhD thesis, University of Maryland (1982)
16. Dunn, J.: The concept of trust in the politics of John Locke. Philosophy in History: Essays on the Historiography of Philosophy, 279–301 (1984)
17. Gambetta, D.: Can we trust trust. Trust: Making and Breaking Cooperative Relations, 213–237 (2000)
18. Glass, A., McGuinness, D.L., Wolverton, M.: Toward establishing trust in adaptive agents. In: IUI 2008: Proc. of the 13th International Conference on Intelligent User Interfaces, pp. 227–236. ACM, New York (2008)
19. Grandison, T., Sloman, M.: A survey of trust in internet applications. IEEE Communications Surveys and Tutorials 3(4), 2–16 (2000)
20. Hasselbring, W., Reussner, R.: Toward trustworthy software systems. Computer 39(4), 91 (2006)
21. Hofstede, G.J., Jonker, C.M., Verwaart, T.: A Multi-agent Model of Deceit and Trust in Intercultural Trade. In: Nguyen, N.T., Kowalczyk, R., Chen, S.-M. (eds.) ICCCI 2009. LNCS, vol. 5796, pp. 205–216. Springer, Heidelberg (2009)
22. IEEE. IEEE Standard 610.12-1990: Glossary of Software Engineering Terminology
23. Jones, S., Morris, P.: TRUST-EC: Requirements for Trust and Confidence in E-Commerce: Report of the Workshop held in Luxembourg, April 8–9 (1999)
24. Kini, A., Choobineh, J.: Trust in electronic commerce: definition and theoretical considerations. In: Proc. of the Hawaii International Conference on System Sciences, vol. 31, pp. 51–61 (1998)
25. Kramer, R.M., Brewer, M.B., Hanna, B.A.: Collective trust and collective action. Trust in organizations: Frontiers of theory and research, 357–389 (1996)
26. Luck, M., McBurney, P., Shehory, O., Willmott, S.: Agentlink Roadmap. Agenlink. org. (2005)
27. Luhmann, N.: Trust and power. Wiley, Chichester (1979)
28. Luhmann, N.: Familiarity, confidence, trust: Problems and alternatives. Trust: Making and Breaking Cooperative Relations, 94–107 (2000)
29. Lutz, R.R.: Software engineering for safety: a roadmap. In: Proc. of the Conference on The Future of Software Engineering, pp. 213–226. ACM, New York (2000)
30. Marsh, S., Meech, J.: Trust in design. In: Proc. of the Conference on Human Factors in Computing Systems, pp. 45–46. ACM, New York (2000)

31. McKnight, D.H., Cummings, L.L., Chervany, N.L.: Initial trust formation in new organizational relationships. The Academy of Management Review 23(3), 473–490 (1998)
32. Moebius, N., Reif, W., Stenzel, K.: Modeling Security-Critical Applications with UML in the SecureMDD Approach. International Journal On Advances in Software 1, 59–79 (2009)
33. Mui, L., Mohtashemi, M., Halberstadt, A.: A computational model of trust and reputation. In: Proc. of the 35th Hawaii International Conference on System Sciences, pp. 188–196 (2002)
34. Müller-Schloer, C.: Organic computing: on the feasibility of controlled emergence. In: CODES+ISSS, pp. 2–5 (2004)
35. Mundie, C., de Vries, P., Haynes, P., Corwine, M.: Trustworthy computing. Whitepaper, Microsoft Corporation (2002)
36. Musa, J.D., Iannino, A., Okumoto, K.: Software reliability: measurement, prediction, application. McGraw-Hill, Inc., New York (1987)
37. Poslad, S., Charlton, P., Calisti, M.: Specifying standard security mechanisms in multi-agent systems. In: Falcone, R., Barber, S.K., Korba, L., Singh, M.P. (eds.) AAMAS 2002. LNCS (LNAI), vol. 2631, pp. 163–176. Springer, Heidelberg (2003)
38. Ramchurn, S.D., Huynh, D., Jennings, N.R.: Trust in multi-agent systems. The Knowledge Engineering Review 19(01), 1–25 (2005)
39. Rotter, J.B.: A new scale for the measurement of interpersonal trust. Journal of Personality 35(4), 651–665 (1967)
40. Rousseau, D.M., Sitkin, S.B., Burt, R.S., Camerer, C.: Not so different after all: A cross-discipline view of trust. Academy of management review 23(3), 393–404 (1998)
41. Ryan, A.J.: Emergence is coupled to scope, not level. Complexity 13(2), 67–77 (2007)
42. Schneider, F.B.: Trust in Cyberspace. National Academy Press, Washington (1998)
43. Storey, N.R.: Safety Critical Computer Systems. Addison-Wesley Longman Publishing Co., Inc., Boston (1996)
44. Sydow, J.: Understanding the constitution of interorganizational trust. Trust within and between organizations: Conceptual issues and empirical applications, 31–63 (1998)
45. Tschannen-Moran, M., Hoy, W.K.: A multidisciplinary analysis of the nature, meaning, and measurement of trust. Review of Educational Research 70(4), 547 (2000)
46. Valmari, A.: The state explosion problem. In: Lectures on Petri Nets I: Basic Models, Advances in Petri Nets, pp. 429–528. Springer, London (1998)
47. van de Bunt, G.G., Wittek, R.P.M., de Klepper, M.C.: The evolution of intra-organizational trust networks: The case of a German paper factory: An empirical test of six trust mechanisms. International Sociology 20(3), 339 (2005)
48. Wang, Y., Vassileva, J.: Trust and Reputation Model in Peer-to-Peer Networks. In: Proc. of the 3rd International Conference on Peer-to-Peer Computing (2003)
49. Wong, H.C., Sycara, K.: Adding security and trust to multiagent systems. Applied Artificial Intelligence 14(9), 927–941 (2000)
50. Yan, Z., Holtmanns, S.: Trust modeling and management: from social trust to digital trust. Computer Security, Privacy and Politics: Current Issues, Challenges and Solutions (2008)
51. Yan, Z., MacLaverty, R.: Autonomic trust management in a component based software system. In: Yang, L.T., Jin, H., Ma, J., Ungerer, T. (eds.) ATC 2006. LNCS, vol. 4158, pp. 279–292. Springer, Heidelberg (2006)

Adaptive Control of Sensor Networks

Sven Tomforde, Ioannis Zgeras, Jörg Hähner, and Christian Müller-Schloer

Leibniz Universität Hannover
Institute of Systems Engineering
Appelstr. 4, 30167 Hannover, Germany
{tomforde,zgeras,haehner,cms}@sra.uni-hannover.de

Abstract. In recent years many algorithms and protocols for applications in wireless sensor networks (WSN) have been introduced. These include, e.g, solutions for routing and event notifications. Common among them is the need to adjust the basic operation to particular operating conditions by means of changing algorithmic parameters. In most applications, parameters have to be set carefully before nodes are deployed to a particular environment. But what happens to the system performance, if the operating conditions change to unforeseen situations at runtime?

In this paper, we present the Organic Network Control (ONC) system and its application to WSNs. ONC is a system for adapting network protocols in response to environmental changes at runtime. Being generic in nature, ONC regards existing protocols as black box systems with an interface to changeable protocol parameters. ONC detects environmental changes locally at each node and applies changes to the protocol parameters by means of lightweight machine learning techniques. More complex exploration of possible parameters is transferred to powerful nodes, such as sink nodes. As an example we show how ONC can be applied to an exemplary WSN protocol for event detection and how performance in the ONC controlled system increases over fixed settings of the protocol.

1   Introduction

In the past decade, many protocols and algorithms have been proposed for applications of wireless sensor networks (WSN). Just like in other application areas, these proposals cover a wide range of tasks which can be located at all layers of the protocol and application stack. Most of the proposed algorithms and protocols have been evaluated in various situations either by means of network simulation or in real WSN deployments. One of the major goals of these evaluations is to carefully choose appropriate settings for the numerous parameters these protocols and algorithms typically have. These variable settings allow for tuning the behaviour of the algorithm in particular operating conditions. However, in many applications, unforeseen changes of these operating conditions are frequently encountered at runtime. Depending on the method of node deployment, the node distribution in the field may differ from what was expected in the design phase. Environmental conditions, e.g. unexpected frequencies of detected events, may lead to node failure and different patterns than expected. In turn,

B. Xie et al. (Eds.): ATC 2010, LNCS 6407, pp. 77–91, 2010.

the pattern of node failures also leads to topology changes in the network. In summary, these occurrences often lead to a degradation of system performance. If these changes were predictable at design time (i.e. before node deployment), engineers could evaluate them in advance and experimentally or analytically prepare parameter settings for the algorithms during deployment preparations. In many cases, however, these changes are just as unpredictable as the particular nature of many WSNs, which, after all, depend on changes in their environment.

The idea of the generic Organic Network Control (ONC) system was initially presented in [1] and since has been applied to various protocols from different domains, e.g. MANets [2] and peer-to-peer applications [3]. The task of the ONC system is to dynamically adapt protocols and algorithms to changing environmental conditions at runtime without requiring details of their internal structure. The only interface between ONC and the particular protocol needs to provide means for changing algorithmic parameters. Examples for such parameters include values for timeouts and the maximum number of message retransmissions. Additionally, the ONC system requires access to observable environmental attributes that may influence the system performance. Examples for such attributes are the number of (one-hop) neighbours in a wireless network and the frequency of messages being forwarded locally. So essentially, the task of the ONC system is to *observe a set of environmental attributes*, which describe the current situation of a node, and *map it to a set of appropriate algorithmic parameters* at runtime. Most importantly, this mapping is discovered using machine learning (ML) techniques, such as Learning Classifier Systems [4]. Note that the particular semantics of the parameters is not of concern to the ONC system. Instead, the application of ML techniques ensures that situations are mapped to suitable parameters. Partially, a mapping between situations and parameters may be found in advance at design time as many (yet not all) aspects of the application are known then. For the remainder of mappings, the ONC system employs ML techniques at runtime, partially on the individual sensor nodes for lightweight adaptation and on more powerful nodes, e.g. sink nodes, for more complex ML.

In this paper we show that ONC can be successfully applied to the domain of WSN and that it improves the performance of existing algorithms in the presence of varying system conditions. As an example we chose the Adaptive Distributed Resource Allocation Scheme (ADRA) presented by Lim et al. in [5]. The remainder of this paper is structured as follows. In Sec. 2 we discuss proposals that are related to the idea of the ONC systems. A particular emphasis is given to related approaches that use ML techniques in the domain of system adaptation. In Sec. 3.1 we will briefly introduce the generic ONC framework, before providing details on how to apply it to the domain of WSNs in Sec. 3.2. In Sec. 4 we provide detailed experimental results of the performance improvements achieved by applying the ONC framework to the ADRA algorithm. We conclude the paper in Sec. 5 with a summary and an outlook to future work.

2   Related Work

Dynamic and adaptive control of wireless sensor network protocols touches three basic fields of research: On-line adaptation of network protocols, wireless sensor network protocols, and machine learning in these networks. On-line adaptation combined with on-line learning and self-optimisation is the goal of the Organic Network Control (ONC) framework. To the best of our knowledge, there are currently no other systems fulfilling the task in a comparable manner. Other approaches to allow for a dynamic adaptation usually rely on developing specialised adaptive protocols (see, e.g., [6]), exchange the protocol itself or the complete stack of protocols (*protocol composition*, e.g. in [7,8]), or using centralised systems that lead to further problems like bottlenecks, lower reaction times, loss of information, and more complex computational models (see, e.g., [9,10]). A detailed differentiation compared to ONC and further details on the approaches named before can be found in [3]. Within the remainder of this section, we will give a brief introduction to the usage of machine learning within these networks.

Although sensor nodes have hard restrictions in terms of resource usage and energy consumption, complex adaptation and optimisation mechanisms using machine learning techniques have been applied to the nodes before. Mainly, four major fields of research have been focused using these mechanisms for WSNs: Design and deployment of WSNs (e.g. [11]), localisation (e.g. [12]), security (e.g. [13]), routing and clustering. Since the former three aspects are covered using centralised approaches without applying the learning techniques to the sensor nodes, they are not of interest for this paper. The latter aspect affects the protocol logic and the communication within the network and is therefore closely related to the Organic Network Control (ONC) system.

Förster studied the restrictions of applying popular learning techniques to sensor nodes [14]. She states that especially *Reinforcement Learning* is well suited for this domain, since it is characterised by medium memory requirements, a high tolerance to dynamic topology changes, and low cost by simultaneously achieving promising results. Besides these general considerations, some examples can be found in literature where authors already investigated an integration of machine learning for routing or clustering tasks. One of the first attempts has been presented by *Boyan and Littman* in 1994 [15]. They introduced a simple Q-learning-based algorithm that learns the best paths locally at each node depending on the least latency to the destination. Another approach is discussed by *Rossi et al.* in [16]. Their framework *SARA* provides a set of statistically assisted routing protocols mainly based on energy-dependent greedy forwarding techniques. Additionally, they introduce an algorithm that learns path cost estimations using on-line heuristic search. Here, a proof of concept, details on the overheads, and an application to real-world problems are still missing. Besides these two approaches, several others can be found in literature. Also, approaches for mobile ad-hoc networks are closely related and might be adapted for usage in WSNs. A more detailed survey of existing approaches using machine learning in both fields can be found in [14]. Although machine learning techniques have been successfully applied to sensor nodes and some approaches already focused on increasing the network's communication performance, an on-demand adaptation of existing protocols in order to adapt the communication behaviour to changing environments is still missing.

3   Dynamic Control of Sensor Node Protocols

This paper demonstrates the increase of the WSN's performance achieved by applying the Organic Network Control system to dynamically adapt protocol configurations of the particular sensor nodes. Within the previous section, we presented a short introduction of machine learning techniques applied to sensor nodes in order to outline the work already done in this domain. In this section, we will start with a brief overview of the ONC system itself and explain what has to be done to enable the control of sensor nodes.

3.1   Organic Network Control

Initially, the Organic Network Control (ONC) system has been presented in [1,3]. Inspired by the generic Observer/Controller architecture [17], the design of the system distinguishes between observation and control tasks and assigns different responsibilities to the three layers as depicted in Fig. 1: Processing of the particular instance of a network protocol (Layer 0), immediate response to observed changes by using pre-evaluated solutions in combination with real-world learning (Layer 1), and planning and optimisation by accepting possibly delayed responses due to a sandbox principle (no direct influence on real world).

Layer 0 encapsulates an existing network protocol instance, e.g. a broadcast algorithm for mobile ad-hoc networks or a mode-selection protocol for sensor nodes. Since the ONC framework provides a basic solution to control existing protocols dynamically, there is no need of knowing internals of the particular protocol or interfering with the protocol logic. However, it is required that the parameters of the protocol can be altered by the ONC system. Additionally, the current status of the protocol instance and the environment it acts in have to be observable and accessible locally. For WSNs – like for mobile ad-hoc networks – the most important factor describing the current status of the protocol instance's environment, is

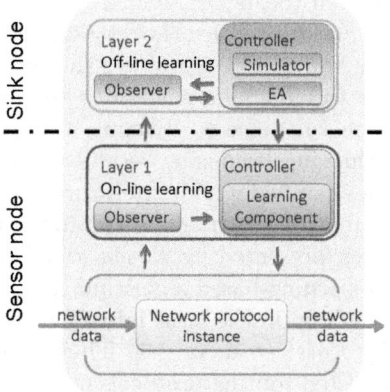

Fig. 1. Architecture of the Organic Network Control system

the neighbourhood of other nodes. Besides this observable environment, a performance measure (also called fitness or evaluation function) quantifying good and bad performance has to be provided in order to evaluate the current performance of the protocol.

Layer 1 of the ONC architecture is responsible for adapting the observed network protocol instance to changes in the environment. Therefore, it contains two basic components: an Observer and a Controller. The Observer is in charge of collecting status information about the network protocol instance and its settings locally, aggregating and augmenting this information with optional further knowledge (e.g. prediction values, historic knowledge, etc.), and building a vector describing the current situation at the node. This situation vector then serves as input to the Controller which has to evaluate the system's performance within the last evaluation cycle and choose an appropriate action to be applied to Layer 0. The main part of the Controller is a machine learning component, currently realised as a Learning Classifier System (LCS - an adapted variant of Wilson's XCS [4]). In our architecture, the LCS is responsible for selecting a new parameter set for the network protocol instance and predicting how the system will perform after applying the action. To evaluate the system's performance, the Controller compares the system's performance measure (the fitness function) with the last prediction and calculates the reward for the LCS to enable the automated learning. In contrast to the original LCS algorithm, our LCS variant is not allowed to create new classifiers (pairs of situation/conditions or parameters/actions) randomly by Genetic Algorithms. Instead, control is transferred to Layer 2 of the ONC architecture.

Layer 2 of the ONC system follows a sandbox principle, i.e. it tests large numbers of possible solutions within a closed environment (the *sandbox*) using a model of the real environment to evaluate the fitness function. It is designed using the same Observer/Controller pattern as before: The Observer monitors the Layer 1 component and realises the need of a new classifier. Based upon the same situation vector as processed by Layer 1, it activates the Controller which contains two main components: a simulation tool and an Evolutionary Algorithm (EA). The situation vector is transformed into an appropriate simulation scenario and applied to the simulator. Afterwards, the EA repeatedly evolves a number of parameter sets for the network protocol and tests them using the simulator. This bears the advantage that newly created parameter sets are not directly used in the live system, as this can cause the system to perform badly or even malfunction. Only those parameter sets that qualify in the simulator of Layer 2 are passed back to Layer 1 and may then be applied in the real world.

ONC provides a black-box solution to control different types of network protocols. To apply ONC to a new protocol, three major tasks have to be covered: Define a performance metric, specify a situation description accompanied by a distance function, and develop a simulation model for Layer 2. Additionally, the assignment of tasks and layers to locations has to be considered in case of restricted hardware, e.g. for WSNs.

3.2 Application to Sensor Networks

Based upon the previously named tasks, the details for ONC's adaptation to control WSNs are explained in the following. Within this paper we focus on mode-selection protocols (see, e.g. [18], chapter 16) as one possible example for protocols in WSNs. In order to keep the same organisation as before, we distinguish between the three layers again and describe what has to be done on each layer. Since the focus of Layer 0 is to integrate an existing protocol into the framework, two interfaces have to be defined: one for accessing the protocol's parameters and one for collecting information about the local system status. The local status of the system (the *situation*) has to take into account the distribution of neighbours within its sending and sensing range and their energy levels.

Fig. 2 describes the classification of an observed neighbourhood and its representation as done by each node using the interface provided by Layer 0. The rule-based learning component relies on a classification of similar situations in order to keep the rule base small and reuse rules for similar situations without the need of an exact matching (which is infeasible for continuous values). Here, a sector-based approach has been developed classifying different distributions of neighbouring nodes within sensing range of the particular sensor node (Fig. 2). For each of these sectors (see Sec 1 to Sec 8 as depicted in Fig. 2) four different values are stored in the situation description: the number of neighbours in active or passive (standby) mode with more/equal or less energy than the current node. In total, 32 values are stored representing a counter of nodes (4 types of nodes, 8 sectors - 32 different entries).

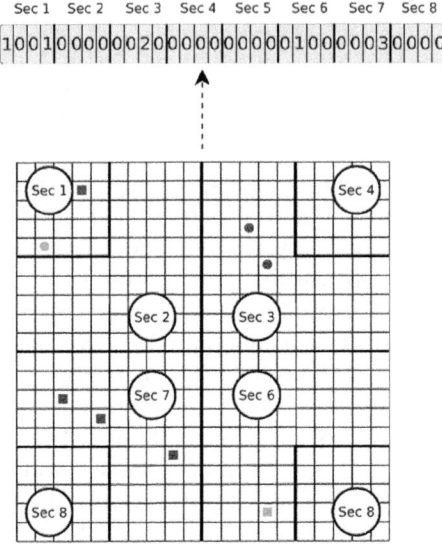

Fig. 2. Encoding of the situation

Based on this description, a distance measurement is needed. Considering the setup of the situation description, the situation for the learning component is the same, if the sectors are, e.g., shifted clockwise. This means, the influence of rotation and reflection have to be deducted before determining the distance by searching for the most similar match. Afterwards, the absolute difference between all corresponding values of the situation description is added up and used as distance measurement (e.g. another situation description with configuration 0000 in Sec. 1 would lead to a difference of 2 for this sector). The higher the distance value is, the less similar are situations.

The Layer 1 component is responsible for the adaptation and learning process. Therefore, a learning feedback (the fitness function) is needed. For mode-selection protocols in WSNs, the fitness function has to take three main aspects into account: 1. the distribution of neighbours within sending distance (goal: minimise number of active nodes), 2. the overlap rate of the environment (ensure complete coverage of environment), and 3. the energy status (minimise energy consumption). All three aspects are measured locally at each node by taking the neighbours' status into account (available due to mode-selection process). The heuristic formula is then: $Fit(n) = \frac{x+y+z}{3}$, with n identifying the currently observed network protocol instance, x being the part of the fitness function rating the node availability, y evaluating the degree of environment coverage, and z determining the energy consumption. The fitness value is calculated for the complete area which is covered by the particular sensor node (we assume that the status messages exchanged for the mode-selection process can easily be augmented with further data without significantly increasing the overhead). The formulas for these three aspects are depicted in the following:

$$I.)\ x = e^{-(x_i-a)^2+b}; \quad II.)\ y = e^{-(y_i-c)^2}; \quad III.)\ z = d + e * z_i - f * z_i^2$$

The variables $a, b, \ldots, f$ are configured empirically, whereas the resulting curves are chosen to achieve a specific behaviour: The x value as defined in part $I.$ of the formula provides a Gaussian distribution for the interval between 0 and 100% of active nodes within the sensing range of the particular node. Thereby, 50% defines the maximum of the curve, since we want to achieve that values towards the extreme values are suppressed (mode-selection has to find a trade-off between active and standby nodes). Second, the y value (see part $II.$ of the previous formula) is defined between 0 and 100% coverage rate of the environment. It describes an normal distribution type curve that has its maximum at 100% and drops strongly towards 0 when reducing the fraction of the environment that is covered by active sensor nodes. Finally, the z value defines the influence of the energy consumption of all nodes within sensing range on the fitness value. Based on the theoretical minimum and maximum values for the energy consumption and the number of nodes in sensing range, a ratio between the determined energy consumption and the aspired one can be determined. Therefore, a parabolic curve of the ratio is used which penalises the extreme values (all nodes being active or in standby mode), but favours low consumption values.

Each classifier of the learning component contains eight sectors of 4 values encoded in Byte-format. In combination with four values encoding the action in floating-point-format (see protocol overview in Sec. 4.1), 48 Byte are needed to encode one classifier. Our Learning Classifier System at Layer 1 contains 48 classifiers (see, again, Sec. 4.1), which means that a maximum of 2.5KByte of RAM is needed. The system does not rely on having the whole rule-base in RAM, instead it can be stored in the node's flash-memory. The selection of a rule, based on the set of classifiers and the distance measurement as presented before, relies on 48 comparisons (number of classifiers) of 32 values in Byte-format (situation description) – in total about 1536 simple Byte-comparisons have to be processed in each cycle which is feasible for nearly all types of sensor nodes. As summary, we can state that the application of ONC's Layer 0 and Layer 1 are possible for wireless sensor nodes.

3.3   Allocation Aspects for the Usage in Wireless Sensor Networks

An optimisation of new parameter sets using a simulation tool on Layer 2 is not feasible for sensor nodes due to resource restrictions. Therefore, we assign Layers 1 and 2 to different locations: Layer 1 remains at the sensor node, but Layer 2 is removed and transferred to a) the sink node and b) the design-time for pre-configuration of the nodes learning component. Since all nodes have similar characteristics, perform the same protocol, and their adaptation decisions are based on the same observation model, all nodes can use the same rules. For part *a*, we assume that long-lasting WSNs will have the possibility to distribute updates from the sink node to all sensor nodes using broadcast messages. Since rules for the learning component are simple pairs of situation/action and both can be serialised using only a few Byte and floating-point values with separators, the effort for communicating these new rules is low. Backwards, the communication of new needs as observed by single nodes can be done by extending the already existing status and event messages by adding data about needed rules. In total, this means that an active managing of the nodes' rule bases can be done without significant new overhead.

Since an on-demand generation of new parameter sets is not possible for sensor nodes (although an update mechanism can be used as outlined before) due to resource restrictions, the ONC system has to be configured in advance to be able to cope with arising situations during runtime (part *b*). Hence, the Layer 2 component is used at design-time generating rules for varying situations. Here, the developer has to decide how many rules he wants to use initially: The more different situations are covered by one rule, the higher is the possible benefit for the control task. But contrary to the positive effect on the system's performance, the computational overhead will also increase and therefore affect the energy consumption of the node. For each defined situation the simulator is used in combination with an EA in order to evolve a matching parameter set.

In general, a trade-off between adaptivity aspects and effort due to resource needs can be observed. In case of wireless sensor network, hard restrictions for energy resources and computation power exist - the adaptivity is decreased for the benefit of making it easier to compute. In contrast, e.g. high-loaded routers in the Internet can be equipped with additional computation power in order to achieve a higher adaptivity and consequently increase the performance. Typically, a situation between these two extreme positions occurs.

4   Evaluation

The ONC system in combination with the adaptations as described in the previous section is able to control mode-selection protocols for WSNs. Within this section, we describe the experimental setup, introduce the considered protocol, and analyse the achieved results.

4.1   Experimental Setup

In order to simulate a WSN and allow for a comparison of the system's performance using ONC-controlled or uncontrolled sensor nodes, we implemented the simulation environment in JAVA using the Multi-Agent Simulation toolkit *Repast Simphony*, see [19]. The node's protocol instance represents Layer 0 of the architecture as depicted in Fig. 1. The respective Layer 1 Controller is an adapted Learning Classifier System as described in [3]. Due to the restrictions in terms of energy consumption and computational resources, nodes have no Layer 2. Instead, the LCS is initialised with a population of classifiers that has been created in advance using different situations and matching parameter sets. Since the possible configuration for situations is infinite, this can be done only for a small fraction of possible situations. Based on the distance measurement as introduced in Sec. 3.2, we restricted the node's rule-base to 48 different classifiers which is a very small population compared to standard LCS-populations. By increasing the population size, more specialised classifiers can be created leading to a potentially increasing system performance. 150 nodes (149 sensor nodes and one sink node) have been created and applied to the simulated area, which has dimensions of 100 x 100 cells (corresponds to 2500 x 2500 meters). The Physical/Mac layer is assumed to be an IEEE 802.11 in ad-hoc mode, therefore, the sending distance is 10 cells (corresponds to 250 meters).

In order to demonstrate the benefit of ONC-control, we chose the exemplary mode-selection protocol *ADRA* (Adaptive Distributed Resource Allocation Scheme) as presented by Lim et al. in [5]. Mode-selection means to determine whether a node will be in standby mode within the next cycle or not. The ADRA protocol has a relative simple logic and offers just a few parameters to be adapted: Its algorithm contains three consecutive phases: 1) initialisation, 2) processing, and 3) decision. During the first phase, the node queries the neighbours' mode status, gets information about detected events (if any), updates its local variables (e.g. battery life), and sends information on detected targets to its neighbours. Afterwards, the information is processed in phase 2: The node receives the queried information on events, compares own information about events with the received ones, computes its mode-scheme, and sends this to its neighbours. Finally, the decision about the mode-selection is done in phase 3 by receiving the neighbours' planned schemes, resolving the own plan with neighbours' influence, and executing the plan (e.g. select standby or active mode).

The range of possible modifications performed by ONC is characterised by the *configuration space* of the System under Observation and Control (SuOC - the ADRA scheme): The configuration of the SuOC is determined by the possible values for all attributed that are subject to control action by the control mechanism (ONC). These attributes are also called configuration attributes - typically, these are the variable parameters of the particular protocol under ONC-control. The set of all the (theoretically) possible configurations constitutes the *configuration space* of the SuOC (for details on the terminoly, see [20]).

The mode-selection is done by determining a so-called *potential* value (*pot*). After initialising *pot* for the next cycle, it is increased using *priority* values depending on the special needs for three influencing aspects: localisation, coverage, and battery. The *localisation priority (LocPrio)* is used, if the node has to locate an event (e.g. triangulation using different nearby nodes). In contrast, the *coverage priority (CovPrio)* is needed to ensure complete sensing of the environment (the less nodes in the neighbourhood, the higher is *CovPrio*). Additionally, the *battery priority (BatPrio)* covers the aspect of different energy levels of the nodes. Finally, a *threshold (Thsd)* is needed defining whether the node will be in active or standby mode within the next cycle. For the standard ADRA protocol, all four values (*LocPrio*, *CovPrio*, *BatPrio*, and *Thsd*) are pre-defined and constant - here, they define the configuration space as introduced before. By applying ONC to the sensor node, they become subject to control actions allowing for situation-dependent individual settings. More details about the protocol and its parameters are given by *Lim et al.* in [5].

Like the authors of the ADRA protocol, we use an abstract representation of energy (the energy unit e) and its consumption. Additionally, simulation of nodes leads to the usage of an abstract unit of time, called *ticks*. All nodes start with an initial energy level of $20,000e$. At each *tick*, all nodes consume a defined amount of energy depending on their current mode: $5e$ in active and $0.5e$ in standby mode. The additional effort for the communication is neglected which does not influence the results, since this effort is the same for all scenarios. The mode-selection algorithm is processed every 50 *ticks*.

4.2   Experimental Results

In order to analyse the impact of ONC's dynamic adaptation of the variable protocol parameters, we performed a comparison of the static protocol version and the version with additional ONC-control. Therefore, we set up three scenarios: 1) a static distribution of nodes with periodically repeating events, 2) a static distribution of nodes with varying events, and 3) a dynamic distribution of nodes with varying events. These experiments and the received results are explained in the remainder of this section. Initially, the effect of ONC-control on the two basic aspects energy consumption and event detection are evaluated and the resulting fitness value (see Sec. 3.2) is determined. Energy consumption is measured by determining the network's operating time (approach: last node dies), the event detection by counting the number of successfully reported events. All figures show the results of 480 consecutive simulations using the same configuration.

Based upon the scenario with a static distribution of nodes and periodically repeating events (every 500 *ticks*), the standard protocol version reported 10 *events* (of 14 in total), corresponding to 7241 *ticks* until the last node of the network died. Fig. 3 describes the measured values for all 480 consecutive runs: The standard protocol version shows constant results, while the ONC-controlled version changes steadily due to the learning and update effect of the LCS. But even more important is the observation that the learning capability of ONC leads to a positive effect in terms of the system's performance: In relation to the performance using standard settings, the ONC-controlled system tends to an increasing performance over time.

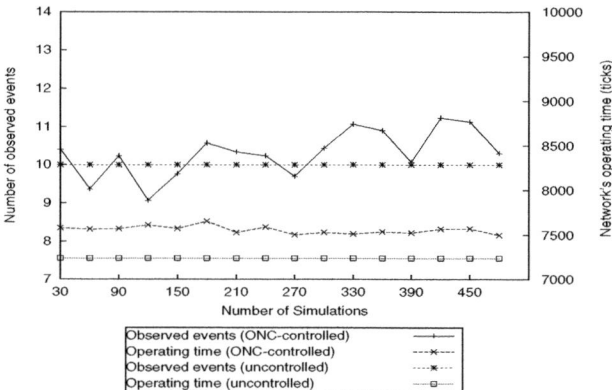

Fig. 3. Comparison of uncontrolled and ONC-controlled system performance within the static scenario: The upper curves correspond to the left scale and the lower curves to the right scale

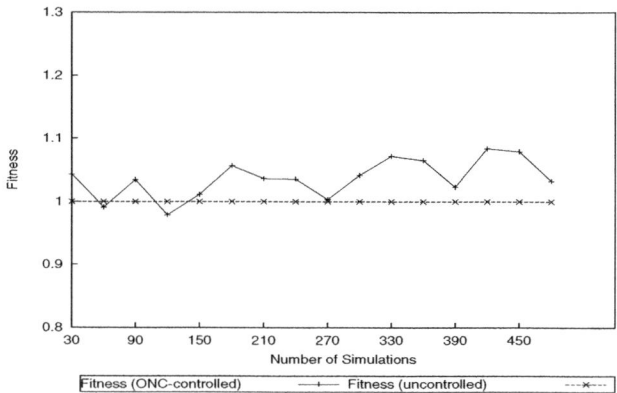

Fig. 4. The resulting fitness value for the ONC-controlled system in comparison to the standard configuration which serves a basis for a normalisation

The additional ONC-control for the same scenario resulted in an average detection of 10.3 *events* (increase of 3%) for all 480 runs and an averaged operating time of 7556 *ticks* (increase of 4.4%). Considering the curve as depicted in Fig. 3, the learning effect is visible: The ONC systems starts with a pre-defined set of classifiers, but it has to learn which one fits the current situation better. Due to this learning effect, the overall performance increases steadily and is always better than the reference solution from simulation 280 on. Considering only the experiments 280 to 480, the increase in performance is even more significant: The network's operating time stays the same, but the number of detected events increases to 10.6 *events*. To achieve a better comparability for all experiments,

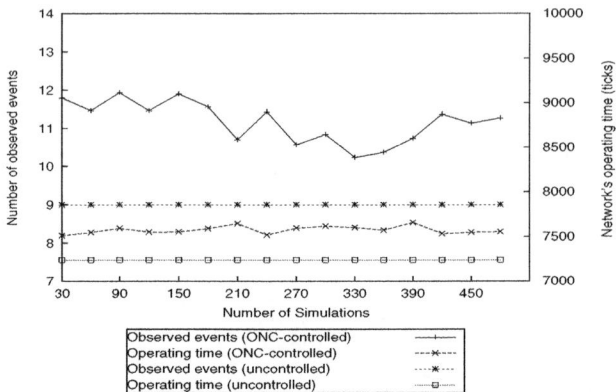

Fig. 5. Comparison of uncontrolled and ONC-controlled system performance within the second scenario with dynamic events

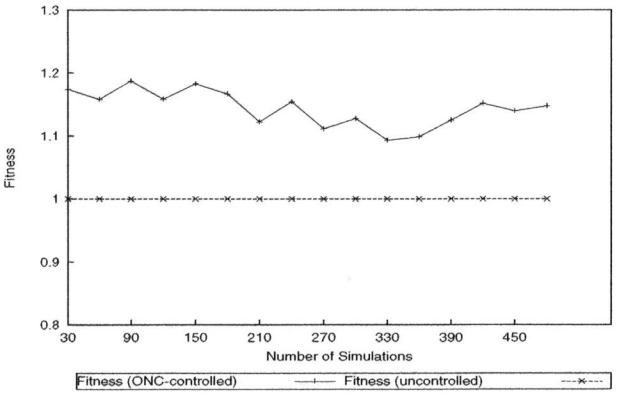

Fig. 6. The resulting fitness value for the ONC-controlled system in comparison to the standard configuration within the second scenario

we normalised the resulting fitness values as depicted in Fig. 4: Since the fitness value of the standard configuration stays the same for all 480 experiments, it is defined to be 1 in all cases – ONC's fitness value is then calculated in relation to the standard value. In this scenario the fitness value of the ONC-controlled protocol instance has been increased by 3.7% compared to the standard protocol configuration – again, the learning effect is visible.

The second evaluation scenario keeps the setup of the previous one, but events are arising randomly now. This reflects a dynamic environment compared to the static one before. As depicted in Fig. 5, the ONC-controlled solution results in an increase of 4.6% (7575 *ticks* compared to 7241 *ticks*) for the network's

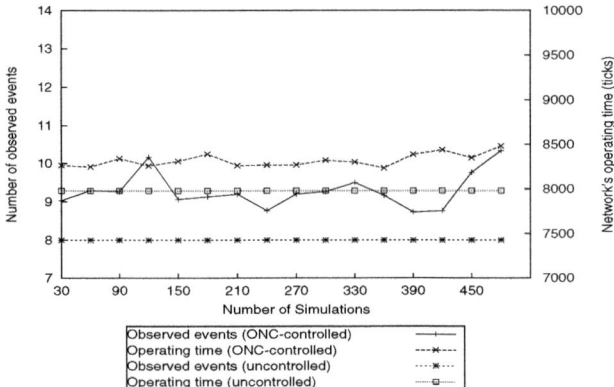

Fig. 7. Comparison of uncontrolled and ONC-controlled system performance within the third scenario with dynamic events and random node-failures

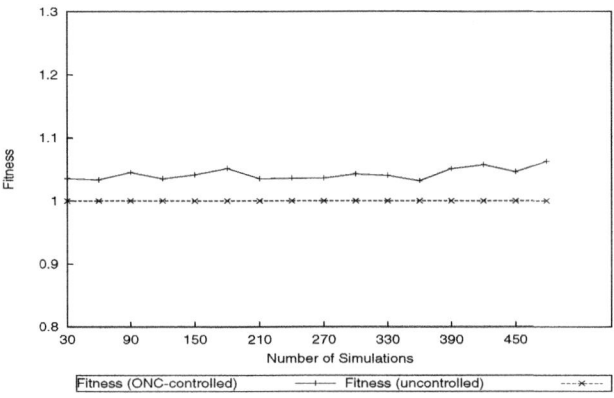

Fig. 8. The resulting fitness value for the ONC-controlled system in comparison to the standard configuration within the third scenario

operation time and in an averaged increase of 22.2% (11.2 *events* compared to 9 *events*) in the number of reported events. This leads to an increase in terms of the normalised fitness function of 15% (1.15 compared to 1 - see Fig. 6). This observation confirms the assumption that ONC will perform better and identify potential benefits for dynamic adaptation in changing environments.

The third evaluation scenario provides an even more dynamic setting: During one run of the simulation, 18 sensor nodes are selected randomly and disabled for 2000 *ticks*. In disabled mode, they consume the energy as defined for the standby mode. As depicted in Fig. 7, the number of observed events can be increased by using the additional ONC-control from 8 *events* to 9.3 *events* on average (growth of 16.3%). Simultaneously, the network's operating time is increased from 7982 *ticks* to 8321 *ticks* in average which corresponds to a benefit of 4.2%. The corresponding normalised fitness value results in a win of 10.2%, see Fig. 8. Summarised, the results of the evaluation demonstrate the benefit of the additional ONC component for sensor nodes. The system's performance can be increased significantly in dynamic environments, but there is also a noticable postive effect for static solutions.

5   Conclusion

This paper introduced the exemplary application of the Organic Network Control (ONC) system to wireless sensor networks. Based upon a short overview of the ONC system, the main adaptations to control sensor node protocols are explained. Afterwards, a protocol from the field of mode-selection algorithms with four variable parameters is chosen to demonstrate the benefit of the additional ONC-component. We analysed the behaviour of ONC in comparison to a manually optimised standard protocol configuration that provides a trade-off for all possible situations. Especially for dynamic environments, the increase in terms of the system's performance is shown to be significantly.

The system as introduced in this paper is a first investigation for the field of wireless sensor networks. Current and future work addresses several main topics: We started with a very restricted version of the ONC system, namely using only few classifiers and only few classes for the abstraction of situations. Here, a detailed investigation of the influence on both - resource usage and possible benefit - will follow. Additionally, the update mechanism has only been drafted in this paper - we plan to develop an algorithm for this simulation scenario.

References

1. Tomforde, S., Cakar, E., Hähner, J.: Dynamic Control of Network Protocols - A new vision for future self-organised networks. In: Proc. of the 6th Int. Conf. on Informatics in Control, Automation, and Robotics (ICINCO 2009), pp. 285–290 (2009)
2. Tomforde, S., Hurling, B., Hähner, J.: Dynamic control of mobile ad-hoc networks - network protocol parameter adaptation using organic network control. In: Proceedings of the 7th International Conference on Informatics in Control, Automation, and Robotics (ICINCO 2010), vol. 1, INSTICC ,pp. 28–35 (2010)
3. Tomforde, S., Steffen, M., Hähner, J., Müller-Schloer, C.: Towards an Organic Network Control System. In: González Nieto, J., Reif, W., Wang, G., Indulska, J. (eds.) ATC 2009. LNCS, vol. 5586, pp. 2–16. Springer, Heidelberg (2009)
4. Wilson, S.W.: Classifier fitness based on accuracy. Evolutionary Computation 3(2), 149–175 (1995)
5. Lim, H.B., Lam, V.T., Foo, M.C., Zeng, Y.: An adaptive distributed resource allocation scheme for sensor networks. In: Cao, J., Stojmenovic, I., Jia, X., Das, S.K. (eds.) MSN 2006. LNCS, vol. 4325, pp. 770–781. Springer, Heidelberg (2006)
6. Whiteson, S., Stone, P.: Towards autonomic computing: adaptive network routing and scheduling. In: Proc. of the Int. Conf. on Autonomic Computing (ICAC 2004), pp. 286–287 (2004)

7. Schöler, T., Müller-Schloer, C.: Design, implementation and validation of a generic and reconfigurable protocol stack framework for mobile terminals. In: Proc. of the 24th Int. Conf. on Distributed Computing Systems Workshops, pp. 362–367 (2004)
8. Rosa, L., Rodrigues, L., Lopes, A.: Appia to R-Appia: Refactoring a Protocol Composition Framework for Dynamic Reconfiguration. Technical report, Department of Informatics, University of Lisbon (2007)
9. Ye, T., Harrison, D., Mo, B., Sikdar, B., Kaur, H.T., Kalyanaraman, S., Szymanski, B., Vastola, K.: Network Management and Control Using Collaborative On-line Simulation. In: Proceedings of IEEE ICC, 06 2001, IEEE, Helsinki (2001)
10. Georganopoulos, N., Lewis, T.: A framework for dynamic link and network layer protocol optimisation. Mobile and Wireless Communications Summit, 2007. 16th IST, 1–5 (2007)
11. Carballido, J.A., Ponzoni, I., Brignole, N.B.: Cgd-ga: A graph-based genetic algorithm for sensor network design. Inf. Sci. 177(22), 5091–5102 (2007)
12. Marks, M., Niewiadomska-Szynkiewicz, E.: Two-phase stochastic optimization to sensor network localization. In: Proceedings of the International Conference on Sensor Technologies and Applications (SensorComm 2007), Octber 2007, pp. 134–139 (2007)
13. Kulkarni, R.V., Venayagamoorthy, G.K.: Neural network based secure media access control protocol for wireless sensor networks. In: Proceedings of the International Joint Conference on Neural Networks (IJCNN 2009), pp. 1680–1687 (June 2009)
14. Foerster, A.: Machine Learning Techniques Applied to Wireless Ad-Hoc Networks: Guide and Survey. In: Proc. of the 3rd Int. Conf. on Intelligent Sensors, Sensor Networks and Information (ISSNIP 2007), pp. 365–370 (2007)
15. Boyan, J.A., Littman, M.L.: Packet routing in dynamically changing networks: A reinforcement learning approach. In: Advances in Neural Information Processing Systems, vol. 6, pp. 671–678. Morgan Kaufmann, San Francisco (1994)
16. Rossi, M., Zorzi, M., Rao, R.R.: Statistically assisted routing algorithms (sara) for hop count based forwarding in wireless sensor networks. Wirel. Netw. 14(1), 55–70 (2008)
17. Richter, U., Mnif, M., Branke, J., Müller-Schloer, C., Schmeck, H.: Towards a generic observer/controller architecture for Organic Computing. In: Tagungsband der GI Jahrestagung, pp. 112–119 (2006)
18. Raghavendra, C.S., Znati, T., Sivalingam, K.M.: Wireless Sensor Networks, 2nd edn. ERCOFTAC Series. Springer, Netherlands (2004)
19. North, M.J., Collier, N.T., Vos, J.R.: Experiences creating three implementations of the repast agent modeling toolkit. ACM Trans. Model. Comput. Simul. 16(1), 1–25 (2006)
20. Schmeck, H., Müller-Schloer, C.: A characterization of key properties of environment-mediated multiagent systems. In: Weyns, D., Brueckner, S.A., Demazeau, Y. (eds.) EEMMAS 2007. LNCS (LNAI), vol. 5049, pp. 17–38. Springer, Heidelberg (2008)

Design of Location-Based Hierarchical Overlay Network Supporting P2PSIP Conferencing Service

Hui-Kai Su[1,*], Chien-Min Wu[2], and Wang-Hsai Yang[3]

[1] Department of Electrical Engineering, National Formosa University
No.64, Wenhua Rd., Huwei Township, Yunlin 632, Taiwan (R.O.C.)
hksu@nfu.edu.tw
[2] Dept. of Computer Science and Information Engineering, Nan-Hua University
No.32, Chung Keng Li, Dalin, Chia-Yi 622, Taiwan (R.O.C.)
cmwu@mail.nhu.edu.tw
[3] Dept. of Information Networking Technology, Hsiuping Institute of Technology
No.11, Gongye Rd., Dali City, Taichung 412, Taiwan (R.O.C.)
yangwh@mail.hit.edu.tw

Abstract. Most VoIP (Voice over IP) conferencing services are based on centralized architecture. Consequently, the issues of single-point failure and loading aggregation are incurred. Therefore, if the concept of P2P (Peer-to-Peer) resource sharing can be used on conferencing services, the system loading will be distributed and the system fault torrent will be improved. However, in a general DHT (Distributed Hash Table) P2P network, e.g. Chord, the geographical location of IP address and the relative position of P2P logical ID are mismatched. Long resource discovery time is needed for P2P real-time applications, especially for P2PSIP conferencing service. Thus, we proposed a hierarchical overlay network based on regional location of IP address. The hierarchical P2PSIP conferencing network is constructed by several regional overlay networks. Additionally, a hierarchical re-source-discovery mechanism was design in our paper. Finally, the system performance was simulated that can reduce resource-discovery time and total call-setup time for P2P conferencing services.

1 Introduction

With the matured Internet technology, the people's lifestyle has been changed. In a Chinese adage, it said "scholars do not go out, to know world affairs". This sentence is appropriate to describe the convenience of current Internet. People depend on Internet applications to communicate each other and obtain various required information. VoIP (Voice over IP) conferencing is one of the popular applications that can support audio and video real-time communication such as a face-to-face talking in a meeting room. However, most VoIP conferencing

---

* Corresponding author.

B. Xie et al. (Eds.): ATC 2010, LNCS 6407, pp. 92–106, 2010.

systems are based on centralized architecture that is easy to incur the problems of single-point failure and single-point heavy loading. If the concept of P2P resource sharing is used into VoIP conferencing service, some tasks of users' profile storage and audio/video mixing can be dispatched to terminal devices. The total service cost can be decreased hugely. In a ideal case, no central infrastructure has to be established by VoIP conferencing service provider. Thus, the system scalability and the resource efficiency can be improved.

However, in a general DHT (Distributed Hash Table) P2P network, the mapping of IP address and P2P logical ID is dispersed randomly. Two adjacent nodes in P2P overlay network may be far away in IP network. If it sends a resource discovery message to its neighbor node, it may spend much transmission time rather than message proccesion time on the destination node. The traditional P2P ID allocation mechanisms are suitable for file sharing applications, but they are not applicable to real-time conferencing applications. Not only the conference setup time would be increased, but also the net-work bandwidth would be wasted to deliver messages.

Thus, we proposed a hierarchical overlay network for P2PSIP conferencing services based on regional location of IP address. The hierarchical P2PSIP conferencing network is constructed by several regional overlay networks. The scope of regional overlay network may be limited in a domain or a sub-network. Additionally, a hierarchical resource-discovery mechanism was also design in this paper. Finally, the resource-discovery performance of P2P conferencing services was simulated. The results show that the hierarchical P2PSIP conferencing network can reduce resource-discovery time and total call-setup time for P2P conferencing services well.

This paper is organized below. In Section 2, we introduce the related works about conferencing system architecture. In Section 3, we propose a hierarchical overlay network for P2PSIP conferencing services. The scheme of system operations is shown in Section 4. And, the simulation and result are explained in Section 5. Finally, we give some conclusions in Section 6.

2   Related Works

In the recent years, many researches about centralized conferencing framework are discussed. The framework is divided into three models by IETF[1]. They are shown below:

- Tightly coupled model
- Loosely coupled model
- Fully distributed model

In the tightly coupled model, several entities are implemented as servers in the network, such as Focus and Mixer. These entities are deployed to enforce the conference management and control. The reliability and stability can be guaranteed well, since the states and memberships of conferences are maintained in the centralized servers. However, the model should deploy more centralized servers and apply hierarchical management to a large-scale environment, but this needs many powerful servers and may increase higher communication cost. Additionally, the IETF working groups, i.e. XCON[2] and MMUSIC[3], focus on this model. Many documents about system architectures and protocols were proposed.

The loosely coupled model is usually based on IP multicast, and there is no central point of control or conference server. This model is suitable for applying in a large-scale environment, but it is lack of reliability.

The fully distributed multiparty model so-called a peer-to-peer conference model is discussed recently. Each participant contacts to other participants in order to negotiate in a conference. There is no central point of control in this model.

The IETF P2PSIP working group[4] was organized in 2007. Based on fully distributed multiparty model, P2PSIP framework was proposed to improve the problems of single-point failure and system bottleneck of traditional SIP. Besides, the establishing cost of service infrastructure could also be reduced. Nowadays, several drafts[5,6,7] and articles[8] about P2PSIP have been proposed.

In this paper, according to the geographic characteristic of IP address structure, we proposed a hierarchical overlay network for P2PSIP conferencing services. Our motivations are to share users' resource and reduce the cost of infrastructure establishment, such as storage and media processing resources. Additionally, in the hierarchical overlay network, the single-point failure and the single-point performance bottleneck of centralized conferencing architecture would be improved.

3   System Architecture

3.1   System Environment

Our location-based hierarchical overlay network for P2PSIP Conferencing Service is shown in Fig. 1. The overlay network is constructed by peer UAs (User Agents). The P2PSIP conference service provider just needs to establish the infrastructure of conferencing backbone network. After P2PSIP UAs are booted, they will login and register to the overlay network, and join to the nearest local overlay network according to their IP address.

Additionally, each local overlay network selects one or more than one super nodes to join the common overlay network. The super nodes have to deal with P2P network routing, and control message processing between local overlay networks. For example, if a resource-discovery message is sent from a local overlay network to another, super nodes will deliver the message to the destination local-overlay network according to the framework of location-based hierarchical overlay network.

In the overlay network, P2PSIP UA will share their resource to each other, such as storage, computing and audio/video mixer resources. Unfortunately, if the resources of peers are not enough to provide conferencing services, the powerful servers in the conferencing backbone network will support them.

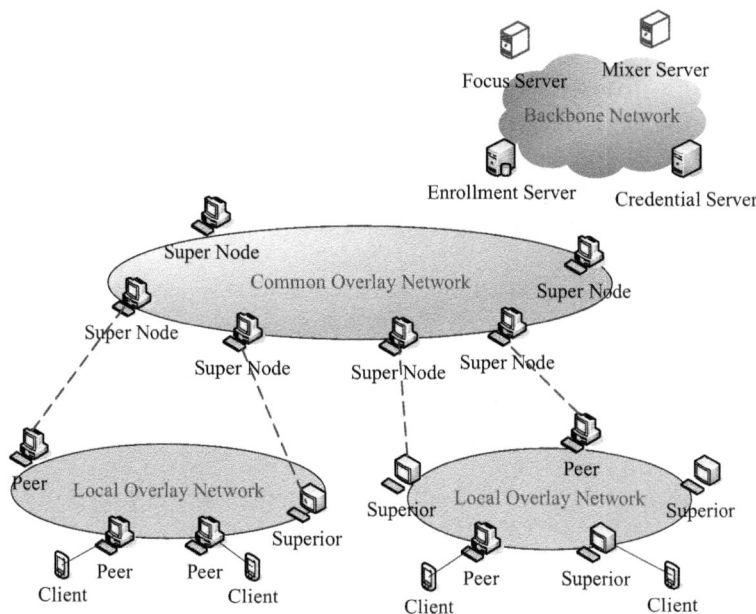

Fig. 1. A location-based hierarchical overlay network for P2PSIP Conferencing Service

The powerful servers are deployed by a P2P conferencing service provider. Therefore, the P2PSIP UAs are divided into three categories. They are defined below:

1. *Peer*: in the overlay network, peers are the major members. They share their computing and storage resources to others, and provide P2P message processing and routing.
2. *Superior*: besides the basic capabilities of peers, superiors have more resources of powerful computing and large storage than peers. They can play a P2P focus to handle establishment, modification and release of a conference, or play a P2P mixer to provide the functionalities of audio and video mixer.
3. *Client*: except for peers and superiors, clients are low-end devices. They cannot provide resources to others. They access the location-based hierarchical overlay network via peers or superiors.

3.2   Hierarchical ID Allocation

In a general DHT P2P network, i.e. Chord, Node ID is generated by a hash function according to its IP address and TCP/UDP port number. Because a hash function would disrupt the dependency of input and output values, two neighboring hosts in IP networks may be far away in P2P overlay network. The general ID allocation mechanisms are suitable for file sharing applications, but they are not applicable to real-time conferencing applications. If the structures of

(a) 140.130.19.9:5050

->H("140.130") = 986e02a28d6012d478fa3bbdcff5a0f8a3f7014d

->H("19.9:5050") = 688bcc96ebd2684abff93d7fe8be45f5138b9b5f

(b) H("140.130")+H("19.9:5050")

= 986e02a28d6012d4 688bcc96ebd2684a

H("140.130")+H("19.8:5050")

= 986e02a28d6012d4 0a187b7f1d747ac0

Fig. 2. Examples of hierarchical ID allocation; (a) two ID segments of a node; (b) the hierarchical IDs of two nodes

IP network and overlay network are mismatched, not only the conference setup time would be increased, but also the network bandwidth would be wasted to deliver messages.

Thus, we proposed a hierarchical ID allocation shown in Fig. 2. The input value of IP address and TCP/UDP port number is divided into two parts. Finally, the node ID is the combination of two hash-function results according to the first part and the last input part of input value.

For an example of 128-bit node ID using SHA1 hash function shown in Fig. 2 (a), the input value of "140.123.107.9: 5050" is separated into "140.123" and "107.9:5050". The first 64 bits of H("140.123") and the first 64 bits of H("107.9:5050") are combined as a complete node ID. In Fig. 2 (b), two hosts belong to the same domain "140.123.0.0", and they are allocated in the same 64-bit prefix node ID. Therefore, their logical distance in P2P overlay network would be shorted.

3.3   Super Node Selection

In the location-based hierarchical overlay network, super nodes have to join a local overlay network and the common overlay network simultaneously. They have to deal with message exchange between local overlay networks. One local overlay network would select one or more than one super nodes. In the framework, the issue of single cluster head failure would be avoided.

The location-based hierarchical overlay network is based on "REsource LOcation And Discovery (RELOAD) Base Protocol"[6] and Chord algorithm[9,10]. In the Chord algorithm, a peer node is aware of successor and predecessor, and maintains a finger table to keep message routing information. Besides the functionalities of Chord algorithm, the 16 specific IDs for super nodes selection are defined in each local overlay network, and decided by the first 4 bits of local ID. A peer node, which manages the resource of one of the 16 specific IDs, will be selected as a super node.

An example of 128-bit Node ID is shown in Fig. 3. The node ID can be separated into Common ID and Local ID. The Common ID equals the first 68 bits of the Node ID, and the Local ID equals the last 64 bits of the Node ID. Super nodes are decided according the 65th to 68th bits of the Node ID.

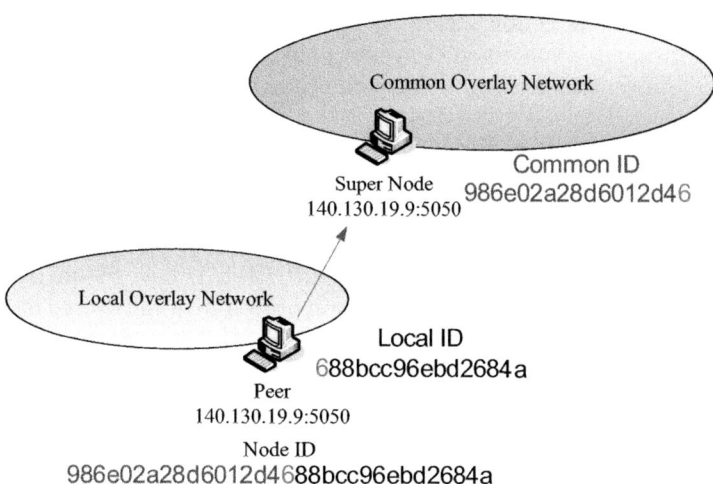

Fig. 3. The Node ID, common ID and local ID of a node

Additionally, Overlay-Prefix is defined to the first 64 bits of the Node ID, i.e. 986e02a28d6012d4 in Fig. 3.

In order to simplify the explanation, an example of 16-bit local ID in a local overlay network is illustrated in Fig. 4. If there is only one peer node in the local overlay network, it would manage all resources containing 16 specific IDs. Thus, it will be selected as a super node. By the same way, if a local overlay network has enough peer nodes, 16 super nodes at most will be selected.

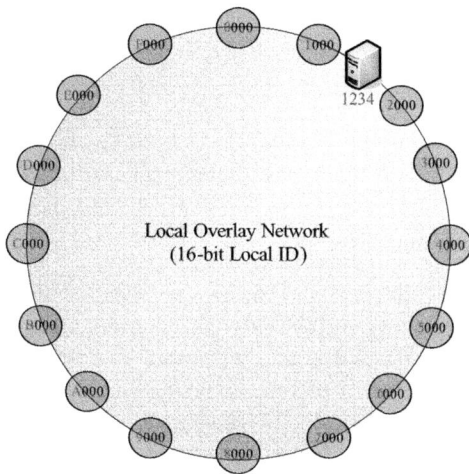

Fig. 4. The specific IDs of super nodes

The super node selection scheme is simple and compatible with the current Chord algorithm. If a super node leaves or joins, a new super node can be selected quickly, and a central decision point is unneeded.

4   System Operations

4.1   Login Procedure

Before using the conferencing service, new P2P SIP UAs have to join the location-based hierarchical overlay network. The login procedure is illustrated in Fig. 5 and explained below.

1. The P2P SIP UA decides as a peer, superior or client by itself, and sends an authentication request to Credential Server.
2. Credential Server replies a certification, which includes a unique Node ID, Enrollment Server and related system information, to the P2P SIP UA.
3. After authentication, the P2P SIP UA sends a request message with its profile to Enrollment Server to query configuration profiles of the overlay network.
4. After receiving UA profile, Enrollment Server has to decide a local overlay, which the P2P SIP UA belongs to. Except for client type, Enrollment Server replies two configuration profiles with XML format. One is common overlay network, and the other is local overlay network. Otherwise, if the P2P SIP UA is client type, it would only receive the configuration profile of local overlay network.
5. According to the configuration profile of local overlay network, if the local overlay network is non-existent, the P2P SIP UA will create the local overlay network. Otherwise, it will join the existent overlay network via bootstrap peers listed in the configuration profile.
6. If the P2P SIP UA is a super node, it will create or join the common overlay network via bootstrap peer listed in the configuration profile of common overlay network.

Finally, after finishing the join procedure, the states of common overlay network and local overlay network would be updated to Enrollment Server periodically.

4.2   Resource Registration

After joining, the new P2P SIP UA has to register new resources into the location-based hierarchical overlay network. Consequently, other P2P SIP UAs can search and obtain the new resource information based on the resource discovery mechanism that presented in the next subsection. The registered resources are divided into three classes that listed below.

- SIP URI
- Conference resources, i.e. P2P Mixer and P2P Focus
- Overlay-Prefix ID

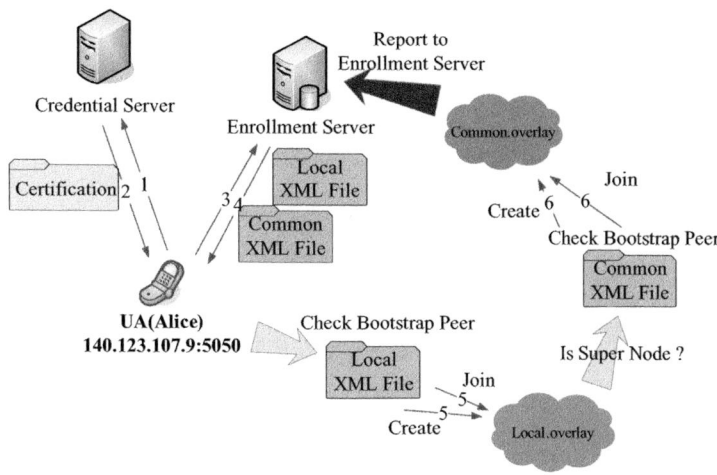

Fig. 5. The login procedure for a new UA

The registration of SIP URI is to store the mapping information of SIP URI and Node ID on the location-based hierarchical overlay network. P2PSIP UA in the overlay network makes a call or a conference by using SIP URI to identify its callee. Unfortunately, there is no central SIP server to maintain the database of user profiles. Contrarily, SIP P2P UAs can look up the Node ID by callee's URI by RELOAD scheme[6].

The URI of P2P SIP UAs is expressed as "sip://<userinfor>@<domain>" in a local overlay network. <userinfo> indicates a user name, and <domain> is the domain name of its local overlay network. In the overlay network, each P2P SIP UA has a unique URI. However, because P2P focus and P2P mixer are shared resources, their <userinfo> is fixed to "focus" and "mixer" respectively, and the URI is presented as "sip://focus@<domain>" or "sip://mixer@<domain>". Actually, there is more than one mixer or focus in a local overlay network, so the URI of focus and mixer is multiple.

The registration of conference resources is to store the P2P focus and P2P mixer profiles, such as the information of location and capabilities, on the location-based hierarchical overlay network. Based on the resource discovery mechanism that presented in the next subsection, a P2P focus and a P2P mixer can be selected to manage the conference and deal with the audio and video mixing.

The registration of Overlay-Prefix ID is to store the mapping information of Overlay-Prefix ID and domain name into the common overlay network. If a P2P SIP UA wants to look up a resource (identified as an URI) stored at another local overlay network, super nodes in the common overlay network would search its Overly-Prefix ID by the domain name of the resource's URI. The Overly-Prefix ID indicates the local overlay network of the destination peer that maintains the resource information.

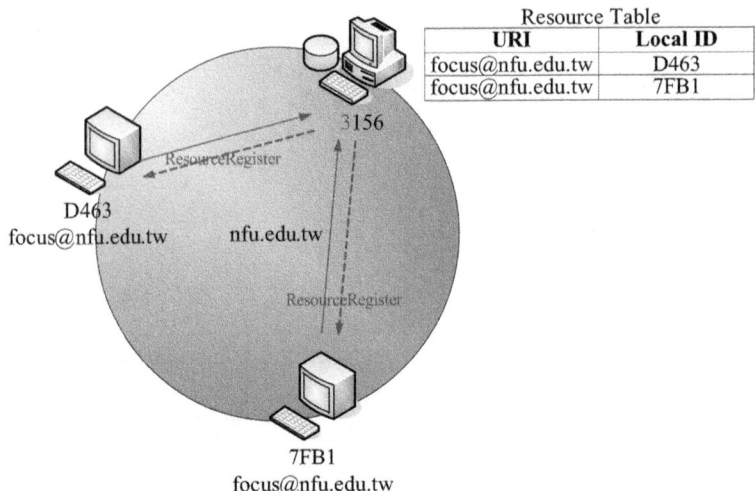

Fig. 6. The resource registration of a focus in a local overlay network

In order to simplify the explanation, 32-bit node ID is used in the below example. The 32-bit node ID is separated into 20-bit Common ID and 16-bit Local ID. Figure 6 illustrates that two P2P focuses in a local overlay network are to register their resource, i.e. the mapping of URI and Local ID, to other peers. According to SHA1 hash function, the first 16 bits of H("focus@nfu. edu.tw") equals "3156". Both resources of the focuses are maintained in the resource table of the peer "3156". Additionally, in this example, the focus list of the local overlay network is only kept in single peer. In order to improve the data availability, the method of Chord replicating data can be used in our local overlay network.

The resource in common overlay network indicates the mapping of domain name and common ID. Figure 7 shows the resource registration in a common overlay network. There are two local overlay networks in the environment. The domain "nfu.edu.tw" has two super nodes; the domain "ccu.edu.tw" has only one super node. According to the SHA1 hash function, the first 20 bits of H("nfu.edu.tw") equals "F3254", and the first 20 bits of H("ccu.edu.tw") is equal to "0A345". Thus, the resources of "nfu.edu.tw" and "ee.ccu.edu.tw" are stored on the peer "F3254" and the peer "0A345" individually. Additionally, Chord replicating data can also be applied to our common overlay network to enhance its data availability.

4.3   Resource Discovery

Based on the resource discovery of Chord algorithm, our resource discovery mechanism is enhanced for the location-based hierarchical overlay architecture. The procedure of conference setup can be divided into two stages. The first stage is that caller initializes a session to focus, and the second stage is that the focus invites callees to join the conference.

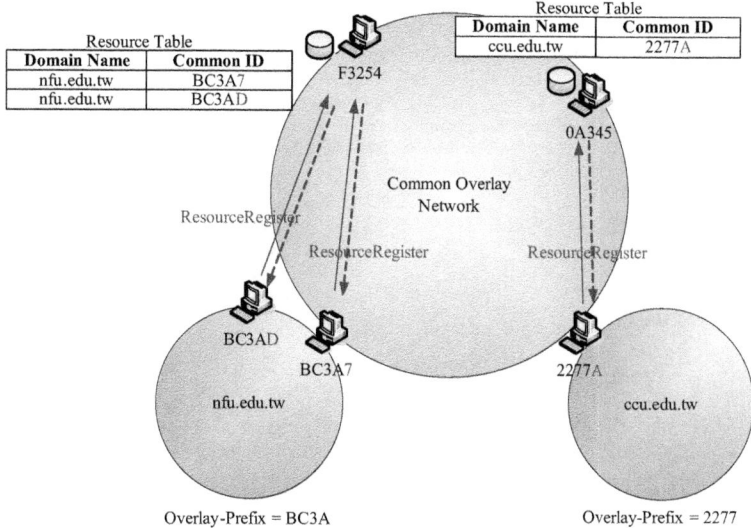

Resource Table

Domain Name	Common ID
ccu.edu.tw	2277A

Resource Table

Domain Name	Common ID
nfu.edu.tw	BC3A7
nfu.edu.tw	BC3AD

Fig. 7. The resource registration in common overlay network

The resource discovery of the first stage is illustrated in Fig. 8. In the scenario, Allen (allen@nfu.edu.tw) makes a conference call to his friends, and one of his friends is Tom (tom@ccu.edu.tw). The data flows are explained below.

1. First, Allen has to select a P2P focus to handle this conference call. According to Chord algorithm, he sends an UriGetRequest message to look up a focus (focus@nfu.edu.tw) in his local overlay network. Because of the hash result of "focus@nfu.edu.tw equals "3156". The UriGetRequest message would be delivered to the peer "3156" via other peers.
2. The focus list of this local overlay network is maintained by the peer "3156". It would randomly select one of the focuses, and reply a UriGetResponse message with a focus information (e.g. "7FB1") to Allen.
3. After that, Allen sends an AttachRequest message to the peer "7FB1" based on Chord algorithm. Finally, the peer "7FB1" would response its IP Address to Allen.
4. After receiving the IP address of focus, Allen would send an INVITE message to "focus@nfu.edu.tw" with URI-LIST according to the current SIP standard. Unlike the INVITE message for a two-way VoIP call, the participants would be listed in the URI-LIST that the caller would like to invite them to join this conference.
5. Finally, the Focus would reply an OK message to Allen, and their session would be initialized.

The resource discovery of the second stage is presented in Fig. 9. After the Focus received the conference request, it would look up each callee listed in the

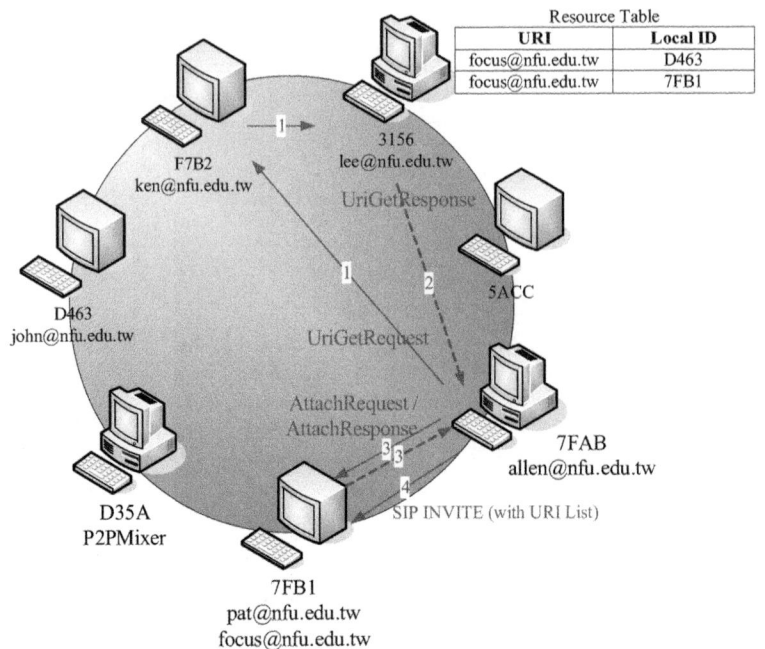

Fig. 8. The resource discovery for a P2P Focus

URI-LIST[11]. An example of discovering Tom located in other local overlay network is illustrated in Fig. 9, and the steps are described below.

1. According to the domain name of URI, the Focus (focus@nfu.edu.tw) knows that Tom is located in difference local overlay network. Therefore, the Focus would send an UriGetRequest message to its nest super node. In the clockwise direction, the nest super node of peer "7FB1" is "8000", and the resource "8000" is maintained on the peer "D463". The Focus would send the UriGetRequest message to the peer "D463" based on its finger table.
2. The node ID of John equals "BC3AD463". He joined the local overlay network (nfu.edu.tw) and the common overlay network simultaneously. Because Tom is located on the domain name "ccu.edu.tw" and the result of H("ccu.edu.tw") equals "0A345", he would send another UriGetRequest message to the peer "0A345" to obtain the super node of the domain "ccu.edu.tw", i.e. "2277A".
3. Therefore, John would forward the original UriGetRequest message to the peer "2277A" according to Chord algorithm.
4. Because the hash function H("tom@ccu.edu.tw") is equal to "C3B1", Ken would deliver the UriGetRequest message to the peer "C3B1".
5. Lee would reply the node ID of the callee (tom@ccu.edu.tw) to the Focus.
6. Consequentially, the Focus would send an AttachRequest message to the peer "227723A2" to obtain its IP address over the location-based hierarchical

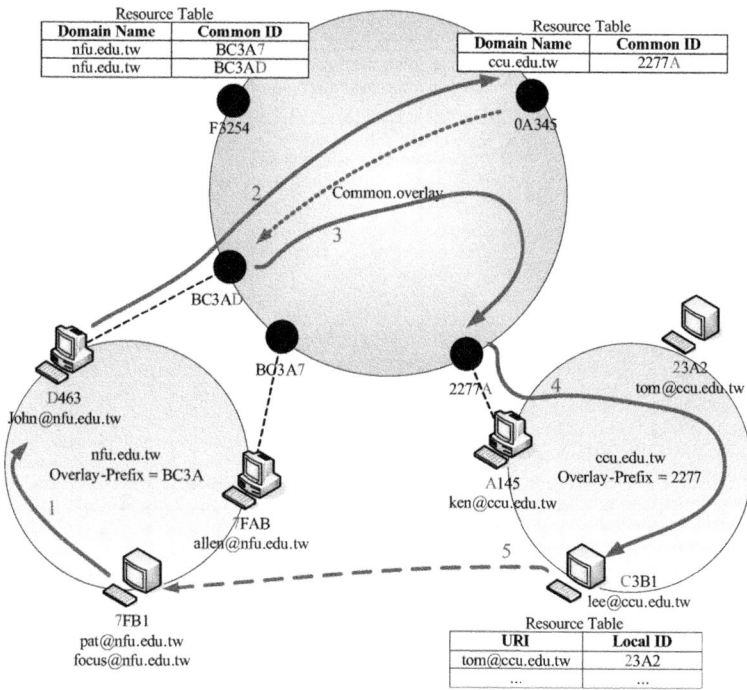

Fig. 9. The resource discovery to a callee

overlay network by the above way. Finally, the Focus would an INVITE message to Tom, and wait for his answer.

Based on our resource discovery mechanism, the session of a conference call over the location-based hierarchical overlay network would be initialized. After completing the session establishment, the Focus would look up a mixer, i.e. "mixer@nfu.edu.tw", to mix the audio/video streams according to our resource discovery scheme. Finally, this conference is going on.

5   Simulation Result

Our system is demonstrated by OverSim[12,13]. We enhanced the functionalities of OverSim, and implemented the modules of RELOAD [6] and our system operations. Additionally, two P2PSIP conference models were simulated. One is based on RELOAD specification, and the other performs our scheme.

The conference services with the above both models provided in one day are simulated. In general, because conferencing service is a VoIP value-added service, two-way VoIP service and conferencing service would be co-operated. Therefore, we assumed that each UA will make two conference calls per day averagely. Each conference call will uniformly and randomly invite two to ten participants to join

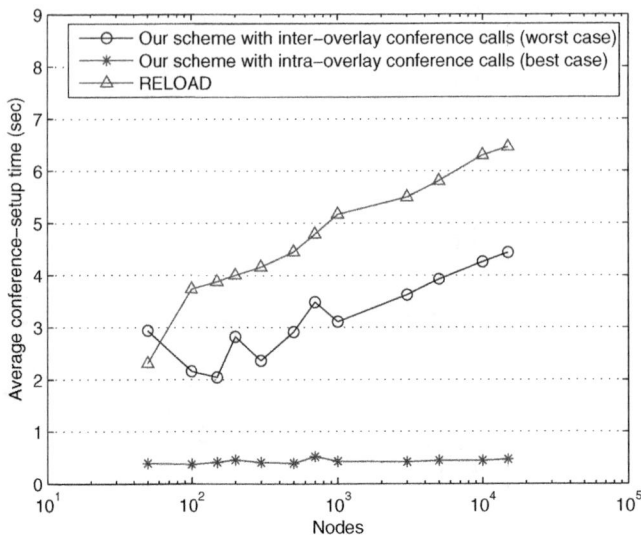

Fig. 10. The comparison of average conference-setup time

its conference. Additionally, each UA will also make four two-way VoIP calls per day as background traffic.

Figure 10 shows the performance compression of RELOAD and our scheme. The performance metric is average conference setup delay that contains the resource-discovery times for focus and callees and the SIP call setup time. The conference setup delay starts at sending the first UriGetRequest message to lookup P2P Focus (shown in Fig. 8), and ends at receiving SIP OK message from the last answerer when the last participant picks up this call.

The worst case of our scheme is that every participant of a conference is located in different local overlay network from others, called an inter-overlay conference call. The resource discovery delay and call setup delay are longer than other cases. Otherwise, the best case means that each participant of a conference is located in the same local overlay network, called an intra-overlay conference call. Moreover, because just one Chord ring is constructed by RELOAD scheme, we only discuss the random distribution of participants here.

In Fig. 10, we can observe that all performances of our scheme are better than RELOAD, except for very small scale (i.e. 50 nodes). Additionally, the performances of RELOAD and our scheme with inter-overlay conference call are increasing exponentially with overlay network scale. However, our scheme with intra-overlay conference calls is not sensitive with overlay network scale; the average conference setup delays are below 0.6 seconds. Thus, the hierarchical overlay network for P2PSIP conferencing services can improve the mismatching problem of IP network and P2P overlay network, and our scheme is appropriate for a huge P2P conferencing overlay network.

6   Conclusion

This paper proposed a hierarchical overlay network for P2PSIP conferencing services based on regional location of IP address. Moreover, a hierarchical resource-discovery mechanism was also design and presented in this paper. Finally, the resource-discovery performance of P2P conferencing services was simulated. The results show that the hierarchical P2PSIP conferencing network can reduce resource-discovery time and total call-setup time for P2P conferencing services well. Our scheme is compatible with service network increasing and suitable for a huge P2P conferencing overlay network. However, the location distribution of participants would affect our performance. In the future, we are going to investigate the distribution ratio of inter-overlay conference calls and intra-overlay conference call, and the scale ratio of common overlay network and local overlay network to against performances.

Acknowledgment

We would like to thank the National Science Council (NSC) in Taiwan. This research was supported in part by the NSC under the grant number NSC-97-2221-E-343-003 and NSC-98-2218-E-150-006. Additionally, we also thank Dr. Kim-Joan Chen and Mr. Jian-Wei Lin, Department of Electrical Engineering, National Chung-Cheng University, for their offer to this research.

References

1. Rosenberg, J.: A framework for conferencing with the session initiation protocol (SIP). RFC 4353 (2006)
2. XCON, IETF working group
3. MMUSIC, IETF working group
4. P2PSIP, IETF working group
5. Bryan, D., Matthews, P., Shim, E., Willis, D., Dawkins, S.: Concepts and Terminology for Peer to Peer SIP. draft-ietf-p2psip-concepts-02.txt (2008)
6. Jennings, C., Lowekamp, B., Rescorla, E., Baset, S., Schulzrinne, H.: REsource LOcation And Discovery (RELOAD) Base Protocol. draft-ietf-p2psip-base-08.txt (2010)
7. Jennings, C., Lowekamp, B., Rescorla, E., Baset, S., Schulzrinne, H.: A SIP Usage for RELOAD. draft-ietf-p2psip-sip-04.txt (2010)
8. Oredope, A., Liotta, A., Roper, I., Morphett, J.: Peer-to-peer session initiation protocol in highly volatile environments. In: Next Generation Mobile Applications, Services and Technologies (NGMAST 2008), pp. 76–82 (2008)
9. Stoica, I., Morris, R., Liben-Nowell, D., Karger, D., Kaashoek, M., Dabek, F., Balakrishnan, H.: Chord: a scalable peer-to-peer lookup protocol for internet applications. IEEE/ACM Transactions on Networking 11(1), 17–32 (2003)
10. Dougherty, M., Kimm, H., sang Ham, H.: Implementation of the distributed hash tables on peer-to-peer networks. In: 2008 IEEE Sarnoff Symposium, pp. 1–5 (2008)

11. Camarillo, G., Johnston, A.: Conference Establishment Using Request-Contained Lists in the Session Initiation Protocol (SIP). draft-ietf-sipping-uri-list-conferencing-05.txt (2006)
12. Baumgart, I., Heep, B., Krause, S.: Oversim: A flexible overlay network simulation framework. In: 2007 IEEE Global Internet Symposium, pp. 79–84 (2007)
13. Baumgart, I., Heep, B., Krause, S.: Oversim: A scalable and flexible overlay framework for simulation and real network applications. In: IEEE Ninth International Conference on Peer-to-Peer Computing, pp. 87–88 (2009)

Effects of Displaying Trust Information on Mobile Application Usage

Zheng Yan[1], Conghui Liu[2], Valtteri Niemi[3], and Guoliang Yu[2]

[1] Nokia Research Center, Helsinki, Finland
zheng.z.yan@nokia.com
[2] Institute of Psychology, Renmin University of China, China
liuconghui2001@gmail.com; yugllxl@sina.com
[3] Nokia Research Center, Lausanne, Switzerland
valtteri.niemi@nokia.com

Abstract. As trust helps users overcome perceptions of uncertainty and engages in usage, visualizing trust information could leverage usage behavior and decision. This paper explores the effects of trust information's visualization on mobile application usage in Finland and China with three steps: (1) Studying users' opinion on mobile application's importance. (2) Evaluating a trust indicator's effect on mobile application usage. (3) Evaluating a trust/reputation indicator's effect on mobile application usage. Although the results achieved in above two countries showed differences, both indicated that displaying an application's reputation value and/or a user's individual trust value could assist in the usage of mobile applications with different importance. We also discuss the possible reasons that caused the different effects in two countries.

1 Introduction

A mobile device has been becoming an open computing platform to run various applications. A mobile application is a software package that can be installed and executed in a mobile device (e.g. a mobile phone). Generally, this software package developed by various vendors can be downloaded for installation. A number of similar functioned mobile applications would be available for selection and usage. Future market could be very competitive. Which mobile application is more trustworthy for a user to consume becomes a crucial issue that impacts both the user's usage and the application's final success.

A user's decision is required during practical consumption of a mobile application, for example, whether it is safe to conduct an important task via using an application; if it is worth continuing usage, etc. Nowadays, mobile users are not given any cue that could help their usage decision. In fact, trust is an important factor that impacts usage. It helps consumers overcome perceptions of uncertainty and engages in trust behavior (i.e. a trusting subject's actions to depend on, or make her/him vulnerable to a trusting object). In the literature, numerous researchers have found a positive correlation between trust and use [1-4]. Some have conceptualized trust as a behavior [8-10]. Prior research has also confirmed a strong correlation between behavioral intentions and actual behavior, especially for human - software system interaction [11, 12]. However,

B. Xie et al. (Eds.): ATC 2010, LNCS 6407, pp. 107–121, 2010.

few existing studies explore the effects of visualizing trust information in the context of mobile application usage.

In this paper, we study the effects of displaying trust information on mobile applications. We hypothesize that visualizing trust information could leverage users' usage decision. We validate that displaying a mobile application's reputation (public trust) value and/or a user's individual trust value could enhance the user's ability to perform appropriate actions in various usage contexts. Detailed trust information about how trust/reputation values are generated can be accessed in an additional way during application execution for the purpose of usability. Our validation is based on a three-stage experiment conducted in both Finland and China.

In the rest of this paper, we firstly give a brief review on related work. Then, we introduce our research questions and experiments followed by experimental details and results. We further discuss the possible reasons that caused the difference of results in two countries. Finally, conclusions are presented in the last section.

2   Background and Related Work

Trust is firstly a social phenomenon. With the rapid growth of computer and networking technology, human – computer trust has been paid attention to. Trust has been defined by researchers in many different ways, which often reflect the paradigms of particular academic disciplines. In this paper, we derived our understanding of trust in mobile applications that has its roots crossing multiple disciplines [6]. A user's trust is defined as his/her belief on a mobile application that could fulfill a task as expectation. Reputation is public trust derived from direct and indirect knowledge or experiences. In our study, it is defined as the public belief on a mobile application that could fulfill a task according to many people's expectations.

Trust is an integral component in many kinds of human interaction, allowing people to act under uncertainty and with the risk of negative consequences [14]. Recently, researchers in Human-Computer Interaction (HCI) and human factors have studied trust in an on-line context, but few in the mobile application domain. The realization that design can affect the trust of a user has had implications for user interface design, web sites and interactivity in general [15]. Some researchers examined the cues that may affect trust. These cues range from design and interface elements, to perceived website credibility, to the extent to which the technology is perceived and responded to as a social actor (e.g. photographs and other indicators of social presence) [16]. Research focuses on the cues that convey trustworthiness to users. Interface design can give cues about trust or signal trustworthiness [16, 17]. However, this part of research did not consider how to confer computational trust values to the users.

Highly related to our work, notification systems attempt to deliver current, important information to users in an efficient and effective manner without causing unwanted distraction to ongoing tasks [18]. McCrickard et al. commented that the effects of incoming notifications on ongoing computing tasks have been relatively unexplored [18]. Notification without interruption of usage still lacks investigation, especially for mobile and ubiquitous devices that include a small display element. Antifakos, et al. conducted experiments to show that displaying confidence information increases the user's trust in a system in various contexts classified by criticalness [19].

But Rukzio et al. proved that the user needs slightly more time and produces slightly more errors when the system confidence is visualized [20]. The contradictory results implied that the visualization of system confidence seems questionable or works differently in different situations.

Recently, trust and reputation mechanisms have been proposed in various fields of distributed systems, such as ad hoc networks, peer-to-peer systems, Grid and pervasive computing, web services and e-commerce [6]. In many existing web services (e.g. eBay.com and Amazon.com), reputation values (mostly in a Likert scale) are displayed based on rating in order to assist users' decision. However, few work in the past, as we know, studied mutual effects of visualizing both individual trust value and public trust (i.e. reputation) value to the mobile application users during its execution.

In addition to all above, the third party, and cultural factors are also important variables affecting trust and its development [21]. It was found that Japanese have a generally low level of trust compared with Americans [22]. Karvonen found that Finnish consumers are the most cautious and Icelandic consumers are the most trusting in e-commerce in Nordic countries [23].

A lot of work has been conducted regarding user interface design in order to improve user's trust, mainly for web sites and in the context of e-commerce. Still, prior art left rooms for further studies on the effects of trust information on usage behaviors and, in particular, on how to provide trust information for mobile users. In the work presented in this paper, we use a trust indicator to indicate a user's individual trust value and a trust/reputation indicator to indicate both the individual trust value and reputation value. They are interface design elements that provide the cue of trust information through a mobile application trust management system [7]. Particularly, a user's individual trust value could play as valuable credibility for the user's contribution (e.g. his/her rating) to the reputation of a mobile application. In addition, the individual trust value and the reputation value could serve as credibility with each other. But no previous researches investigated these two pieces of information's mutual effects on users, which is one of our research targets. What is more, the above effects could also be impacted by region and culture (e.g. western and eastern cultures), and context (e.g. the importance of the mobile application), which is also what we aim to explore in our study.

3   Research Questions and Experiment Overview

3.1   Displaying Trust Information for Mobile Application Usage

A user's trust in a mobile application is built up over time and changes with the use of the application due to the influence of many factors. We developed a system to calculate the device's estimate on its user's individual trust based on his/her usage behaviors (e.g. using behavior about normal usage statistics, reflection behavior related to application performance and user experience, and correlation behavior regarding similar functioned applications) [7, 13]. We achieved an individual trust model by mathematically formalizing trust behavior measures that were investigated in a large scale user study [13]. The individual trust is calculated by the user's mobile device based on trust behavior observation.

The application's reputation value is generated through aggregating the users' individual trust and ratings together. It is issued by a reputation service provider, as designed in [7]. We use a number to indicate the individual trust value and the reputation value, respectively. Their value range is from 0 to 1, representing from full distrust to full trust. We use a rectangle bar to indicate the trust value and a trapezoid bar to indicate the reputation value in our experiments. Concretely, the user's individual trust value is presented by the trust indicator. The trust/reputation indicator presents both values.

We also assumed that detailed trust information is available through an additional access, either from a device menu or by touching the indicator or via a short-cut key. This is because providing comprehensive information and necessary explanation could increase users' trust [24]. But directly displaying the detailed trust information (e.g. how these values are generated and who provides this information) could influence the user's usage experience due to the limited screen size of mobile devices.

Although application reputation is very helpful for the users to select an application for purchase and installation, we still faced an important system design issue: is it helpful for the users if we display the real time trust information (i.e. trust and/or reputation values) during the application usage or consumption? The work presented in this paper aims to evaluate the effects of displaying trust information on mobile application usage. Concretely, we try to explore the following research questions:

1. How important do people think in using various mobile applications?
2. How does the individual trust information affect mobile application usage?
3. How does the individual trust and public reputation information affect mobile application usage?

3.2 Experiment Overview

We developed an experiment toolkit and conducted a three-stage user study to investigate the above research questions in both China (CN) and Finland (FI). We adopted 48 mobile applications and recorded their usage videos. The 48 mobile applications were selected from real products or prototypes, which provide a diverse sample of various mobile application scenarios and usage contexts. Examples include mobile enterprise solutions (e.g. corporate email checking); mobile personal business solutions (e.g. mobile payment, wallet, and safe box); mobile entertainment solutions (e.g. mobile TV, mobile video/audio/radio/music, gaming and camera); mobile life and social networking solutions (e.g. mobile search, location based services, maps, instant messaging and VoIP applications, travel aids, and mobile diary); mobile education solutions (e.g. e-book reader and multi-language translator); and integrated applications that provide an easy access to various mobile Internet services, e.g. Nokia WidSets; and Yahoo! Go.

In the first experiment we assessed the importance of mobile application scenarios. Using this result we selected a small set of 9 applications based on their importance rates (low, medium and high) and showed them in the later two experiments. In the second and the third experiments with different participants, the trust indicator or the trust/reputation indicator was displayed in one experiment block, while in the other block no information about trust was given. For each application usage scenario (showed as a video) we asked the participants to rate their willingness to continue consumption and check trust information. Thereby, the effects of three variables: the availability of trust information, trust information itself (either a trust value indicator or a trust/reputation values indicator), and the specific mobile application scenario (with different importance rates) were studied, respectively. Meanwhile, the results achieved in both countries were also compared. Table 1 shows the design of Experiment 2(E2) and Experiment 3 (E3).

Table 1. The design of Experiment 2 and 3

	Experiment variables	Block 1	Block 2
E2	Indicated trust value	Low, mid, high	Low, mid, high
	Indicator availability	No	Yes
	Application importance	Low, mid, high	Low, mid, high
	Region (test sites)	Finland & China	Finland & China
E3	Indicated (trust value) × (reputation value)	(low, mid, high) × (low, mid, high)	(low, mid, high) × (low, mid, high)
	Indicator availability	No	Yes
	Application importance	Low, mid, high	Low, mid, high
	Region (test sites)	Finland & China	Finland & China

4 Experiments and Results

4.1 Experiment 1: Application's Importance

We define importance as how important a specific task that can be fulfilled by a mobile application is to the participant concerning its usefulness and personal interest. To determine it, each participant's preferred scale is assessed in Experiment 1.

Experimental Toolkit, Participants and Procedure
The experimental toolkit contains a number of testing slides. Each testing slide is divided into four parts under the application name, as shown in Fig. 1. Part 1 is a brief introduction of the mobile application. Part 2 is the explanation of assumed application scenario and an underlying task. Part 3 is a video record of the application usage. The videos last from 48 seconds to 3 minutes and 17 seconds. Part 4 is a feedback area where the participant can use the scroll bars to provide his/her feedback. The experiment data were automatically recorded.

In Finland, 26 participants mainly from a university participated in this study. We selected 23 valid samples (39.1% female) for data processing. This group ranged in age mostly from 19-29 years old, and 87.0% majored in science and technology, but also arts (8.7%) and business (4.3%). In China, we selected 26 valid samples (61.5% female) from a total of 31 participants for data processing. The sample was composed of 13 graduates and 13 undergraduates. This group ranged in age from 19-29 years old, and 7.7% majored in science and technology, while 57.7% in arts, and 34.6% in business. Each participant in both countries was rewarded a gift after the testing.

Warm Up Example 1: Animated SMS

- A SMS allows you to send SMS with animated emotions and animations.
- Application scenario and underlying task:
  - You send an animated SMS to your friend for e.g. a birthday celebration

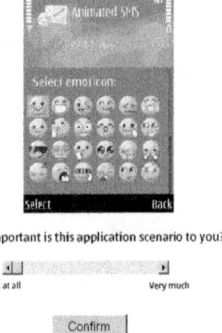

How important is this application scenario to you?

Not at all   Very much

Application Importance Test   Confirm

Fig. 1. Example testing slide of experiment 1

In this experiment, each participant completed a series of application scenarios to assess his/her opinion on application importance. For each scenario, shown as a text description and a video, the participant was asked to answer the following question: How important is this application scenario to you?

A scroll bar was provided for the experiment participants to indicate the importance rate (IR) from 'not at all' to 'very much'. The corresponding values attached to them are 0 and 1, respectively. After answering these two questions, the participant pressed "Confirm" button. Then the test automatically went to the next scenario. After each user test, the display order of the application scenarios was shifted by two. Meanwhile, all the scroll bars' values were reset to 0.

Results

The importance rates of the 48 application scenarios varied between .224 and .777, with an average of .487 in Finland, and between .314 and .887, with an average of .553 in China, respectively. This showed that the applications adopted in the experiment covered the continuum of importance well.

Table 2. Selected mobile applications (FI and CN)

Application groups	IR low		IR medium		IR high	
	FI	CN	FI	CN	FI	CN
Application names	LifeBlog Video Download Shozu	LifeBlog TextTV **Web-Browser**	Gizmo Yahoo!Go; M-realplayer	Mobi-Reader Yahoo!Go M-realplayer	Nokia Maps Gmail **Web-Browser**	Camera Fring Music player
IR average	**.292**	**.341**	**.478**	**.539**	**.719**	**.773**
IR stdev	.010	.038	.059	.008	.042	.014

We grouped and selected the applications based on the importance rate. As shown in Table 2, the results in Finland and China are different, implying that people's opinions on mobile applications' importance could be different in different regions. Surprisingly, one of the high important applications (i.e. mobile web browser) in Finland was treated unimportantly in China although its usage experience rate is not low (73.9% in Finland and 49.2% in China). We further conducted paired samples t test to evaluate our grouping. The t and p values of high importance group and medium importance group are 25.666 and <.005 in Finland; 9.517 and ☐ .001 in China, respectively. The t and p values of medium importance group and low importance group are 4.775 and <.05 in Finland; 9.678 and <.001 in China, respectively. The t and p values of high importance group and low importance group are 14.405 and <.005 in Finland; 11.16 and <.001 in China, respectively. The results showed that our groupings in both countries are valid.

4.2 Experiment 2: Trust Indicator's Effects on Mobile Application Usage

The goal of this experiment is to study the trust indicator's effects on mobile application usage. We try to investigate if displaying the device self-recognized individual trust value could assist in the usage of mobile applications.

Design

We applied a design with three independent variables: application scenario (with an importance rate), the trust indicator, and indication-availability, i.e. whether or not the indicator is displayed. We also tried to investigate regional influence in our study.

This part of experiment was conducted in two blocks. In Block 1, no information about trust was given whilst in Block 2 the trust indicator was displayed. The independent variable application scenario was randomized in both blocks. We made use of the previously chosen 9 applications from Experiment 1. The scenarios in Block 1 and Block 2 were different regarding the same application. But inside Block 2, we applied the same scenarios for each application to indicate different trust values. Thus, the selected 9 scenario sequences were repeated at 3 different individual trust values (Low - 0.15, Medium – 0.5, and High – 0.9). This resulted in 9*3 trials in Block 2. The application scenario order was counterbalanced across participants.

Experimental Toolkit, Participants and Procedure

Each testing slide in Experiment 2 contains the test for one mobile application scenario and its structure is the same as that of Experiment 1. The application usage videos last from 34 seconds to 2 minutes and 1 second. An example testing slide is provided in Fig. 2.

In Finland, 31 university students participated in this study. We selected 29 (27.6% female) valid samples for data processing. This group ranged in age from 18-30 and came from mainly the science and technology departments (82.8%). In China, 30 Chinese university students participated in this study. We selected 26 (57.7% female) valid samples for data processing. This group ranged in age from 19-29 and mainly major in arts (77.0%), but also science and technology (11.5%), and business (11.5%). Each participant in both countries was rewarded a gift after the testing.

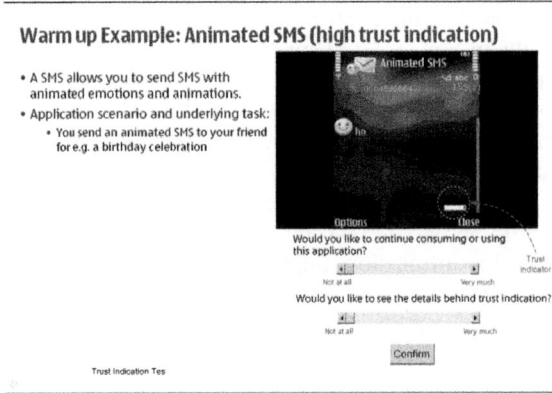

Fig. 2. Example testing slide of experiment 2

In Experiment 2, each participant completed a series of scenarios without the trust indicator in Block 1 and with the trust indicator in Block 2 to assess his/her willingness of continuous consumption and the willingness to see the trust value of the application (in Block 1) or the detailed trust information (in Block 2). For each scenario, the participant was asked to answer the following two questions:

- Would you like to continue consuming or using this application? (Block 1 & 2)
- Would you like to see the trust value of this application? (Block 1)
- Would you like to see the details behind the trust indicator? (Block 2)

After each user test, the test order of the application scenarios in Block 1 and Block 2 was shifted by 1 and 3 respectively in a counterclockwise way. Meanwhile, all the scroll bars' values were reset to 0.

Results
Usage willingness with and without trust indicator
An analysis of variance (ANOVA) was performed to test the effects of the trust indicator on the usage of mobile application, with the importance rate (high, medium, and low) and the trust indicator value (high, medium, and low) as within-subject factors, as reported in Table 3. We found significant main effects of the importance rate (IR) and the trust value (TV), indicating that the willingness of continuously using a mobile application increased from the importance rate low to high and from the trust value low to high, as shown in Fig. 3 with standard errors. However, the interaction between IR and TV was not significant in both countries. This indicated that the effect

Table 3. Experiment 2 ANOVA results on usage willingness

Factors	Effects in Finland (FI)	Effects in China (CN)
IR	$F(2,56)=30.447, p<0.005$	$F(2,50)=6.830, p=0.005$
TV	$F(2,56)=1035.187, p<0.001$	$F(2,50)=17.651, p<0.001$
IR × TV	$F(4,112)=0.183, p=0.941$	$F(4,100)=0.275, p=0.830$

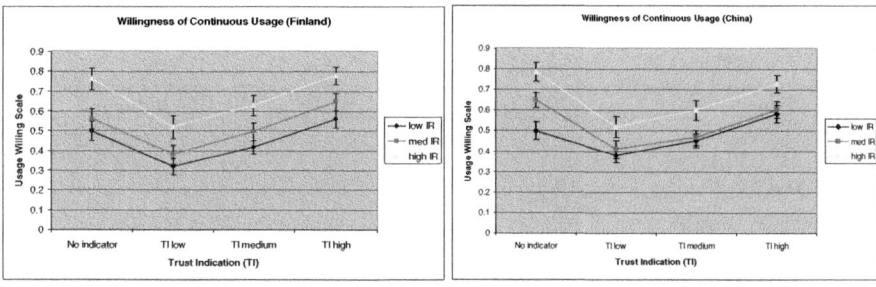

Fig. 3. Usage willingness with and without trust indicator (Finland and China)

of trust value did not differ over application scenarios with different importance rates. Table 4 compared the results of paired samples t test to examine the effect of the trust indicator on the usage of mobile application in two countries.

Table 4. Paired-samples t test on usage willingness with and without a trust indicator

Pairs	Finland		China	
	t	*p*	*t*	*p*
NO_TI - TV_L	9.546	<.000	4.679	<.001
NO_TI – TV_M	3.977	<.005	4.455	<.001
NO_TI - TV_H	-1.867	.099	2.287	.077

Willingness of checking trust information with and without trust indicator

We conducted a two-way (importance rate × trust value) repeated measure ANOVA to test the effects of the trust indicator on the user's willingness to check detailed information behind trust indication. We only found very significant effect of trust indicator [$F (2, 56) = 124.777$, $p < 0.000$] in Finland. This indicated that the willingness to check the detailed trust information behind trust indicator did not vary over the importance rate and the indicated trust value in China, but varied over the indicated trust value in Finland, as shown in Fig. 4 (with standard errors). We also found from paired sample t test that the trust indicator affects the check willingness according to its displayed values. But the effects are different in two countries, as shown in Table 5.

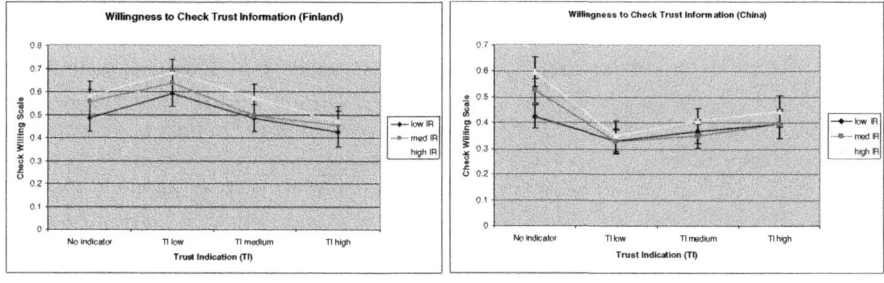

Fig. 4. Willingness to check trust information (Finland and China)

Table 5. Paired-samples t test on trust information check willingness with and without a trust indicator

Pairs	Finland		China	
	t	*p*	*t*	*p*
NOTI - TV_L	-4.390	<.005	4.731	<.001
NOTI - TV_M	.862	.411	4.898	<.001
NOTI - TV_H	3.888	<.005	2.699	<.05

4.3   Experiment 3: Trust/Reputation Indicator's Effects on Mobile Application Usage

Based on the literature study, public trust and other people's usage information could be very helpful for mobile application consumption. Experiment 2 only investigated the effects of displaying individual trust information on mobile application usage. Experiment 3 further explored the effects of displaying both individual trust and public trust (reputation) on mobile application usage. We try to investigate the mutual influence of visualizing these two pieces of information and study if the trust/reputation indicator (TRI) could assist in the usage of mobile applications.

Design

The design of this experiment is very similar to that of Experiment 2. Three independent variables were applied: application scenario (with an importance rate), the trust/reputation indicator, and indication-availability. The same as Experiment 2, this experiment was conducted in two blocks. In Block 1, no information about trust/reputation was given whilst in Block 2 the trust/reputation indicator was displayed. The selected 9 application scenario sequences were repeated at 9 different trust/reputation values (Low – 0.15, Medium – 0.5, and High – 0.9 × Low – 0.15, Medium – 0.5, and High – 0.9). This resulted in 9*9 trials in Block 2.

Experimental Toolkit, Participants and Procedure

The same toolkit was used. In the test, letter T and R were marked beside the rectangle bar and the trapezoid bar to make the participants easily identify the trust value and the reputation value. Fig. 5 shows an example testing slide.

In Finland, most of participants were university students. We selected 25 valid samples (28% female) from 26 participants for data processing. This group ranged in age from 18-35 and majored in science and technology (68.0%), but also arts (8%) and business and law (12%). In China, we selected 28 valid samples (67.9% female) from 31 university participants for data processing. This group ranged in age from 19-29 and majored mostly in arts (67.9%), but also science and technology (10.7%) and business (21.4%). Each participant in both countries was rewarded a gift after the testing.

The procedure of this experiment is the same as that of Experiment 2. For each scenario, the participant was asked to answer similar questions to E2. After each user test, the test order of the application scenarios was shifted by 1 and 9 in Block 1 and Block 2 in a counterclockwise way, respectively. Meanwhile, all the scroll bars' values were reset to 0.

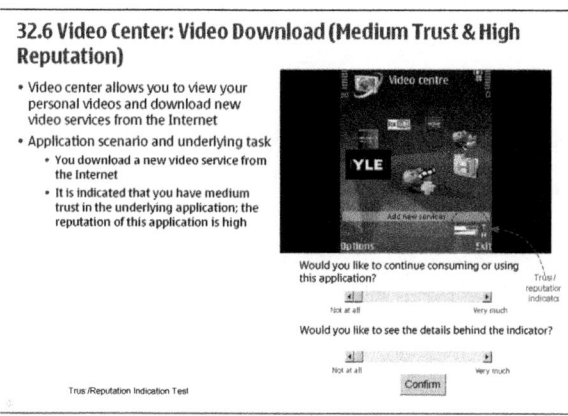

Fig. 5. Example testing slide of experiment 3

Results

Usage willingness with and without trust/reputation indicator

The usage willingness scale was subjected to an analysis of variance (ANOVA) with three within-subject factors: the importance rate (IR) (high, medium, and low), the indicated trust value (TV) (high, medium, and low), and the indicated reputation value (RV) (high, medium, and low), as reported in Table 6. We found significant main effects of IR, TV and RV, indicating that the willingness of continuous usage increased from the importance rate low to high, from the indicated trust value low to high, and from the indicated reputation value low to high in both countries, as shown in Fig. 6 with standard errors. There was a significant interaction between IR and TV in China; but not significant in Finland. There was a significant interaction between IR and RV in China; but not significant in Finland. However, there was a significant interaction between TV and RV in both countries. The interaction effect among IR, TV and RV was significant in China; but not significant in Finland. This indicated that the effect of trust value and/or reputation value did not differ over application scenarios with different importance rates in Finland, but the situation is different in China. The effects of TV differ over RV significantly in both countries, and vice versa. The paired sample t test also indicated that the trust/reputation indicator has significant impact on the usage willingness according to its displayed values, as shown in Table 7.

Table 6. Experiment 3 ANOVA results on usage willingness

Factors	Effects in Finland (FI)	Effects in China (CN)
IR	$F(2,48)=13.202, p<0.02$	$F(2,54)=4.629, p=0.05$
TV	$F(2,48)=707.86, p<0.000$	$F(2,54)=42.148, p<0.001$
RV	$F(2,48)=1009.887, p<0.000$	$F(2,54)=28.734, p<0.001$
IR × TV	$F(4,96)=0.951, p=0.483$	$F(4,108)=14.614, p<0.001$
IR × RV	$F(4,96)=1.513, p=0.286$	$F(4,108)=3.212, p=0.05$
TV × RV	$F(4,96)=8.317, p=0.006$	$F(4,108)=8.780, p=0.001$
IR × TV × RV	$F(8,192)=0.364, p=0.925$	$F(8,216)=2.388, p=0.05$

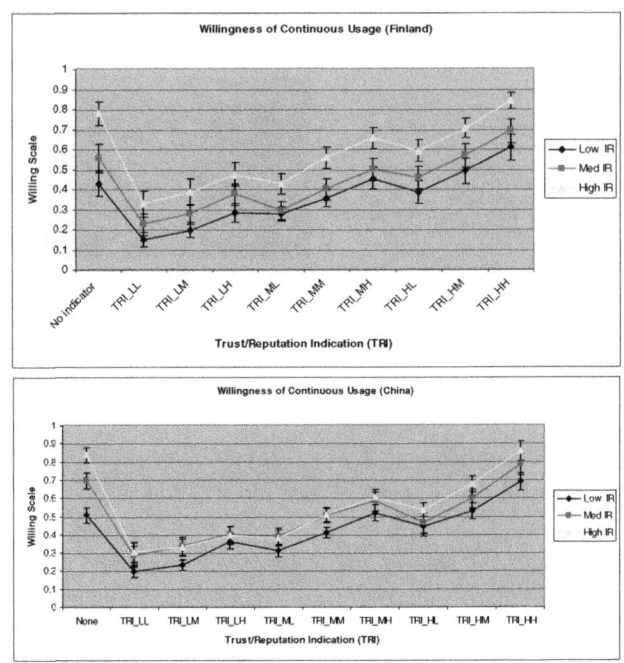

Fig. 6. Usage willingness with and without trust/reputation indicator (Finland and China)

Table 7. Paired-samples t test on usage willingness with and without a trust/reputation indicator

Pairs	Finland		China	
	t	*p*	*t*	*p*
NO_TRI - TRI_LL	11.690	.000	8.304	.000
NO_TRI - TRI_LM	9.783	.000	9.616	.000
NO_TRI - TRI_LH	7.311	.000	7.058	.000
NO_TRI - TRI_ML	7.981	.000	7.217	.000
NO_TRI - TRI_MM	5.908	.000	5.700	.000
NO_TRI - TRI_MH	1.974	.084	2.924	.007
NO_TRI - TRI_HL	4.678	.002	3.859	.001
NO_TRI - TRI_HM	-.048	.963	1.806	.082
NO_TRI - TRI_HH	-5.917	.000	-2.459	.021

Willingness of checking trust information with and without trust/reputation indicator
We conducted a three-way (IR × TV × RV) repeated measure ANOVA to test the effect
of the trust/reputation indicator on the user's willingness to check detailed trust information behind the indicator. As shown in Fig. 7 (with standard errors displayed), we found
a significant main effect of TV [$F (2, 54) = 9.809$, $p < 0.01$ in China; $F (2, 48) = 13.840$,
$p < 0.05$ in Finland]. The main effect of RV reached marginal significant level [$F (2, 54)$
$= 3.293$, $p = 0.069$] in China and significant level [$F (2, 48) = 77.646$, $p < 0.005$] in
Finland. No other main effects and interactions reached statistical significance in China.
But in Finland, The main effect of IR reached marginal significant level [$F (2, 48) =$
3.037, $p = 0.158$]. In addition, there was a significant interaction between TV and RV

$[F\ (4,\ 96) = 64.817,\ p < 0.000]$ in Finland, implying that the effects of TV differ over RV significantly, and vice versa.

As shown in Table 8, the paired samples t test implied that the sharper difference between the trust value and the reputation value, the higher willingness is to check the detailed trust/reputation information in Finland. However, the check willingness is generally lower with the trust/reputation indicator than without any indicator in China. The results indicated that the trust/reputation indicator has positive impact on the check willingness according to its displayed values.

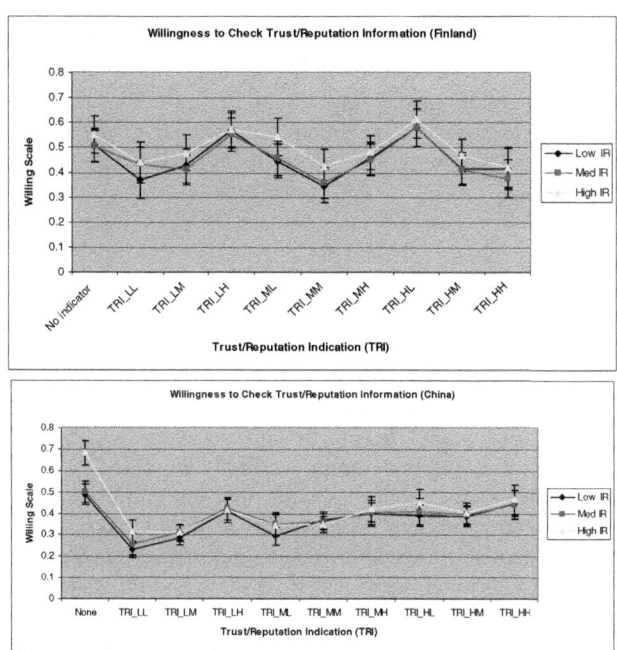

Fig. 7. Willingness to check trust information (Finland and China)

Table 8. Paired-samples t test on trust information check willingness with and without a trust/reputation indicator

Pairs	Finland		China	
	t	*p*	*t*	*p*
CW_NOTRI - TRI_LL	4.061	.004	6.022	.000
CW_NOTRI - TRI_LM	4.275	.003	7.306	.000
CW_NOTRI - TRI_LH	-2.155	.063	3.166	.004
CW_NOTRI - TRI_ML	1.433	.190	4.966	.000
CW_NOTRI - TRI_MM	6.673	.000	6.086	.000
CW_NOTRI - TRI_MH	2.691	.027	3.371	.002
CW_NOTRI - TRI_HL	-2.113	.068	2.901	.007
CW_NOTRI - TRI_HM	3.536	.008	4.867	.000
CW_NOTRI - TRI_HH	7.314	.000	2.216	.035

5   Discussion on Other Impact Factors

Obviously many other factors would influence the participant's mobile application usage in addition to providing useful trust information. We found that the participants' opinions could be sharply different in the same situations. Personality is one of the important factors that may affect usage decision and usage behavior. Different personalities attribute different importance levels to each of the accepted trust cues (such as branding and professional user interface design, etc). Extroversion and openness to experience lead to a higher disposition to trust. However, neuroticism and conscientiousness lead to a lower disposition to trust [5]. We also notified that the results we got are different in Finland and China, especially on the willingness to check trust information. Since the selected participants' ages and occupations are similar in both countries, the potential reasons that would cause the difference could be culture deviation, past usage experiences, technical background of the participants, and regional technology development status. We will investigate the above factors' influence in future research.

6   Conclusions

Trust can greatly overcome uncertainty, thus influences users' usage confidence. In this paper, we proposed displaying trust/reputation information to assist mobile application usage. The effectiveness of the visualization was shown from our three-stage user study conducted in both China and Finland.

We contribute a user study design for investigating participants' opinions on mobile application usage. Using this design, we firstly identified the importance of various mobile applications in two countries with different culture and technology background. This, as we know, has not been studied in the literature. We then selected a number of candidate applications with different importance rate to examine how users react to the display of their own individual trust value and the display of both the individual trust and public trust (reputation). We found that displaying the trust value and the trust/reputation values makes a significant difference. Users tend to change their usage behavior and decision. The experimental results indicated that both the trust indicator and the trust/reputation indicator have significant impact on the usage willingness according to their displayed values. These two indicators also have valuable impact on the willingness to check detailed trust information although the results in two countries are different. We found different usage willingness patterns and trust information check patterns in two countries with different cultural and regional background. Our results suggest displaying trust information's assistance on mobile application usage and its potentiality to improve the usability of mobile applications. Particularly, our experiments investigated the interaction effects among application importance, trust value, and/or reputation value on application usage and trust information check.

References

1. Sheridan, T.: Computer Control and Human Alienation. Technology Review, 61–73 (1980)
2. Muir, B.M.: Trust in Automation Part I: Theoretical Issues in The Study of Trust and Human Intervention in Automated Systems. Ergonomics 37(11), 1905–1922 (1994)

3. Muir, B.M., Moray, N.: Trust in Automation Part II: Experimental Studies of Trust and Human Intervention in a Process Control Simulation. Ergonomics 39(3), 429–469 (1996)

4. Lee, J., Moray, N.: Trust, Control Strategies and Allocation of Function in Human-Machine Systems. Ergonomics 35(10), 1243–1270 (1992)

5. Lumsden, J., MacKay, L.: How Does Personality Affect Trust in B2C E-commerce? In: Proc. of 8th Int. Conf. on E-Commerce, pp. 471–481 (2006)

6. Yan, Z., Holtmanns, S.: Trust Modeling and Management: from Social Trust to Digital Trust. In: Subramanian, R. (ed.) Computer Security, Privacy and Politics: Current Issues, Challenges and Solutions. IGI Global (2008)

7. Yan, Z., Niemi, V.: A Methodology Towards Usable Trust Management. In: González Nieto, J., Reif, W., Wang, G., Indulska, J. (eds.) ATC 2009. LNCS, vol. 5586, pp. 179–193. Springer, Heidelberg (2009)

8. Anderson, J.C., Narus, J.A.: A Model of Distributor Firm and Manufacturer Firm Working Partnerships. Marketing 54(1), 42–58 (1990)

9. Fox, A.: Beyond Contract: Work, Power, and Trust Relations. Faber, London (1974)

10. Deutsch, M.: The Resolution of Conflict: Constructive and Destructive Processes. Yale University Press, New Haven (1973)

11. Sheppard, B.H., Hartwick, J., Warshaw, P.R.: The Theory of Reasoned Action: a Meta Analysis of Past Research with Recommendations for Modifications in Future Research. Consumer Res 15(3), 325–343 (1988)

12. Venkatesh, V., Davis, F.D.: A Theoretical Extension of The Technology Acceptance Model: Four Longitudinal Field Studies. Management Sci. 46(2), 186–204 (2000)

13. Yan, Z., Yan, R.: Formalizing Trust Based on Usage Behaviours for Mobile Applications. In: González Nieto, J., Reif, W., Wang, G., Indulska, J. (eds.) ATC 2009. LNCS, vol. 5586, pp. 194–208. Springer, Heidelberg (2009)

14. Artz, D., Gil, Y.: A Survey of Trust in Computer Science and the Semantic Web. In: Web Semantics: Science, Services and Agents on the World Wide Web, vol. 5(2), pp. 58–71 (2007)

15. Nielsen, J.: Trust or Bust: Communicating Trustworthiness in Web Design (1999), http://www.useit.com/alertbox/990307.html

16. Corritore, C.L., Kracher, B., Wiedenbeck, S.: On-Line Trust: Concepts, Evolving Themes, a Model. Int. J. of Human-Computer Studies: Trust and Technology 58(6), 737–758 (2003)

17. Riegelsberger, J., Sasse, A.M., McCarthy, J.D.: The Mechanics of Trust: a Framework for Research and Design. Int. J. of Human-Computer Studies 62(3), 381–422 (2005)

18. McCrickard, D.S., Czerwinski, M., Bartram, L.: Introduction: Design and Evaluation of Notification User Interfaces. Int. J. of Human-Computer Studies 58(5), 509–514 (2003)

19. Antifakos, S., Kern, N., Schiele, B., Schwaninger, A.: Towards Improving Trust in Context-aware Systems by Displaying System Confidence. In: Proc. of the 7th Int. Conf. on Human Computer Interaction with Mobile Devices & Services, pp. 9–14 (2005)

20. Rukzio, E., Hamard, J., Noda, C., Luca, A.D.: Visualization of Uncertainty in Context Aware Mobile Applications. In: Proc. of Mobile HCI, pp. 247–250 (2006)

21. Baba, M.L., Falkenburg, D.R., Hill, D.H.: Technology Management and American Culture: Implications for Business Process Redesign. Research Technology Management 39(6), 44–54 (1996)

22. Yamagishi, T., Yamagishi, M.: Trust and Commitment in the United States and Japan. Motivation and Emotion 18, 129–166 (1994)

23. Karvonen, K.: Designing Trust for a Universal Audience: a Multicultural Study on the Formation of Trust in the Internet in the Nordic Countries. In: Proc. of First Int. Conf. on Universal Access in Human-Computer Interaction, vol. 3, pp. 1078–1082 (2001)

24. Nielsen, J., Molich, R., Snyder, S., Farrell, C.: E-Commerce User Experience: Trust. Nielsen Norman Group (2000)

Context Based Trust Normalization in Service-Oriented Environments

Lei Li and Yan Wang

Department of Computing,
Macquarie University,
Sydney, NSW 2109,
Australia
{lei.li,yan.wang}@mq.edu.au

Abstract. With the development of information technology, the issue of trust becomes more and more important. In e-commerce or service-oriented environments, when there are a few sellers or service providers providing the same product/service, the buyer or service client would like to request the trust management authority to provide trust values of sellers or service providers, which are based on the ratings reflecting the quality of previous transactions. In addition, trust is context dependent, i.e. for different context of transactions, there are different factors influencing the trust result. In this paper, we propose a fuzzy comprehensive evaluation based method for building up a projection from the trust ratings in the transaction history of a service provider to an upcoming transaction depending on the similarity between previous transactions and the upcoming one, and the familiarity between each rater and the service client of the upcoming transaction. This process is termed as *context based trust normalization*. After trust normalization, normalized trust ratings are used for trust evaluation, the results of which would be closely bound to the upcoming transaction. Finally, we introduce the results of our conducted experiments to illustrate how our proposed method can detect some typical risks.

1 Introduction

Trust has always been a vitally important issue in the field of information technology (IT), but with the rise of service-oriented computing (SOC), social network and cloud computing, the issue of trust has grown in prevalence [12,15,18]. In these environments, the trust management authority is responsible for collecting available information (e.g. ratings, transaction cost, social relationships), evaluating trust values with these information and providing trust results to clients by publishing them on web or responding to their requests [15,16].

The concept of trust varies in different disciplines. In sociology and psychology, the degree with which one party trusts another is a measure of belief in the capabilities, self-confidence, willingness, persistence, morality and goals of another party [4]. In economics, trust can often be conceptualized as reliability

B. Xie et al. (Eds.): ATC 2010, LNCS 6407, pp. 122–138, 2010.
© Springer-Verlag Berlin Heidelberg 2010

in transactions. In all cases, trust involves many heuristic decision rules, requiring the trust management authority to handle a lot of complex information with great effort in rational reasoning [4].

Conceptually, trust is the measure taken by one party on the willingness and ability of another party to act in the interest of the former party in a certain situation [15]. If the trust value is in the range of [0,1], it can be taken as the subjective probability with which, one party expects that another party performs a given action [12].

In recent years, with the development of IT, the computer-mediated trust is especially actively studied. In e-commerce (EC) or SOC environments, the reputation-based trust value is a very important indication for a buyer or a service client to make the selection from a pool of sellers or service providers providing the same product or service, because the buyer or service client usually would like to order from the seller or service provider with the best transaction reputation. This is particularly important when the buyer or service client has to select from unknown sellers or service providers [20].

The issue of trust has also been actively studied in Peer-to-Peer (P2P) information-sharing networks[1] (e.g. [12,30]). In P2P systems, it is quite natural for a client peer to doubt if a serving peer can provide the complete file prior to any download action, which may be quite overhead-consuming (e.g. time and network bandwidth). Different from some trust evaluation methods in EC, in the P2P trust management system, a requesting peer needs to request the trust information of a serving peer from other peers which may have transacted with the serving peer [13,19,31]. The trust evaluation of the serving peer from the collected ratings is then performed by the requesting peer, not a central management server, because of the decentralized architecture of P2P systems.

Trust is a critical issue in EC or SOC environments [12,15]. Some applications (such as eBay[2]) have introduced simple trust management mechanisms to provide valuable trust information to service clients prior to placing orders and making payment. However, malicious service providers and fraudulent transactions may widely exist in simple trust management enabled environments with the following types of risks.

Type 1 risk. In EC or SOC environments, a typical risk is to accumulate a good reputation by offering cheap and attractive products/services, then may cheat clients with expensive products/services [27,28].

Type 2 risk. This risk is to accumulate a good reputation by providing products/services in a similar category (e.g. cameras), then may cheat clients by offering products/services in a different category (e.g. watches) which s/he has no sufficient experience [27,28].

Type 3 risk. This risk is to collude within a small group to earn a good reputation, then may cheat victims out of the group [33,34].

---

[1] http://www.gnutella.com

[2] http://www.eBay.com/

Thus, it requires a novel trust management system that can provide useful information to indicate to some extent the trust level of the service provider about the upcoming transaction.

Considering trust is context dependent, i.e. for different context of transactions (e.g. transaction cost, product/service category, clients), there are different factors influencing the trust result [27,28], in this paper, we propose a method for building up a projection from the trust ratings in the transaction history of a service provider to an upcoming transaction depending on the similarity between previous transactions and the upcoming one, and the familiarity between each rater and the service client of the upcoming transaction, which process is termed as *context based trust normalization*. After trust normalization, normalized trust ratings are used for trust evaluation, the results of which would be closely bound to the upcoming transaction. Namely, different upcoming transactions may lead to different final trust values of the same service provider.

Generally speaking, it is a difficult task to provide a comprehensive trust evaluation method, because trust evaluation involves fuzziness and tremendous amount of context factors [4,27,28]. In this paper, based on the analysis of multiple factors which affect trust evaluation, first, we propose a comprehensive evaluation index system including all influencing factors. Second, with this index system, we propose a fuzzy comprehensive evaluation based method to compute the similarity between previous transactions and the upcoming one, and the familiarity between each rater and the service client of the upcoming transaction. With this method, the trust ratings can be normalized for computing the final trust value that would be closely bound to an upcoming transaction.

This paper is organized as follows. In Section 2, we review the concept of trust, trust evaluation and subjective probability. Section 3 presents our context based trust normalization method and evaluates the trust value that would be closely bound to the upcoming transaction. Some experiments are presented in Section 4 for illustrating that our proposed method can detect some typical risks. Finally Section 5 concludes our work.

2   Related Work

2.1   Trust Evaluation in Computer-Mediated Environments

For e-commerce (EC) applications, in [35], a trust evaluation approach is proposed based on the trust ratings of transactions in a recent period, rather than all of them. In this method, recent ratings are taken as more important in trust evaluation. In [24], fuzzy logic is applied to trust evaluation, which divides sellers or service providers into multiple classes of reputation ranks.

Trust is also an important issue in Peer-to-Peer (P2P) information-sharing network[1], because a client peer needs to know prior to download actions whether a serving peer can provide complete files. Trust evaluation in P2P systems can rely on a polling algorithm (e.g. [5]), a binary rating system for calculating the trust value of a given peer (e.g. [13,31]), or a voting reputation system (e.g. [19]) that calculates the final trust value by combining the values returned by responding peers and the requesting peer's experience with the given peer.

In the literature, trust issue receives a lot of attention in service-oriented computing (SOC) research. In [26], Vu et al present a model to evaluate and rank the reputation and trust of QoS-based services. In [14], a trust vector approach is proposed to SOC applications, which includes final trust level (FTL), service trust trend (STT), and service performance consistency level ($SPCL$). This approach can depict trust rating history more exactly and offer more information to service clients for their decision-making in the selection of trustworthy service providers.

Trust also has drawn much attention in the field of multi-agent systems. In [7], Griffiths proposes a multi-dimensional trust model which allows agents to evaluate the trust value of others according to various criteria. In [23], Sabater et al propose a model discussing the trust development between groups. When calculating the trust from individual A to individual B, a few factors are considered, e.g., the interaction between A and B, the evaluation of A's group to B and B's group, and A's evaluation to B's group.

2.2   Trust Evaluation and Subjective Probability

As we have pointed out in Section 1, trust is the *subjective probability* by which, one party expects that another party performs a given action [12], and it is better to adopt *subjective probability theory* to deal with trust evaluation.

Subjective probability is one of the most popular interpretations of the concept of probability [9]. Subjective probability interprets the concept of probability as the subjective degree of belief in a proposition, rather than a frequency (frequency interpretations of probability) or a physical property of a system (propensity interpretations of probability) [9].

Subjective probability is the actual personal judgment about a proposition, normally representing what a person believes his/her judgment should be, in view of his/her own information to date and of his/her sense of information provided by other people. However, of course a person are not always clear about what his/her judgment should be. The most important questions in the subjective probability theory concern ways and means of constructing reasonably satisfactory probability assignments to fit his/her present state of mind [10].

In the early 20th century, the definition of subjective probability was first proposed [10]. The most initial work of subjective probability theory focused on Bayesian inference. A primary goal of Bayesian inference is summarizing available information about unknown parameters that define statistical models through the specification of probability density functions [8]. Later on, non-Bayesian inference methods in subjective probability theory were proposed and attracted much more attention. For example, Jeffrey [10] proposes the rule of probability kinematics, which is the typical non-Bayesian inference method.

In the literature, there are some existing works to deal with subjective ratings. In [11], Jøsang proposes a framework for combining and assessing subjective ratings from different sources based on Dempster-Shafer belief theory, which is a generalization of the Bayesian theory of subjective probability. Based on Bayesian inference, Wang et al [29] set up a bijection from subjective ratings to trust values with a mathematical understanding of subjective trust in multiagent systems. Both models use either a binary rating (positive or negative) system or a triple rating (positive, negative or uncertain) system that is more suitable for security-oriented or P2P file-sharing trust management systems [16].

In composite services, assuming that the trust ratings of each service component conform to a normal distribution, Li et al [16] propose a Bayesian inference based subjective trust evaluation approach which aggregates the subjective ratings from other service clients. However, in most existing rating systems[2,3,4], trust ratings are discrete numbers, making the number of occurrences of ratings of each service component conform to a multinomial distribution [15]. Hence, Li and Wang [15] propose a subjective trust estimation method for service components based on Bayesian inference, which can aggregate the non-binary discrete subjective ratings given by service clients and keep the subjective probability property of trust ratings and trust results.

3   Trust Normalization

Trust is context dependent, i.e. for service-oriented transactions, there are different factors (e.g. transaction cost, service category) influencing the trust result [27,28]. These factors should be considered comprehensively to adjust strategies in trust evaluation.

In order to evaluate the trust value that would be closely bound to an upcoming transaction, we need the ratings reflecting the quality of previous transactions about the service provider. However, these trust ratings of previous transactions with different context should not be aggregated without considering context difference to obtain the trust value [27,28]. In our proposed method, a projection is built up from the trust ratings in the transaction history of the service provider to the upcoming transaction depending on the similarity between previous transactions and the upcoming one, and the familiarity between each rater and the service client of the upcoming transaction, which process is named as *context based trust normalization*. After trust normalization, normalized trust ratings are used for trust evaluation, the results of which would be closely bound to the upcoming transaction.

In fact, trust normalization is a preprocessing before trust evaluation. This makes trust normalization totally different from any trust evaluation methods. In addition, this also makes it be easily transferable upon any trust evaluation method without a lot of modifications.

Trust is a very complicated issue, including many uncertain factors [4]. Hence, with the fuzziness, fuzzy comprehensive evaluation provided by fuzzy set theory [3] can deal with context based trust normalization in a reasonable manner. The fuzzy comprehensive evaluation based method analyzes complicated questions

---

[3] http://www.epinions.com/

[4] http://www.youtube.com/

in terms of factors, by decomposing the question into several factors, stipulating every score of each factor and weighting the evaluated results with certain scale. In particular, the fuzzy comprehensive evaluation based method is superior to other evaluation methods in dealing with subjective factors [3,6].

3.1 Comprehensive Evaluation Index System

In order to provide an effective fuzzy comprehensive evaluation based method in context based trust normalization, it is necessary to firstly establish a systematic and comprehensive index system. This index system includes all influencing factors, analyzes the relationships of factors and finds out the main factors which influence context based trust normalization the most. The criteria for developing the comprehensive evaluation index system are as follows [6]:

- The index system must be capable of reflecting every aspect of influencing context based trust normalization, i.e. every aspect of determining the similarity between previous transactions and the upcoming one, and the familiarity between each rater and the service client of the upcoming transaction.
- The data for the factors in the index system must be capable of being collected from reliable sources and being consistent.
- The index system must be capable of accommodating the relationship between factors and the evaluation criteria, especially generating corresponding main factors at the request of evaluators.

According to the aforementioned definition of trust, the difference of context based trust in SOC environments is determined by both the difference of transactions and the difference of involved parties. Therefore, following the above criteria, in context based trust normalization, in order to determine the similarity between previous transactions and the upcoming one and the familiarity between each rater and the service client of the upcoming transaction, we set up a comprehensive evaluation index system, which consists of

Transaction cost relativity: In economics and related disciplines, the transaction cost is the cost incurred in making an economic exchange [1]. The larger the cost of the previous transaction is than the cost of the upcoming transaction, the higher the transaction cost relativity is, and vice versa.

Transaction category similarity: The more similar to the category of product/service in the upcoming transaction the category of product/service in the previous transaction, the higher the transaction category similarity, and vice versa.

Social relationship influence: The social relationship influence is determined by social relationships, such as the social intimacy degree and the role impact factor [18]. The higher the social intimacy degree, the larger the social relationship influence. The larger the role impact factor value, the larger the social relationship influence.

3.2 Fuzzy Comprehensive Evaluation Model

Fuzzy comprehensive evaluation model is a synthetical application of analytical hierarchy process and fuzzy mathematics by inspecting many influencing factors.

Single-level and Multi-level Fuzzy Comprehensive Evaluations. Fuzzy comprehensive evaluation can be divided into single-level and multi-level. Generally, single-level fuzzy comprehensive evaluation is adopted to evaluate the case that there are few factors involved in the evaluation process. The steps of single-level fuzzy comprehensive evaluation are as follows.

- First, determine the *affiliation score of each factor* in the comprehensive evaluation index system, then a *fuzzy affiliation matrix* is obtained.
- Second, an *affiliation vector* which evaluates the similarity between previous transactions and the upcoming one and the familiarity between each rater and the service client of the upcoming transaction can be obtained by the composition operation of the affiliation matrix and the *weight vector of factors*.
- Last, evaluation results can be obtained with different principles.

The steps of multi-level fuzzy comprehensive evaluation are as follows.

- First, the *factor set* is divided into several sub-factor sets.
- Second, as for the sub-factor sets, the single-level evaluation method is adopted to obtain some affiliation vectors.
- Third, combine the vectors to obtain a matrix, then composition operation is performed on this matrix and its immediate higher level weight vector. The evaluation vector can be obtained until the aforementioned three steps are adopted to achieve the highest level.

In this paper, we set up {Transaction Cost Relativity, Transaction Category Similarity, Social Relationship Influence} as our comprehensive evaluation index system. We take this factor set as an example to illustrate our proposed single-level fuzzy comprehensive evaluation based method for context based trust normalization. If there is any necessary to process the more detailed analysis involving more factors with multiple levels, we can follow the aforementioned three steps for multi-level fuzzy comprehensive evaluation, which is similar to our single-level fuzzy comprehensive evaluation in this paper.

Establishing Affiliation Score Set. In real systems, the trust rating scores of a service provider given by raters are represented by a series of fixed numbers [15]. For example, the rating scores at eBay[2] are in the set of $\{-1, 0, 1\}$. At Epinions[3], each rating score is an integer in $\{1, 2, 3, 4, 5\}$. At YouTube[4], each rating score is in $\{-10, -9, \ldots, 10\}$. In this paper, we take the five-level scale at Epinions[3] as an example and the affiliation score set is $\{1, 2, 3, 4, 5\}$. With linguist interpretation for these scores, the rater's corresponding comment set can be labeled as {terrible, poor, medium, good, excellent}.

Establishing Fuzzy Affiliation Matrix. Here we establish the affiliation score of each factor in the comprehensive evaluation index system.

Considering transaction cost relativity, firstly let $C_{previous}$ denote a previous transaction cost of the service provider and $C_{upcoming}$ denote the upcoming transaction cost, then the transaction cost relativity value can be evaluated by

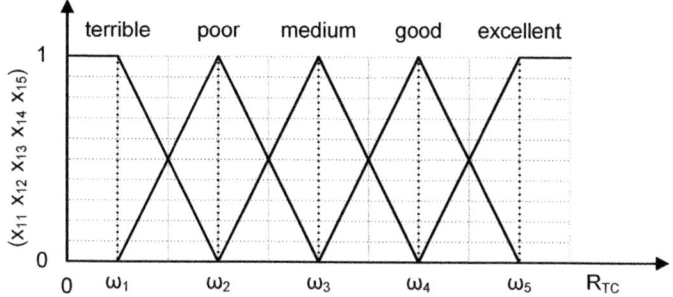

Fig. 1. Triangular membership functions with five levels

$$R_{TC} = \frac{C_{previous}}{C_{upcoming}}. \tag{1}$$

To determine the corresponding frequency $\{(x_{11}\ x_{12}\ x_{13}\ x_{14}\ x_{15})|\sum_{i=1}^{5} x_{1i} = 1\}$ about the comment set {terrible, poor, medium, good, excellent} of the transaction cost relativity, we introduce the triangular membership functions with five levels [3] as follows, which is also illustrated in Fig. 1.

$$(x_{11}\ x_{12}\ x_{13}\ x_{14}\ x_{15}) =$$

$$\begin{cases} x_{11} = 1; x_{12} = x_{13} = x_{14} = x_{15} = 0; & \text{if } R_{TC} \leq \omega_1; \\ x_{11} = \frac{R_{TC}-\omega_2}{\omega_1-\omega_2}; x_{12} = \frac{R_{TC}-\omega_1}{\omega_2-\omega_1}; x_{13} = x_{14} = x_{15} = 0; & \text{if } \omega_1 < R_{TC} \leq \omega_2; \\ x_{12} = \frac{R_{TC}-\omega_3}{\omega_2-\omega_3}; x_{13} = \frac{R_{TC}-\omega_2}{\omega_3-\omega_2}; x_{11} = x_{14} = x_{15} = 0; & \text{if } \omega_2 < R_{TC} \leq \omega_3; \\ x_{13} = \frac{R_{TC}-\omega_4}{\omega_3-\omega_4}; x_{14} = \frac{R_{TC}-\omega_3}{\omega_4-\omega_3}; x_{11} = x_{12} = x_{15} = 0; & \text{if } \omega_3 < R_{TC} \leq \omega_4; \\ x_{14} = \frac{R_{TC}-\omega_5}{\omega_4-\omega_5}; x_{15} = \frac{R_{TC}-\omega_4}{\omega_5-\omega_4}; x_{11} = x_{12} = x_{13} = 0; & \text{if } \omega_4 < R_{TC} \leq \omega_5; \\ x_{15} = 1; x_{11} = x_{12} = x_{13} = x_{14} = 0; & \text{if } R_{TC} > \omega_5; \end{cases} \tag{2}$$

where ω_1, ω_2, ω_3, ω_4 and ω_5 are the parameters for determining the membership function curves. The values of these parameters are assessed by the subjective knowledge of domain experts [3] in advance and stored in the trust management authority. In this paper, we adopt the triangular membership functions with five levels in Eq. (2) as an example to illustrate our method, and it is a similar process to adopt any other membership functions.

For calculating transaction category similarity, firstly it is necessary to build up the category system based on connectivity in the network and lexicosyntactic matching [21,22]. With this domain independent taxonomy, the similarity between transaction categories can be evaluated [22]. By applying the triangular membership functions with five levels [3], the corresponding frequency

$$\{(x_{21}\ x_{22}\ x_{23}\ x_{24}\ x_{25})|\sum_{i=1}^{5} x_{2i} = 1\} \tag{3}$$

about the comment set {terrible, poor, medium, good, excellent} of the transaction category similarity can be determined.

Social relationship influence can be determined by both social intimacy degree and role impact factor. Social intimacy degree is defined to describe the extent to which two parties have intimate social relationships, because we usually trust the party with more intimate social relationships [2,18]. The value of social intimacy degree can be estimated by collecting the information of social relationships [25]. Role impact factor is defined to reflect the impact of a party's recommendation role on trust propagation, because we usually put greater reliance on the party with particular social positions where his/her actions weigh heavily on his/her social position [1,18]. The value of role impact factor can be estimated with the PageRank model [25]. By combining the social intimacy degree and the role impact factor and applying the triangular membership functions with five levels [3], the corresponding frequency

$$\{(x_{31} \ x_{32} \ x_{33} \ x_{34} \ x_{35})| \sum_{i=1}^{5} x_{3i} = 1\} \tag{4}$$

about the comment set {terrible, poor, medium, good, excellent} of the social relationship influence can be determined.

Therefore, we can obtain the fuzzy affiliation matrix M in Eq. (5).

$$M = \begin{bmatrix} x_{11} \ x_{12} \ x_{13} \ x_{14} \ x_{15} \\ x_{21} \ x_{22} \ x_{23} \ x_{24} \ x_{25} \\ x_{31} \ x_{32} \ x_{33} \ x_{34} \ x_{35} \end{bmatrix} \tag{5}$$

Establishing Weight Vector. The weights in weight vector $W = (\omega_6 \ \omega_7 \ \omega_8)$ of factors in the index system reflect the importance of each factor, and $\omega_6 + \omega_7 + \omega_8 = 1$. These weights are specified in the service client's preference or fulfilled by domain experts [3] based on their own knowledge and experience.

Establishing Affiliation Vector. As we have pointed out, the affiliation vector, which evaluates the similarity between previous transactions and the upcoming one, and the familiarity between each rater and the service client of the upcoming transaction, can be obtained by the composition operation of the affiliation matrix and the weight vector of factors. Let the affiliation vector $R = (R_1 \ R_2 \ R_3 \ R_4 \ R_5)$, then we have

$$R = W \times M = (\omega_6 \ \omega_7 \ \omega_8) \times \begin{bmatrix} x_{11} \ x_{12} \ x_{13} \ x_{14} \ x_{15} \\ x_{21} \ x_{22} \ x_{23} \ x_{24} \ x_{25} \\ x_{31} \ x_{32} \ x_{33} \ x_{34} \ x_{35} \end{bmatrix} = (R_1 \ R_2 \ R_3 \ R_4 \ R_5) \tag{6}$$

i.e.
$$R_i = \omega_6 x_{1i} + \omega_7 x_{2i} + \omega_8 x_{3i}, \quad i = 1, 2, 3, 4, 5. \tag{7}$$

Hence, the similarity between previous transactions and the upcoming one and the familiarity between each rater and the service client of the upcoming transaction can be evaluated, and the affiliation vector is obtained.

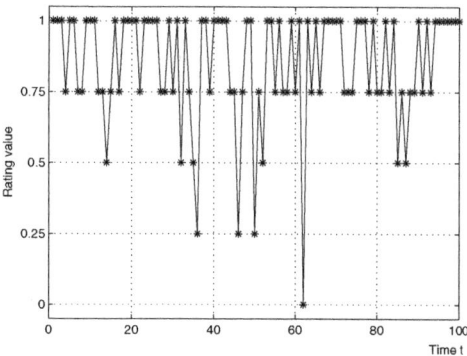

Fig. 2. Ratings from Epinions

Discounting Rate. Since in this section the five-level scale at Epinions[3] is adopted as an example, ratings are scaled to be in $\{0, 0.25, 0.5, 0.75, 1\}$ [15], which correspond to comments {terrible, poor, medium, good, excellent} respectively. Then the *discounting rate* can be determined

$$D_r = (R_1\ R_2\ R_3\ R_4\ R_5) \times (0\ 0.25\ 0.5\ 0.75\ 1)^T = 0.25R_2 + 0.5R_3 + 0.75R_4 + R_5 \quad (8)$$

Therefore, the projection from the trust ratings in the transaction history of the service provider to the upcoming transaction is well established, where *the trust ratings of the service provider can be normalized by multiplying the discounting rate*. Then normalized trust ratings can be used for trust evaluation, the results of which would be closely bound to the upcoming transaction. For the details of context based trust normalization process, please refer to the example of context based trust normalization proposed in Section 4.1.

4   Experiments

In this section, we first illustrate the details of our proposed context based trust normalization method, after which we present the results of our conducted experiments for studying our proposed method and explain why the context based trust normalization method can detect some typical risks.

In these experiments, ratings are taken from Epinions[3], which is a popular online reputation system, and each rating is an integer in $\{1, 2, 3, 4, 5\}$. Since ratings as numerical values in $[0, 1]$ are more suitable for trust evaluation [15,32], all Epinions ratings are scaled to be in $\{0, 0.25, 0.5, 0.75, 1\}$ in advance, which correspond to comments {terrible, poor, medium, good, excellent} respectively.

In these experiments, we set $\omega_1 = 0.1$, $\omega_2 = 0.5$, $\omega_3 = 1$, $\omega_4 = 5$ and $\omega_5 = 10$, which are the thresholds for determining triangular membership functions with five levels in Eq. (2) (depicted in Fig. 1).

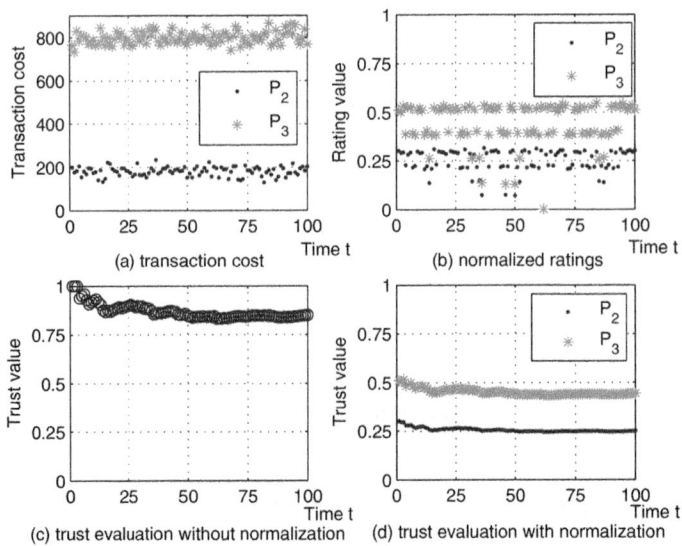

Fig. 3. Experimental results about Type 1 risk

4.1   An Example of Context Based Trust Normalization

In this experiment, we take the ratings at Epinions[3] as an example to illustrate the details of our context based trust normalization method, including establishing the affiliation score set, the fuzzy affiliation matrix, the weight vector and the affiliation vector in the fuzzy comprehensive evaluation, and determining the discounting rate.

Let us consider a scenario as follows. Service client A plans to buy a Nokia 6085 cell phone (denoted by transaction TR_{AP_1}) from service provider P_1. Hence, A needs the ratings reflecting the quality of previous transactions about P_1, and requests the trust management authority to provide valuable information prior to placing orders and making payment. Assume we randomly select a rating $r_{BP_1} = 0.75$ of a previous transaction TR_{BP_1} about service provider P_1 rated by rater (client) B. In TR_{BP_1}, B bought an Olympus EVOLT E-300 digital camera from P_1.

In order to normalize all relevant ratings, we need build up a projection from the ratings in the transaction history of P_1 to the upcoming transaction TR_{AP_1} depending on the fuzzy affiliation matrix, which consists of both the similarity between transaction TR_{BP_1} and transaction TR_{AP_1} and the familiarity between service client A and rater B. In order to obtain the fuzzy affiliation matrix M (defined by Eq. (5)), we need establish affiliate scores of each factor (defined by Eqs (2)(3)(4)).

Considering the affiliate score of the transaction cost relativity, let $C_{TR_{AP_1}}$ and $C_{TR_{BP_1}}$ denote the transaction costs of TR_{AP_1} and TR_{BP_1} respectively.

Since in SOC the price of a product is the major part of the transaction cost and the big concern of clients, we take this price as the transaction cost in this paper. Hence, we have $C_{TR_{AP_1}} = \$100$ and $C_{TR_{BP_1}} = \$900$. According to Eq. (1), the transaction cost relativity is $R_{TC} = 9$. With the thresholds for determining triangular membership functions in Eq. (2) $\omega_1 = 0.1$, $\omega_2 = 0.5$, $\omega_3 = 1$, $\omega_4 = 5$ and $\omega_5 = 10$, we can have the affiliate score of the transaction cost relativity $(x_{11}\ x_{12}\ x_{13}\ x_{14}\ x_{15}) = (0\ 0\ 0\ 0.2\ 0.8)$. Considering the affiliate scores of the transaction category similarity and the social relationship influence respectively, since this paper does not focus on the detailed data mining techniques, we will just list the results of the affiliate scores of the transaction category similarity and the social relationship influence without any computational details. Hence, we can have the affiliate score of the transaction category similarity $(x_{21}\ x_{22}\ x_{23}\ x_{24}\ x_{25}) = (0\ 0\ 0.4\ 0.6\ 0)$ and the affiliate score of the social relationship influence $(x_{31}\ x_{32}\ x_{33}\ x_{34}\ x_{35}) = (0\ 0\ 0.5\ 0.5\ 0)$.

Here we assume the weight vector specified in A's preference is $W = (0.2\ 0.5\ 0.3)$. The affiliation vector R can be obtained by the composition operation of the weight vector of factors W and the affiliation matrix M defined by Eq. (5). Following Eq. (6), we have

$$R = W \times M = (0.2\ 0.5\ 0.3) \times \begin{bmatrix} 0\ 0\ 0\ 0.2\ 0.8 \\ 0\ 0\ 0.4\ 0.6\ 0 \\ 0\ 0\ 0.5\ 0.5\ 0 \end{bmatrix} = (0\ 0\ 0.35\ 0.49\ 0.16).$$

In addition, following Eq. (8), the discount rate is

$$D_r = (0\ 0\ 0.35\ 0.49\ 0.16) \times (0\ 0.25\ 0.5\ 0.75\ 1)^T = 0.7025. \tag{9}$$

Therefore, the normalized rating N_{P_1} from r_{BP_1} can be obtained

$$N_{P_1} = r_{BP_1} \times D_r = 0.75 \times 0.7025 \approx 0.53.$$

Trust is context dependent, and different upcoming transactions may lead to different trust levels of the same service provider. Therefore, after trust normalization, the rating r_{BP_1}, which is 0.75 for the transaction with the product of an Olympus EVOLT E-300 digital camera, becomes 0.53 for the transaction with the product of a Nokia 6085 cell phone.

4.2   Experiment on Type 1 Risk

In this experiment, we aim to illustrate how our proposed method can detect Type 1 risk, with which a malicious seller accumulates a good reputation by offering cheap and attractive services, then may cheat clients with expensive services [27,28].

In this experiment, after trust normalization, we take the average of ratings as the trust evaluation method, which has been widely adopted in many trust evaluation models [12,17].

Service client A plans to buy a Canon PowerShot A640 digital camera, which is provided by two service providers P_2 and P_3 with the same transaction cost

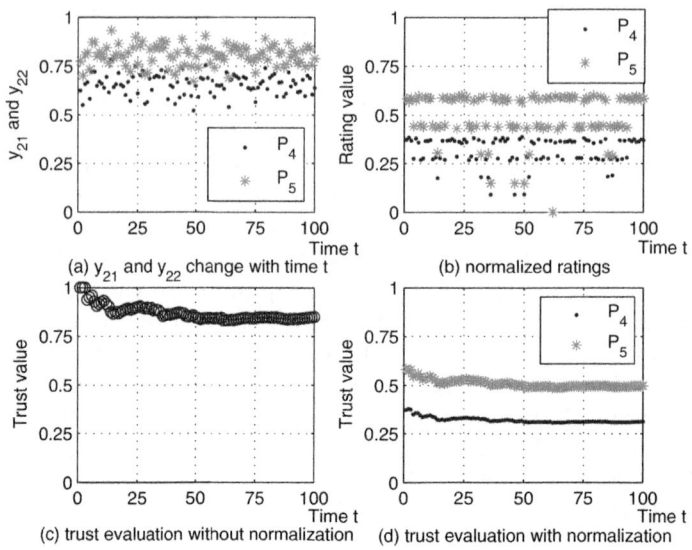

(a) y_{21} and y_{22} change with time t

(b) normalized ratings

(c) trust evaluation without normalization

(d) trust evaluation with normalization

Fig. 4. Experimental results about Type 2 risk

$C_{TR_{AP_2}} = C_{TR_{AP_3}} = \$900$. We assume that they both have the same ratings illustrated in Fig. 2. Their transaction costs are listed in Fig. 3 (a). We can observe that $C_{TR_{P_2}}$ is much smaller than $C_{TR_{P_3}}$, which means P_2 accumulates a good reputation by offering cheap services and starts to provide expensive services now, i.e. Type 1 risk.

For the sake of simplicity, we assume P_2 and P_3 have the same affiliate scores of the transaction category similarity and the social relationship influence. Then we have the fuzzy affiliation matrices

$$M_{P_2} = \begin{bmatrix} y_{11} & 1-y_{11} & 0 & 0 & 0 \\ 0 & 0 & 0.4 & 0.6 & 0 \\ 0 & 0 & 0.5 & 0.5 & 0 \end{bmatrix}, \quad M_{P_3} = \begin{bmatrix} 0 & 1-y_{12} & y_{12} & 0 & 0 \\ 0 & 0 & 0.4 & 0.6 & 0 \\ 0 & 0 & 0.5 & 0.5 & 0 \end{bmatrix}, \quad (10)$$

where y_{11} and y_{12} is determined by triangular membership functions in Eq. (2) with the values of $C_{TR_{P_2}}$ and $C_{TR_{P_3}}$. With the weight vector $W_1 = (0.6\ 0.2\ 0.2)$, the corresponding normalized ratings of P_2 and P_3 are listed in Fig. 3 (b). For the details of context based trust normalization, please refer to Section 4.1.

Without trust normalization, P_2 and P_3 have the same trust evaluation results, which are depicted in Fig. 3 (c). However, considering the evaluated trust results with trust normalization plotted in Fig. 3 (d), service client A prefers P_3 to P_2, because the final trust value of P_3 is much larger than that of P_2. That preference results from the fact that P_2 may be a malicious service provider who cheats service clients. Therefore, we can observe that our proposed context based trust normalization method can detect Type 1 risk.

4.3   Experiment on Type 2 Risk

In this experiment, we also take the average of ratings as the trust evaluation method [12,17] to illustrate that our proposed context based trust normalization method can detect Type 2 risk, which is to accumulate a good reputation by providing services in a similar category, then may cheat clients by offering services in a different category which s/he has no sufficient experience [27,28].

Service client A plans to buy a Canon PowerShot A640 digital camera, which is provided by two service providers P_4 and P_5. We assume that they both have the same ratings illustrated in Fig. 2. However, P_4 used to sell watches while P_5 used to sell camcorders. We can observe that the transaction category similarity between camcorders and digital camera is larger than that between watches and digital camera, because camcorders and digital camera belongs to the electronics category without watches. That means P_4 accumulates a good reputation by providing services in a similar category, then starts to provide services in a different category, i.e. Type 2 risk.

For the sake of simplicity, we assume P_4 and P_5 have the same affiliate scores of the transaction cost relativity and the social relationship influence. Then we have the fuzzy affiliation matrices

$$MP_4 = \begin{bmatrix} 0 & 0 & 0 & 0.2 & 0.8 \\ y_{21} & 1-y_{21} & 0 & 0 & 0 \\ 0 & 0 & 0.5 & 0.5 & 0 \end{bmatrix}, \quad MP_5 = \begin{bmatrix} 0 & 0 & 0 & 0.2 & 0.8 \\ 0 & 1-y_{22} & y_{22} & 0 & 0 \\ 0 & 0 & 0.5 & 0.5 & 0 \end{bmatrix}, \quad (11)$$

where the values of y_{21} and y_{22} are listed in Fig. 4 (a). With the weight vector $W_2 = (0.2\ 0.6\ 0.2)$, the corresponding normalized ratings of P_4 and P_5 can be obtained as in Fig. 4 (b).

With these normalized ratings, the evaluation results are illustrated in Fig. 4 (d). Compared with the same trust values of P_4 and P_5 obtained by trust evaluation without normalization depicted in Fig. 4 (c), from Fig. 4 (d) we can observe that the evaluated trust value of P_4 is much smaller than that of P_5. This results from the fact that P_4 may be a malicious service provider who cheats service clients. Therefore, our proposed context based trust normalization method can detect Type 2 risk.

4.4   Experiment on Type 3 Risk

In this experiment, by adopting the average of ratings as the trust evaluation method [12,17] we aim to illustrate that our context based trust normalization method can detect Type 3 risk, which is to collude within a small group to earn a good reputation, then may cheat victims out of the group [33,34].

Service client A plans to buy a Canon PowerShot A640 digital camera, which is provided by two service providers P_6 and P_7. We assume that they both have the same ratings illustrated in Fig. 2. However, P_6 used to have frequent transactions with a few clients who have transactions only among them. In contrast, P_7 used to have transactions with a large variety of clients. Hence, we can observe that social relationship influence of P_6 is much smaller than that of P_7. That means

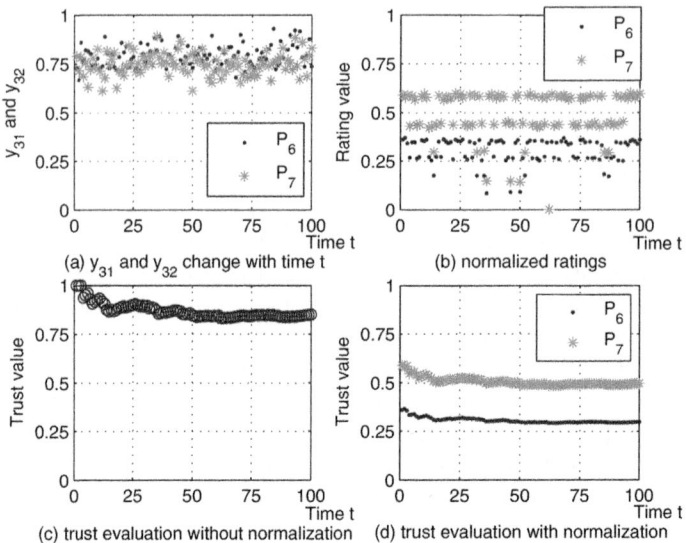

Fig. 5. Experimental results about Type 3 risk

P_6 collaborates in a small group to earn a good reputation, then starts to cheat victims out of the group, i.e. Type 3 risk.

For the sake of simplicity, we assume P_6 and P_7 have the same affiliate scores of the transaction cost relativity and the transaction category similarity. Then we have the fuzzy affiliation matrices

$$M_{P_6} = \begin{bmatrix} 0 & 0 & 0 & 0.2 & 0.8 \\ 0 & 0 & 0.4 & 0.6 & 0 \\ y_{31} & 1-y_{31} & 0 & 0 & 0 \end{bmatrix}, \quad M_{P_7} = \begin{bmatrix} 0 & 0 & 0 & 0.2 & 0.8 \\ 0 & 0 & 0.4 & 0.6 & 0 \\ 0 & 1-y_{32} & y_{32} & 0 & 0 \end{bmatrix}, \quad (12)$$

where the values of y_{31} and y_{32} are listed in Fig. 5 (a). With the weight vector $W_3 = (0.2\ 0.2\ 0.6)$, the corresponding normalized ratings can be obtained as in Fig. 5 (b).

With these normalized ratings, the evaluation results are illustrated in Fig. 5 (d). Compared with the same trust values of P_6 and P_7 obtained by trust evaluation without normalization depicted in Fig. 5 (c), we can observe from Fig. 5 (d) that the evaluated trust value of P_6 is much smaller than that of P_7. This results from the fact that P_6 may be a malicious service provider who cheats service clients. Therefore, our proposed context based trust normalization method can detect Type 3 risk.

5   Conclusions

In this paper, we proposed a fuzzy comprehensive evaluation based method for building up a projection from the trust ratings in the transaction history of a service provider to an upcoming transaction. This process is named as context based trust normalization. After trust normalization, normalized trust ratings are used directly for trust evaluation, the result of which would be closely bound to the upcoming transaction, and thus is more accurate and objective. Hence, trust normalization is a preprocessing before trust evaluation, which makes it be easily transferable upon any trust evaluation method without a lot of modifications. From our experimental results, we can observe that our proposed context based trust normalization method can detect some typical risks in transactions that can hardly be identified by existing trust evaluation methods calculating the general and global trust value only.

The context based trust normalization in this paper focuses on the applications in service-oriented environments. In our future work, the context based trust normalization will be generalized to be applied in other environments, such as: P2P networks, multi-agent systems and social networks.

References

1. Adler, P.S.: Market, hierarchy, and trust: The knowledge economy and the future of capitalism. Organization Science 12(2), 215–234 (2001)
2. Ashri, R., Ramchurn, S.D., Sabater, J., Luck, M., Jennings, N.R.: Trust evaluation through relationship analysis. In: AAMAS 2005, pp. 1005–1011 (2005)
3. Azar, A.T.: Fuzzy Systems. Intech (2010)
4. Castelfranchi, C., Falcone, R.: Trust is much more than subjective probability: Mental components and sources of trust. In: HICSS 2000 (2000)
5. Damiani, E., di Vimercati, S.D.C., Paraboschi, S., Samarati, P., Violante, F.: A reputation-based approach for choosing reliable resources in peer-to-peer networks. In: ACM Conference on Computer and Communications Security (CCS 2002), pp. 207–216 (2002)
6. Feng, S., Xu, L.D.: Decision support for fuzzy comprehensive evaluation of urban development. Fuzzy Sets and Systems 105(1), 1–12 (1999)
7. Griffiths, N.: Task delegation using experience-based multi-dimensional trust. In: AAMAS 2005, pp. 489–496 (2005)
8. Hamada, M.S., Wilson, A.G., Reese, C.S., Martz, H.F.: Bayesian Reliability. Springer, Heidelberg (2008)
9. Hójek, A.: Probability, Logic, and Probability Logic. The Blackwell Guide to Philosophical Logic, pp. 362–384. Blackwell Publishing, Malden (2001)
10. Jeffrey, R.: Subjective Probability: The Real Thing. Cambridge University Press, Cambridge (April 2004)
11. Jøsang, A.: Subjective evidential reasoning. In: IPMU (2002)
12. Jøsang, A., Ismail, R., Boyd, C.: A survey of trust and reputation systems for online service provision. Decision Support Systems 43(2), 618–644 (2007)
13. Kamvar, S.D., Schlosser, M.T., Garcia-Molina, H.: The eigentrust algorithm for reputation management in p2p networks. In: WWW 2003, pp. 640–651 (2003)
14. Li, L., Wang, Y.: A trust vector approach to service-oriented applications. In: ICWS 2008, pp. 270–277 (2008)
15. Li, L., Wang, Y.: Subjective trust inference in composite services. In: AAAI 2010, pp. 1377–1384 (2010)
16. Li, L., Wang, Y., Lim, E.-P.: Trust-oriented composite service selection and discovery. In: Baresi, L., Chi, C.-H., Suzuki, J. (eds.) ICSOC-ServiceWave 2009. LNCS, vol. 5900, pp. 50–67. Springer, Heidelberg (2009)

17. Li, L., Wang, Y., Varadharajan, V.: Fuzzy regression based trust prediction in service-oriented applications. In: González Nieto, J., Reif, W., Wang, G., Indulska, J. (eds.) ATC 2009. LNCS, vol. 5586, pp. 221–235. Springer, Heidelberg (2009)

18. Liu, G., Wang, Y., Orgun, M.A.: Optimal social trust path selection in complex social networks. In: AAAI 2010, pp. 1391–1398 (2010)

19. Marti, S., Garcia-Molina, H.: Limited reputation sharing in p2p systems. In: ACM EC 2004, pp. 91–101 (2004)

20. Papazoglou, M.P., Traverso, P., Dustdar, S., Leymann, F.: Service-oriented computing: a research roadmap. Int. J. Cooperative Inf. Syst. 17(2), 223–255 (2008)

21. Ponzetto, S.P., Navigli, R.: Large-scale taxonomy mapping for restructuring and integrating wikipedia. In: IJCAI 2009, pp. 2083–2088 (2009)

22. Ponzetto, S.P., Strube, M.: Deriving a large-scale taxonomy from wikipedia. In: AAAI 2007, pp. 1440–1445 (2007)

23. Sabater, J., Sierra, C.: REGRET: reputation in gregarious societies. In: Agents 2001, pp. 194–195 (2001)

24. Song, S., Hwang, K., Zhou, R., Kwok, Y.-K.: Trusted p2p transactions with fuzzy reputation aggregation. IEEE Internet Computing 9(6), 24–34 (2005)

25. Tang, J., Zhang, J., Yao, L., Li, J., Zhang, L., Su, Z.: Arnetminer: extraction and mining of academic social networks. In: KDD 2008, pp. 990–998 (2008)

26. Vu, L.-H., Hauswirth, M., Aberer, K.: QoS-based service selection and ranking with trust and reputation management. In: Meersman, R., Tari, Z. (eds.) OTM 2005. LNCS, vol. 3760, pp. 466–483. Springer, Heidelberg (2005)

27. Wang, Y., Lim, E.-P.: The evaluation of situational transaction trust in e-service environments. In: ICEBE 2008, pp. 265–272 (2008)

28. Wang, Y., Lin, K.-J.: Reputation-oriented trustworthy computing in e-commerce environments. IEEE Internet Computing 12(4), 55–59 (2008)

29. Wang, Y., Singh, M.P.: Formal trust model for multiagent systems. In: Proceedings 20th International Joint Conference on Artificial Intelligence (IJCAI 2007), pp. 1551–1556 (2007)

30. Wang, Y., Varadharajan, V.: Trust^2: Developing trust in peer-to-peer environments. In: IEEE SCC 2005, pp. 24–34 (2005)

31. Xiong, L., Liu, L.: PeerTrust: Supporting reputation-based trust for peer-to-peer electronic communities. IEEE Trans. Knowl. Data Eng. 16(7), 843–857 (2004)

32. Yu, B., Singh, M.P., Sycara, K.: Developing trust in large-scale peer-to-peer systems. In: 2004 IEEE First Symposium on Multi-Agent Security and Survivability, pp. 1–10 (2004)

33. Yu, H., Kaminsky, M., Gibbons, P.B., Flaxman, A.D.: Sybilguard: defending against sybil attacks via social networks. IEEE/ACM Trans. Netw. 16(3), 576–589 (2008)

34. Yu, H., Shi, C., Kaminsky, M., Gibbons, P.B., Xiao, F.: Dsybil: Optimal sybil-resistance for recommendation systems. In: IEEE Symposium on Security and Privacy, pp. 283–298 (2009)

35. Zacharia, G., Maes, P.: Trust management through reputation mechanisms. Applied Artificial Intelligence 14(9), 881–907 (2000)

A Framework for Trust Enabled Software Asset Retrieval

YanZhen Zou[1,2], SiBo Cai[1,2], Meng Li[1,2], Lijie Wang[1,2], and Bing Xie[1,2]

[1] Software Institute, School of Electronics Engineering and Computer Science,
Peking University, Beijing 100871, China
[2] Key Laboratory of High Confidence Software Technologies, Ministry of Education,
Beijing 100871, China
{zouyz,caisb06,Limeng,wanglj07,xiebing}@sei.pku.edu.cn

Abstract. With the development of Internet technology, a lot of software assets emerge on the Internet, but it is difficult to predict or control the quality of these software assets. Therefore, an effective asset retrieval mechanism is needed to select and reuse trustworthy software assets. In this paper, we introduce the idea of trust management into Software Asset Repository (SAR) and propose a framework for trust-enabled software assets retrieval. The framework decomposes trust management into evidence collection, trust evaluation, trust recommendation and asset retrieval support, supporting dynamical and personalized asset trustworthiness evaluation and retrieval in SAR. We present the experiments of this framework in Trusted Software Asset Repository of Peking University, and a case study is given in this paper.

Keywords: Software Asset, Software Asset Repository, Trust management, Recommendation System.

1 Introduction

Software Asset Repository (SAR) is a fundamental software reuse facility to manage reusable software asset. With the development of Internet technology, a large number of software assets emerge on the Internet, and the service of SAR becomes more open, public and dynamic than before. In this situation, users can compose various assets efficiently, but it is difficult to predict and control the quality of assets. As a result, users could not trust the candidate asset in SAR though amount of software assets are available [1-3]. Therefore, an effective asset retrieval mechanism should be provided for assisting users select and reuse trustworthy software assets.

Currently, there are many works on software asset repository [4-7] and software asset retrieval [8-13]. However, few works present a good solution for trustworthy software assets retrieval. In our study, we found that the main difficulties of this problem lie in:

a) The diversity of software asset entities. The software asset is defined as all reusable software products in the software life cycle, such as software requirements, source

B. Xie et al. (Eds.): ATC 2010, LNCS 6407, pp. 139–153, 2010.

code, and test cases [14]. Therefore, we need a trustworthiness evaluation method that appropriate to all kinds of software assets, which could not be implemented by the traditional approaches of software analysis and software testing. In the same time, the evolution of software asset (such as Web Services) adds the difficulty of evaluation further.

b) The incompleteness of certificate information. In the process of software reuse, the role of asset developer, asset maintainer (SAR) and asset user are independent, and the phases of asset publish, asset discovery and asset reuse are separated. The asset users could only look into a candidate asset by its description information before download or reuse it. However, researchers have found that in many cases the descriptions of some software assets are insufficient and inaccurate [15].

c) The relativity of asset evaluation. More uncertainties, which affect a software asset's credibility, are added because of the difference of application environments. Different users have different requirements, and a user may have different requirements in different scenarios. Therefore, we could not access the trustworthiness of software asset using absolute standards in different scenarios, but measure the degree that the software asset meets a user's requirement in a given time, environment, and limited knowledge constraints. Namely, it is defined as the **trust relationship** from user to asset [16].

Based on the above analysis, this paper introduces the idea of trust and trust management [17-21] into SAR and proposes a framework for trust-enabled software assets retrieval. The **trust** in this paper stressed the confidence of an asset user on a software asset in completing one or more operations. The **trust management** collects trust evidence, builds trust evaluation engine and supports trust recommendation among different users. Based on the trust management framework, we implemented the trust-enabled software assets retrieval system in Trusted Software Asset Repository of Peking University, which help users select credible software asset in the retrieval process.

The rest of this paper is organized as follows: In section 2, we briefly introduce the background and the concepts in trust management. In section 3, we give the details of our proposed trust management framework. In section 4, we present a case of our framework. In section 5, related work and some discussions are addressed. Finally, in section 6, we conclude this paper and look into our future work.

2   Background and Concepts

In general, the trustworthiness of software can be decomposed into a group of trust properties. If a software system meets a user requirement in all trust properties, it is said that the software is reliable. However, the trust properties may have different content in practice. For example, from the view of avoiding unacceptable software failure, Avizienis et al. [22] define the trust properties includes Availability, Reliability, Safety, Integrity and Maintainability; But from the view of end users, the Microsoft [23] defines the trust properties should contain Security, Privacy, Reliability, Business Integrity. Therefore, in most of the existing works, only some specific trust properties are selected according to the application environment.

In SAR, users always retrieve software assets based on specific application environment. Different users may have different trust properties preference in different scenario. For example, a user using a logging asset may concern about the response time of the asset when developing real-time applications, while the other user engaged in developing e-commerce applications may pay more attention on the maintainability of the asset. Therefore, a concept of **trust requirement** should be introduced into trust management of SAR, which is used to describe the trust properties and the constraints on these trust properties such as weight, value constraint, and so on. Thus user can define his trust requirement based on different application environments. It improves the flexibility of trust management.

The trust from a user to a software asset depends on the relevant evidence, known as trust evidence. In general, **trust evidence** includes all facts that can be used to prove the truth conditions of a software asset. In SAR, the common tools to gather evidence include software testing, QoS (Quality of Service) monitoring, usage report, etc. The trust management framework needs an evidence description model to store evidence collected by different tools.

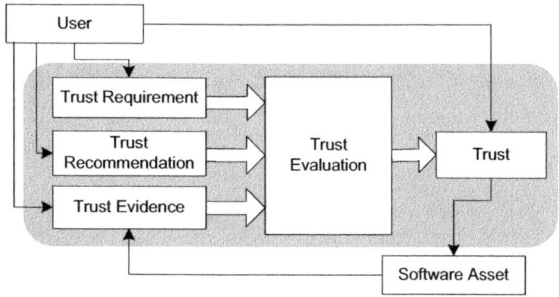

Fig. 1. The concepts in trust management of Software Asset Repository

Fig.1 describes the concepts of trust management in SAR, in which thick arrows represent data flows, while thin arrows represent relationships among the concepts. The **trust evaluation** here can be defined as the process of accessing the trustworthiness of a software asset according a user's trust requirement and analyzing the relevant trust evidence. In this process, a user may establish trust with a software asset depended on the available evidences collected by himself (direct trust) or by other users (indirect trust). The evidences are delivered among users through **trust recommendation**. That is, we need to establish trust recommendation policy for evidence sharing and transmission among users.

Based on these concepts, we proposed a framework for managing the trust relationship between users and their trustworthy software asset and supporting trust-enabled software assets retrieval.

3   Trust Management Framework

As shown in Fig.2, in consideration of the framework should be scalable and easy to use, we decompose trust management into four parts:

- **Evidence Collection.** Evidence Collection is the basis of the framework, which is used to collect, store and display trust evidence;
- **Trust Evaluation.** Trust Evaluation is used to describe and express the user's trust requirement firstly, then we propose a trust model for software assets;
- **Trust Recommendation.** Trust Recommendation is used to establish trust recommendation relationships among users, supporting evidence sharing and transitive for trust evaluation;
- **Asset Retrieval Support.** Asset Retrieval Support is used to provide the application interface of trust management that assists users in selecting trustworthy candidate software assets. On this basis, a trust enabled software asset retrieval mechanism is established and implemented.

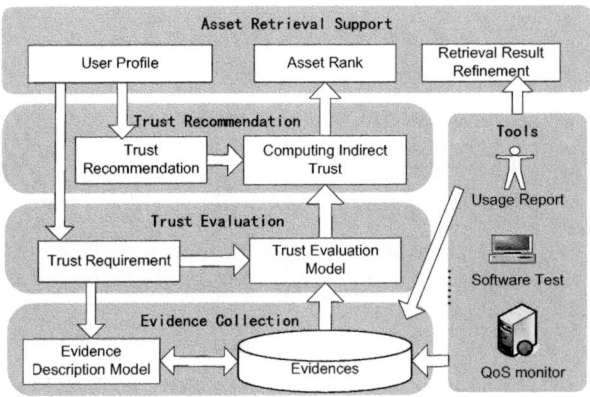

Fig. 2. The trust management framework of Software Asset Repository

3.1   Evidence Collection

In SAR, the tools of software testing, QoS monitoring or usage report are usually used to feedback the related trust evidence. It is not difficult to find that these tools focus on different quality attributes of the software asset. For example, usage report often reflects the reliability and security of an asset, but a test tool may only report the number of memory leaks. Therefore, the evidence description model here should be customized and extended to store the evidences collected by a variety of tools.

In this paper, we propose an evidence description model with a group of customized evidence template. Every evidence template describes a class of evidence by a kind of evidence collection tool. When the system needs to support new evidence collection tools, we need only to establish a new evidence template but affect the existing evidence description.

In details, every **evidence template** can be defined as a five-tuple form, which is
$evidT = <etName, etKey, certificationPoint, EvidAttrSet, EvidAttrValueSet >$

- *etName* defined the name of the evidence template;
- *etKey* defined the key that uniquely identifies the template;
- *certificationPoint* defined the validation side of the template, it can be the asset repository administrator or a network *URL*;
- *EvidAttrSet* defined all the evidence attributes in the template. *EvidAttrSet=<eaName, eaValue, eaKey, parent, isLeaf>*, where *eaValue* defines the feedback value on the evidence attribute; *parent* defines the parent node of the evidence attribute in the template; *isLeaf* mark whether the attribute is leaf node. When a template is used to describe an evidence instance, all of its leaf node will be fed back.
- *EvidAttrValueSet =<type, max, min>* defined the value set to evaluate the value on an evidence attribute. For example, define the value set of "reliability" is float (*type*) values range from 0 (*min*) to 1(*max*). It means the value is closer to 1, the reliability of the asset is better.

Based on this evidence model, we developed feedback based evidence collection mechanism. Here we distinguish two kinds of feedback: subjective feedback and objective feedback. The subjective feedback is used to describe all usage report from asset users, which may include unfair feedback because there is subjectivity in asset users; the objective feedback is used to describe all information collected by test or monitoring tools, which may need integrate the information collected further to prove evidence. In this situation, all feedback is associated to a user or a tool, and the unfair feedback could be handled easily.

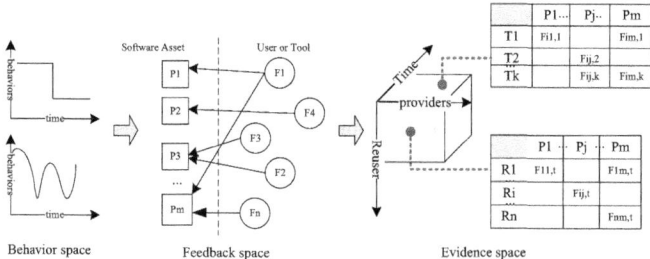

Fig. 3. Evidence collection process in trust management

As shown in Fig. 3, the evidence collection process is divided into the following steps: 1) Feedback collection. From behavior space to feedback space, all feedbacks (such as execution time) from asset users or specific tools are collected to describe the condition of software asset. These feedback data are the origin of trust evidence; 2) Evidence aggregation. From feedback space to evidence space, all feedback data are aggregated to get the evaluation on the evidence attribute, then is stored with an evidence template in SAR. Particularly, values on some evidence attributes should be normalized for the different units and ranges, which are used to compare different evidence instances described by different evidence templates.

3.2 Trust Evaluation

As mentioned earlier, different users have different trust requirements in SAR because of their different application environments. To help users select and define their favorite trust properties, we also provide a customized trust requirement model and propose a trust model for software assets.

3.3 Trust Requirement

The trust requirement model is defined with a group of customized requirement template. Every **requirement template** is a six- tuple, which is *requT=<user, rtKey, TrProperty, TrPropValSet, TrPropCons, Association>*

- *user* defines the user id that published and used this template;
- *rtKey* defines the key that uniquely identifies the template;
- *TrProperty* defines the trust properties in a requirement template. *TrProperty=<trPropName, trPropKey, trPropParent, trPropWeight, trPropIsLeaf>*, where *trPropWeight* defined the weight of the property, which is in range of [0,1]. The sum of all the property weight with the same parent should be 1; *trPropIsLeaf* mark whether the trust property is leaf node in the template. When a trust property is leaf node, it must be associated with one or more evidence attributes.
- *TrPropValSet =<type, max, min>* defines the value set of a trust property, including type (*type*), maximum (*max*) and minimum (*min*) .
- *TrPropCons =<trPropKey, OP, trPropValue>*, where *OP* is a valid comparison operators, such as ">"; *trPropValue* defines the boundary value on the particular trust property marked by *trPropKey* .
- *Association=<trPropKey, eaKey, associateType>* defines the value on the trust property rely on the responding the value on the corresponding evidence attribute. Here *associateType* describes the type of association, such as "pessimistic", "optimist" and "cautious". The "pessimistic" means all the evidence attributes associated with the trust property must meet the restrictions, "optimist" means as long as one attribute associated with the trust property meet the restrictions; and "cautious" means computing a value based on all the attributes associated with the trust property, then this value should meet the restrictions.

Here we can see that *Association* elements bridge the gap from user's trust requirement to evidence information. When a user has defined his trust requirement template, he submits his query as a set of trust properties and the constrictions on these trust properties. To get the evaluation on particular trust property, a map must be built from a trust property to relevant data source - evidence described by evidence template. As shown in Fig. 4, the value of the "reliability" in trust requirement template relies on the evidence from both QoS monitoring and usage report, and the

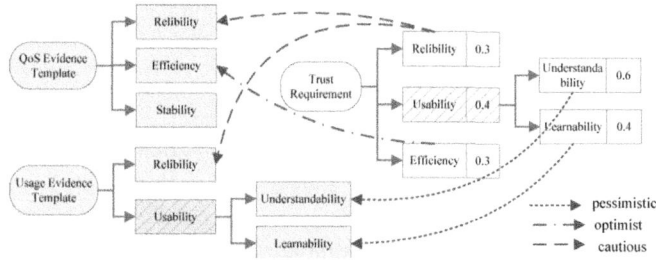

Fig. 4. Examples of association from trust property to evidence attribute

associateType is set as "cautious". The value of the "Efficiency" relies on the evidence from QoS monitoring only, and the *associateType* is set as "optimist". As a result, evidences collected by usage report and QoS monitoring tool can be analyzed.

3.3.1 Trust Evaluation Model

Based on the trust requirement, a trust evaluation model is needed to analyze related evidence information. These evidences have a certain degree of ambiguity, which reflected in two aspects: firstly, users often give ambiguous feedbacks, such as "fine", "medium", "poor"; Secondly, some evidence attribute has a certain ambiguity, such as reusability and usability. Therefore, we introduce the idea of the fuzzy processing into trust evaluation and propose a trust model based on Fuzzy Comprehensive Evaluation. The trust model includes the steps in follow:

1) Building Factor Set, Evaluation Set and Weight Set Based on User's Trust Requirement

Factor Set is composed of the trust properties in user's trust requirement template. According the father-son relationship between trust properties, we decompose the corresponding factor set into several levels. The solution is given from the bottom level of the factor set. For example, the factor set based on the trust template in Fig.4 can be described as $U = (u_1, u_2, u_3) = (reliability, usability, efficiency)$, where $u_2 = (u_{21}, u_{22}) = (understandability, learnability)$. Thus we obtain the fuzzy comprehensive evaluation of u_2 firstly.

Evaluation Set is composed of the value set of the trust property. In this paper, this value set is normalized into [0,1]. For example, the evaluation set of 5-point scale can be described as $V = (v_1, v_2, ...,v_5) = (1,2,3,4,5)$, which can be normalized as $V = (0.2, 0.4, 0.6, 0.8, 1)$.

Weight Set described the influence of the factors in the comprehensive evaluation. Different evaluation result is got with the same factor set but different weight set. In this paper, weight set is composed of the corresponding weight of trust properties. Thus in Fig.4, the weight set $W=(w_1, w_2, w_3)=(0.3, 0.4, 0.3)$, $w_2=(u_{21}, u_{22})=(0.6, 0.4)$.

2) Set up Evaluation Matrix

Based on factor set and evaluation set, we obtain a evaluation matrix named R, where r_{ij} denotes the evaluation result of the factor u_i ($i = 1, 2, ..., m$) on the evaluation factor

v_j ($j= 1, 2, ..., n$). The valuation result is got though a numerical function. Usually, the numerical function can be defined as:

$$f(u_i, v_j) = \sum_{l=1}^{N} rw_l / \sum_{k=1}^{M} rw_k \tag{1}$$

Here M is the total number of trust evidence, N is the number of evidence that have value v_j ($j= 1, 2, ..., n$) on the factor u_i ($i = 1, 2, ..., m$), rw_k ($k=1, 2,..., M$) is the recommendation weight of the trust evidence.

This numerical function used a very simple ratio model, which is not sensitive to changes of evidences. In this paper, we update this function because:

- Consideration of recent evidence. In general, the most recent evidence is able to illustrate the asset's current state. Thus, more attention needs to be paid on the recent evidence in order to reflect the trustworthiness of the asset;
- The effectiveness of evidence decrease with time. For example, the evidence gathered a month ago is not sufficient to explain the current situation of the asset.
- The amount of evidence is important. As we known, the more evidence we got, the more reliable evaluation result we got. In other words, we only have inaccurate evaluation result if there are only one or two evidence instances.

Formula 2 gives the improved function, where t and $t-1$ is two time points, the logical distance between them is Δt; M is the total number of trust evidence involved in the evaluation, where $N_{\Delta t}$ evidence give value v_j ($j= 1, 2, ..., n$) on the factor u_i ($i = 1, 2, ..., m$) from $t-1$ to t; δ is a constant, $e^{-\delta \Delta t}$ is the attenuation factor. When the system does not detect new evidence, the trust value will decay with time. In a period of time, the more evidence is gathered, the larger is the trust value.

$$f_t(u_i, v_j) = e^{-\delta \Delta t} \times f_{t-1}(u_i, v_j) + (1 - e^{-\delta \Delta t}) \times \sum_{l=1}^{N_{\Delta t}} rw_l / \sum_{k=1}^{M} rw_k \tag{2}$$

For example, suppose 10 users that have fed back to a candidate software asset in Fig.4. For "*understandability*", 3 users gave 5 stars, 4 users gave 4 stars and 3 users gave 3 stars. For "*learnability*", 2 users gave 5 stars, 4 users gave 4 stars and 4 users gave 3 stars. All the recommendation weight is set 1. Then we can got $R_{21} = (0, 0, 0.4, 0.3, 0.3)$, $R_{22}=(0, 0, 0.4, 0.4, 0.2)$. Based on this, we can compute $R_2 = [R_{21}, R_{22}]^T$.

3) Compute Fuzzy Comprehensive Evaluation
Based on the evaluation matrix R and the weigh set W, we can compute the fuzzy comprehensive evaluation $E = W * R$, where w_i ($i = 1, 2, ..., m$) is normalization and non-negative. Thus in Fig.4, we can compute

$$E_2 = w_2 \bullet R_2 \Leftrightarrow [e_{21}, e_{22}] = [w_{21}, w_{22}] \bullet \begin{bmatrix} R_{21} \\ R_{22} \end{bmatrix} = [0.6, 0.4] \bullet \begin{bmatrix} 0, 0, 0.3, 0.4, 0.3 \\ 0, 0, 0.4, 0.4, 0.2 \end{bmatrix}$$

$$= [0, \ 0, 0.34, 0.4, 0.26]$$

4) Get Evaluation Results
Based on fuzzy comprehensive evaluation $E = (e_1, e_2, ..., e_m)$, the final trust evaluation result is computed through the largest membership method, the weighted average

method or the fuzzy distribution method. In the above example, the final evaluation result on the "understandability" index to:

- Using the largest membership method, the $V = \{v_L | v_L \to \max_j e_j\} = 4$
- Using the weighted average method, then $V = \sum_{j=1}^{n} e_j v_j / \sum_{j=1}^{n} e_j = 3.92$
- Using the fuzzy distribution method, then $V = E_2 = [0, 0, 0.34, 0.4, 0.26]$

Notes: 1) If the evaluation set is qualitative, only the largest membership method could be used. If the evaluation set is quantitative, it can also use the weighted average method or fuzzy distribution method. 2) In multi-level fuzzy comprehensive evaluation, the number of evaluation set should be same among the brother trust properties, and the map from the son factor evaluation result to parent factor evaluation matrix should be built. In the above example, the evaluation result of " understandability" is obtained using fuzzy distribution method, which will be next used to compose the evaluation matrix of $U = (u_1, u_2, u_3) = (reliability, usability, efficiency)$.

3.3.2 Trust Recommendation

As introduced above, a user can only get limited trust evidence by himself. On one hand, a user cannot use, test or monitor all the assets in SAR; on the other hand, a user can not call or download a software asset repeatedly in a long span. Especially for a user who has newly registered, gets and learns from others is more practical and possible. Therefore, we need to establish and maintain the trust relationships between users in the software asset repository.

In our study, we found that there are often such flaws in the existing trust recommendation policies: Although a recommender has higher trust value, but his recommendation is not accepted by the other users because they focus different technical areas. Therefore, we build personalized user preference model to describe the user's favorite technical areas and compute the similarity between users. Then based on the similarity, we initial the recommendation weight and establish the recommendation relationships between users.

Note that few users will call or download the same assets repeatedly. When there are a amount of assets in SAR, calculate the condition of every asset will also have a greater cost in time and space. Therefore, this paper will classify all the software assets into several disjoint asset categories according to their function and application field. If an asset belongs to a category has been frequently used or downloaded, then all the assets in the same category will be assigned to have a higher preference value. Then according to a user's query and download history in a period of time, a user's preferences can be expressed as a vector $V = <m_1, m_2, \ldots, m_n>$, where m_i represents the number of the users download the assets in category i $(i=1,2,\ldots, n)$. As a result, the similarity between users can be calculated as formula (3) and formula (4) below. Here N is the total number of asset categories, $m_i(u)$ that the number of user u downloaded the assets in category i.

$$R(a,b) = dist(V(a),V(b)) = \frac{1}{N} * \sum_{i=1}^{N} dist(m_i(a), m_i(b)) \qquad (3)$$

$$dist(m_i(a), m_i(b)) = \begin{cases} 1 & m_i(a) = m_i(b) = 0 \\ \dfrac{m_i(b)}{\max\{m_i(a), m_i(b)\}} & else \end{cases} \tag{4}$$

Recommend is asymmetrical. We can see from the above formula, if user j used more assets in all asset categories than user i, then $rw_{ij} = 1$; on the contrary, rw_{ij} will be relatively small. When a user does not use any assets, he recommendation weigh to any other users will be zero. This is reasonable.

In practice, the recommendation weight is also considered in the following four aspects: 1) the evidence is provided by a authorized third-party agency, or is collected by a user favorite tools ; 2) the difference of users on their application environment, such as network environment; 3) the reliability of evidence, such as a user may provide boast feedback. Thus, we also support users in the trust evaluation system build and maintain their own recommendation relationships.

4 Experiments

Based on our work, we implemented a trust-enabled software asset retrieval system in the Trusted Software Asset Repository of Peking University[1], which is used to recommend trusted software asset in the process of software asset retrieval. In this section, we illustrate our work with a case study of web service selection.

As shown in table 1, we selected 5 Web Services that provide weather forecast functions in the software asset repository. Now suppose a software developer login our software asset repository (as a user), build his trust requirement and maintain his trust recommendation relationships. Then in his software asset retrieval process, the system will recommend him the trustworthy software assets according the trust evaluation results.

Table 1. Five candidate Web services

ID	Name	Provider	WSDL address
WS 1	CDYNE Weather	CDYNE	http://ws.cdyne.com/WeatherWS/Weather.asmx?wsdl
WS 2	City Weather Forecast Web Service	Web.Xml	http://www.webxml.com.cn/WebServices/WeatherWebService.asmx?WSDL
WS 3	Weather Web Service	Ws.79777.cn	http://ws.79777.cn/Weather.asmx?wsdl
WS 4	National Weather Service	NOAA	http://www.weather.gov/forecasts/xml/DWMLgen/wsdl/ndfdXML.wsdl?wsdl
WS 5	Weather	Deep Training	http://www.deeptraining.com/webservices/weather.asmx?wsdl

---

[1] http://tsr.trustie.net/

4.1   Evidence Instances

For these web services, two tools are supported for evidence collection, which are QoS monitoring and usage report from the end user. Therefore, we built both QoS evidence template and usage evidence template in our evidence model. As shown in Fig.5, the QoS evidence template contains four evidence attributes: Performance, Robustness, Response Time, availability, reliability, where only three leaf nodes in the template is used to get evidence instances; the usage evidence template contains five evidence attributes: Security, Effectiveness, Reliability, Usability and Satisfaction, they are all leaf node that could be used to get evidence instances. The usage evidence template is built based on ISO/IEC 9126 [24]. The value set on all the evidence attributes in these two templates is in range of [0, 1] except of "Response Time".

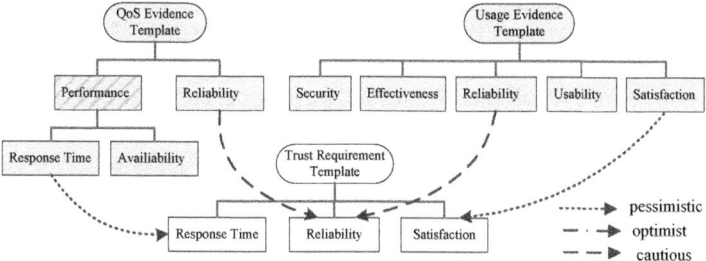

Fig. 5. QoS evidence template, usage evidence template and user's trust requirement

Based on the QoS evidence template, we described the evidence instances collected by QoS monitoring. As shown in table 2, we get two evidence instances for every Web Services, one instance is got at public network and the other is got at education network. In the same time, some usage evidence instances are fed back in SAR. Here we do not list them in detail.

Table 2. Trust evidence collected by QoS monitoring

ID	Reliability (Pub/Edu)	Response time (Pub/Edu)	Availability (Pub/Edu)
WS 1	100% / 100%	654ms / 3174ms	100% / 99.6%
WS 2	100% / 100%	1166ms / 225ms	99.9% / 100%
WS 3	100% / 100%	178ms / 249ms	100% / 99.7%
WS 4	100% / 100%	1238ms / 4089ms	95% / 100%
WS 5	100% / 100%	590ms / 3700ms	100% / 99.5%

4.2   Trust Recommendation

To simply the problem, we classify users into two categories: users in public network and users in education network. Users in education network will more favorite the QoS data (as trust evidence) monitored in education network, the corresponding recommendation weight is set as 0.9; To the same user, the QoS data monitored in public network is less to be considered relatively. Therefore, the recommendation weight between users in different network is set as 0.1

Suppose that our retrieval user is a new registered user, and he accepts all the recommendation from other users with a default recommendation weight of 0.4. As the user call or download more software assets, our system will log his query and use history to update the recommendation weight.

4.3 Trust Evaluation and Trust-Enabled Software Asset Retrieval

Suppose the retrieval user submit his trust requirement template shown in Fig. 5, the requirement template contains 3 trust properties: Reliability, Response Time and Satisfaction. Here the constraints include: (Reliability, >, 0.9), (Response Time, <, 1), (Satisfaction, >, 0.9). The attribute associations include: (reliability, reliability@QoS Template, cautious), (reliability, reliability@Usage Template, cautious), (Response Time, Response Time@QoS Template, pessimistic), and (Satisfaction, Satisfaction @Usage Template, pessimistic).

Based on the above requirement template, trust evidence and trust recommendation relationships, we got the trust evaluation result at each trust properties. As shown in table 3, only WS2 and WS3 could meet the user's trust requirement, and they would be recommended to this retrieval user. In the next step, the system will normalize all the evaluation results on the three trust properties and get a final trust value that be used to rank all the candidate software assets.

Table 3. Trust evaluation result

ID	Reliability	Response time	Satisfaction
WS1	100%	2915 ms	95%
WS2	**100%**	**307 ms**	**93%**
WS3	**100%**	**242 ms**	**95%**
WS4	100%	3804 ms	85%
WS5	100%	3389 ms	95%

Based on the case study, we found our proposed framework is very practicable. Users could point out what trust property they care about and what evidence they favorite on, multiple evidence collection tools could be supported and integrated in the software asset repository. In this paper, we do not show how the evaluation results finally take effect as trust evidence evolution, which is our next step work to do. But we believe that with the trust evidence and trust recommendation increased, the final trust evaluation results will be improved and ultimately facilitate the software asset retrieval and selection.

5   Related Work and Discussion

Trust management technology has been widely discussed in recent years. Early trust management research began in the security field [17], where representative works include Policymaker, KeyNote, and so on. However, when subjectivity is pointed out as an important characteristic of trust, more and more researches turn to evidence-based trust evaluation and management. Typically, Gradison [18] proposed SULTAN trust management framework to support the trust in distributed web applications; Xiong [19] proposed a reputation-based trust management system peerTrust. In the same time, there have been a lot of trust models, such as Abudul-Rahman model [20], Jøsang model [21], and so on. In application, Wang [25] proposed the trust model apply to grid computing, Standifird [26] the trust models apply to e-commerce, Xu and Wang [27, 28] proposed the trust models apply to Netware, and so on.

In these work, trust embodies a dynamic features: the system dynamically collect evidence, dynamically evaluate trust value, and dynamically establish and revoke the trust based on the evaluation results. This dynamic trust assessment and decision-making mechanism provides a good idea for our trustworthy software asset retrieval problem. However, some problems still need to be addressed: 1) the existing work on evidence collection is lack of multiple-level description model support, and the reliability of the evidence is also rarely concerned; 2) the evaluation method is coupled highly with the evidence, limiting the scalability of the system; 3) the trust model could not deal with the variability of user needs in the software repository. To solve these problems, this paper proposed our trust management framework and gave corresponding solutions.

There are also a lot of works on software asset recommendation and retrieval. For example, Frank [8] proposed a recommendation method using Collaborative Filtering, which collects usage history of all users and then use IR techniques to calculate the similarity between users. A. Mockus [9] proposed an Expertise Browser to help users locate experts to consult. Ye [10] proposed CodeBroker to foster software reuse by actively recommending methods that are suitable in a context. Cubranic [11] proposed an Eclipse plug-in tool named Hipikat to locate user cared information by log and text similarity matcher. Zhao [12] proposed comprehensive trust management architecture for web services. Sarma [13] proposed interactive visual exploration of Socio-Technical Relationships in Software *Development*. Different from these methods, our work start from user's trust requirement and support collaborative filtering though trust recommendation, making the software asset retrieval results have better accuracy and availability.

6 Conclusion

This paper introduced a trust management framework to recommend user trusted software assets in the retrieval process. It analyzed and defined the concepts of trust, decomposed trust management into evidence collection, trust evaluation, trust recommendation, and software asset retrieval support. On this basis, it also proposed a trust model applicable to software asset, and the evaluation result is used to select candidate assets effectively. In the next step, we will focus on an automated or semi-automatic approach to associate user's trust requirement and related trust evidence and a trust recommendation policy integrated application environment.

Acknowledgment

This research was sponsored by the National Basic Research Program of China (973) under Grant No. 2005CB321805 and the National Key Technology R&D Program of China (863) under Grant No. 2007AA010301.

References

1. Jøsang, A., Ismail, R., Boyd, C.: A Survey of Trust and Reputation Systems for Online Service Provision. Decision Support Systems (2006)
2. ComponentSource, http://www.componentsource.com/
3. SourceForge, http://www.sourceforge.net/
4. IEEE standard for information technology -software reuse - data model for reusable library interoperability: Basic interoperability data model (BIDM). IEEE std. 1420.1 (1995)
5. UDDI Version 3.0, UDDI Specification Technical Committee Specification
6. Reusable Asset Specification, OMG Adopted Specification, ptc/04-06-06 (2004), http://www.omg.org/issues/
7. The Electronic Industry Standard of china SJ/T 11371-2007, Software component management - The first part - Management information model (published in November 2007), put in practice (January 2008)
8. McCarey, F., Cinnéide, M.Ó., Kushmerick, N.: Recommending Library Methods- An Evaluation of the Vector Space Model (VSM) and Latent Semantic Indexing. In: The 8th International Conference on Software Reuse, Torino, Italy, pp. 217–230 (June 2006)
9. Mockus, A., Herbsleb, J.D.: Expertise Browser: A quantitative approach to identifying expertise. In: Proceedings of the International Conference on Software Engineering, pp. 503–512 (2002)
10. Ye, Y., Fischer, G.: Reuse conductive development environments. Automated Software Engineering 12(2), 199–235 (2005)
11. Cubranic, D., Murphy, G.C.: Hipikat: A Project Memory for Software Development. IEEE Transactions on Software Engineering 31(6), 446–464 (2005)
12. Zhao, W., Varadharajan, V.: Trust Management for Web Services. In: IEEE International Conference on Web Services, pp. 819–821 (2008)
13. Sarma, A., Maccherone, L., Wagstrom, P., Herbsleb, J.: Tesseract: Interactive Visual Exploration of Socio-Technical Relationships in Software Development. In: IEEE 31st International Conference on Software Engineering, Vancouver, BC, Canada (2009)
14. Cai, S., Zou, Y., Shao, L., Xie, B., Shao, W.: A Framework Supporting Software Assets Evaluation on Trustworthiness. Journal of Software 21(2), 359–372 (2010)
15. Fan, J., Kambhampati, S.: A Snapshot of Public Web Services. ACM SIGMOD Record 34(1), 24–32 (2005)
16. Chang, E., Dillon, T.S., Hussain, F.K.: Trust and reputation relationships in service-oriented environments. In: Proceeding of the Third International Conference on Information Technology and Applications (ICITA), pp. 4–14 (2005)
17. Blaze, M., Feigenbaum, J., Lacy, J.: Decentralized trust management. In: Proceeding of the 1996 IEEE Symp. On Security and Privacy, Washington, pp. 164–173. IEEE Computer Society Press, Los Alamitos (1996)
18. Grandison, T.W.A.: Trust Management for Internet Applications. Department of Computing. London, University of London. Ph.D thesis (2003)

19. Xiong, L., Liu, L.: PeerTrust: supporting reputation-based trust for peer-to-peer electronic communities. IEEE Transactions on Knowledge and Data Engineering 16(7), 843–857 (2004)
20. Abdul-Rahman, A., Hailes, S.: A distributed trust model. In: Proceedings of the 1997 Workshop on New Security Paradigms, Langdale, Cumbria, United Kingdom, pp. 48–60 (1997)
21. Jøsang, A., Gray, L., Kinateder, M.: Simplification and Analysis of Transitive Trust Networks. Web Intelligence and Agent Systems Journal 4(2), 139–161 (2006)
22. Avizienis, A., Laprie, J.C., Randell, B., Landwehr, C.: Basic Concepts and Taxonomy of Dependable and Secure Computing. IEEE Transactions on Dependable and Secure Computing 1(1), 11–33 (2004)
23. http://www.microsoft.com/mscorp/twc/twc_whitepaper.mspx (2002)
24. ISO/IEC 9126-1:2001 Software engineering - Product quality - Part 1: Quality model, http://www.iso.org/iso/iso_catalogue/catalogue_tc/catalogue_detail.htm?csnumber=22749
25. Wang, D.: Research on Trust Model and Trust-based Application for Grid Computing. Institute of Computing Technology, Chinese Academy of Science, Beijing, China. Ph.D thesis (2006)
26. Standifird, S.S.: Reputation and E-commerce: eBay Auctions and the Asymmetrical Impact of Positive and Negative Ratings. Journal of Management 27, 279–295 (2001)
27. Xu, F., Lv, J., Zheng, W., Cao, C.: Design of a trust valuation model in software service coordination. Journal of Software (in Chinese with English Abstract) 14(6), 1043–1051 (2003)
28. Wang, Y., Lv, J., Xu, F., Zhang, L.: A Trust Measurement and Evolution Model for Internetware. Journal of Software 17(4), 682–690 (2006)

Opportunistic Trust Based P2P Services Framework for Disconnected MANETs

Basit Qureshi, Geyong Min, and Demetres Kouvatsos

School of Computing, Informatics and Media
University of Bradford, United Kingdom
{b.qureshi,g.min,d.kouvatsos}@bradford.ac.uk

Abstract. In delay-tolerant disconnected Mobile Ad-hoc Networks (MANETs), mobile devices communicate with each other as they meet opportunistically establishing peer-to-peer (P2P) connections. Trust management in this type of networks is a challenging task due to the dynamic topology and decentralized nature and has attracted mant recent research interests. In this paper we propose a trust based framework for P2P services in a delay-tolerant disconnected MANET. The proposed framework utilizes a decentralized trust model and a P2P communication protocol for secure file exchange in an opportunistic store-carry and forward mechanism. We discuss the implementation of the framework and experiment with a gnutella style P2P file sharing application in a disconnected MANET. Our results provide important insight into the key challenges and short-comings face by researchers and engineers when designing and deploying such systems.

Keywords: Opportunistic routing, Peer-to-peer services, Disconnected MANETs, Trust Management, Pervasive devices.

1 Introduction

Due to advances in micro-electronic wireless technologies, mobile devices with ever increasing capabilities of processing, storage and communications are being made available. Devices such as multi-function phones, personal digital assistants, wearable devices and handheld sensor devices are considered as pervasive devices. These devices when used in urban computing scenarios bring a lot of unknown people together allowing discovery of other people and possible communication and sharing of information. Personal handheld devices carried by people can communicate with embedded servers to obtain relevant information thus forming an open and a dynamic network. The networks formed in these open and dynamic environments are delay tolerant ad-hoc peer to peer networks [1, 2]. These networks are categorized by not having a pre-deployed fixed infrastructure nor centrally administered space controlled users. Rather, these pervasive devices are resource constrained, self-organized and dynamically self-configured to set up in the network by both consuming and providing services as peers.

Delay tolerant disconnected mobile ad-hoc network (MANET) is a type of MANET characterized by long delay paths and frequent disconnections and network

B. Xie et al. (Eds.): ATC 2010, LNCS 6407, pp. 154–167, 2010.
© Springer-Verlag Berlin Heidelberg 2010

partitions [3]. In a disconnected MANET, information may be carried by a mobile node and forwarded opportunistically across partitions, therefore allowing communication between areas of the network that are never connected by an end-to-end path. Recently, this kind of opportunistic forwarding scenarios have become popular in the research area investigating delay-tolerant networks (DTN). Mobile nodes enable indirect data exchange among disconnected portions of the overall network, typically using a store-and-forward approach and some form of opportunistic forwarding [4, 5, 7]. To assume trustworthy interaction in this kind of networks is unrealistic due to the fact that most entities in the network are unknown. Consequently, trust has recovered a big interest as a basis to secure and manage peer to peer relationships [6].

Trust can be used to establish new connections between unknown entities, or to measure certain parameters such as cooperation ability, Quality of Service, individual behavior and social environment. Recent studies have already demonstrated the feasibility of using distributed trust techniques in self-organized, distributed and re-source-constrained networks. TRAVOS [8] is a trust model that is built upon prob-ability theory and based on observations of past interaction between nodes. Yu and Singh [9] developed an approach for social reputation management, in which they represented a node's ratings as a scalar and combined them with testimonies using combination schemes. Hang et. al. [10] proposed an adaptive probabilistic trust model that combines probability and certainty and offers a trust update mechanism to esti-mate the trustworthiness of users in a de-centralized distributed network. Authors in [11] proposed a reputation-based decentralized trust management middleware. The reputation information of every peer is stored in its neighbors and piggy-backed on its replies to requests for data or services. eBiquity Group proposes a trust based data management framework, in order to enable mobile devices access to the available distributed computation, storage, and sensory resources [12]. This also includes a reputation system from the history of prior encounters.

In this paper we propose a light weight trust based framework for secure digital content sharing in pervasive devices. The main contribution of this paper is to allow providing non-existing security services to the applications in a dynamic way by mak-ing pervasive devices act as secure peers. The proposed framework allows peers to store, carry and forward shared content in an opportunistic manner. A secure file ex-change protocol for file sharing in ad hoc environment is also proposed. We con-ducted user trials with a set of users to test the framework and provide results and recommendations based on our experiments.

The rest of the paper is organized as follows, section 2 presents the proposed framework, and section 3 presents management consideration and requirements for the framework. In section 4, we give details about the experiments and user trials. Section 5 presents the results obtained followed by closely related work in section 6. Finally, the summary and conclusions are presented in section 7.

2   Proposed Framework Architecture

The main motivation of the proposed trust-based framework is to provide flexible security services to the peer to peer applications in a disconnected MANET. The pro-posed architecture is based on the concept of distributed decentralized trust models that eliminates the complexity of establishing new relationships, the dependence on a central server, the need for frequent manual setting and always-on global connectivity. Any device that can participate in a P2P communication model can establish connections in a secure way using an opportunistic communication protocol. Figure 1 shows an overview of the proposed framework in use by mobile and stationary users.

Users mainly operate in mobile ad hoc mode, as the devices come within each other's range, files are shared among users. We assume that a mobile user may physically change location to an area with Internet accessibility providing an opportunity to synchronize data or upload / download latest versions of files. A user can also move to a new location and establish connection with a cluster of mobile ad hoc users while sharing the latest version of the downloaded files thus utilizing the notion of exchanging files with an opportunistic store-carry and forward mechanism. The neighborhood discovery method depends on the radio technology being used: commonly available options with today's mobile device hardware include Bluetooth device discovery or broadcast beacons on a well known WiFi SSID. We illustrate the ad hoc mode by the circle in the center of Figure 1 where two devices move in the vicinity of each other and engage in interaction. Of course the neighborhood can, and usually will, contain more than two devices; the system must therefore manage multiple simultaneous connections. In a delay tolerant MANET, nodes discover each other as long as they can communicate in a limited range depending on the device capability and radio technology used. Nodes can frequently appear or disappear depending on various environmental factors or device limitations.

We assume that in ad hoc mode, each node executes a periodic loop that consists of three steps: (1) neighborhood discovery, (2) user identification (and authentication), and (3) data exchange. Upon discovery of a new device in the neighborhood, the system enters the identification phase where the devices open a communication link between each other to exchange the user identity information. Each device using the framework runs a digital content sharing application based on the communication protocol, discussed in section 2.2. Upon a first encounter the devices running the application exchange their profiles during the identification phase. The system stores the profiles persistently along with other contact statistics to avoid unnecessary profile updates and to make subsequent decisions, e.g., to forward messages between nodes. During subsequent contacts the profiles are exchanged only if the profile has changed since the last encounter (i.e., user changed his nickname or status etc.), otherwise the nodes only exchange their user identifiers. Once the identification is successfully completed, the last step of the interaction is the data exchange phase. The application running on connected devices transfer / update the profile and exchange files. These files are stored persistently on the devices within the limits of storage space and forwarded to other devices as contact opportunities arise. These opportunistic exchanges combined with human mobility create a temporal communications network as in Pocket Switched Network (PSN) [13] where messages travel from device to device over multiple hops without any infrastructure connectivity.

Figure 2 depicts the architecture of the proposed framework. We consider three layers in the proposed framework to decouple applications from security and opportunistic user discovery issues. The main advantage of using this design is the application developers can rely on the framework for security, trusted user discovery and interaction and file sharing. We discuss the three layers in detail.

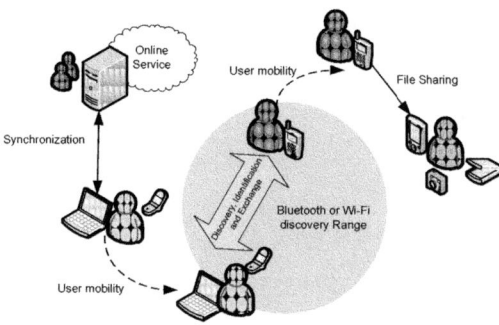

Fig. 1. Proposed System Overview

2.1 Content Sharing Applications

We have developed three applications to exchange messages and files between pervasive devices using the communication API shown in Figure 3.

Mobile Social Networking. This application shows the user the current set of neighboring devices with related information such as user profile. A user may search for new neighbors; remove users from this list of neighbors and send messages. User can tag a neighboring user as a trusted friend. The user can also enable distinct alerts to be notified when a friend is in the neighborhood.

Epidemic Newsgroup. This application is an opportunistic equivalent of the traditional Usenet messaging service. It enables discussions among multiple disconnected participants sharing some specific interest. As with asynchronous messaging, a message consists of text and an optional file.

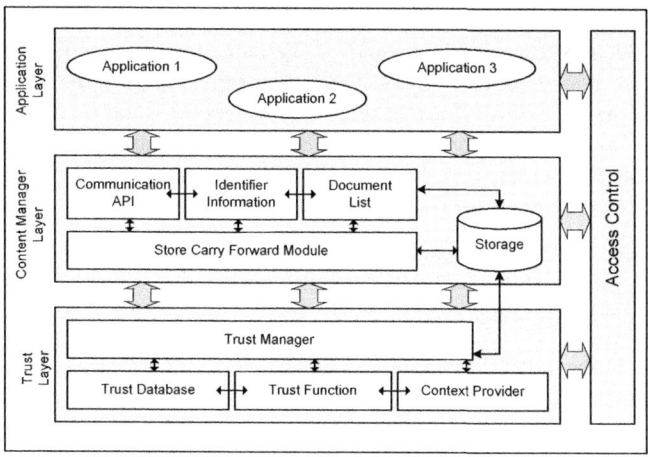

Fig. 2. Framework Architecture

P2P File Sharing. This application is an implementation of file sharing. When two neighbors communicate, they can share list of files in the user storage. If willing, users can share the files. In an opportunistic manner, a user can store, carry and forward files and share with other users.

```
Reg_application(app_no)
Set_identifier(OSCF_UID)
[get|set]document_list(OSCF_dir)
[get|set]user_list(OSCF_UID)
message(dest, ttl_timestamp, message, OSCF_dir)
```

Fig. 3. Communication API

2.2 Content Management Layer

Content management layer is the middle layer of the framework. This layer is responsible for user discovery, identification (authentication), document exchange and managing documents in the storage area. It is composed of four modules, identifier information, document list, storage area and the store-carry-forward module. The store-carry-forward module is a communication protocol and is the modified and improved version of the eMule [www.emule.com]. Details of these modules are as follows.

Identifier Information: Each user maintains a unique identifier. This identifier is used to search for neighbors along with maintaining a list of neighbors. Furthermore this identifier is also used to compute trust values based on recommendations from neighboring nodes.

Document List: is a list of documents stored at a host. A document list consists of certain attributes of documents stored in the device storage area. These attributes include but are not limited to a Unique Identifier for the document, Document size, Document type, ownership and a Timestamp. Each document stored in the device's storage has this information. A Unique identifier uniquely identifies a document, where each document name is the standard file name format i.e. (filename.extension). Document size is mentioned in bytes. Document type relates to the particular interest and contains the description for that interest. Ownership is the unique user identifier. A Timestamp is the date and time for the document creation and indicates when the document was last updated. A list of documents is announced whenever two users with similar interests decide to share files.

Storage area: Each node maintains a document repository for documents to be shared. Since most mobile devices have limited storage for documents, a limit is set to the size of a device's storage area.

Store Carry Forward Module: The framework implements a simple three step process for all transmissions. It is assumed in ad hoc mode, each node executes a periodic loop that consists of three steps: (1) neighborhood discovery, (2) user identification (and authentication), and (3) data exchange. Upon discovery of a new device in the neighborhood, the system enters the identification phase where the devices open a communication link between each other to exchange the user identity information.

Upon a first encounter the devices running the application, exchange their profiles during the identification phase. The system stores the profiles persistently along with other contact statistics to avoid unnecessary profile updates and to make subsequent decisions, e.g., to forward messages between nodes. During subsequent contacts the profiles are exchanged only if the profile has changed since the last encounter (i.e., user changed his nickname or status etc.), otherwise the nodes only exchange their user identifiers. Once the identification is successfully completed, the last step of the interaction is the data exchange phase.

It is possible that many adjacent nodes would request the same document from a host. In this case a unicast message needs to be sent to all requesting nodes. This however would greatly decrease the performance due to overhead of repeatedly sending the same message. As a solution to this problem the n-list is used. The n-list is a list of adjacent neighboring nodes that have been contacted in the past interactions. If a simple majority of hosts request the same document, a broadcast message is sent to all immediate neighbors, instead of individual unicast messages, thus flooding the corresponding group of users. This is to ensure that all members of the group would keep forwarding the content until everyone has received a copy of the document and no copy of the document is sent to a user who is not a member of the group. This provides a minimum of guarantee on privacy and also helps as a incentive mechanism.

2.3 Trust Management Layer

In the absence of a centralized server for trust management and security credentials verification, providing trusted interaction among users is a challenging task. Decentralized reputation based models depend on periodically updating trust values of a node based on local knowledge gained from neighboring nodes. We have included a light weight trust manager, based on Pervasive Trust Management (PTM) model [14]. PTM allows establishing trust relationships in an ad hoc manner between nodes. Each node has its own public/private key pair, a protected list of trustworthy and untrustworthy users, and behavioral information.

Trust Management Layer is responsible for providing and storing trust ratings for neighboring nodes. Each node in a cluster of connected nodes periodically asks for trust ratings from its neighbors and updates trust values defined in a list. The Trust layer consists of four components, trust manager, trust function calculations, trust values list and context provider.

Trust Manager: A trust relationship between two nodes is established based on direct interaction trust values. It is possible to have two scenarios for direct trust interactions, (1) trust establishment determined by contextual information, (2) trust establishment determined by recommendations from direct neighbors. In the first scenario two nodes having no history of encounters can trust each other based on contextual information. Contextual information is gathered often as a consequence of a complex set of beliefs, perceptions and interpretations based on periodic monitoring of the behavior of nodes in direct interactions. The context provider component of the trust management layer controls this information. In the second scenario, a node i requiring trust value for another node j, will request recommendation from its neighbors. Recommendation replies are sent if there already exists a trust relationship between some neighboring nodes. Such replies are only accepted if they come from trusted peers.

We consider recommendations from a trusted peer if it has a trust value bigger than a threshold σ, for instance, $\sigma > 0.5$. At the moment we only accept recommendations from directly trusted nodes. Long recommendation chains are avoided to minimize security and scalability problems.

The unauthorized access to a resource is avoided via the Access Control. The Trust Manager enables to distinguish among different authenticated users. It checks whether the user is trusted or not and subsequently requests the Access Control module to grant access.

Trust Function: Trust variable $T_{i,j}(t)$ is defined to identify the level of trust a node i, has for a target node j after t interactions between agent i and agent j, while $T_{i,j}(t) \in [-1, +1]$ and $T_{i,j}(0) = 0$. One agent in the view of the other agent can have one of the following levels of trustworthiness: Trustworthy, Not Yet Known, or Untrustworthy. The trust value is calculated as the sum of all the available ratings weighted by the rating relevance and normalized to the range of $[-1, +1]$ (by dividing the sum by the sum of all the weights).Trust value for an agent is given by the function

$$T(x) = \frac{\sum_{i \in t\_list} (Trust(i) * opinion_i(x))}{\sum_{i \in t\_list} Trust(i)} \tag{1}$$

Whereas x is the node whose trust is to be computed, i is a node in the list of trusted users (t_list) and the function $opinion_i(x)$ indicates the opinion of user i towards user x. The value of $opinion_i(x)$ is determined by the context provider component. Value for $T(x)$ is always in the interval $(1, -1)$, i.e. a Trustworthy user will obtain a positive value, whereas a negative value indicates a untrustworthy node.

Trust Values List: The trust values for all users in contact are stored in the t_list and are updated frequently. If a trust rating is requested for a particular user, the latest value stored in t_list is forwarded to the requesting user. If a node i has requested trust value for node j from neighboring nodes, trust values received are stored in the t_list, only if a trust value for the recommending node exists in the t_list provided the $T_{i,j}$ is greater than 0.5.

Context provider: We monitor the nodes behavior through their actions and store it in the trust value list t_list. As a node takes into consideration recommendations to decide about trustworthy node selection, it updates its recommendation trust and also records the interaction results in its t_list. The interaction history gives a reflection of the relevant past transactions of a node. Since each record in the history has a timestamp ttl value for each trust recommendation, older values can be discarded to reduce the size of the t_list.

To determine if a service performed in an interaction was to the desired expectation we compare the desired value of service to the actual value after the interaction and we increment the value of two variables, α and β accordingly. Based on the number of positive interactions α or negative interactions β the $opinion_i(x)$ function provides the context information as a positive or negative value thus affecting the trust value for a target node. As mentioned earlier, the value of $T_{i,j}$ determines if a node i is trustworthy, untrustworthy or not yet known. A node whose trust value $T_{i,j}$ falls below -0.2 ($T_{i,j}(t) < 0.2$) due to poor opinions, is considered untrustworthy. Untrustworthy nodes are removed from the t_list and their membership is effectively revoked. It is however possible that an untrustworthy node gains enough confidence in later transactions with other nodes to improve its trust value in neighbors and thus can be forgiven.

3 Prototype Implementation Details

We implement the prototype using the J2ME Personal Profile. Figure 4 shows the Classes diagram for our implementation. The developed prototype has been success-fully tested on HP iPAQ 211 PDA running Microsoft Windows Mobile 6.0. The size of the prototype binary is 280KB which is an acceptable size for devices with limited capabilities. For our experiments we enable Bluetooth connectivity due to its energy efficiency. We observed that while running Wi-Fi interface, the battery drains in a couple of hours whereas with Bluetooth interface we can run the device for up to 6 hours. The Bluetooth device discovery is performed every 2 minutes (+/- small delays for synchronization purpose) for the duration of 10.24 seconds, which is recom-mended minimum duration by the Bluetooth standard. We allow only 3 device-to-device connections at a time with RFCOMM links although Bluetooth permits up to 7 connections.

We implement the three applications in J2ME and interface the applications with the prototype using the communications API.

4 Experimental Setup and Results

The objective of the experiments is to validate the design on the proposed framework and to gain information on contact opportunities in peer to peer mobile applications. Furthermore testing of the trust module in the proposed framework would provide important information of users trust ratings for other users. We conducted user trials with 7 users each equipped with a Bluetooth enabled HP iPAQ 211 PDA running the prototype. Each PDA has all the three applications installed on it however for the ex-periments conducted all users run the p2p file sharing application, where users can announce their files and share. User trials were run for an average of 3 days (approx. 35 work hours) in a campus setting where users move between classes in the same building, twice for the framework with and without the trust module. For the purpose of quantifying the number of connections made, active and inactive times are used. If the device is active while any of the prototype applications were used for duration of

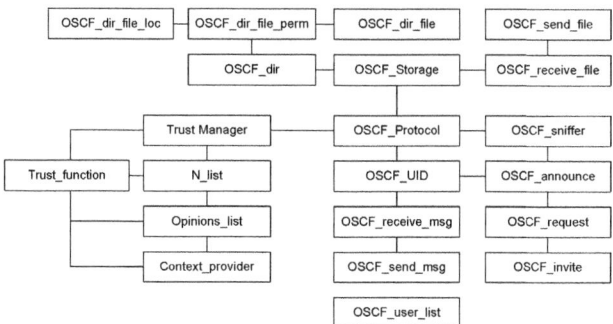

Fig. 4. Prototype Classes Diagram

time, we call this as *active time*. Each device is re-charged whenever the battery is depleted. We consider the time when the prototype application is not used as *inactive time*. Not all the users previously know each other and a few have pre-existing social relationship, we tend to exploit this with our framework to view the opportunities created for interaction. Table 1 shows the characteristics of collected data set for both sets of user trials.

4.1 Opportunistic Contacts

In our initial experiment we do not consider trust management and freely allow all users to make contacts. During the trial period the average active time for all devices was 21.2 hours (60%). The average inactive time was 13.6 hours (40%). It can be noted that the amount of inactive time is lower due to the battery depletion consequently making user go off-line for recharging. While this can also be partly due to normal use of mobile devices, or because our prototype adds to the energy consumption due to frequent Bluetooth operations.

During the trial period a total of 529 Bluetooth contacts were made between all devices of which 271 (51%) were successful connections while the rest were refused or dropped. This is due to the fact that we used Bluetooth for discovery prior to RFCOMM connection establishment for exchange of document lists and files. A total of 155 messages were successfully received (75% success rate). Maximum size of a file is set to be 1 MB for transfer, a total of 55 files was successfully received (58% success rate) with a size of 1MB or lesser. Figure 5 shows a relationship between successful connections established, messages and files received by all devices.

Despite all of these limitations we were able to obtain interesting results in terms of opportunistic relationship building and communication. In Figure 6(a) we present a friendship graph for all the users before and after the experiment. The initial friendship graph has a mixture of connected and disconnected nodes. After the completion of the experiment, the user friendship graph has a high degree of connectivity (average 4.8 connections per user) which shows that users were able to contact almost all other users and establish connections thus evolving a well defined community.

Table 1. Characteristics of collected data sets

	without trust	with trust
Duration	35 approx.	35 approx.
Active time	21.2	20.9
Inactive time	13.6	13.7
Bluetooth connections	529	491
Successful connections	271	247
Total messages sent	252	217
Total messages received	155	136
Total files sent	94	81
Total files received	55	42

4.2   Trust Based Contacts

In the second experiment we also record the trustworthiness of users in their interactions. Three users introduce three levels of untrustworthy behavior. User M1 is always deceptive and provides false information and false recommendations. User M2 is frequently deceptive and provides false information 50% of times. User M3 is rarely deceptive and provides false information rarely (10% of times). The rest of the users are considered to be honest in their interactions.   With similar parameters and limitations in the first experiment we observe the number of Bluetooth connections to be 491 of which 247 were successful (50%). A total of 136 messages were successfully received (72% success rate). A total of 42 files were successfully received (52% success rate). The average success rate for messages delivered and file transfers completed is similar to the first experiment as can be seen from figure 5. This shows the additional burden of calculations for trust management module has a negligible effect on the performance.

Figure 6(b) shows the friendship graph before and after using the trust based framework prototype. As before the normal (honest) nodes are able to create contacts

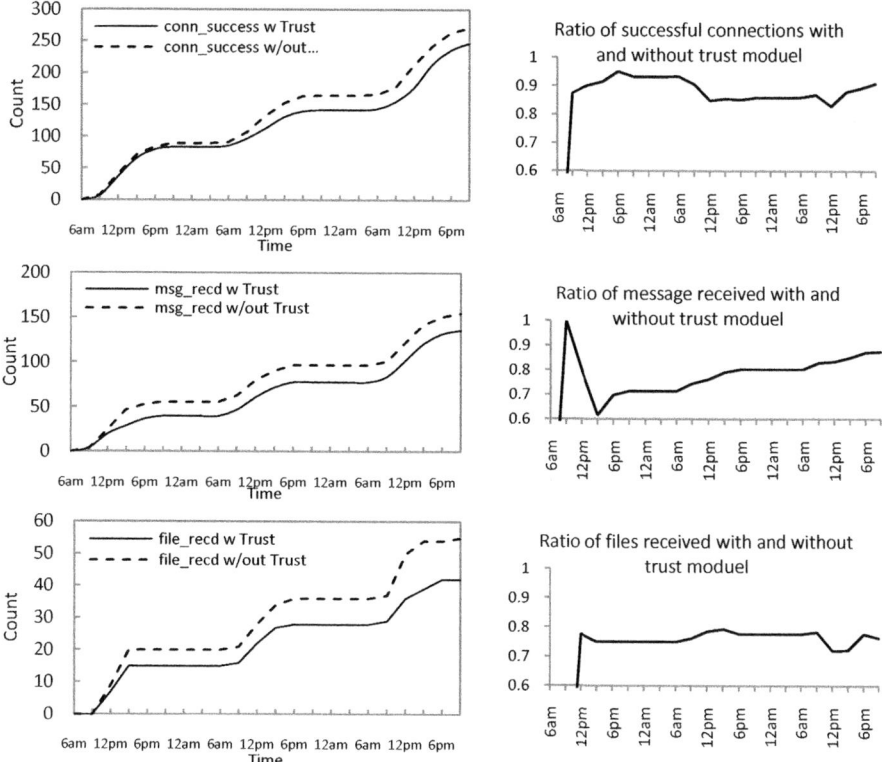

Fig. 5. The sum and ratio of successful connections, messages and files received over time

with other nodes whereas malicious nodes are isolated due to the untrustworthy behavior. The average value of trust between two nodes is computed and shown as edge
value in the graph. The average trust value between honest nodes is higher (>0.5)
where as between an honest and malicious node is significantly lower. It can be seen
that node M3 initially had two contacts but lost connection with all nodes except node
M2 which is also a malicious node.

The average trust rating between M2 and M3 is a negative value (-0.1) which suggests that the connection between M2 and M3 would be broken if the trust value fall
below -0.2. The friendship graph for our prototype utilizing the trust module proves that
the experiment was successful in identifying untrustworthy nodes. Figure 7 shows the
trust matrix for trust values (t_list) in all nodes at the end of the experiment. For the
purpose of acknowledging the existence of connection between an honest user and a
malicious user, if the trust rating falls below -0.2 we didn't remove it from the t_list
although this rating was never used in computing the trust values. It can be seen from
figure 7, the trust rating of malicious user M3 is -0.9 in (t_list) of user 1, however the
rating is +0.1, yielding an average of -0.4 which identifies M3 as an untrustworthy user.

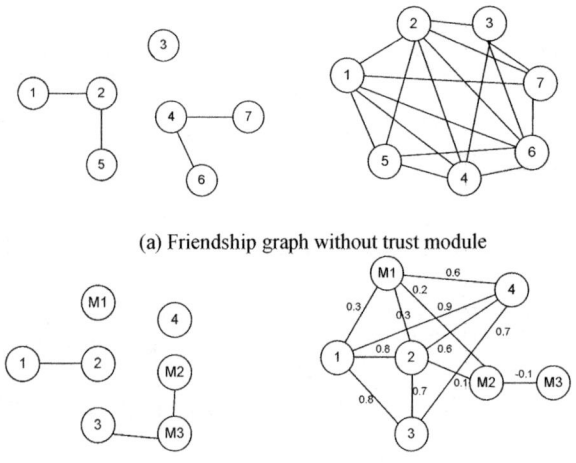

(a) Friendship graph without trust module

(b) Friendship graph with trust module

Fig. 6. Initial (left) and final (right) friendship graphs with and without trust component

	1	2	3	4	M1	M2	M3
1	1.0	0.8	0.7	0.8	0.2	-0.8	0.0
2	0.7	1.0	0.8	0.6	0.3	-0.4	0.0
3	0.8	0.6	1.0	0.7	0.0	0.0	-0.9
4	1.0	0.6	0.7	1.0	0.4	0.0	-0.7
M1	0.4	0.3	0.0	0.8	1.0	0.2	0.0
M2	-0.2	0.0	0.0	0.0	0.2	1.0	-0.5
M3	0.0	0.0	0.1	-0.2	0.0	0.3	1.0

Fig. 7. Trust Matrix for trust ratings ($T_{i,j}$) in (t_list) for all users

5   Related Work

Most of the work in mobile social communications has been commercial and centered around sending location and status updates from mobile devices towards centralized (and proprietary) activity aggregation services (and then possibly again back to the mobile devices as notifications). Examples include Dodge-ball[1], Twitter[2], and facebook[3]. In contrast to these our framework functions mainly in ad hoc mode. MIT's Serendipity [15] was a socially motivated project based on Bluetooth proximity detection. Similar projects based on the basic idea of Bluetooth based contact discovery were also presented in [16, 17] where the proximity data is stored on a central server and can be later visualized through a Facebook application. Mobile Social network middleware architectures have been proposed in [18] and a technique for profile based query routing presented in [19]. Both these techniques rely on centralized servers.

MobiClique [20] presents a middleware for mobile social networking using opportunistic contacts and Bluetooth node discovery. It utilizes the user proximity to detect new contacts and help create new types of communities in a mobile social network. It does not however consider trust management in messages and data transfer and is thus susceptible to security flaws. Authors in [21] address the security issues in a delay tolerant network based on social contacts. Using trust model and trust ratings between users of a social network, they are able to identify untrustworthy users. Comparatively, the proposed trust based framework addresses the trust management issues by leveraging social trust ratings and applies opportunistic contact discovery protocol and allows content transfer between nodes. Furthermore the framework can be used to study mobility and social contact behavior of users.

6   Conclusions and Future Work

The framework proposed allows forming of trust based communities in a disconnected and delay tolerant mobile ad hoc networks. Users can share content and transfer files in an opportunistic manner utilizing store-carry-forward paradigm. A framework was designed in J2ME Personal Profile and tested on devices using Windows Mobile 6.0. Using the framework we were able to demonstrate through two experiments, the successful construction of communities between nodes that contact each other opportunistically in close proximity and ad hoc manner. We also showed using a light weight trust model to identify trustable and untrustworthy users based on social contacts. The trust management module manages trust ratings based on reputation from neighboring users. Results prove the effectiveness of trust management module, nevertheless various factors having an impact on results need further investigation.

Due to many limitations the experiments were carried out with a rather small dataset and limited resources, the framework needs to be tested in a large scale environment to fully investigate the social contact and file transfer opportunities without pre-existing social contacts. The current trust module also considers trust ratings from immediate

---

[1] http://www.dodgeball.com
[2] http://www.twitter.com
[3] http://www.facebook.com

neighbors that may collude together to provide collective false ratings to artificially boost the ratings of a malicious user. Moreover in the experiments carried out we also limited the number of Bluetooth connections per device to 3, although in a mobile ad hoc network setting a node can maintain connections not only to the immediate neighbors but also to distant nodes over a multihop network. Consequently a user may receive ratings of other from distant parts of the network thus increasing the chances of a collusion attack. To prevent such attack the trust model needs to accommodate not only direct interaction trust ratings from immediate neighbors but also witness trust ratings from distant node in the network.

In future we would like to extend features in the proposed framework. The limitations of battery drainage due to extensive Bluetooth protocol usage, permitted size for files and clustering of larger files for transfer will be addressed. An improved version of the trust module that considers trust ratings from distant nodes also needs further investigation.

References

[1] Hui, P., Crowcroft, J., Yoneki, E.: Bubble rap: social-based forwarding in delay tol-erant networks. In: Proceedings of the 9th ACM international symposium on Mobile ad hoc networking and computing SIGMOBILE 2008, pp. 241–250 (2008)

[2] Almenarez, F., Marin, A., Diaz, D., Cortes, A., Campo, C., Garcia-Rubio, C.: A Trust based middleware for providing security to ad hoc peer to peer applications. In: Proceedings of the sixth annual IEEE International Conference on pervasive Computing and communications (PERCOMM 2008), pp. 531–536 (2008)

[3] Jain, S., Fall, K., Patra, R.: Routing in a Delay Tolerant Network. In: Proceedings of ACM SIGCOMM 2004, Portland, OR (August 2004)

[4] Zhang, Z., Zhang, Q.: Delay disruption tolerant mobile ad hoc networks: latest developments. Wireless Communications and Mobile Computing 7(10), 1219–1232 (2007)

[5] Daly, E.M., Haahr, M.: Social network analysis for routing in disconnected delay-tolerant MANETs. In: MobiHoc 2007: Proceedings of the 8th ACM int. symposium on Mobile ad hoc networking and computing (2007)

[6] Pietilainen, A.-K., Diot, C.: Experimenting with opportunistic communications. In: MobiArch 2009: The 4th ACM International Workshop on Mobility in the Evolving Internet Architecture (2009)

[7] Chaintreau, A., Fraigniaud, P., Lebhar, E.: Opportunistic spatial gos-sip over mobile social networks. In: Proceedings of the first workshop on Online social networks WOSN in SIGCOMM 2008, pp. 73–78 (2008)

[8] Teacy, W.T.L., Patel, J., Jennings, N.R., Luck, M.: Coping with inaccurate reputation sources: experimental analysis of a probabilistic trust model. In: AAMAS 2005, pp. 997–1004. ACM, New York (2005)

[9] Yu, B., Singh, M.P.: Detecting deception in reputation management. In: AAMAS 2003, pp. 73–80. ACM, New York (2003)

[10] Hang, C.-W., Wang, Y., Singh, M.P.: An adaptive probabilistic trust model and its evaluation. In: AAMAS, vol. (3), pp. 1485–1488 (2008)

[11] Patwardhan, A., et al.: Active Collaborations for Trustworthy Data Management in Ad Hoc Networks. In: Proceedings of the 2nd IEEE International Conference on Mobile Ad-Hoc and Sensor Systems (November 2005)

[12] Repantis, T., Kalogeraki, V.: Decentralized Trust Management for Ad-hoc Peer-to-peer Networks. In: Proceedings of the 4th International Workshop on Middleware for Pervasive and Ad- Hoc Computing (MPAC 2006) in conjunction with MIDDLEWARE 2006 (November 2006)

[13] Su, J., Scott, J., Hui, P., Crowcroft, J., de Lara, E., Diot, C., Goel, A., Lim, M., Upton, E.: Haggle: Seamless networking for mobile applications. In: Krumm, J., Abowd, G.D., Seneviratne, A., Strang, T. (eds.) UbiComp 2007. LNCS, vol. 4717, pp. 391–408. Springer, Heidelberg (2007)

[14] Almenárez, F., Marín, A., Díaz, D., Sánchez, J.: Developing a Model for Trust Management in Pervasive Devices. In: Third IEEE International Work-shop on Pervasive Computing and Communication Security (PerSec 2006) held in conjunction with IEEE PerCom 2006 (March 2006)

[15] Eagle, N., Pentland, A.: Social serendipity: Mobilizing social software. IEEE Pervasive Computing 4(2) (2005)

[16] Miklas, A., Gollu, K., Chan, K., Saroiu, S., Gummadi, K., de Lara, E.: Exploiting socialinteractions in mobile systems. In: Krumm, J., Abowd, G.D., Seneviratne, A., Strang, T. (eds.) UbiComp 2007. LNCS, vol. 4717, pp. 409–428. Springer, Heidelberg (2007)

[17] Nicolai, T., Yoneki, E., Behrens, N., Kenn, H.: Exploring social context with the wireless rope. In: Meersman, R., Tari, Z., Herrero, P. (eds.) OTM 2006 Workshops. LNCS, vol. 4277, pp. 874–883. Springer, Heidelberg (2006)

[18] Chang, Y.-J., Liu, H.-H., Chou, L.-D., Chen, Y.-W., Shin, H.-Y.: A General Architecture of Mobile Social Network Services. In: proceedings of the International Conference on Convergence Information Technology, November 21-23, pp. 151–156 (2007)

[19] Tomiyasu, H., Maekawa, T., Hara, T., Nishio, S.: Profile-based Query Routing in a Mobile Social Network. In: Proceedings of the 7th International Conference on Mobile Data Management (MDM 2006), pp. 105–109 (2006)

[20] Pietiläinen, A.-K., Oliver, E., LeBrun, J., Varghese, G., Diot, C.: MobiClique: middleware for mobile social networking. In: Proceedings of the 2nd ACM workshop on Online social networks WOSN in SIGCOMM 2009, pp. 49–54 (2009)

[21] El Defrawy, K., Solis, J., Tsudik, G.: Leveraging Social Contacts for Mes-sage Confidentiality in Delay Tolerant Networks. In: 33rd Annual IEEE International Computer Software and Applications Conference (COMPSAC), Seattle, July 20-24 (2009)

A Risk-Aware Resource Service Decision Strategy
for Global Computing

Wei Du[1,2], Guohua Cui[1], and Wei Liu[2,3,4]

[1] College of Computer Science & Technology,
Huazhong University of Science and Technology, Wuhan, China
[2] College of Computer Science & Technology, Wuhan University of Technology, Wuhan, China
[3] State Key Lab of Software Engineering, Wuhan University, Wuhan 430072, China
[4] State Key Laboratory for Novel Software Technology, Nanjing University, Nanjing, P.R. China
wdhust07@gmail.com, cgh3986@126.com, wliu@whut.edu.cn

Abstract. In an unreliable environment such as global computing, resource providers are faced with the problem of making decision autonomously with partial information before providing services for resource requesters. Although many trust management models have been proposed to deal with security concerned in resource service, few of them take risk into consideration. In those schemes involving risk, either risk is discussed conceptually, or methods for calculating risk and trustworthiness are not described clearly. This paper presents a risk-aware resource service decision strategy for global computing. The paper not only explores the pivotal source of risk and the relationship between trust and risk, but also quantifies risk to facilitate the resource service decision. The paper proposes the reputation inference based on probability theory and risk degree algorithm based on Chernoff Bound theorem. In the simulation, the performance of our risk-aware resource service decision strategy is evaluated.

Keywords: reputation, risk, Chernoff Bound, global computing.

1 Introduction

Global computing (GC) refers to computation over "global computers", i.e. computational infrastructures available globally and able to provide uniform services with variable guarantees for communication, co-operation and mobility, resource usage, security policies and mechanisms, etc. [1]. It is characterized by a mass of free participants and the absence of a globally administrative authority like CA in PKI. So, resource providers in such an unreliable environment are faced with following problems. Firstly, resource requesters usually are not acquainted with or even strange to resource providers. Before providing resources for users, providers are required to make security decisions. Secondly, for centralized security infrastructure does not exist, decision should be made by resource providers autonomously. Thirdly, entities, i.e. resource providers and requesters, can freely join or leave a GC environment. Thus, it is impossible to collect and maintain integrated information about entities. In a word, how to make trust decision autonomously with partial information is one of the challenges towards secure resource service in GC.

B. Xie et al. (Eds.): ATC 2010, LNCS 6407, pp. 168–181, 2010.

A trust decision is based on the balance between trust and risk [2]. Furthermore, trust and risk are intrinsically related in the sense that there is no need for a trust decision unless there is risk involved [3]. So, a trust model suitable for GC should involve risk and reflect the relationship between trust and risk adequately. Trust management [4] seems a promising approach for dealing with secure resource services in GC. But, most existing models ignore risk and its effect on trust. Even in those schemes involving risk, either risk is discussed conceptually, or methods for calculating risk and trustworthiness are not described clearly. This paper presents a risk quantification algorithm and a risk-aware decision strategy for resource service in GC.

The rest of the paper is structured as follows. In Section 2, based on analysis of existing schemes for trust management, the research motivations are provided. Section 3 describes concepts for inferring reputation. Subsequently, risk involved in reputation is derived and analyzed by Chernoff Bound theorem. In section 4 three proper metrics are listed and simulation results are evaluated. Finally, we summarize our work and make a few suggestions for future research in Section 5.

2 Related Work

Many work have been carried out on the relationship between trust and risk. Currently, there are three views on such problem. The first view regards trust as a form of risk acceptance. [5] introduces the concept of risk into the work [6]. Risk is exposed by the trusting behavior and influences the trusting intentions and possibly the situational decision to trust. [7] adjusts the work [5] slightly. A trust policy takes trust metrics, costs and utility functions as parameters to produce trust decision. However, this view seems to be invalid in the case that a highly risky recommendation is probably given by a highly trusted party. The second view recognizes that the level of trust has an approximately inverse relationship to risk degree [3, 8, 9, 10]. In SECURE project [3], risk is evaluated on every possible outcome of a particular action and is represented as a family of cost-PDFs. But constructing suitable cost-PDFs to model applications is usually difficult. In [8, 9], the authors define risk as a probability of failure. But the damage caused by each failure does not be included in the definition. In [10], the authors refine Manchala's model [11] to derive a computational model integrating trust and risk. However, the generality of this model is weakened by the absence of universal mathematical definition for the important components. The third view argues that it is not enough to consider trust only and then say that trust is risk acceptance, or trust is inverse to risk, or the like [12]. The trust level and the consequence of risk are two factors that should be presented to calculate the risk. Such an opinion opens up possibilities in explore the relationship between trust and risk more dynamically and deeply. However, all conclusions in the work [12] are based on well-founded trust, which is not suitable for GC.

The quantification of risk in trust management has recently become hot research area. A revised risk model for SECURE [13] is based on the economic theory of decision and Hirshleifer's state-preference approach [14]. However a lower-bound for the number of bits of information known about the chosen action has to be set by policy-writer. Since counting the number of bits of information is difficult, it seems a trouble for this model to choose the suitable bound objectively. Mui et al. [15] propose a computational trust model based on sociological and biological understandings. However the simplifications made in the paper [15] are so idealized that the final model is unpractical in parallel and distributed environments like GC. The work [16, 17, 18, 19] respectively present their approaches to model and compute risk. But it seems that these work concern more on the framework or concepts than on the computational methods. In [20, 21], Liang and Shi propose a personalized trust model consisting of reputation evaluation and risk evaluation. The formulae for risk computation are given clearly. However the model takes value of reputation as trustworthiness directly and ignores entity's opinion derives from direct experience. It would be dangerous when recommendation is from malicious entity. Although the scheme to avoid such situation is mentioned in risk evaluation, it seems that such risk control is gained by loss of efficiency of model.

The methods and contributions of this paper are different from above work. The goal of the paper is not only to explore the pivotal source of risk and the relationship between trust and risk, but also to quantify risk to facilitate the resource service decision. We introduce the concept of risk into Mui's model [15] and expand it to facilitate resource provider to make autonomous service decision in GC. Meanwhile, our work is inspired by SECURE project and our contribution in this paper is to propose a novel model for resource service decision. Moreover, in order to compute trustworthiness of resource requester, we propose a method to infer reputation and analyze risk involved in reputation by Chernoff Bound theorem.

3   Risk-Aware Resource Service Decision Strategy

3.1   Concepts

In this section, relative concepts are introduced to facilitate the modeling of computationally risk-aware resource service decision strategy.

Assuming that e_1, e_2 are two entities in a certain GC environment. e_1 is a resource provider and e_2 is a resource requester.

Community as far as e_2, denoted by C^{e_2}, is an entity set. If $e \in C^{e_2}$, then e_2 has requested resource from e. e can be distinguished by the same identification at a certain moment.

In the *ith* resource service request, e_1 decides whether to provider resource for e_2 depending on trustworthiness of e_2. This is a resource service decision process and result of such a decision, denoted by $d_i^{e_1 e_2}$, is an element of resource service decision set D, i.e. $d_i^{e_1 e_2} \in D$. $d_i^{e_1 e_2}$ takes on the value 'provide' if e_1 decides to provide resource for e_2 and 'refuse' otherwise.

Random variable $RR_i^{e_1 e_2}$ denotes the *ith* resource request of e_2 to e_1. The value of $RR_i^{e_1 e_2}$ is taken on as follows:

$$RR_i^{e_1 e_2} = \begin{cases} 1, & d_i^{e_1 e_2} = provide \\ 0, & d_i^{e_1 e_2} = refuse \end{cases}$$

Resource service decision process is a injective function: $D \rightarrow RR$, where RR represents a set of all resource requests.

Before the ith resource service request, C^{e_2}'s current experience to e_2, denoted by $ES^{e_2}\left(C^{e_2}\right)$, is a set consisting of all e_2's requests to the providers in C^{e_2}, i.e.:

$$ES^{e_2}\left(C^{e_2}\right) = \{RR^{e_\beta\, e_2}_\alpha \mid \alpha, \beta \in \mathbb{N}, and\ 1 \leq \alpha \leq i-1, e_\beta \in C^{e_2}\}.$$

Reputation of e_2 in the ith request, as far as C^{e_2} is concerned, represents the overall expectation about the reliability of e_2 depending on $ES^{e_2}\left(C^{e_2}\right)$. Hereafter, $ES^{e_2}\left(C^{e_2}\right)$ is simplified as ES^{e_2}. The value of such reputation, denoted by $V^{e_2}_{RE}\left(C^{e_2}, ES^{e_2}\right)$, is described by the successful probability of e_2's resource requests from entities in C^{e_2} depending on $ES^{e_2}\left(C^{e_2}\right)$, i.e.,

$$V^{e_2}_{RE}\left(C^{e_2}, ES^{e_2}\right) = p\left(RR^{e_\beta e_2}_\alpha = 1 \mid ES^{e_2}\right) = E\left(\widetilde{V^{e_2}_{RE}} \mid ES^{e_2}\right),$$

where $\widetilde{V^{e_2}_{RE}}$ is an estimator for $V^{e_2}_{RE}$. Especially, if $ES^{e_2} = \varnothing$, $V^{e_2}_{RE}\left(C^{e_2}, ES^{e_2}\right) = 0$.

Risk concerning to e_1 is a deviation of trust, which arose from calculating trustworthiness of e_2 depending on ES^{e_2}. Therefore, the risk degree, denoted by γ, is defined to describe the error between the estimator of reputation $\widetilde{V^{e_2}_{RE}}$ and the actual reputation $V^{e_2}_{RE}$, and $\gamma \in [0,1]$.

3.2 Model for Risk-Aware Resource Service Decision

In most literatures, evidence is defined as any kind of information about entities' past manifestations in certain context. It is usually classified as direct and indirect ones according to the source of information. Direct evidence is usually reliable. But fraud, disguise or misplace are easily successful if provider only depends on direct evidence to decide whether to collaborate with requester. Furthermore, requester is often strange to provider in context like GC and thus direct evidence can not be fetched. Under these situations, provider has to gather information from third party. Indirect evidence refers to such information, which reflects the overall evaluation about requester from a certain community. In this paper, the former is defined as witness and the latter reputation. Compare with witness, the validity of reputation is usually questionable and should be treated cautiously. Different entities may evaluate differently the same facts, and someone or some communities may even distort the facts for individual or organizational benefits. Consequently, reputation is considered as the pivotal source of risk.

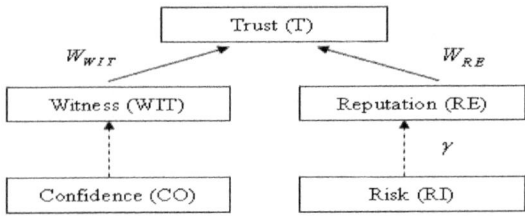

Fig. 1. Relationships of trust, witness, reputation and risk

In this paper, the relationships of trust, witness, reputation and risk are shown in Fig. 1. Trust T is derived from witness WIT (i.e. direct evidence) and reputation RE (i.e. indirect evidence). W_{WIT} and W_{RE} are adjustable weights for WIT and RE respectively. Confidence CO represents resource provider's self-opinion about direct evidence, which is reflected by W_{WIT}. Risk RI embodies the unreliability of RE, which is quantified by γ. W_{RE} affects the portion of RE in T. Consequently, the trust value V_T is formulated as follows:

$$V_T = \begin{cases} \left(W_{WIT}, W_{RE}\right) \times \left(V_{WIT}, (1-\gamma)V_{RE}\right)^T \\ \qquad W_{WIT}, W_{RE}, V_{WIT}, V_{RE} \in \mathbb{R} \\ \qquad and \;\; W_{WIT}, W_{RE}, V_{WIT}, V_{RE} \in [0,1] \\ V_{WIT} \qquad\qquad , \;\; if \;\; V_{RE} = 0 \\ V_{RE} \qquad\qquad\; , \;\; if \;\; V_{WIT} = 0 \end{cases} \tag{1}$$

Here $W_{WIT} + W_{RE} = 1$, V_{WIT} is the value of witness, and V_{RE} is the value of reputation.

A resource service decision is made according to the result of (1). Whereas W_{WIT} and W_{RE} are usually configured subjectively, and V_{WIT} is self-determined and regarded usually by decision maker as valid and facts, how to evaluate these parameters falls outside the scope of this paper. In following sections, inference of V_{RE} and γ is discussed in detail.

3.3 Inference of Resource Requester's Reputation

Consider a resource provider x and a resource requester y in a certain GC environment. Assume that this is the *ith* request. In order to accomplish such a resource service decision process, x need to gather the reputation information of y. Hereafter, $ES^y\left(C^y\right)$ is simplified as ES^y and $V_{RE}^y\left(C^y, ES^y\right)$ as V_{RE}^y.

Consider different resource providers e_β in C^y, $ES^y = \bigcup_{e_\beta \in C^y} ES^{e_\beta y}$, where

$ES^{e_\beta y} = \left\{ RR_1^{e_\beta y}, RR_2^{e_\beta y}, \dots, RR_k^{e_\beta y} \right\}$, $k \in \mathbb{N}$, and $1 \le k \le i-1$ is e_β's current experience to y.

Let $\left| ES^y \right|$ represent the size of ES^y, and $provision\_Num$ be the number of $RR_\alpha^{e_\beta y} = 1$ in ES^y, $RR_\alpha^{e_\beta y} \in ES^y$. According to the definition in section 3.1, V_{RE}^y should be a function of both $\left| ES^y \right|$ and $provision\_Num$, i.e. $f: \left| ES^y \right| \times provision\_Num \to V_{RE}^y$. In this paper, the frequency of $RR_\alpha^{e_\beta y} = 1$ in ES^y is taken as f. Then a simple estimator for V_{RE}^y can be obtained:

$$\widetilde{V_{RE}^y} = \frac{provision\_Num}{\left| ES^y \right|} \qquad (2)$$

Here, $\widetilde{V_{RE}^y}$ is a proportion random variable, which can be modeled as a Beta distribution [22], i.e.:

$$p\left(\widetilde{V_{RE}^y}\right) = Beta\left(\lambda_1, \lambda_2\right) \qquad (3)$$

where λ_1 and λ_2 are parameters determined by prior assumptions.

To avoid misplacing decision by experience, each decision made by a provider is independent to others. It means that the value of each $RR_\alpha^{e_\beta y}$ in the same $ES^{e_\beta y}$ is obtained independently. Decisions made by different resource providers are also independent to others. It means that the value of each $RR_\alpha^{e_\beta y}$ in the different $ES^{e_\beta y}$ is obtained independently too. Then among $\left| ES^y \right|$ requests, the probability of $provision\_Num$ $RR_\alpha^{e_\beta y} = 1$ and $\left(\left| ES^y \right| - provision\_Num \right)$ $RR_\alpha^{e_\beta y} = 0$ can be calculated as follows:

$$p\left(ES^y \mid \widetilde{V_{RE}^y}\right) = \binom{\left| ES^y \right|}{provision\_Num} \cdot \widetilde{V_{RE}^y}^{\,provision\_Num} \cdot \left(1 - \widetilde{V_{RE}^y}\right)^{\left| ES^y \right| - provision\_Num} \qquad (4)$$

The Beta distribution is the conjugate prior for $p\left(ES^y \mid \widetilde{V_{RE}^y}\right)$ [23].

According to (3) and (4), the posterior estimate for $\widetilde{V_{RE}^y}$ can be obtained [24]:

$$p\left(\widetilde{V_{RE}^y} \mid ES^y\right) = Beta\left(\lambda_1 + provision\_Num, \lambda_2 + \left|ES^y\right| - provision\_Num\right) \tag{5}$$

Subsequently, the expectation of above posterior estimator is obtained:

$$E\left(\widetilde{V_{RE}^y} \mid ES^y\right) = \frac{\lambda_1 + provision\_Num}{\lambda_1 + \lambda_2 + \left|ES^y\right|} \tag{6}$$

Combining concept of reputation and (6), the reputation of y in C^y depending on ES^y can be formulated as follows:

$$V_{RE}^y\left(C^y, ES^y\right) = E\left(\widetilde{V_{RE}^y} \mid ES^y\right) = \frac{\lambda_1 + provision\_Num}{\lambda_1 + \lambda_2 + \left|ES^y\right|} \tag{7}$$

3.4 Risk Analysis and Risk Degree Algorithm Description

In our model for risk-aware resource service decision described in subsection 3.2, the risk degree γ is regarded as the quantification of unreliability of reputation. Such risk should be analyzed and computed to facilitate the resource service decision process.

As explained in subsection 3.3, the value of each $RR_\alpha^{e_\beta y}$ in the same $ES^{e_\beta y}$ is obtained independently. Thus each y's request for e_β's resource can be regarded as an independent Bernoulli trial, i.e. $RR_1^{e_\beta y}$, $RR_2^{e_\beta y}$, $\cdots$, $RR_k^{e_\beta y}$ form a sequence of k independent Bernoulli trials. Suppose probability of $d_\alpha^{e_\beta y} = provide$ for each trial is ω, i.e.

$$p\left(RR_\alpha^{e_\beta y} = 1 \mid ES^{e_\beta y}\right) = \omega, \ \alpha=1,2,...,n, \ n \leq k \tag{8}$$

and define a random variable $\widetilde{\omega}$ to represent the frequency of $d_\alpha^{e_\beta y} = provide$ in k trials, i.e.:

$$\widetilde{\omega} = \left(RR_1^{e_\beta y} + RR_2^{e_\beta y} + ... + RR_k^{e_\beta y}\right)/k \tag{9}$$

then $E\left(\widetilde{\omega}\right) = \omega$ can be obtained. Consequently, for $0 \leq \varepsilon \leq 1$ and $0 \leq \xi \leq 1$, the following bound exists:

$$p\left(\left|\omega - \widetilde{\omega}\right| \geq \varepsilon\right) \leq 2e^{-2k\varepsilon^2} \leq \xi \tag{10}$$

Above result can be proofed by a straightforward application of the additive form of the Chernoff Bound for Bernoulli trails [15, 25]. Note that ω can refer to V_{RE}^{y} and $\tilde{\omega}$ to $\widetilde{V_{RE}^{y}}$ by comparing (9) with (2). So $\left|\omega - \tilde{\omega}\right|$ refers to the error of the estimator from the actual reputation, namely, the risk. In this sense, ε and ξ can be considered as fixed parameters, which are chosen by resource providers to satisfy their special security requirements. k is required to be larger than a lower bound to guarantee an acceptable risk. According to (10), this lower bound can be calculated as follows:

$$k \geq -\frac{ln\left(\xi/2\right)}{2\left(\varepsilon\right)^{2}} \tag{11}$$

In the same way, for each $e_{\beta} \in C^{y}$, an equation similar to (11) can be obtained as follows:

$$k_{j} \geq -\frac{ln\left(\xi_{j}/2\right)}{2\left(\varepsilon_{j}\right)^{2}}, j = 1, 2, ..., \left|C^{y}\right| \tag{12}$$

Where $0 \leq \varepsilon_{j} \leq 1$, $0 \leq \xi_{j} \leq 1$, $k_{j} = \left|ES^{e_{\beta} y}\right|$.

Let $\psi_{j} = -\frac{ln\left(\xi_{j}/2\right)}{2\left(\varepsilon_{j}\right)^{2}}$ represent the minimum number of resource service decision processes necessary to achieve the acceptable γ and desired level of ε_{j}, γ can be obtained by Algorithm 1. The complexity of algorithm 1 is $O\left(\left|C^{y}\right|\right)$.

Algorithm 1: $RD(\partial, j, k_{j}, \psi_{j}, \left|C^{y}\right|)$

1. Initialize counter ∂, i.e. let $\partial = 0$
2. **For** $j = 1$ to $\left|C^{y}\right|$
3.   Compare actual number of resource service decision processes k_{j} with lower bound of frequency ψ_{j}
4.   **if** $k_{j} \geq \psi_{j}$
5.   **then** accumulate counter, i.e. let $\partial = \partial + 1$
6.   **End if**
7. **End for**

8. Calculate risk degree $\gamma = 1 - \dfrac{\partial}{\left|C^{y}\right|}$

Submit the results of algorithm 1 and (7) to (1), V_T of y, as far as x is concerned, can be derived. Then x can make a resource service decision depending on V_T.

4   Simulations

In this section, we first describe the experimental setup. Then we present and analyze simulation results. Note that, in our simulation, we only care about the reputation inference and risk analysis, which are independent of any underlying network resource, like bandwidth etc.

4.1   Simulation Setup and Parameter Settings

As Grid is one of typical applications for global computing [26], we simulate a grid system on top of the JAVASIM network simulator [27]. The grid system consists of 10 clusters. The number of nodes of these clusters is a random variable normally distributed with the mean of 30 and the standard deviation of 10. Each node is regarded as an entity in simulation, which can be a resource provider or a requester. In each resource service process, the simulation system chooses two entities randomly. The first one acts as a resource provider and the second one as a resource requester. Two types of entities, i.e., positive entity and malicious entity, are considered in the simulations. A malicious entity rates a positive entity as the malicious and rates a malicious entity as the positive. Malicious recommendation ratio μ is defined as the percentage of malicious entities in all entities, i.e.

$$\mu = \frac{Number \ of \ malicious \ entities}{Total \ Number \ of \ entities} \times 100\%$$

In the simulations, malicious recommendation ratio varies from 20%, 50% to 80%. In order to start up a reputation inference and risk analysis mechanism, 50% entities are designed to have requested resources from or provided resources to other 10 entities during simulation initialization. Each of 50% entities and each of its corresponding 10 entities are defined as a pair of familiar entities. Initial trustworthiness between them is taken randomly from the uniform distribution in the interval [0, 1]. The rest 50% entities are regarded as strangers to all the others. Initial trustworthiness of each of them is set by 0.6 when it requests or is requested resource. Acceptable trustworthiness threshold is set by 0.8. Acceptable error of estimator from the actual reputation ranges from 0.01 to 1. Chernoff Bound is set by 0.5. Weight of witness is set by 0.5. Simulation parameters are listed in Table 1.

The performance of decision strategy is evaluated by risk sensitiveness (RS), Resource service decision turnaround ratio (RSDTR) and Resource provision success ratio (RPSR). Perception to the existence and change of risk is regarded as risk sensitiveness of a mechanism. According to algorithm 1, k, ψ and $\left|C^y\right|$ are crucial factors influencing the value of γ. By varying these factors, how they affect the risk degree

Table 1. Simulation Parameters

Simulation parameter	Value
Number of clusters	10
Number of nodes in each cluster	30
Number of experiment rounds	[3, 10]
Number of decisions in one experiment round	1000
Number of entities	[200, 300, 400]
Malicious recommendation ratio	[20%, 50%, 80%]
Number of familiar entities for each of 50% entities	10
Initial trustworthiness between a pair of familiar entities	[0,1]
Initial trustworthiness of each of 50% entities strange to all the others	0.6
Acceptable trustworthiness threshold	0.8
Error	[0.01, 1.0]
Chernoff Bound	0.5
Weight of witness	0.5

can be studied and the risk sensitiveness of a mechanism can be implied. A resource service process consists of three phrases: request, decision and response (i.e. service provision if request is accepted or refuse information if request is refused). Denote the total number of resource service processes by RSP ($RSP \in N$ and $RSP \geq 1$). Each process corresponds to a resource request. In the ith resource service process, denote the resource request arrival time for an entity e_j ($j \in N$ and $j \geq 1$) by at_i, the service decision finish time by dt_i and the response completion time by ct_i. Then, the average turnaround time can be defined as $\left(\sum_{i=1}^{RSP} \left(ct_i - at_i \right) \right) / RSP$, and the average decision time as $\left(\sum_{i=1}^{RSP} \left(dt_i - at_i \right) \right) / RSP$. The resource service decision turnaround ratio is defined as the ratio of the average turnaround time to the average decision time, i.e.,

$$RSDTR = \frac{\left(\sum_{i=1}^{RSP} \left(ct_i - at_i \right) \right) / RSP}{\left(\sum_{i=1}^{RSP} \left(dt_i - at_i \right) \right) / RSP} = \frac{\sum_{i=1}^{RSP} \left(ct_i - at_i \right)}{\sum_{i=1}^{RSP} \left(dt_i - at_i \right)}$$

Since physical network delay and service resource scheduling time are ignored, the delay time is due to computation time of a mechanism. So, RSDTR can indicate the time complexity of a reputation inference and risk analysis mechanism. In the ith resource service process, a resource provider evaluates a requester's trustworthiness. By comparing the evaluation result with the acceptable trustworthiness threshold, the provider can decide whether or not to provide resource for the requester. If this request is accepted, it is a successful resource provision. Otherwise, it is failed. Denote the number of accepted requests by D_s. Then resource provision success ratio is defined as the percentage of the number of accepted requests in the total number of resource service processes, i.e.,

$$RPSR = \frac{D_S}{RSP} \times 100\%$$

For RPSR can represent the decision correct ratio, it can indicate the effectiveness of a reputation inference and risk analysis mechanism.

4.2 Results and Evaluations

The first series of experiments are conducted to evaluate the risk sensitiveness of our strategy and Fig. 2 show the results. Intuitively, less resource service processes, higher malicious recommendation ratio μ or smaller acceptable error ε would increase the risk degree γ. Under the condition of fixed ε ($\varepsilon = 0.03$) and ξ ($\xi = 0.5$), Fig. 2 illustrates the impact of different number of resource service process and malicious recommendation ratio on the risk degree. Obviously, the greater μ is, the higher of γ. Contrarily, the more resource services carry out, the lower of γ. The result demonstrates that our mechanism accords with human intuition and thus is valid.

The second series of experiments aim at comparing our strategy to other decision mechanisms involving risk or not. We choose Mui's mechanism [15] (abbreviated as Mui) and Liang's trust model [21] (abbreviated as PET) to compare with ours (abbreviated as RDS). Fig. 3 shows the results of resource service decision turnaround ratio.

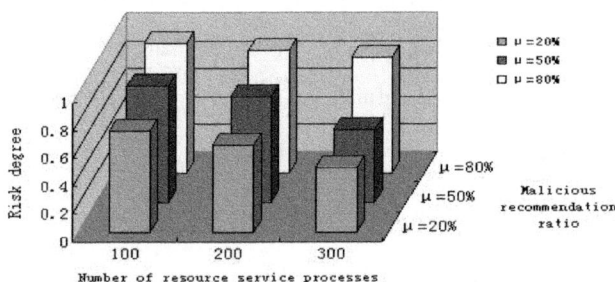

Fig. 2. Impact of different number of resource service processes and malicious recommendation ratios on risk degree

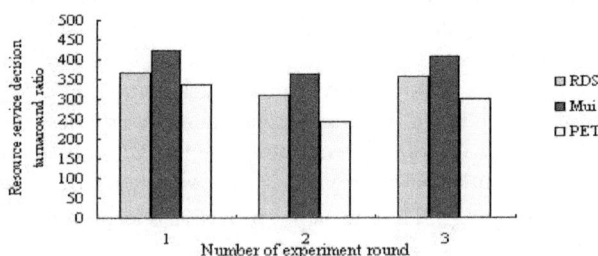

Fig. 3. Comparison of resource service decision turnaround ratio of three mechanisms

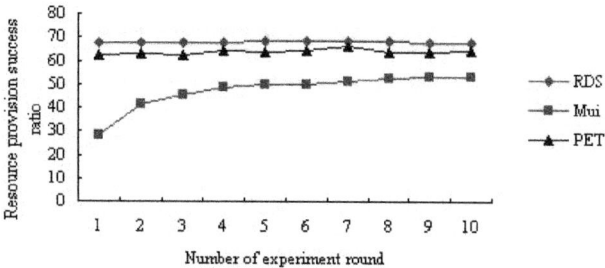

Fig. 4. Comparison of resource provision success ratio of three mechanisms

We observe that resource service decision turnaround ratio of RDS is lower than that of Mui's mechanism. Such performance degradation is ascribed to RDS's risk analysis which Mui's mechanism ignores. On the other hand, resource service decision turn-around ratio of RDS is higher than that of Liang's model in which risk is considered. It means the lower complexity of RDS. Fig. 4 shows the results of resource provision success ratio. Under the condition of the same acceptable trustworthiness threshold, a highly and steadily resource provision success ratio is gained by RDS. The result demonstrates the effectiveness of our strategy.

5   Conclusions and Future Work

Considering the security of resource service in GC, a trust model suitable for it should involve risk, reflect the relationship between trust and risk, and exploit two kinds of evidences, i.e. witness and reputation adequately. More practically, the risk degree should be quantitative and computational for decision. However, most existing schemes can not satisfy these requirements perfectly.

Based on the analysis of evidences affecting trustworthiness, we propose that repu-tation is the crucial source of risk. Then approach to calculate reputation, risk degree and trustworthiness is presented. Simulation results demonstrate validity and effec-tiveness of our strategy in terms of risk sensitiveness during resource service decision in GC.

Our work can be improved in the following aspects. Firstly, other possible types of risk existing in GC should be discussed thoroughly. Secondly, other functions with reasonable computational complexity for reputation estimation would be attempted to generalize our mechanism. Finally, trustworthiness feedback information would be integrated to optimize current risk control process.

Acknowledgments. The authors thank the editors and the anonymous reviewers for their helpful comments and suggestions. The work was partly supported by the National Natural Science Foundation of China (NSF) under Grant nos. 60703048, Open Foundation of State Key Laboratory for Novel Software Technology of Nanjing University (KFKT2009B22), Open Foundation of State Key Lab of Software Engineering of Wuhan University (SKLSE20080720), Educational Research Project of WHUT and Open Laboratory Project of WHUT.

References

1. Global Computing Initiative, http://cordis.europa.eu/ist/fet/gc.htm
2. Ruohomaa, S., Kutvonen, L.: Trust Management Survey. In: Herrmann, P., Issarny, V., Shiu, S.C.K. (eds.) iTrust 2005. LNCS, vol. 3477, pp. 77–92. Springer, Heidelberg (2005)
3. English, C., Terzis, S., Wagealla, W.: Engineering Trust Based Collaborations in a Global Computing Environment. In: Jensen, C., Poslad, S., Dimitrakos, T. (eds.) iTrust 2004. LNCS, vol. 2995, pp. 120–134. Springer, Heidelberg (2004)
4. Blaze, M., Feigenbaum, J., Lacy, J.: Decentralized Trust Management. In: IEEE Symposium on Security and Privacy, pp. 164–173. IEEE Press, New York (1996)
5. Povey, D.: Developing Electronic Trust Policies Using a Risk Management Model. In: Baumgart, R. (ed.) CQRE 1999. LNCS, vol. 1740, pp. 1–16. Springer, Heidelberg (1999)
6. McKnight, D.H., Chervany, N.L.: The Meanings of Trust. Technical Report, MISRC Working Paper Series 96-04, University of Minnesota, Management Information Systems Research Center (1996)
7. Dimitrakos, T.: A Service-oriented Trust Management Framework. In: Falcone, R., Barber, S.K., Korba, L., Singh, M.P. (eds.) AAMAS 2002. LNCS (LNAI), vol. 2631, pp. 53–72. Springer, Heidelberg (2003)
8. Grandison, T., Sloman, M.: A Survey of Trust in Internet Application. IEEE Communication Survey 3, 2–16 (2000)
9. Grandison, T., Sloman, M.: Specifying and Analyzing Trust for Internet Application. In: 2nd IFIP Conference on Towards the Knowledge Society: E-Commerce, E-Business, E-Government, pp. 145–157. Kluwer, Deventer (2002)
10. Jøsang, A., Presti, L.S.: Analysing the Relationship Between Risk and Trust. In: Jensen, C., Poslad, S., Dimitrakos, T. (eds.) iTrust 2004. LNCS, vol. 2995, pp. 135–145. Springer, Heidelberg (2004)
11. Manchala, D.W.: Trust Metrics, Models and Protocols for Electronic Commerce Transactions. In: 18th International Conference on Distributed Computing Systems, pp. 312–321. IEEE Press, New York (1998)
12. Solhaug, B., Elgesem, D., Stølen, K.: Why Trust is Not Proportional to Risk. In: 2nd International Conference on Availability, Reliability and Security, pp. 11–18. IEEE Press, New York (2007)
13. Dimmock, N., Bacon, J., Ingram, D., Moody, K.: Risk Models for Trust-based Access Control (TBAC). In: Herrmann, P., Issarny, V., Shiu, S.C.K. (eds.) iTrust 2005. LNCS, vol. 3477, pp. 1–8. Springer, Heidelberg (2005)
14. Hirshleifer, J., Riley, J.: The Analytics of Uncertainty and Information, Cambridge surveys of economic literature. Cambridge University Press, Cambridge (1992)
15. Mui, L., Mohtashemi, M., Halberstadt, A.: A Computational Model of Trust and Reputation. In: 35th Hawaii International Conference on System and Sciences, pp. 188–196. IEEE Press, New York (2005)
16. Asnar, Y., Giorgini, P., Massacci, F., Zannone, N.: From Trust to Dependability through Risk Analysis. In: 2nd International Conference on Availability, Reliability and Security, pp. 19–26. IEEE Press, New York (2007)
17. Jøsang, A., AlFayyadh, B., Grandison, T., AlZomai, M., McNamara, J.: Security Usability Principles for Vulnerability Analysis and Risk Assessment. In: 23rd Annual Computer Security Application Conference, pp. 269–278. IEEE Press, New York (2007)
18. Kim, D.J., Ferrin, D.L., Rao, H.R.: A Trust-based Consumer Decision Making Model in Electronic Commerce: The Role of Trust, Perceived risk, and Their Antecedents. Decision Support Systems 44, 544–564 (2008)

19. Ryutov, T.: A Socio-cognitive Approach to Modeling Policies in Open Environments. In: 8th IEEE International Workshop on Policies for Distributed Systems and Networks, pp. 29–38. IEEE Press, New York (2007)
20. Liang, Z.Q., Shi, W.S.: Analysis of Rating on Trust Inference in Open Environments. Performance Evaluation 65, 99–128 (2008)
21. Liang, Z.Q., Shi, W.S.: PET: A Personalized Trust Model with Reputation and Risk Evaluation for P2P Resource Sharing. In: 38th Hawail International Conference on System and Sciences, pp. 201.2. IEEE Press, New York (2005)
22. Dudewicz, E.J., Mishra, S.: Modern Mathematical Statistics. John Wiley & Sons, New York (1988)
23. Heckerman, D.: A Tutorial on Learning with Bayesian Networks, Learning in Graphical Models. MIT Press, Cambridge (1999)
24. Mui, L., Mohtashemi, M., Ang, C., Szolovits, P., Halberstadt, A.: Bayesian Rating in Distributed Systems: theories, models and simulations. MIT LCS Memorandum (2001)
25. Ross, S.: Stochastic Process. John Wiley & Sons, New York (1995)
26. Dimmock, N., Belokosztolszki, A., Eyers, D., Bacon, J., Moody, K.: Using Trust and Risk in Role-based Access Control Policies. In: 9th ACM Symposium on Access Control Models and Technologies, pp. 156–162. ACM, New York (2004)
27. JAVASIM, http://javasim.codehaus.org

Message Race Detection for Web Services
by an SMT-Based Analysis

Mohamed Elwakil[1], Zijiang Yang[1], Liqiang Wang[2], and Qichang Chen[2]

[1] Department of Computer Science, Western Michigan University, Kalamazoo, MI 49008, USA
[2] Department of Computer Science, University of Wyoming, Laramie, WY 82071, USA
{mohamed.elwakil,zijiang.yang}@wmich.edu,
{wang,qchen2}@cs.uwyo.edu

Abstract. The success of the cloud computing initiative is heavily dependent on realizing trustworthy Web Services. The trustworthiness of a Web Service is judged by four factors: security, privacy, reliability and business integrity. Web Services use message-passing for communication which opens the door for messages races. Messages race with each other when their order of arrival at a destination is not guaranteed and is affected non-deterministically by factors such as network latencies and scheduling variations. Message races are dangerous to Web Services because they can be unforeseen consequences of bugs, causing messages to arrive in an unexpected ordering. In this paper we present a novel approach for improving the reliability of Web Services by detecting message races using SMT-based analysis. We model a BPEL process as a Web Service Modeling Graph (WSMG). A WSMG model is then encoded into a set of SMT constraints. The satisfiability of these constraints means that message races will occur during the actual execution of the Web Service. Hence, we reduce the message race detection problem to constraint solving problem based on satisfiability modulo theories (SMT).

Keywords: web services, satisfiability modulo theories, symbolic analysis.

1 Introduction

Reliability is one of the four pillars necessary for producing trustworthy Web Services [1]. Writing reliable Web Services is difficult due to the unique challenges of this domain. In particular, Web Services are prone to concurrency errors due to 1) concurrent processing of user/service requests; and 2) complex interaction behavior resulting from diverse communication mechanisms such as synchronous and asynchronous operations. In order to develop reliable Web Services, effective testing, analysis and verification techniques must be available to address these challenges. In this paper we attack the problem of detecting message races in Web Services. Race conditions are listed among the top 25 dangerous programming errors [2]; hence, detecting them is critical for Web Services development.

Fig. 1 illustrates a simple message race. WS1, WS2, and WS3 are three Web Services. WS1 sends messages M1 and M2 to WS2 and WS3, respectively. WS3 reacts to the received message, by sending message M3 to WS2. Since M3 is sent in response to M1,

B. Xie et al. (Eds.): ATC 2010, LNCS 6407, pp. 182–194, 2010.

WS3 would expect receiving M2 before receiving M3 as in scenario A. However, M3 may arrive at WS2 before M2 (scenario B) due to unexpected network latency between WS1 and WS2, or due to unforeseen impediment at WS1 that delays sending M2. Messages M2 and M3 are said to be racing with each other. Intuitively, two messages race with each other if either could be received first due to the unpredictability of schedulers and message delays. Message races should be detected since they may be manifestations of bugs and can cause unpredictable results.

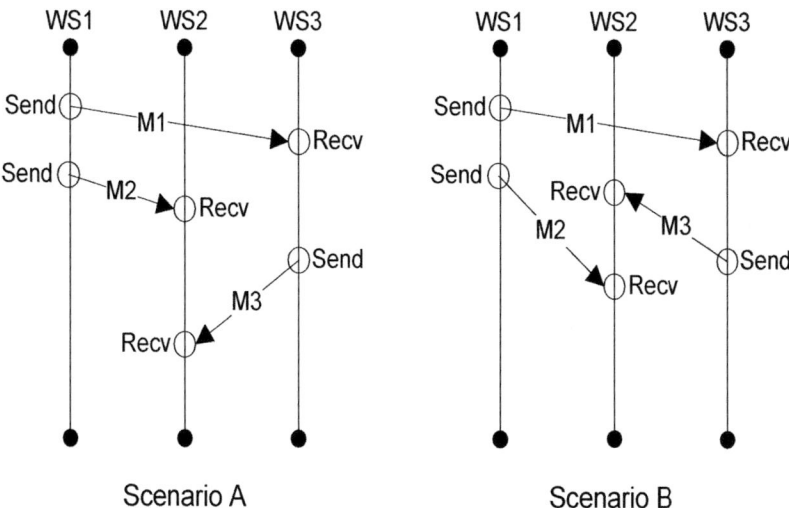

Fig. 1. Messages can arrive at different orderings

Unfortunately, traditional testing approaches that repeatedly execute or simulate a Web Service are not effective in detecting message races. First, such testing can be used to prove the existence of errors, but not the absence of them. Not detecting message races in multiple executions or simulations does not necessarily imply that they can't happen. To completely verify the behavior of a Web Service, all possible scenarios must be examined. Explicitly examining all possible scenarios is a taunting task, if not impossible, as the number of possible scenarios is astronomical. Also, controlled testing can't take into account unpredictable interactions that appear in the field. Second, Web Services testers have to interpret vast amount of output to determine whether there exists message races. This task alone takes non-trivial amount of time, and in many cases the output of an execution or simulation is considered correct by mistake even if there are message races. In the case where a message race is detected, the particular execution sequence that manifested the message race cannot be easily reproduced.

In this paper we present a novel approach that addresses these problems that plague traditional testing approaches. Our approach can be used to prove the absence of message races within a bound specified by the user. Unlike most other static analysis approaches that report large amount of false negatives, only real message races are reported by our approach. In order to explore the astronomical amount of possible scenarios we model Web Services using suitable classes of constraints and reducing various analysis problems to constraint solving. Fig. 2 depicts the steps of our approach. First, a BPEL [3] process is translated to a WSMG model. Second, the WSMG is encoded as an SMT [3] formula. Third, an SMT solver is used to decide the satisfiability of the formula. We chose using SMT solvers as their performance has benefited from recent significant advances in Boolean satisfiability (SAT) solvers (e.g. [5], [6], [7]) and SMT solvers (e.g. [8], [9]).

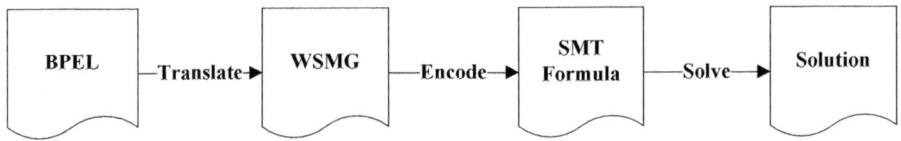

Fig. 2. Steps for finding messages races in a Web Service

The semantics of non-determinism such as network latency is represented implicitly by the SMT formula. The solution reported by the SMT solver offers detailed information that explains how the message race happened. Thus the bug is reproducible in the sense that the user can always simulate Web Service execution based on our bug report to obtain the same message race.

The rest of this paper is organized as follows. Section 2 briefly reviews related work. Section 3 presents our modeling language for Web Services. Section 4 details our approach to reduce message race detection problem to constraint solving problem. Section 5 describes two case studies and we conclude in Section 6 with contributions and limits of this paper.

2   Related Work

Netzer and Miller [10] first characterize message races and design an on-the-fly algorithm for detecting them. Afterwards, Netzer et al. [11] improve their previous approaches by using a two pass hybrid on-the-fly/post-mortem scheme, and remove artifact races that are side effects of non-determinism from the bug report. In [12], Park *et al.* present an on-the-fly detection tool, which detects message races in MPI programs by checking communication concurrency in distributed processes.

In [13], message race is identified as one type of undesirable interactions between Web Services. In that work, Web Services are modeled as feature interactions and then analyzed to discover potential message races. Zhang *et al.* proposed a Petri net based approach to detect race conditions in Web Services [14]. They subsequently presented another model checking based technique using SPIN, where the business process execution language for Web Services (BPEL4WS) is translated to Promela (SPIN model definition language) [15]. The most significant difference between previous work and ours is that most previous work uses existing languages and models that are intended for other domains such as hardware and network protocol designs. On the other hand, we use our Web Service Modeling Graph (WSMG) which is targeted for Web Services. Also, our SMT-based analysis eliminates false positives and produces a trace that facilities pinpointing the source of the message race.

Similar ideas that apply symbolic analysis to detect message races have been reported in [17] [18]. However, the technique has been applied in a different domain on MCAPI (Multicore Association Communication API), which leads to totally different modeling and encoding algorithms.

3 Web Service Modeling Graph

In this section we define the Web Service Modeling Graph (WSMG) that is inspired by hierarchical reactive modules [16]. WSMG is a compact representation that exhibits concurrency and control flow in Web Services.

A WSMG model represents a Web Service as a set of threads that communicate via messages over a set of channels. A thread consists of a set of sequential transitions $\mathcal{T}$. The set of transitions is defined as $\mathcal{T} \subseteq P \times Q \times Guard \times Action$, where P is the state before the transition, Q is the state after the transition, $Guard$ is a conditional expressions and $Action \in Asgn \cup Snd \cup Rcv \cup \{-\}$. $Asgn$ is a set of assignment statements. $Snd \in Ch \times E$ sends the result of expression E over a channel in Ch. $Rcv \in Ch \times Var$ receives a value from a channel and saves the value to a variable in Var. No-op is denoted by $-$. In WSMG there are two types of channels $Ch = Ch_S \cup Ch_A$. Ch_S is a set of synchronous channels, over which both send and receive are blocking. Ch_A is a set of asynchronous channels, over which both send and receive are non-blocking if the buffer in a channel is not full during send action, and not empty during receive action.

We say a transition τ in thread t has a *token*, denoted as $tk_t = \tau$, if it is a candidate for execution in a thread t. At any time one transition per thread can have the token. We say a transition τ is *fired* if it is selected for execution. When τ is fired, the token moves to the next transition in that thread. $succ(\tau)$ denotes the next transition of transition τ. In the following we explain the execution semantics of a WSMG model:

- Let $\tau = (g, v := expr)$ be a transition in thread t. τ can be fired if t is scheduled and $tk_t = \tau \wedge g = true$. After the firing, $tk_t = succ(\tau)$, and the assignment is executed.
- Let $\tau = (g, snd(ch, E))$ be a transition in thread t that sends the value of E to synchronous channel ch, and $\tau' = (g', rcv(ch, v))$ is a transition in thread t' that receives to the variable v from channel ch. Transition τ can be fired if $tk_t = \tau$, $tk_{t'} = \tau'$, t' is scheduled, and both g and g' is true. In this case, τ and τ' are fired simultaneously. After the firings, the value of v is updated by the result of E, and the tokens in t and t' are transferred to $succ(\tau)$ and $succ(\tau')$, respectively.
- Let $\tau = (g, asnd(ch, E))$ be a transition in thread t that sends the value of E to asynchronous channel ch. Transition τ can be fired if t is scheduled, $tk_t = \tau$, g=true and the buffer in ch is not full. After the firing, $tk_t = succ(\tau)$, and the value of E is delivered to ch's buffer.
- Let $\tau = (g, arcv(ch, v))$ be a transition in thread t that receives a value from asynchronous channel ch. Transition τ can be fired if t is scheduled, $tk_t = \tau$,

g=true, and the buffer in ch is not empty. After the firing $tk_t = succ(\tau)$, and the value of v is updated by the removed value from ch.

- Let $\tau = (g, \text{fork } (t'))$ be a transition in thread t that forks thread t', and τ' be the first transition in thread t'. Both τ and τ' will be fired if t is scheduled, g=true and $tk_t = \tau$. After the firings $tk_t = succ(\tau)$ and $tk_{t'} = \tau'$.

- Let $\tau = (g, \text{join } (t'))$ be a transition in thread t that joins thread t with thread t', and τ' be the last transition in thread t'. Both τ and τ' will be fired if $tk_t = \tau \wedge tk_{t'} = \tau'$, g=true and t' is scheduled. After the firings, $tk_t = succ(\tau)$ and $tk_{t'} = \bot$.

4 Symbolic Encoding

In this section we present an encoding approach that converts a given WSMG model G to an SMT formula that consists of initial constraint $\iota_0(G)$, thread scheduling constraint $\chi_B(G)$, transition constraint $\tau_B(G)$ and message race constraint $\rho_B(G)$. Whether there is message race up to the predefined bound B can be checked by the validity of formula 1 which is equivalent to checking the satisfiability for formula 2.

$$\iota_0(G) \wedge \chi_B(G) \wedge \tau_B(G) \wedge \rho_B(G) \tag{1}$$

$$\iota_0(G) \wedge \chi_B(G) \wedge \tau_B(G) \rightarrow \neg \rho_B(G) \tag{2}$$

We use the SMT solver Yices [8] to solve formula 2. If the formula is satisfiable, the solution gives a trace that leads to a message race from the initial state in G; otherwise, it is proved that G has no message race within B steps. In the following we first discuss the symbolic variables needed for the encoding, and then discuss the constraints.

4.1 Symbolic Variables

In our symbolic analysis we check race conditions up to a pre-defined bound B. For each step $i < B$, we add a fresh copy for each variable introduced in this section. That is, $var[i]$ denotes the copy of var at the i-th step. The symbolic variables are:

- *Token variable*: In order to encode the threads interleaving semantics symbolically we identify the set of threads in a given WSMG model and introduce one token variable tk_t for each thread t. A transition τ has a token iff $tk_t = \tau$. Before a thread t is created or after it is terminated, we set tk_t to be $\top$ or $\bot$, respectively.
- *Model variables*: Given a WSMG model G, we introduce a symbolic variable for each model variable in G.
- *Scheduling variable*: To model non-determinism in the scheduler, we add a symbolic variable s whose domain is the set of thread identifiers. The value of $s[i]$ indicates which thread is scheduled to execute at step i. This is an important feature to our symbolic analysis in our approach. As in most cases the value of $s[i]$ is unspecified, the SMT solver is forced to consider the case where any thread can be scheduled to execute at step i.

- *Asynchronous channel buffers*: In our encoding we only consider channels with finite size buffers. Let the size of the buffer in ch be F, we introduce F symbolic variables $buf_1^{ch} \ldots buf_F^{ch}$, each of which represents a cell in the buffer of ch. A buffer is treated as a queue with buf_1^{ch} and buf_F^{ch} as its tail and head, respectively. We use a sentinel value $stnl$ to denote a cell without valid information. The buffer in ch is full iff $buf_1^{ch} \neq stnl$ and is empty iff $buf_F^{ch} = stnl$.

4.2 Initial Condition Constraint

The initial condition constraint $\iota_0(G)$ specifies the starting locations for each thread as well as the initial values of model variables, including the values set by the input vector.

4.3 Scheduling Constraint

Our approach analyzes all possible valid interleavings, and excludes invalid ones. Therefore, we add thread scheduling constraint $\chi_B(G)$ to prevent invalid interleavings from being considered. In a WSMG model, a thread t must not be scheduled at step i in four cases: 1) before its creation, or after its termination (formula 3), 2) when an asynchronous send transition is pending and the relevant buffer is full, or when an asynchronous receive transition is pending and the relevant buffer is empty (formula 4), 3) when a synchronous send transition is pending, and there is no corresponding pending receive transition at another thread (formula 5), or 4) when a synchronous receive transition is pending, and there is no corresponding pending send transition at another thread (formula 6). τ_{as} is an asynchronous send transition, τ_{ar} is an asynchronous receive transition, τ_{ss} is a synchronous send transition, and Rv is all potential receive transitions of τ_{ss}, τ_{sr} is a synchronous receive transition, and Sd is all potential send transitions of τ_{sr}.

$$(tk_t[i] = \top \vee tk_t[i] = \bot) \rightarrow s[i] \neq t \tag{3}$$

$$\begin{aligned}(tk_t[i] = \tau_{as} \wedge buf_1^{ch} \neq stnl) \\ \vee (tk_t[i] = \tau_{ar} \wedge buf_F^{ch} = stnl) \rightarrow s[i] \neq t\end{aligned} \tag{4}$$

$$(tk_t[i] = \tau_{ss} \wedge \bigwedge_{(t',p') \in Rv} (tk_{t'}[i] \neq p')) \rightarrow s[i] \neq t \tag{5}$$

$$(tk_t[i] = \tau_{sr} \wedge \bigwedge_{(t',p') \in Sd} (tk_{t'}[i] \neq p')) \rightarrow s[i] \neq t \tag{6}$$

The thread scheduling constraint is encoded as in formula 7, where $\chi_B[i]$ is the conjunction of the constraints listed in formulas 3, 4, 5, and 6.

$$\chi_B(G) = \bigwedge_{i=1}^{B} \chi_B[i] \tag{7}$$

4.4 Transition Constraint

The execution semantics of a thread is specified by the encoding of its transitions in a WSMG model. In the following we discuss the translation from transitions to SMT formulas based on the types of transitions:

1. An assignment transition in the format of $\tau = (g, v := expr)$ where g is a guard, and $v := E$ assigns the results of E to variable v is encoded as in formula 8.

$$s[i] = t \wedge tk_t[i] = \tau \wedge g[i] \rightarrow tk_t[i] = succ(\tau) \wedge v[i+1] = E[i] \wedge \\ \delta(\{s, tk_t, v\}) \tag{8}$$

Formula 8 states that at step i, τ is fired under the following conditions: Thread t is selected $(s[i] = t)$, τ has token $(tk_t[i] = \tau)$ and guard is true $(g[i])$. Note that $g[i]$ (or $E[i]$) means that all variables in the guard g (or expression E) are replaced by their corresponding versions at step i. The following updates occur at step $i+1$ when τ is fired at step i: the transition that succeeds τ in t will have the token $(tk_t[i+1] = succ(\tau))$, the value of v at step $i+1$ is the result of E at step i $(v[i+1] = E[i])$ and the values of all variables except s, tk_t, v remain unchanged from step i to $i+1$. Note that $\delta_t(S)$ means that all the variables except those listed in set S keep their values step i to $i+1$.

2. A synchronous send/receive transition pair in the format of $\tau = (g, snd(ch, E))$ and $\tau' = (g', recv(ch, v))$, will be encoded as:

$$s[i] = t \wedge tk_t[i] = \tau \ \wedge g \wedge g' \wedge tk_{t'}[i] = \tau' \rightarrow (tk_t[i+1] = succ(\tau) \wedge \\ tk_{t'}[i+1] = succ(\tau') \wedge v[i+1] = E[i] \wedge \delta(\{s, tk_t, tk_{t'}, v\})) \tag{9}$$

3. An asynchronous send transition in the format of $\tau = (g, asnd(ch, E))$, is encoded as:

$$s[i] = t \wedge tk_t[i] = \tau \wedge \ g \wedge buf_1^{ch}[i] = stnl \rightarrow (tk_t[i+1] = succ(\tau) \wedge \\ \delta(\{s, tk_t, buf_F^{ch}, \dots, buf_1^{ch}\}) \wedge (buf_F^{ch}[i] = stnl? buf_1^{ch}[i+1] = \\ E[i]: \dots buf_2^{ch}[i] = stnl? buf_2^{ch}[i+1] = E[i]: buf_1^{ch}[i+1] = E[i])) \tag{10}$$

4. An asynchronous receive transition in the format of $\tau = (g, arcv(ch, v))$, is encoded as:

$$s[i] = t \wedge tk_t[i] = \tau \wedge \ g \ \wedge buf_F^{ch}[i] \neq stnl \rightarrow (tk_t[i+1] = succ(\tau) \wedge \\ v[i+1] = buf_F^{ch}[i] \wedge \bigwedge_{f=2}^{F}(buf_f^{ch}[i+1] = buf_{f-1}^{ch}[i]) \wedge buf_1^{ch}[i+1] = \\ stnl \wedge \delta(\{s, tk_t, buf_F^{ch}, \dots, buf_1^{ch}, v\})) \tag{11}$$

5. A fork transitions in the format of $\tau = (true, fork(t'))$, will be encoded according to formula 12, such that τ' is the first transition in thread t'.

$$s[i] = t \wedge tk_t[i] = \tau \to tk_t[i + 1] = succ(\tau) \wedge tk_{t'}[i + 1] = \tau' \wedge \\ \delta(\{s, tk_t, tk_{t'}\}) \tag{12}$$

6. A join transitions in the format of $\tau = (true, join\,(t'))$, will be encoded according to formula 13, such that τ' is the last transition in t'.

$$s[i] = t' \wedge tk_t[i] = \tau \wedge tk_{t'}[i] = \tau' \to tk_t[i + 1] = succ(\tau) \wedge tk_{t'}[i + \\ 1] = \bot \wedge \delta(\{s, tk_t, tk_{t'}\}) \tag{13}$$

Let $\gamma_\tau[i]$ denote the constraint for transition τ at step i and T be the set of all transitions in a WSMG model, the transition constraint can be specified as

$$\gamma_B(G) = \bigwedge_{\tau \in T} (\bigwedge_{i=1}^{B} \gamma_\tau[i]) \tag{13}$$

4.5 Message Race Constraint

A message race occurs on a synchronous channel ch when two conditions exist: a receive operation on ch is pending, and two or more send operations simultaneously attempt to deliver messages on ch. In such case, the received message is non-deterministic. Let SR_{ch} be the set of transitions with synchronous receive from ch and SS_{ch} be the set of transitions with synchronous send to ch. The constraint for synchronous message race at step i on channel ch can be specified as:

$$\alpha_{ch}[i] \equiv \underset{\tau \in SR_{ch}}{\exists} ((s[i] = t \wedge tk_t = \tau) \\ \wedge \underset{\tau_1 \in SS_{ch}}{\exists}\,\underset{\tau_2 \in SS_{ch}}{\exists} (tk_{t1}[i] = \tau_1 \wedge tk_{t2}[i] = \tau_2)) \tag{14}$$

Message race happens on an asynchronous channel ch if ch is not full and there are multiple transitions trying to send messages over ch at the same time. In such case, the message saved in the buffer of ch is non-deterministic. Let AS_{ch} be the set of transitions with asynchronous send to ch. The constraint for asynchronous message race at step i on channel ch can be specified as in formula 15, where $\tau_1 = (g_1, asnd(ch, E_1))$ and $\tau_2 = (g_2, asnd(ch, E_2))$ are transitions in thread t_1 and t_2, respectively.

$$\beta_{ch}[i] \equiv \left(ch \neq full \wedge \underset{\tau_1 \in AS_{ch}}{\exists}\,\underset{\tau_2 \in AS_{ch}}{\exists} (tk_{t1}[i] = \tau_1 \wedge tk_{t2}[i] = \tau_2)\right) \tag{15}$$

Let ACH and SCH be the set of asynchronous and synchronous channels in a WSMG model G. The message race property, up to bound B, can be specified by:

$$\rho_B(G) = \overset{B}{\underset{i=1}{\vee}} \left(\bigvee_{ch \in ACH} \alpha_{ch}[i] \vee \bigvee_{ch \in SCH} \beta_{ch}[i]\right) \tag{16}$$

5   Experiments

To assess the feasibility of our approach, we applied it on the stock-trading and the loan-approval case studies from the BPEL-WS 1.1 standard [2].

As shown in Fig. 3, the stock-trading case study consists of three sub-services: a quote service (SQS), a trading service (STS), and a bank service (Bank). The quote service has two threads that continuously send updated stock prices to the bank and the trading services. The trading service compares a received price to a minimum threshold and a maximum threshold. If the price is less than the minimum threshold, the trading service will send to the bank a buy request message. If the price is greater than the maximum threshold, the trading service will send to the bank a sell request message. Otherwise the trading service does nothing. The bank service updates its database when it receives new stocks prices from the quote service, and performs either selling or buying operations according to the requests received from the trading service.

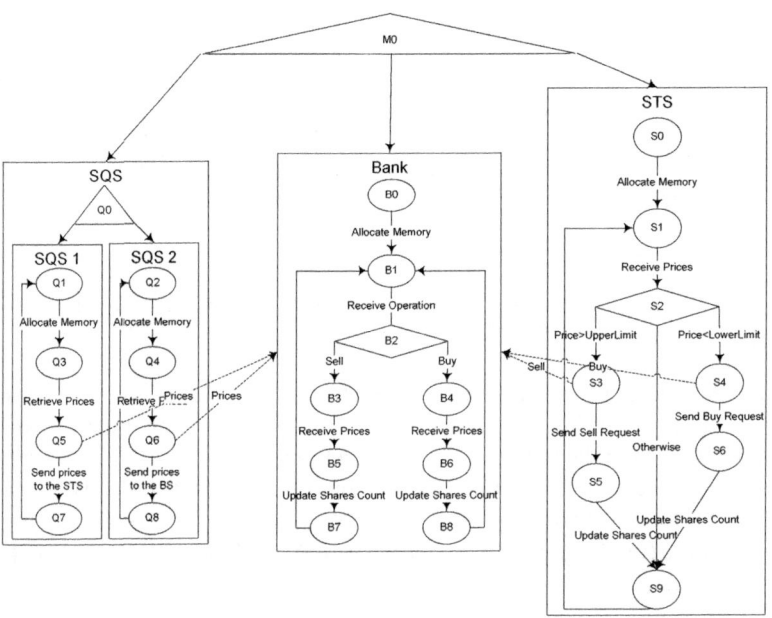

Fig. 3. The stock-trading Web Service

We followed the steps depicted in Fig. 3 and used Yices as the SMT solver. The solution produced by Yices indicates that a message race will occur when two quote services send prices-update messages to the bank service.

Table 1 shows the output of Yices which is an interpreted partial valuation to the symbolic variables in the SMT formula. In particular, we show the values of the token variables and the thread selection variable. The values of token variables indicate which transition is ready to be executed in a thread, and the value of thread selection variable shows which thread is scheduled at a given step. With the values of these two kinds of variables, the trace that leads to a message race can be replayed, thus solving the non-repeatability problem in the debugging of Web Services. According to table 1, at the 10th step, the variable values satisfy the message race constraint: the bank thread is scheduled for execution $(S, T4)$ and its pending transition is a receive operation $(tk_4, B1)$. At the same time, there exist two send operations $(tk_3, Q6)$ and $(tk_5, S3)$ and all the three operations are on the same channel.

Table 1. Partial valuation to the FOL formula translated from the stock-trading WSMG model

Step	Partial Valuation
0	$(tk_0, M0), (tk_1, \top), (tk_2, \top), (tk_3, \top), (tk_4, \top), (tk_5, \top), (S, T0)$
1	$(tk_0, \bot), (tk_1, Q0), (tk_2, \top), (tk_3, \top), (tk_4, B0), (tk_5, S0), (S, T1)$
2	$(tk_0, \bot), (tk_1, \bot), (tk_2, Q1), (tk_3, Q2), (tk_4, B0), (tk_5, S0), (S, T3)$
3	$(tk_0, \bot), (tk_1, \bot), (tk_2, Q1), (tk_3, Q4), (tk_4, B0), (tk_5, S0), (S, T3)$
4	$(tk_0, \bot), (tk_1, \bot), (tk_2, Q1), (tk_3, Q6), (tk_4, B0), (tk_5, S0), (S, T2)$
5	$(tk_0, \bot), (tk_1, \bot), (tk_2, Q3), (tk_3, Q6), (tk_4, B0), (tk_5, S0), (S, T5)$
6	$(tk_0, \bot), (tk_1, \bot), (tk_2, Q3), (tk_3, Q6), (tk_4, B0), (tk_5, S1), (S, T2)$
7	$(tk_0, \bot), (tk_1, \bot), (tk_2, Q5), (tk_3, Q6), (tk_4, B0), (tk_5, S1), (S, T2)$
8	$(tk_0, \bot), (tk_1, \bot), (tk_2, Q7), (tk_3, Q6), (tk_4, B0), (tk_5, S2), (S, T5)$
9	$(tk_0, \bot), (tk_1, \bot), (tk_2, Q7), (tk_3, Q6), (tk_4, B0), (tk_5, S3), (S, T4)$
10	$(tk_0, \bot), (tk_1, \bot), (tk_2, Q7), (tk_3, Q6), (tk_4, B1), (tk_5, S3), (S, T4)$

The second case study is based on the loan-approval Web Service which is shown in Fig. 4. It consists of four sub-services: a customer service (Customer), an approval service (Approval), an approver service (Approver), and an assessor service (Assessor). The approval service receives loan requests from the customer service. If the requested loan amount is less than a predetermined threshold, the loan request is sent to the approver service for automatic approval. Otherwise, the loan request is sent to the assessor service. When the assessor service receives a loan request, it assesses the risk associated with the customer, and then sends the risk assessment to the approval process. If the risk is high, the approval process denies the request; otherwise, the request is forwarded to the approver process. When the approver process receives a request, it automatically stamps the request as approved, and sends it back to the approval process. When the approval process receives an approved request from the approver process, it forwards the request to the customer.

When Yices is fed the SMT formulas corresponding to the loan-approval Web Service, it was able to detect a potential message race that happens when two quote services send prices-update messages to the bank service. Table 2 shows the output of Yices. At the 8th step, the variable values satisfy the message race constraint: $L1$ is scheduled for execution and it is a receive operation. At the same time both the pending transitions of $C4$, and $C5$ are send operations.

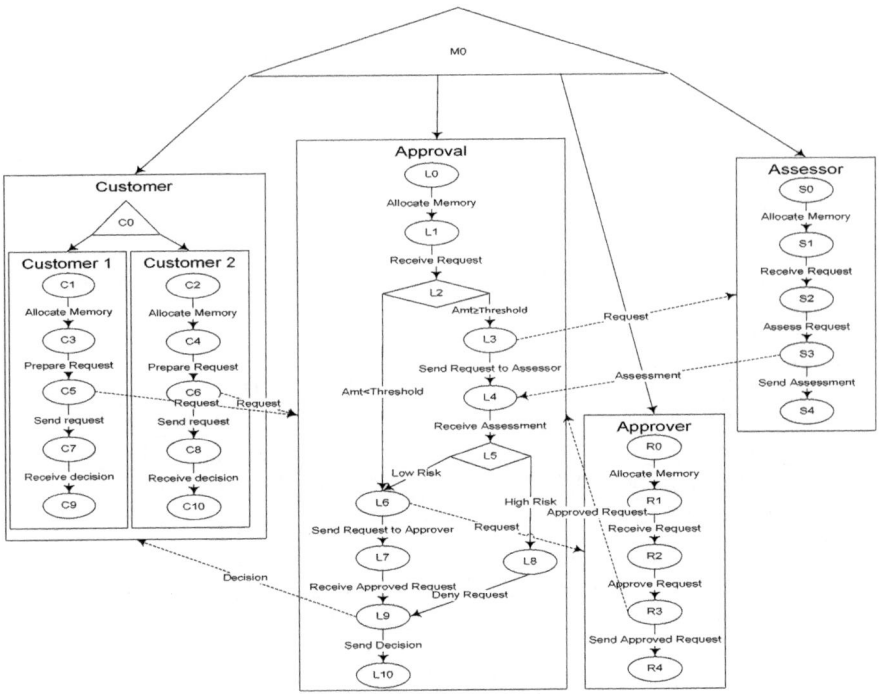

Fig. 4. The loan-approval Web Service

Table 2. Partial valuation to the FOL formula translated from the loan-approval WSMG model

Step	Partial Valuation
0	$(tk_0, M0), (tk_1, \top), (tk_2, \top), (tk_3, \top), (tk_4, \top), (tk_5, \top), (tk_6, \top), (S, T0)$
1	$(tk_0, \bot), (tk_1, C0), (tk_2, R0), (tk_3, L0), (tk_4, S0), (tk_5, \top), (tk_6, \top), (S, T1)$
2	$(tk_0, \bot), (tk_1, \bot), (tk_2, R0), (tk_3, L0), (tk_4, S0), (tk_5, C1), (tk_6, C2), (S, T3)$
3	$(tk_0, \bot), (tk_1, \bot), (tk_2, R0), (tk_3, L1), (tk_4, S0), (tk_5, C1), (tk_6, C2), (S, T5)$
4	$(tk_0, \bot), (tk_1, \bot), (tk_2, R0), (tk_3, L1), (tk_4, S0), (tk_5, C3), (tk_6, C2), (S, T5)$
5	$(tk_0, \bot), (tk_1, \bot), (tk_2, R0), (tk_3, L1), (tk_4, S0), (tk_5, C5), (tk_6, C2), (S, T4)$
6	$(tk_0, \bot), (tk_1, \bot), (tk_2, R0), (tk_3, L1), (tk_4, S1), (tk_5, C5), (tk_6, C2), (S, T6)$
7	$(tk_0, \bot), (tk_1, \bot), (tk_2, R0), (tk_3, L1), (tk_4, S1), (tk_5, C5), (tk_6, C4), (S, T6)$
8	$(tk_0, \bot), (tk_1, \bot), (tk_2, R0), (tk_3, L1), (tk_4, S1), (tk_5, C5), (tk_6, C4), (S, T6)$

The experiments were performed on a computer with Intel Core 2 Duo 2.6GHz processor and 4GB memory. Table 3 reports statistics that are related to solving the SMT formulas in the two case studies, including the number of decisions, number of conflicts, number of Boolean variables and memory usage during the SMT solving procedure. The last two rows list the memory and time usage of the two case studies.

Table 3. Yices statistics

Yices Statistics	Loan-approval	Stock-trading
#Decisions	11833	7954
#Conflicts	6411	869
Boolean variables	8845	5176
Memory used (MB)	20.1	13
CPU Time (sec.)	2.8	0.45

6 Conclusion and Discussion

To improve the reliability and consequently the trustworthiness of Web Services, potential messages races should be detected. We have addressed the problem of detecting message races in BPEL Web Services. The main contribution of this paper is a novel approach that reduces message race detection to constraint solving and uses modern SMT solvers to check the satisfiability of the SMT formula translated from the WSMG models. Given a predefined bound B, our approach is both sound and complete within the bound. Compared with traditional testing approaches that repeatedly execute or simulate a Web Service, the advantages of our approach include 1) ability to prove the absence of message races within a predefined bound, 2) implicit exploration of astronomical amount of possible scenarios, 3) no need to control the non-deterministic factors in Web Services in testing environment, and 4) detailed bug reports.

However, even though all the message races reported by our approach are real, there are benign message races that are allowed by certain Web Services. How to differentiate benign and malicious message races is an important area that is out of the scope of this paper. For the future work, we plan to perform more significant case studies to future investigate the effectiveness of the approach.

Acknowledgements. The work was supported in part by ONR Grant N000140910740 and NSF Grant CCF-0811287.

References

1. Schneider, F.B.: Trust in Cyberspace. National Academies Press, Washington (1999)
2. Christey, S. (eds), Top 25 most dangerous programming errors, CWE/SANS report (2009), http://cwe.mitre.org/top25
3. Klein, J., Leymann, F., Roller, D., Curbera, F., Goland, Y., Weerawarana, S.: Business process execution language for web services, version 1.1 (2003)
4. Satisfiability Modulo Theories, http://en.wikipedia.org/wiki/Satisfiability_Modulo_Theories
5. Marques-Silva, J.P., Sakallah, K.A.: GRASP: A search algorithm for propositional satisfiability. IEEE Transactions on Computers 48(5), 506–521 (1999)
6. Moskewicz, M.W., Madigan, C.F., Zhao, Y., Zhang, L., Malik, S.: Chaff: engineering an efficient SAT solver. In: 38th Design Automation Conference (DAC), pp. 530–535. ACM Press, New York (2001)

7. Een, N., Sorensson, N.: An extensible sat-solver. In: Satisfiability Workshop, pp. 333–336 (2003)
8. Dutertre, B., de Moura, L.: Fast Linear-Arithmetic Solver for DPLL(T). In: Ball, T., Jones, R.B. (eds.) CAV 2006. LNCS, vol. 4144, pp. 81–94. Springer, Heidelberg (2006)
9. Moura, L.D., Bjrner, N.: Z3: An efficient SMT solver. In: Ramakrishnan, C.R., Rehof, J. (eds.) TACAS 2008. LNCS, vol. 4963, pp. 337–340. Springer, Heidelberg (2008)
10. Netzer, R.H.B., Miller, B.P.: Optimal tracing and replay for debugging message-passing parallel programs. In: Super computing 1992: Proceedings of the 1992 ACM/IEEE conference on Supercomputing, pp. 502–511. IEEE Computer Society Press, Los Alamitos (1992)
11. Netzer, R.H.B., Brennan, T.W., Damodaran-Kamal, S.K.: Debugging race conditions in message-passing programs. In: SPDT 1996: Proceedings of the SIGMETRICS symposium on Parallel and distributed tools, pp. 31–40. ACM Press, New York (1996)
12. Park, M.Y., Shim, S.J., Jun, Y.K., Park, H.R.: Mpirace-check: Detection of message races in MPI programs. In: Cérin, C., Li, K.-C. (eds.) GPC 2007. LNCS, vol. 4459, pp. 322–333. Springer, Heidelberg (2007)
13. Weiss, M., Esfandiari, B.: On feature interactions among web services. In: IEEE International Conference on Web Services. IEEE Computer Society, Los Alamitos (2004)
14. Zhang, J., Su, S., Yang, F.: Detecting race conditions in web services. In: AICT ICIW 2006: Proceedings of the Advanced Int'l Conference on Telecommunications and Int'l Conference on Internet and Web Applications and Services, p. 184. IEEE Computer Society, Washington (2006)
15. Zhang, J., Yang, F., Su, S.: Detecting feature interactions in web services with model checking techniques. The Journal of China Universities of Posts and Telecommunications 14(3), 108–112 (2007)
16. Alur, R., NcDougall, M., Yang, Z.: Exploiting Behavioral Hierarchy for Efficient Model Checking. In: Brinksma, E., Larsen, K.G. (eds.) CAV 2002. LNCS, vol. 2404, p. 338. Springer, Heidelberg (2002)
17. Elwakil, M., Yang, Z., Liqiang, W.: CRI: Symbolic Debugger for MCAPI Applications. In: Chin, W.-N. (ed.) ATVA 2010. LNCS, vol. 6252, pp. 353–358. Springer, Heidelberg (2010)
18. Elwakil, M., Yang, Z.: Debugging Support Tool for MCAPI Applications. In: Workshop on Parallel and Distributed Systems: Testing, Analysis, and Debugging (PADTAD - VIII). ACM, Trento (2010)

A User-Oriented Approach to Assessing Web Service Trustworthiness*

Weinan Zhao, Hailong Sun, Zicheng Huang, Xudong Liu, and Xitong Kang

School of Computer Science and Engineering, Beihang University,
Beijing 100191, China
{zhaown,sunhl,huangzc,liuxd,kangxt}@act.buaa.edu.cn

Abstract. Trustworthiness is a synthetic characteristic of Web services, which not only involves objective attributes of software quality, but also subjective perception of users. However accurate assessment for service trustworthiness from user's perception is a difficult problem, since user perception of a particular Web service varies in terms of users, application scenarios and time. In this paper, we present a user oriented Web service trustworthiness assessment approach based on collecting and aggregating user feedbacks. The difference from other research work is that in our approach we consider application and user specific factors including the similarity between contexts of the evaluator and feedback reporter, the timeliness of feedback and the evaluator's preferences on quality properties of a Web service. A prototype of our approach is implemented based on ServiceXchange, a Web service repository and search engine developed by our research team. Experimental results demonstrate that our approach has a significant advantage over other approaches that treat feedbacks equally and ignore the difference among user preferences.

Keywords: SOA, Web service, trustworthiness assessment, user feedback.

1 Introduction

Service oriented architecture (SOA)has been widely accepted in both industry and academia. As an important type of SOA realization technologies, Web services have been successfully adopted in e-commerce, finance, telecommunication and other fields. In practice, individual Web services provide limited functions that are difficult to meet complex business requirements. Therefore by selecting and compositing existing Web services in accordance with a certain business process, service composition becomes the main approach to service-oriented software development.

Among all the challenges faced by service composition, trustworthiness assurance is especially critical to service-oriented software due to highly complicated software structure and uncertain network environments. Typically, trustworthy software means its behaviors and execution results are consistent with user expectations [1], which usually include both functional and non-functional requirements. Therefore, software

---

* This work was partly supported by China 863 program under Grant No. 2007AA010301 and partly supported by China 973 program under Grant No. 2005CB321803.

B. Xie et al. (Eds.): ATC 2010, LNCS 6407, pp. 195–207, 2010.

trustworthiness not only involves objective attributes of software quality, but also subjective perception of users [2]. The most important prerequisite of developing trustworthy software based on service composition is to select individual trustworthy Web services. Hence, an effective Web service trustworthiness assessment approach that can help to locate trustworthy Web services is of paramount importance to service oriented software development.

There have been a lot of research works on software trustworthiness. However, most of them are focusing on the different attributes of software quality while they ignore the user perception of software quality. For example, [3,4,5] study trustworthiness issue from the perspective of automatic monitoring and measuring quality of service (QoS). Compared with trustworthiness of web service, QoS only focus on the objective quality attributes. Those methods are appropriate for measuring the quality properties of a Web service like response time and reliability, but inappropriate for user oriented quality properties like usability and price.

Reputation-based approaches utilize user feedbacks to evaluate a software system including Web services [6,7,8]. The reputation of a Web service is the aggregation of user feedbacks that contain ratings on various software quality properties. Through the use of feedback, these reputation based approaches assess Web service trustworthiness from the user perspective. However, most existing work treats all the user feedbacks equally and ignores the difference among users and application scenarios, which can make the assessment result inaccurate. The feedbacks of a particular Web service from different users may vary greatly due to the following reasons: (a) The quality properties of Web services are context sensitive. In this paper, the *context* denotes the input parameters and invocation environment of Web service. For example, a Web service may have shorter response time to LAN users than Internet users.(b) The user preferences on quality properties can vary greatly. A time-critical user may give higher overall rating to an expensive real-time Web service than other users who are concerned more about price. (c) The quality properties of Web services are dynamically changing due to upgrade and the changing of underlying infrastructure. Therefore, assessment of a Web service by simply aggregating feedbacks without considering specific contexts, user preferences and the timeliness of feedbacks cannot obtain accurate results.

To address these problems, we propose a user oriented approach to assessing Web service trustworthiness. Our approach collects feedbacks that contain reporter's contextual information and multi-dimensional ratings on service quality properties. When a user (*evaluator*) wants to learn the trustworthiness of a specific Web service, he is required to submit his context and preferences. The assessment procedure is divided into two steps. First, quality properties are predicted by aggregating the feedbacks, that are weighted by the timeliness of feedbacks and the context similarity between evaluator and feedback reporter. Second, the predicted quality properties are aggregated into an overall trustworthiness using evaluator's preferences as weight. Finally, we implement a prototype on the basis of our ServiceXchange [9], a Web service repository and search engine developed by our R&D team at Beihang University. The major contributions of this paper are as follow:

- We propose a user oriented approach to assessing Web service trustworthiness from user's perspective, with consideration of the difference among users' contexts and the difference among user preferences on quality properties as well as the time-liness of user feedbacks.

- We design and implement a prototype of our approach base on our previous work, namely ServiceXchange.
- We demonstrate the assessment accuracy of our approach through experimental evaluation.

The remainder of this paper is organized as follows. Section 2 introduces the related work. Section 3 describes the proposed approach in detail. Section 4 describes the prototype of our approach. Section 5 presents experiments and results. Finally we conclude our work in Section 6.

2   Related Work

Generally speaking, the study of Web service trustworthiness assessment is performed along two technical directions, i.e. test-based and reputation-based approaches.

Test-based approaches use monitored QoS attributes to assess Web service trustworthiness. Shao et al [3] propose a user-perceived service availability metric on the basis of service status. The service status is described as *stable up*, *transient down*, and *persistent down*. By analyzing the service-invocation records, the service status feature is recognized and used to measure Web service trustworthiness. Zhang et al [4] present the design and implementation of a Web services testing platform. By utilizing of mobile agent technology, the total testing time and network traffic are reduced. Bai et al. [5] propose an approach to generate Web services test cases automatically based on the WSDL (Web Services Description Language), which carries the basic information of a service including its interface operations and the data transmitted. These approaches effectively and efficiently facilitate Web service testing, but are limited to get network related quality metrics like response time and availability.

The reputation-based approaches measure trustworthiness by collecting and aggregating user feedbacks. Zaki et al. [8] propose a model to compute the reputation of a Web service according to other users' feedbacks, and the user credibility is taken into consideration in the proposed method. Surya et al. [6] present a composite service oriented reputation system. When a rating is given to a composite service, the system will distribute it to the component Web services fairly. Zaki et al. [7] propose two techniques to resolve the reputation bootstrap issue, with which the initial reputation is set up to a new comer service in a fair and accurate manner. Reputation system is also extensively studied in other fields such as E-commerce and P2P networks [10,11,12]. However those works use feedback with overall rating that ignores the difference among user preferences, and aggregates user feedbacks without considering the context sensitivity and timeliness of feedbacks.

Different from the existing methods, we propose a user oriented Web service trustworthiness assessment approach. By collecting feedback with multidimensional ratings on quality properties instead of an overall rating, the misleading effect caused by the difference among user preferences is eliminated. By using context similarity as weight to aggregate feedbacks, we only make use of feedbacks that have similar context with evaluator to predict quality properties of Web services. Additionally, the timeliness of feedbacks is also taken into account so as to differentiate the time effectiveness of user feedbacks.

3   User Oriented Trustworthiness Assessment Approach

3.1   Overview

Fig.1 gives an overview of our approach to assessing Web service trustworthiness. Firstly the feedbacks are collected as a basis. Then the assessment process is divided into two steps:(a) Predict multidimensional quality properties, using feedbacks that are weighted by the timeliness of feedback and the context similarity between evaluator and feedback reporter.(b)Aggregate the predicted quality properties into an overall trustworthiness incorporating evaluator's preferences.

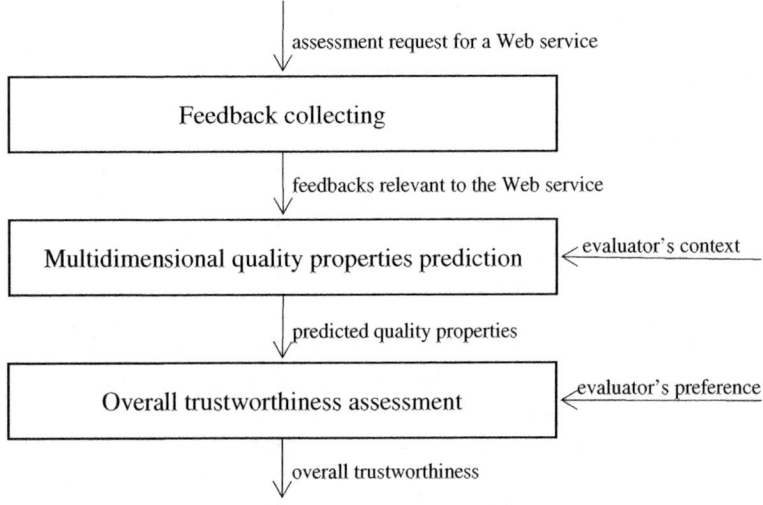

Fig. 1. The overview of our approach

Then we propose our user oriented assessment approach in detail. First, the consideration about feedback collecting is discussed. Second, the method to predict quality properties under a specific context is presented. Third, the timeliness of feedback is taken account into the quality properties prediction. Finally, we introduce the calculation of overall trustworthiness incorporating user preference.

3.2   Feedback Collecting

To assess the Web service trustworthiness under the evaluator's specific context and preference, we collect feedbacks that contain contextual information and multidimensional ratings on quality properties into a *feedback repository*. The collecting of multidimensional ratings instead of an overall rating will clear away the preferences of feedback reporters. And by recording reporter's contextual information and comparing it to evaluator's context, we can know whether a feedback should be involved in the assessment. In addition, throughout this paper we will utilize *context of feedback* and *context of feedback reporter* interchangeably to denote the context in which the Web service is invoked, and *context of evaluator* to denote the context in which the evaluator want to use the Web service.

To collect multidimensional feedbacks, a feedback model should be defined first. A feedback model describes what information should be collected while users submit feedbacks.

We give the formal definition of feedback model and user feedback as follows.

Definition 1. A *feedback model* is defined as *<Context, Quality>* , where *Context*=$<ctx_1, ctx_2, ..., ctx_i>$ defines a set of context factor and *Quality*=$<qlt_1, qlt_2, ..., qlt_i>$ defines a set of quality properties.

Definition 2. A *user feedback* reported by user U at time T about Web service S is defined as $<U,S,T,C,Q>$, where $C=<c_1, c_2, ..., c_i>$ defines a set of context factor values and $Q=<q_1, q_2, ..., q_i>$ defines a set of quality property values. Without loss of generality, the domain of quality property value is set to between 0 and 1. And in this paper we only consider the case where context factors have discrete or categorical values.

In practice, users focus on different quality properties considering services in different categories. Hence a domain specific feedback model should be given for each service category, and this is usually completed by domain experts.

For instance, considering services in *search engine category*, the feedback model may be *<Context, Quality>* where *Context*=*<User Location, Search Language>* and *Quality*=*<Response time, Recall, Precision>*. Then a user feedback of a service in the category may be $<U,S,T,C,Q>$ where $C=<RPC, English>$ and $Q=<0.6, 0.7, 0.7>$.

3.3 Predict Quality Properties under a Specific Context

Based on multidimensional user feedbacks from the feedback repository, the quality properties under a specific context can be predicted. Assuming that a user requests to assess the trustworthiness of a Web service S under the specific context C, we firstly fetch feedbacks related to S from feedback repository into a feedback set FS and for each feedback F in FS, the similarity between C and context of F is calculated. Then we use the similarity as weight to aggregate the feedbacks in FS to predict the multidimensional quality properties of S.

The core part of the prediction is the context similarity calculation. Then we give the consideration and design of the calculation method as follows.

We call two contexts is similar to a Web service iff the difference between service's quality property values under the two contexts is less than a threshold. In practice, the similarity between two contexts is sensitivity to quality properties. For instance, considering the quality property values of a search engine Web service under two context C_1 and C_2, where $C_1=<UK, Chinese>$ and $C_2=<UK, English>$, the values of quality property *Response Time* may be close since the values of context factor *User Location* are same while the values of quality property *Precision* may be obviously different due to the values of context factor *Search Language* vary(e.g. Google performs better while is used to search English information than Chinese).

Therefore C_1 and C_2 are similar to the search engine Web service considering the property *Response Time* and not similar considering the property *Precision*. Based on the above discussion, the similarity between two contexts should be calculated for each quality property individually.

The formal definition and calculation method of context similarity is given as follows.

Definition 3. *The distance between two context factor values* c_i *and* c_j *considering quality property* qlt_k *of service S is* $dis^S_{qlt_k}(c_i, c_j)$ *which is defined as:*

$$dis^S_{qlt_k}(c_i, c_j)= \left| \overline{q^S_k(c_i)} - \overline{q^S_k(c_j)} \right|, \ c_i, c_j \in domain(ctx_m). \tag{1}$$

Where:

$$\overline{q^S_k(c_i)}=\frac{1}{n}\Sigma_{F_i \in FS'} q_k, FS'=\{F_j | S \in F_j \wedge C \in F_j \wedge c_i \in C\}, n=|FS'|. \tag{2}$$

Definition 4. *The similarity of context C_1 and C_2 considering property qlt_k of service S is* $sim^S_{qlt}(C_1,C_2)$ *which is defined as:*

$$sim^S_{qlt_k}(C_1,C_2)=1-\sqrt{\frac{1}{n}\Sigma_{i=1}^n \left[dis^S_{qlt_k}(c_i^1,c_i^2)\right]^2}, c_i^j \in C_j, n=|C_j|. \tag{3}$$

Note that $dis^S_{qlt_k}(c_i, c_j) \in [0,1]$, and larger value of it implies greater change of value of quality property qlt_k when the value of context factor ctx_m vary from c_i to c_j. Then $sim^S_{qlt_k}(C_1,C_2) \in [0,1]$, and larger value of it implies higher similarity between C_1 and C_2 considering property qlt_k of S.

For instance, $dis^S_{Precision}$ (*Chinese, English*) is the distance between context factor values *Chinese* and *English*, and $sim^S_{Precision}(C_1,C_2)$ is the similarity between contexts C_1 and C_2 considering quality property *Precision* of service S.

To predict quality properties of service S under evaluator's specific context C, we average values of the quality properties in feedbacks related to S, using similarity between C and feedback reports' context as weight. A threshold ∂ is used to filter out the feedbacks that have context not similar to C. The following equation gives the formally definition of the prediction, where $pq_k(C)$ denotes the predicted value of quality property qlt_k under context C.

$$pq_k(C)=\frac{\Sigma_{F_i \in FS} sim'^S_{qlt_k}(C_i,C) \times q_k^i}{\Sigma_{F_i \in FS} sim'^S_{qlt_k}(C_i,C)}, C_i, Q_i \in F_i, q_k^i \in Q_i. \tag{4}$$

Where:

$$sim'^S_{qlt_k}=\begin{cases} sim^S_{qlt_k} & , if \ sim'_{qlt_k}>\partial. \\ 0 & ,otherwise. \end{cases} \tag{5}$$

It is worth noting that $dis^S_{qlt_k}(c_i, c_j)$ reflects the Web service's inherent characteristic that is relative stable, so it could be calculated offline and stored in a lookup table to facilitate online context similarity calculation.

3.4 Timeliness Consideration of Feedback

$$\gamma(T_i, T_{now}) = \tau^{T_{now}-T_i}, T_i \in F, \tau \in [0,1] \tag{6}$$

To cope with the dynamic feature of service quality properties, we give less weight to old feedback than more recent ones. A fading factor is introduced as weight to weaken the old feedbacks' importance on prediction [10]. Suppose that the current time is T_{now}, the fading factor of a feedback F is defined as follows.

By adjusting the value of τ, different fading effect can be achieved. It's complete fading when $\tau=0$, that only the latest feedbacks are counted and all previous feedbacks are completely swept out. And having $\tau=1$ is equivalent to not having a fading factor.

Based on the introduced fading factor, we give the formal definition of the quality properties prediction that takes timeliness of feedback into account as follows.

$$pq_k(C, T_{now}) = \frac{\sum_{F_i \in FS} sim^S_{qlt_k}(C_i, C) \times \gamma(T_i, T_{now}) \times q^i_k}{\sum_{F_i \in FS} sim^S_{qlt_k}(C_i, C) \times \gamma(T_i, T_{now})}, T_i, C_i, Q_i \in F_i, q^i_k \in Q_i. \tag{7}$$

3.5 Incorporation of User Preference

By collecting and aggregating the multidimensional feedbacks, the quality properties of a Web service are predicted with the feedback reporter's preference eliminated. The predicted quality properties can be delivered to evaluator as multidimensional trustworthiness, but typically the comparison among candidate services' trustworthiness is conducted to help selecting the most trustworthy Web service, so an overall trustworthiness is required as a sorting index. We give a method to assess the overall trustworthiness of a Web service base on the incorporation of the evaluator's own preference into the predicted quality properties.

First we give the formal definition of user preference on multidimensional quality properties as follows.

Definition 5. *A user preference on quality properties of a Web service* is defined as $P=<p_1,p_2,...p_k>, p_k \in [0,1], \sum p_k =1$, where p_k is the importance to the quality property qlt_k from the user perspective.

Then the aggregation method for overall trustworthiness under user specific context C and preference P at particular time T_{now} is given as follow.

$$T(P,C,T_{now}) = \sum p_k \times pq_k(C,T_{now}), p_k \in P. \tag{8}$$

4   Prototype Design and Implementation

In this section, we will first introduce a Web service repository and search engine that developed by our R&D team, namely ServiceXchange, and then present the implementation of a prototype of the proposed trustworthiness assessment approach based on ServiceXchange.

4.1   ServiceXchange

ServiceXchange is a Web service repository and search engine that provides functions of Web service registering, searching, monitoring,etc.Fig.2 shows the system architecture of ServiceXchange. Web services are collected into ServiceXchange using a crawler, and a UDDI-like registry is also available for software provider to register their Web service into ServiceXchange. By analyzing the WSDL of Web services, the information such as interface operations and data transmitted is stored in Raw Info DB. Further knowledge of Web services such as similarity, connectivity, cluster and the keyword index are discovered leveraging the data mining technology and stored in Mined Info DB. Users can search Web services by keyword or category. To measure QoS of Web services, automatic built clients are used to monitor Web services and measure the response time and availability.

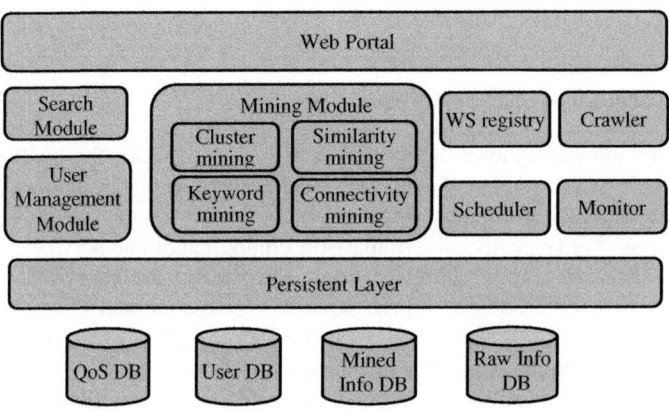

Fig.2. System architecture of ServiceXchange

4.2   Implementation of a Prototype

On the basis of the design presented in section 3, we implement a prototype integrating our trustworthiness assessment approach with ServiceXchange. Fig.3 shows the system architecture of the prototype.

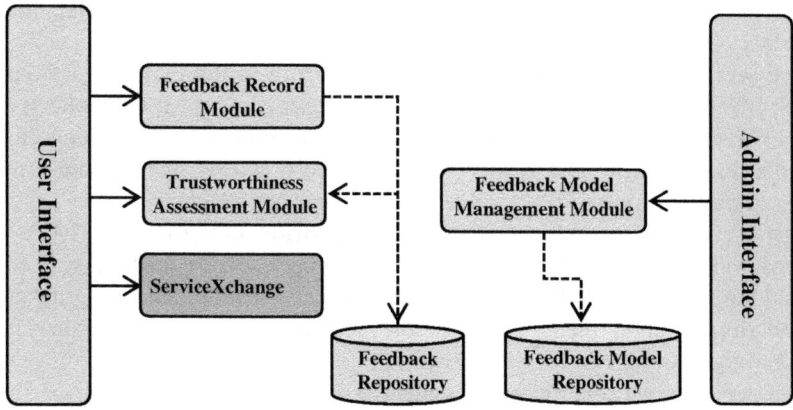

Fig. 3. System architecture of the prototype.

Feedback model management module provides tools to domain experts for building feedback models. For each Web services category in ServiceXchange, a feedback model that contains the contextual factors and quality properties is built leveraging domain knowledge. When a user want to report a feedback about a Web service, the feedback record module automatically generates a HTML form according to feedback model, then the user can report multidimensional feedbacks that will be stored into the Feedback Repository. The trustworthiness assessment module support two interfaces to assessing trustworthiness: (a) Submit a context, then get the assessed multidimensional quality properties of a particular Web service. (b) Submit a context and user preference, then get the assessed overall trustworthiness of a particular Web service or sort the Web services in same category by the overall trustworthiness.

5   Experimental Evaluation

In this section, we present experimental evaluation of our approach for trustworthiness assessment. Since our prototype based on ServiceXchange is not open to public yet, few real-world feedbacks can be used to evaluate our approach. In order to evaluate the assessment accuracy of our proposed methods, we conducted a simulation. The main purpose of this simulation is to measure the performance of our approach in assessing Web service trustworthiness. To clearly show the effectiveness of our approach, we implement the following five different assessment methods and perform comparative analysis of them in terms of assessment accuracy.

- **Web service trustworthiness assessment using user oriented approach** (*WSTA_{UO}*). This approach is proposed in section 3.
- **Web service trustworthiness assessment ignoring user preferences** (*WSTA_{IUP}*). Compared with *WSTA_{UO}*, this method does not consider the difference among user preferences. It collects the overall ratings incorporating the preference of *feedback reporters* that may be different from the preference of the *evaluator*, and then

aggregates them using the context similarity and fading factor to weighting the feedbacks from different users.

- **Web service trustworthiness assessment ignoring context** ($WSTA_{IC}$). Compared with $WSTA_{UO}$, this approach does not consider user contexts. It first collects multidimensional feedbacks, then predicts quality properties using the fading factor of feedbacks as weight, and finally aggregates the predicted quality values into an overall trustworthiness using evaluator's preference as weight.
- **Web service trustworthiness assessment ignoring timeliness** ($WSTA_{IT}$). Compared with $WSTA_{UO}$, this method ignores the timeliness of feedbacks. It collects multidimensional feedbacks, and then predicts quality properties using the context similarity as weight, finally aggregate the predicted quality property values into an overall trustworthiness using evaluator's preference as weight.
- **Web service trustworthiness assessment with overall rating** ($WSTA_{OR}$). This approach collects overall ratings and evaluates trustworthiness simply by averaging the ratings, ignoring all the considerations that are taken into account by $WSTA_{UO}$.

5.1 Simulation Parameters

There are three types of parameters in the simulation:

1. **Simulation environment parameters.** Simulations are run for 100 epochs, and a user assesses a Web service with the probability of 0.5.After a user obtains the assessed trustworthiness value, he invokes the Web service to get the real trustworthiness value and reports a feedback. If the difference between the assessed and real trustworthiness value is less than a threshold ε, the assessment is considered to be accurate. The threshold ε is set to 0.1. The five assessment approaches are used concurrently for each assessment. At the end of each epoch, the ratio of accurate assessment for each approach is record and compared.
2. **User parameters.** The number of users is set to 100. The characteristic of a user consist of two aspects: (a) User's context. A user's context contains two dimensions and each dimension has two possible values, i.e. 0 or 1. Then the space of user context value is $C^*=\{C=<c_1,c_2>|c_i\in[0,1]\}$. (b)User preference on multidimensional service quality properties. The user preference is a tuple whose elements are set to random numbers.
3. **Web service parameters.** Considering the candidate Web service set that contains 20 services, namely service set $S=\{s_1,s_2,...,s_{20}\}$. Each service has three quality properties. When a service is invoked, the user perceived quality properties are determined by the following two factors: (a) The service's inherent feature, which follows normal distribution $N(\mu,\sigma^2)$. The μ and σ is set to a random number between 0 and 1. (b) The context adjustment factor δ_s that is affected by user context. Then the user perceived quality property values of a service s under specific context C is defined as follows.

$$Q_s(C)=<q_1,q_2,q_3>,q_i=N(\mu,\sigma^2)+\delta_s(C). \tag{9}$$

In order to simulate the impact of the context on the quality properties of a service, we divide the services set S into two subset: S_1, S_2 where $S_1 \cap S_2 = \emptyset$, and divide the user context space C^* into two subset: C_1^*, C_2^* where $C_1^* \cap C_2^* = \emptyset$, then set the context adjustment factor δ_s as follows.

$$\delta_s(C) = \begin{cases} -0.2, if\, s \in S_1 \wedge C \in C_1^*. \\ 0.2,\ if\, s \in S_1 \wedge C \in C_2^*. \\ 0.2, if\, s \in S_2 \wedge C \in C_1^*. \\ -0.2, if\, s \in S_2 \wedge C \in C_2^*. \end{cases} \tag{10}$$

The above formula implies that the services in S_1 will the performance better under the contexts in C_1^* than under the contexts in C_2^*, and services in S_2 is just the opposite.

Note that the calculated result of q_i according to the equation 9 and 10 may be out of the range 0 to 1, we just set 1 to result values greater than 1 and set 0 to result values less than 0. To simulate the dynamic feature of Web services, each service is set to have a probability of randomly changing its quality properties, and this probability is set to 0.2.

5.2 Simulation Results

At the beginning of the simulation, the accuracy of all approaches is low since few feedbacks are obtained. As the simulation advanced, more feedbacks are reported and used to assess the trustworthiness of Web services. Fig.4 shows the comparison between simulation results using $WSTA_{UO}$ and $WSTA_{IUP}$. $WSTA_{UO}$ maintains the accuracy of about 0.7 while $WSTA_{IUP}$ only 0.3. $WSTA_{IUP}$ suffers from low accuracy because the ignorance of the difference among user preferences. Fig.5 shows the comparison between the simulation results using $WSTA_{UO}$ and $WSTA_{IC}$, $WSTA_{IC}$ gains poor accuracy about 0.2 for ignoring the difference among user contexts.

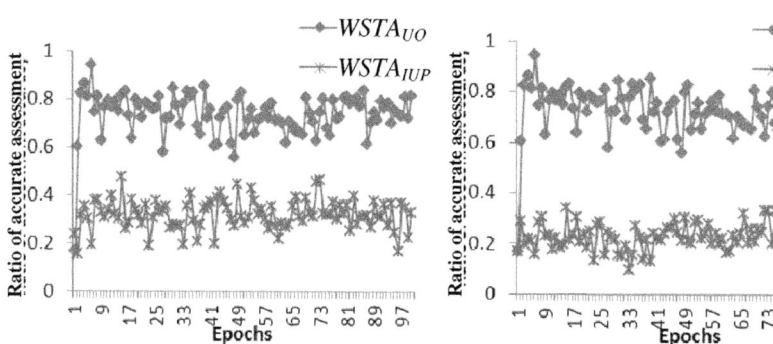

Fig. 4. Simulation results of $WSTA_{UO}$ and $WSTA_{IUP}$

Fig. 5. Simulation results of $WSTA_{UO}$ and $WSTA_{IC}$

Fig. 6shows the comparison between the simulation results using $WSTA_{UO}$ and $WSTA_{IT}$, the accuracy of $WSTA_{IT}$ is same as $WSTA_{UO}$ initially. However, as simulation progress, some services change their quality properties values randomly. Without taking the timeliness of feedbacks into consideration, $WSTA_{IT}$ is misled by outdated feedbacks and its accuracy decreases sharply with time. Fig. 7 shows the comparison between simulation result using $WSTA_{UO}$ and $WSTA_{OR}$. By collecting overall ratings and treating them equally, $WSTA_{OR}$ gets poor accuracy about 0.2.

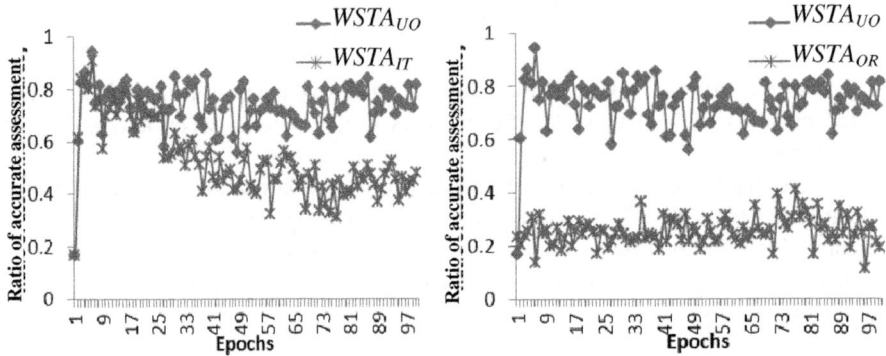

Fig. 6. Simulation results of $WSTA_{UO}$ and $WSTA_{IT}$

Fig. 7. Simulation results of $WSTA_{UO}$ and $WSTA_{OR}$

6   Conclusion

We have presented a user oriented approach to assessing Web service trustworthiness. Different from other approaches, this approach runs the assessment from the perception of users, taking account of the context sensitivity and dynamic feature of service quality properties as well as the difference among user preferences.

A prototype of our approach is implemented on the basis of a Web service repository and search engine, namely ServiceXchange. Users can discover services that meet functional requirements with ServiceXchange, and then our proposed approach can be used to assess the trustworthiness of the Web services.

The simulation results show that our approach has a significant accuracy advantage over other approaches that treat feedbacks equally and ignore the difference among user preferences.

For future work, we plan to release ServiceXchange combining with our trustworthiness assessment approach to public and collect real-world feedbacks to evaluate our approach. Moreover, we will design an algorithm to identity malicious users that report fake feedbacks.

References

1. Wang, H., Yin, G.: Trustworthy software evolution in the Internet era. Communications of the CCF 6(2) (2010) (in Chinese)
2. Mei, H., Cao, D.: Trustworthiness of software: Challenges from Internet. Communications of the CCF 6(2) (2010) (in Chinese)

3. Shao, L., Zhang, J., Xie, T., Zhang, L., Xie, B., Mei, H.: User-Perceived Service Availability: A Metric and an Estimation Approach. In: Proceedings of IEEE International Conference on Web Services, pp. 647–654. IEEE Computer Society, Los Angeles (2009)

4. Zhang, J., Xu, D.: A Mobile Agent-Supported Web Services Testing Platform. In: Proceedings of the 2008 IEEE/IFIP International Conference on Embedded and Ubiquitous Computing, vol. 2, pp. 637–644. IEEE Computer Society, Washington (2008)

5. Bai, X., Dong, W., Tsai, W.-T., Chen, Y.: WSDL-Based Automatic Test Case Generation for Web Services Testing. In: Proceedings of IEEE International Workshop on Service-Oriented System Engineering, pp. 215–220. IEEE Computer Society, Los Alamitos (2005)

6. Nepal, S., Malik, Z., Bouguettaya, A.: Reputation Propagation in Composite Services. In: Proceedings of the 2009 IEEE International Conference on Web Services, pp. 295–302. IEEE Computer Society, Washington (2009)

7. Malik, Z., Bouguettaya, A.: Reputation Bootstrapping for Trust Establishment among Web Services. IEEE Internet Computing 13(1), 40–47 (2009)

8. Malik, Z., Bouguettaya, A.: Evaluating Rater Credibility for Reputation Assessment of Web Services. In: Benatallah, B., Casati, F., Georgakopoulos, D., Bartolini, C., Sadiq, W., Godart, C. (eds.) WISE 2007. LNCS, vol. 4831, pp. 38–49. Springer, Heidelberg (2007)

9. ServiceXchange, http://www.servicexchange.cn

10. Jøsang, A., Ismail, R.: The Beta Reputation System. In: Proceedings of the 15th Bled Electronic Commerce Conference, Bled, Slovenia (2002)

11. Gupta, M., Judge, P., Ammar, M.: A reputation system for peer-to-peer networks. In: ACM 13th International Workshop on Network and Operating Systems Support for Digital Audio and Video, Monterey, CA (2003)

12. Wang, Y., Vassileva, J.: Trust and Reputation Model in Peer-to-Peer Networks. In: Proceedings of IEEE Conference on P2P Computing, Linkoeping, Sweden (September 2003)

Improving the Trustworthiness of Service QoS Information in Service-Based Systems

Stephen S. Yau, Jing Huang, and Yin Yin

Information Assurance Center, and
School of Computing, Informatics, and Decision System Engineering
Arizona State University
Tempe, AZ 85287-8809, USA
{yau,Jing.Huang.5,yin.yin}@asu.edu

Abstract. Service-oriented architecture facilitates rapid development and management of large-scale distributed service-based systems (SBS), where new workflows are composed of available services. Besides services' capabilities, the qualities of services (QoS) also need to be considered in service composition in order to have high-quality workflows. The QoS profiles of services provided by their service providers may be inaccurate. In this paper, an approach is presented to improving the trustworthiness of the QoS information of services to facilitate the development of high-quality workflows in SBS. Our approach is based on identifying the deviation between the QoS profiles of the services claimed by their service providers and the QoS profiles determined by monitors and service user feedbacks. An example is given to illustrate the approach.

Keywords: quality of service (QoS), service QoS, improving trustworthiness, high-quality workflow, service-based system.

1 Introduction

To facilitate the development and management of large-scale distributed applications, service-oriented architecture (SOA) [1] has been adopted for many large-scale distributed applications, including e-commerce, health care, transportation, homeland security and military [2]. Systems developed based on SOA are called *service-based systems (SBS)*. The basic components of SBS are individual services, each of which provides certain capabilities. The workflow for implementing an application is composed of services whose dependency and communication relations are specified in the workflow. With SOA, the development of application systems is to develop workflows composed of available services, instead of from scratch. During workflow composition, SBS developers first need to identify the capabilities required by the application systems, search for available services providing such capabilities, and use them to compose the workflows.

In this development process, besides services' capabilities, the qualities of services (QoS), like throughput, completion time, accuracy and security protection, also need to be considered in service composition in order to have high-quality workflows.

B. Xie et al. (Eds.): ATC 2010, LNCS 6407, pp. 208–218, 2010.

Service-level agreement (SLA) [3] and protection-level agreement (PLA) [4, 5] are provided by service providers to claim their services' QoS in service contracts. In this paper, we will present an approach to improving the trustworthiness of information on the service QoS to facilitate the development of high-quality workflows in SBS. In this approach, service providers provide the information on their services' QoS profiles along with the services they provide. SBS developers use the QoS profiles to select services among the available services providing the needed functionality. Service providers may update the QoS profile of a service when there are changes in the software or underlying hardware supporting the service. We consider in the paper that the QoS profile of each service claimed by its service provider will include both performance and security.

However, the QoS profiles provided by service providers may be questionable since service providers may exaggerate the QoS profiles of their services to attract the interests of developers in using their services. Hence, the developers need to have more trustworthy QoS profiles of the services to make good decisions on selecting the services. Our approach will generate *more trustworthy QoS profiles* (*MTQP*) for services in service-based systems by identifying the deviation of service providers' claimed QoS profiles from the measured QoS profiles through the use of service monitors and service user feedbacks.

In the rest of the paper, we will first discuss the current state of the art on trust evaluation for information systems. In Section 3, we will introduce our overall approach, and the details of certain major steps are elaborated in Sections 4 to 7. An example to illustrate our approach will be given in Section 8. In Section 9, we will discuss future work needed for improving our approach.

2 Current State of the Art

Trust is fuzzy and dynamic in nature, and is a subjective notion describing the degree of belief about a particular entity's behavior [6, 7]. DeFigueiredo, et al., [8] investigated the human's intuitive understanding of trust to better understand the concept of trust in the cyber domain. The trustworthiness of information has been studied in social networking, where peers collaborate together to create and share information [9-12]. The trustworthiness of the information has been evaluated based on the information's quality, the credibility on the information quality, and the pertinence [13, 14].

The measurement of trustworthiness of computer systems and networks has been considered at three levels: infrastructure, understanding, and policy [15]. The infrastructure level emphasizes the trustworthiness of the underlying system, i.e. hardware, software and the network. Remote attestation mechanism defined by Trusted Computing Group (TCG) [16] can provide users with more confidence in a remote cyber system environment. WS-Attestation [5] leverages TCG technologies in Web Services framework. At the understanding level, reputation systems are widely adopted to assist trust establishment [17-20]. While trust is a directional pairwise relationship, reputation is distilled about the information available from the individual's past behavior reported by those having interacted with it. For those agents who do not have direct interactions before, reputation is very important information to help them make trust decisions. To ensure the effectiveness of reputation evaluation mechanisms, dishonest feedback needs to be deleted. Statistical techniques are widely used to detect dishonest feedback, often with a presumed distribution of the collected ratings. Feedback may be screened out or given a weight based on their deviations from the majority opinion [20-22]. Such methods assume that a majority of the users are honest. Vu, et al. [23] used trust/distrust propagation and clustering techniques in assigning the weights to user reports. They made some assumptions on the properties of the service users and distribution of user ratings in the system. The efficiency of their algorithms is not clear. Jurca presented a novel application of reputation systems in SBS [24]. His mechanism targeted economic applications with attackers who aim at making money, but is fragile in hostile environments, where money is not a concern for the attackers. For critical systems, the attackers may try to sabotage the normal functioning of the system at any cost.

3 Our Approach

In this section, we will present the overview of our approach, including the participating entities and their relations of the SBS system and the mechanisms for generating *MTQP* of services in the SBS.

In our SBS with trust and reputation management, there are three types of entities: *service providers*, *service users* and the *administration*. The administration includes all administrative components, such as the *service directories*, *monitors* and *proxies*. Both service providers and service users can be benign or malicious. Therefore, in our approach, we will only trust the administrative components which manage their reputation information, but do not fully trust service providers or users.

Service providers register their services with functionality meta data, claimed QoS and the access point of each of their services at service directories. Services should behave consistently with the registered information, regardless of the invoker, but their QoS may fluctuate around a stable value. Malicious service providers cheat on the QoS or even functional properties of their services either for economic benefits or for impeding system functionality, i.e. the experiences of service users. Some services are composed of other services in the SBS, and we call them *composite services*. Service S_A is called a *partner service* of service S_B if S_A has invoked S_B in any composite service or workflows. There are two types of service users: the end users and the partner services. Service monitors [25-30] are used to remotely monitor and report service QoS. Our approach does not require any specific proportion of services being monitored by a trusted monitor. Therefore, we have two categories of services in the SBS: those with a monitor, and those without. Fig. 1 shows an example of SBS with six services. Assume that services S_3, S_4 and S_5 are provided by the same service provider. The solid arrowheads in the figure represent a workflow in the SBS. The dashed arrowhead from service S_1' to S_2 indicates that S_1' is an alternate of service S_1 because they provide the same functionality. The services placed in a green rectangle are currently monitored by the same service monitor.

Service monitors periodically report the observed QoS of the services they are monitoring. Service users report the observed QoS of the services when they have used them. Since the QoS observations on delay, throughput, etc. need to be made automatically, we assume that the administration makes the observing and reporting code available for the users to submit feedback automatically. However, malicious users may tamper the reporting code and report dishonest QoS feedback for the services. Service proxies, which will be explained in Section 4, may capture some of the dishonest user feedback. Dishonest feedback and feedback from users who have submitted certain amount of dishonest feedback in the past will be deleted.

Using the information collected from monitors and users, we calculate two types of trust values for each service: *Mutual Trust Value (MTV) and Individual Trust Value (ITV)*. They reflect the accumulated reputation of the service provider in providing accurate QoS information for the service. MTV represents the accuracy of a service's QoS profile from the point of view of one of its users. It is based only on the user's experience and only represents the user's opinion. ITV represents the accuracy of an individual service's QoS profile considering its interactions with all users. It is either generated with the information from the monitor or aggregated from all its users' feedbacks. These two types of trust values are generated from two types of information sources and reflect the trustworthiness of the QoS profile from a local view or a holistic view. In our approach, the *ITV* and *MTV* interact and affect each other. We evaluate a service's *MTV* from each of its users through feedbacks from that user. If the service is monitored by a monitor, we compute its *ITV* using the monitor's reports; otherwise, we compute its *ITV* by aggregating all the *MTVs* from all users. The trust values are applied on the latest claimed QoS profile of the service to generate *MTQP* for a service.

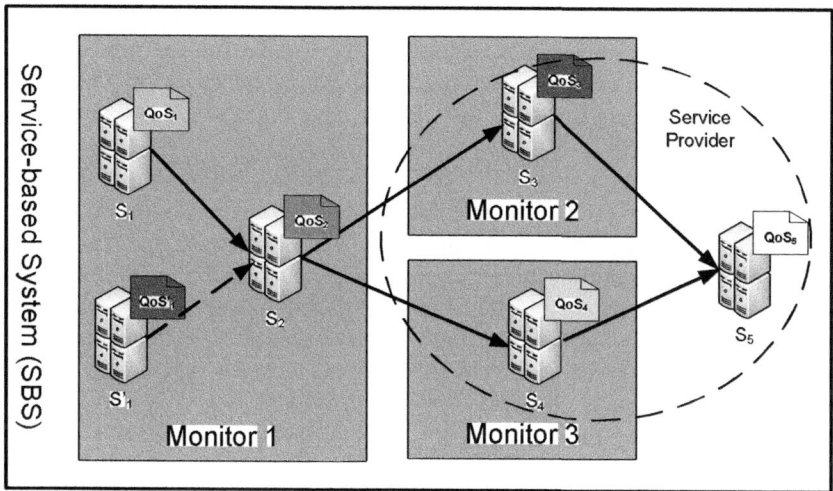

Fig. 1. An example SBS with service monitors

Our approach can be summarized in the following four steps. The operations in Step 1)-3) are performed whenever there is new input information. Step 4) is performed when *MTQP* of a service is needed for service selection. Step 1) receives input from the service monitors and service users; the other steps use the output generated by the previous step.

1) Collect QoS feedback from service monitors and service users.
2) Filter dishonest user feedback for service proxies.
3) Calculate two types of trust values for each service: *MTV* and *ITV*.
4) When *MTQP* of a service is needed for service selection, it is computed using the latest claimed QoS profile of the service and either its *ITV* or one of its *MTV*.

Step 2) will be explained in Section 4. Sections 5 and 6 will give the details of Step 3) and Section 7 will elaborate Step 4).

4   Detection of Dishonest Feedback Using Service Proxies

Service proxies are special types of services hosted by the administration. They are registered in the service directory as regular third party services and are not recognizable to service users. However, a service proxy does not hold particular functionalities itself, but acts as a proxy between the user and another service. It provides the same interfaces as the third service, and when invoked, it will invoke that service to fulfill the functionality instead. However, the service users do not know how the service proxy provides the requested functionality, and will submit QoS feedback for the service proxy.

The purpose of using service proxies is to detect dishonest feedback without much overhead. When a user invokes a service proxy, it provides the opportunity to collect both the QoS of a service observed by the administration and the feedback submitted by the user for the service proxy. The difference between them should not exceed the small communication overhead between the user and the service proxy, plus some possible random noise. A large difference between them indicates dishonest feedback from the service user. The specific threshold is determined based on the QoS aspect and application scenario.

To allow dynamic binding in SBS, services with the same or similar functionality usually have similar interface. The administration can host one service proxy for each group of such services, and periodically change the service it invokes among the group of services without much development and configuration overhead. Since service proxies do not perform functionalities themselves, developing and hosting service proxies do not consume much effort and system resources. Therefore, it does not increase the system complexity much although the number of service proxies needed may grow with the number of types of services in the SBS.

It is noted that using service proxies to detect dishonest users is not based on any assumptions on the distribution of collected feedback or the percentage of dishonest users among all users.

5   Generation of Mutual Trust Value *(MTV)*

Because services' qualities are manifold, we define the *QoS profile of a service* as a vector with *n* elements, each of which represents the QoS of the service on one of the n QoS aspects, such as accuracy, delay, and security. For a service *S*, let the QoS profile of the given service *S* provided or claimed by its service provider be denoted by

$$cQoS = <cQ_1, cQ_2, ..., cQ_n>, \tag{1}$$

where cQ_i is the *ith* QoS aspect provided by the service provider, $i = 1, 2, ..., n,$. Let the QoS profile based on the feedback of user U_j of S be denoted by

$$fQoS_j = <fQ_{1j}, fQ_{2j}, ..., fQ_{nj}>, \tag{2}$$

where fQ_i is the *ith* QoS based on the feedback of the user, $i = 1, 2, ..., n,$.

The mutual trust value (*MTV*) of S from user U_j is denoted by

$$MTV_j = <mtv_{1j}, mtv_{2j}, ..., mtv_{nj}>, \tag{3}$$

where mtv_{ij} is given by

$$mtv_{ij} = F_{tl} (fQ_{ij} - cQ_i), \tag{4}$$

and the function F_{tl} satisfies the following three properties.

- **The value of mtv_{ij} is in the range (-1, 1).** The QoS fQ_i based on the feedback of partner service S_j may be better or worse than cQ_i. If fQ_i is as good as cQ_i, mtv_{ij} is equal to 0. A negative mtv_{ij} means that the value of fQ_i is smaller than that of cQ_i, and a positive mtv_{ij} means larger.
- **For a constant cQ_i, the value of mtv_{ij} increases as fQ_i increases.** A larger QoS in the feedback will lead to a larger mtv_{ij}.
- **For a constant cQ_i, the value of mtv_{ij} increases faster as $|fQ_i - cQ_i|$ increases, until asymptotically approaching the upper or lower bound.** When fQ_i is closer to cQ_i, the value of mtv_{ij} is insensitive to the difference $|fQ_i - cQ_i|$. This property is to model the normal variation of quality. First, it is difficult for service providers to accurately specify their services' QoS, which is usually an estimation based on historical data. Second, services' QoS is not stable and will vary in a small scale. On the other hand, the value of mtv_{ij} will increase faster as the award or penalty for better or worse fQ_i.

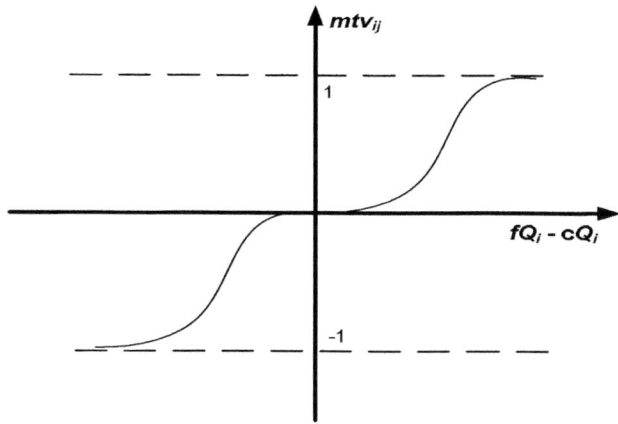

Fig. 2. The variation of mtv_{ij} based on $fQ_i - cQ_i$

Based on the above three properties, mtv_{ij} can be expressed in Fig. 2 and (5).

$$F_{tl}(x) = \frac{2}{1+\exp(-x/\mu)} - 1 \qquad (5)$$

where μ is a parameter which depends upon the range of a certain QoS aspect. This parameter can be used to tune the growing speed of the curve.

6   Generation of Individual Trust Value (ITV)

6.1   Generation of ITV with Monitors

For a service S with a monitor, the QoS profile reported by its monitor is denoted by

$$mQoS = <mQ_1, mQ_2, ..., mQ_n>, \qquad (6)$$

where mQ_i is the ith QoS reported by the monitor, $i = 1, 2, ..., n,$. The ITV of S is denoted by

$$ITV = <itv_1, itv_2, ..., itv_n>, \qquad (7)$$

where itv_i is given by

$$itv_i = F_{tl}(mQ_i - cQ_i), \qquad (8)$$

where the function F_{tl} was discussed in Section 5.

6.2   Generation of ITV without Monitors

When there is no monitor monitoring the service S, we evaluate the service's ITV using all its MTVs between the service and its users.

Assume that service S has interacted with m ($m \geq 1$) users and each of them may have a different MTV about the trustworthiness of S's claimed QoS profile based on their own experiences. The ITV of S is denoted by

$$ITV = <itv_1, itv_2, ..., itv_n>, \qquad (9)$$

where itv_i is given by

$$itv_i = F_{ag}(mtv_{i1}, mtv_{i2}, ..., mtv_{im}), \qquad (10)$$

where F_{ag} depends on mtv_{ij}'s distribution. For example, if mtv_{ij} has the uniform distribution, the simple average function is a good candidate for F_{mtv}. If mtv_{ij} has normal distribution, F_{mtv} should give higher weights for mtv_{ij} close to the average of the means of all mtv_{ij}. The time duration since the interaction between the service and its user that produces mtv_{ij} can also be used as its weighting factor.

7   Generation of MTQP of Services

At the time of service selection, a service's MTQP can be derived from its latest claimed QoS profile and either its ITV or its MTV. We consider the following two types of applications. In the first application type, the QoS of a service is independently of the partner services it interacts with, and we use the service's *ITV* and its latest QoS profile claimed by its provider to generate its *MTQP*.

The *MTQP* of *S* can be computed as follows:

$$tQoS = <tQ_1, tQ_2, ..., tQ_n>$$

$$= <F_{t2}(cQ_1, itv_1), F_{t2}(cQ_2, itv_2) ..., F_{t2}(cQ_n, itv_n)> \quad (11)$$

where tQ_i is the *ith* QoS generated by our approach, and the function F_{t2} inverses the result of function F_{t1} in (5), and is given by

$$F_{t2}(x, y) = x - \mu \cdot \log_e\left(\frac{1-y}{1+y}\right). \quad (12)$$

In the second application type, the QoS of a service is particularly sensitive to its partner service. In this case, we use the service's *MTV* to estimate its QoS profile instead of *ITV* because the *MTQP* of a service cannot be determined before choosing its partner service. If *S* is expected to be invoked by service S_j, we will use the *MTV* of *S* from S_j and the latest claimed QoS profile of *S* to generate its *MTQP*.

The *MTQP* of *S* can be computed as follows:

$$tQoS = <tQ_1, tQ_2, ..., tQ_n>$$

$$= <F_{t2}(Q_1, mtv_{1j}), F_{t2}(Q_2, mtv_{2j}) ..., F_{t2}(Q_n, mtv_{nj})>. \quad (13)$$

8   An Example

Consider the example *SBS* given in Fig. 1, which has 6 services and 5 are monitored by monitors. In this example, we will consider only one QoS aspect, the completion time, because other QoS aspects can be handled similarly. We will generate the *MTQP*s of the six services, for the application type where services' QoS is independent of their partner services for composing workflows. Hence, we compute the *ITVs* for all the services.

The completion time of these services claimed by their service providers and reported by their monitors and partner services is given in Table 1.

Table 1. Computation results of the example

Service	S_1	S_1'	S_2	S_3	S_4	S_5
Claimed completion time	0.25	0.40	0.15	0.20	0.35	0.25
Monitored completion time	0.40	0.35	0.20	0.30	0.30	
User feedback						0.15, 0.20
ITV	0.64	-0.25	0.25	0.46	-0.25	-0.36
More trustworthy completion time	0.40	0.35	0.20	0.30	0.30	0.18

• **Generating *ITVs* for services monitored by service monitors.** First, we set the parameter   = 0.10, assuming that a difference of 1 second or more between the claimed and actual completion time is considered unacceptable. Using (5), we obtain the *ITV* of S_1

$$ITV_1 = F_{t1}\,(0.4\text{-}0.25) = \frac{2}{1+\exp\left(-\frac{(0.4-0.25)}{0.1}\right)} - 1 = 0.64 \tag{14}$$

Similarly, we find the *ITVs* of S_1 to S_4, which are also included in Table 1. Note that the negative trust values indicate worse QoS for the completion time because smaller completion time is more desirable.

• **Generating *ITVs* for services not monitored by service monitors.** For service S_5, assume that S_3 and S_4 have interacted with S_5 and provided their feedback on its completion time as 0.15 and 0.20, respectively. Using (5) we obtain the *MTVs* of S_3 to S_5 and S_4 to S_5 -0.46 and -0.25, respectively. We choose the average *MTV* as the service's *ITV*, which is -0.36.

• **Generating *MTQPs*.** The more trustworthy completion time of S_1 is computed using (13) and is given below:

$$F_{t2}\,(0.25, 0.64) = 0.25 - 0.1 \times \log_e\!\left(\frac{2}{0.64+1} - 1\right) = 0.4. \tag{15}$$

Note that the more trustworthy completion time of all the services, except S_5, is the same as the monitored completion time. However, if their service providers have updated the QoS profiles to claim a different completion time, the more trustworthy completion time will be different from the monitored value, but maintains the same *ITV* with regard to the new QoS profile, until new data is collected by the monitors and integrated in the *ITVs*.

Assume that S_2 and S_5 provide the same functionality. S_2 has shorter completion time based on the QoS profiles provided by their service providers, but the result of our approach indicates that S_5 is likely to have a shorter completion time, and hence S_5 is more desirable.

9   Discussions

In this paper, we have presented an approach to improving the trustworthiness of service QoS profiles in SBS to facilitate the development of high-quality workflows. In our approach, we assume that some services in the SBS are monitored by service monitors, but do not require that all the services are monitored. We will investigate how the proportion of monitored services and different ways of choosing services to be monitored affect the effectiveness of our approach.

Since service proxies cannot detect all the dishonest feedback submitted by service users, we will study the detection of dishonest feedback through inconsistencies between the QoS feedback of a composite service and that of its component services.

In the future, we will also evaluate the effectiveness of the more trustworthy QoS profiles and the techniques for detecting dishonest feedback through simulation and experiments.

Acknowledgment

This work reported here is sponsored by National Science Foundation under Grant No. CCF-0725340. The authors would like to thank Dazhi Huang of Arizona State University for many valuable discussions of this research.

References

1. IEEE Service-Oriented Architecture Standards,
   http://www.soa-standards.org/
2. Bartoletti, M., Degano, P., Ferrari, G.L.: Enforcing Secure Service Composition. In: Proc. of 18th IEEE Computer Security Foundations Workshop (CSFW), pp. 211–223 (2005)
3. Rajan, H., Hosamani, M.: Tisa: Towards Trustworthy Services in a Service-Oriented Architecture. In: IEEE Trans. on Services Computing, vol. 1(4), pp. 201–213 (2008)
4. Alam, M., Zhang, X., Nauman, M., Ali, T.: Behavioral Attestation for Web Services (BA4WS). In: Proc. of 2008 ACM Workshop on Secure Web Services, pp. 21–28 (2008)
5. Yoshihama, S., Ebringer, T., Nakamura, M., Munetoh, S., Maruyama, H.: WS-Attestation: Efficient and Fine-Grained Remote Attestation on Web Services. In: Proc. of 2005 IEEE Int'l Conf. on Web Services, pp. 750–757 (2005)
6. Chang, E.J., Hussain, F.K., Dillon, T.S.: Fuzzy Nature of Trust and Dynamic Trust Modeling in Service Oriented Environment. In: Proc. of 2005 Workshop on Secure Web Services, pp. 75–83 (2005)
7. Cook, K.S. (ed.): Trust in Society, New York. Russell Sage Foundation Series on Trust, vol. 2 (2003)
8. DeFigueiredo, D.B., Barr, E.T., Wu, S.F.: Trust Is in the Eye of the Beholder. In: Proc. of Int'l Conf. on Computational Science and Engineering, pp. 100–108 (2009)
9. Thuraisingham, B. M.: Trust Management in a Distributed Environment. In: Proc. of Annual IEEE Computer Software and Applications Conf., pp. 561—562 (2005)
10. Thuraisingham, B.M.: Assured Information Sharing between Trustworthy, Semi-trustworthy and Untrustworthy Coalition Partners. In: Proc. of the 4th Int'l Symp. on Info., Computer, and Comm. Security, Keynote (2009)
11. Hamlen, K.W., Thuraisingham, B.M.: Secure Peer-to-peer Networks for Trusted Collaboration. In: Proc. of Int'l Conf. on Collaborative Computing: Networking, Applications and Worksharing, pp. 58–63 (2007)
12. Layfield, R., Kantarcioglu, M., Thuraisingham, B.M.: Incentive and Trust Issues in Assured Information Sharing. In: Proc. of Int'l Conf. on Collaborative Computing: Networking, Applications and Worksharing, pp. 113–125 (2008)
13. Moturu, S.T., Yang, J., Liu, H.: Quantifying Utility and Trustworthiness for Advice Shared on Online Social Media. In: Proc. of Symp. on Social Intelligence and Networking, IEEE Int'l Conf. on Social Computing (2009)
14. Moturu, S.T., Liu, H.: Evaluating the Trustworthiness of Wikipedia Articles through Quality and Credibility. In: Proc. of 5th Int'l Symp. on Wikis and Open Collaboration (2009)
15. Yang, S.J.H., Hsieh, J.S.F., Lan, B.C.W., Chung, J.-Y.: Composition and Evaluation of Trustworthy Web Services. Int'l J. of Web and Grid Services 2(1), 5–24 (2006)
16. Trusted Computing Group Specification Architecture Overview, Revision 1.2,
   https://www.trustedcomputinggroup.org/downloads/TCG_1_0_
   Architecture_Overview.pdf

17. Emekci, F., Sahin, O.D., Agrawal, D., Abbadi, A.E.: A Peer-to-Peer Framework for Web Service Discovery with Ranking. In: Proc. of IEEE Int'l Conf. on Web Services, pp. 192–199 (2004)
18. Kalepu, S., Krishnaswamy, S., Loke, S.W.: Reputation = F(User Ranking, Compliance, Verity). In: Proc. of IEEE Int'l Conf. on Web Services, pp. 200–207 (2004)
19. Zeng, L., Benatallah, B., Dumas, M., Kalagnanam, J., Sheng, Q.Z.: Web Engineering: Quality Driven Web Service Composition. In: Proc. of Int'l World Wide Web Conf., pp. 411–421 (2003)
20. Malik, Z., Bouguettaya, A.: RATEWeb: Reputation Assessment for Trust Establishment among Web services. The VLDB J. 18(4), 885–911 (2009)
21. Dellarocas, C.: Immunizing Online Reputation Reporting Systems against Unfair Ratings and Discriminatory Behavior. In: Proc. of 2nd ACM Conf. on Electronic Commerce, pp. 150–157 (2000)
22. Whitby, A., Josang, A., Indulska, J.: Filtering Out Unfair Ratings in Bayesian Reputation Systems. The Icfain J. of Management Research 4(2), 48–64 (2005)
23. Vu, L.-H., Hauswirth, M., Aberer, K.: QoS-based Service Selection and Ranking with Trust and Reputation Management. In: Meersman, R., Tari, Z. (eds.) OTM 2005. LNCS, vol. 3760, pp. 466–483. Springer, Heidelberg (2005)
24. Jurca, R.: Truthful reputation mechanisms for online systems. PhD dissertation, Ecole Polytechnique Fédérale de Lausanne (EPFL), Lausanne, Switzerland (2007)
25. Yau, S.S., Ye, N., Sarjoughian, H., Huang, D.: Developing Service-Based Software Systems with QoS Monitoring and Adaptation. In: Proc. of 12th Int'l Workshop on Future Trends of Distributed Computing Systems, pp. 74–80 (2008)
26. Yau, S.S., Yin, Y., An, H.G.: An Adaptive Model for Tradeoff between Service Performance and Security in Service-Based Environments. In: Proc. of Int'l Conf. on Web Services, pp. 287–294 (2009)
27. Yau, S.S., Ye, N., Sarjoughian, H., Huang, D., Roontiva, A., Baydogan, M., Muqsith, M.: Towards Development of Adaptive Service-Based Software Systems. IEEE Trans. on Services Computing 99, 247–260 (2009)
28. Raimondi, F., Skene, J., Emmerich, W.: Efficient Online Monitoring of Web-Service SLAs. In: Proc. of the 16th ACM SIGSOFT Int'l Symp. on Foundations of Software Engineering (2008)
29. Ezenwoye, O., Sadjadi, S.M.: RobustBPEL2: Transparent Autonomization in Business Processes through Dynamic Proxies. In: Proc. of the 8th Int'l Symp. on Autonomous Decentralized Systems (2007)
30. Moser, O., Rosenberg, F., Dustdar, S.: Non-Intrusive Monitoring and Service Adaptation for WS-BPEL. In: Proc. of the 17th Int'l Conf. on World Wide Web (2008)

Using ELECTRE TRI Outranking Method to Evaluate Trustworthy Software

Gang Lu, Huaimin Wang, and Xiaoguang Mao

Computer School, National University of Defense Technology,
410073 ChangSha, China
lugang@263.net

Abstract. Trustworthy software evaluation is taken as the multi-criteria decision aiding process in this paper. The use of ELECTRE TRI method for evaluating software trustworthiness is presented. Software under evaluation is compared with some predefined norms and is assigned to one of trust levels. The entire evaluating process is described, including definition of problem situation and formulation, determination of the model and its parameters, and the application of the model. A metric for trustworthiness and an attributes weighting method are also presented. Some practical considerations are discussed in the final part of the paper.

Keywords: trustworthy software, evaluation, models, ELECTRE TRI method, MCDA.

1 Introduction

In the past few years there has been increased in the demand for more trustworthy software and services to cope with the growing scale and complexity of computing systems. Evaluating trustworthiness is getting more important in research on trustworthy software and services. Generally, software trustworthiness is viewed as a composite attribute; it's a multidimensional concept [1][2][3]. A lot of researches on trustworthiness evaluation focus on a single or a few features, and little attention is paid to evaluating it in a comprehensive way.

During our study on trustworthy resources management on internet, we found that if the potential users lack an easy, effective, and trustworthy process to justify the software trustworthiness, they will be confronted with considerable complexity in making a decision on software selection. Rating the software trustworthiness can not only reduce the cognitive effort required from the users in evaluating phase, but also guide the developing projects to the direction of trustworthiness evolution.

Since software trustworthiness is a multidimensional concept, the Multicriteria Decision Aid (MCDA) approach is adopted as a powerful tool taking several concerns into account to achieve a compromise evaluation solution. Roy distinguished four types of MCDA problems [4]:

1. Choice problematic $P.\alpha$: help choose a best alternative;
2. Sorting problematic $P.\beta$: help sort actions according some predefined norms;

B. Xie et al. (Eds.): ATC 2010, LNCS 6407, pp. 219–227, 2010.

3. Ranking Problematic $P.\gamma$: help rank alternatives with partial order;
4. Description Problematic $P.\delta$: help describe alternatives in a formalized way.

$P.\alpha$ and $P.\gamma$ base their results on the pairwise comparisons of alternatives, but in $P.\beta$ each alternative is considered independently from others and the result only depends on the intrinsic values of the alternative and the predefined norms. Evaluating and selecting software packages is normally $P.\alpha$ or $P.\gamma$ for acquisition managers. However, from the perspective of our management on trustworthy resources, rating software trustworthiness is $P.\beta$.

Based on their aggregation procedures, MCDA methods are classified into two categories: compensatory and noncompensatory. The weighted average sum (WAS) aggregation technique used in everyday evaluations is compensatory, so are some other techniques based on multi-attribute utility theory. ELECTRE TRI outranking method [5][6] is a noncompensatory MCDA method and suitable for the features of our trustworthiness evaluation:

1. dimensions of trustworthiness are not generally considered to compensate each other;
2. the measurements of trustworthiness dimensions may be imprecise, and/or uncertain, and/or inaccurate.

In addition, software submission mode on the internet is open for every supplier in our study. The supplier often does not present sufficient evidences for proving that the software can be justified trustworthy, and providing each software package with some specific evaluators was neither practical nor necessary. Therefore, the automation or less labor during the evaluation is desired.

2   Software Trustworthiness Evaluation

For nearly 30 years, numerous models and methodologies have been developed for evaluating and selecting software [7][8]. These models and methodologies focus on different features of software and evaluation process to meet the needs of different motivations and purposes of evaluation. Morisio and Tsoukias design a methodology to evaluate software products in a formal and rigorous way, namely Iusware, which is based on the MCDA approach and encompasses the activities during a software product evaluation process [9]. Stamelos and Tsoukias provide a partial list of software evaluation problem situations based on Mosirio's work [10]. Following the terminology defined in [9][10], we describe the software trustworthiness evaluation process (STEP) as:

1. define problem situation of trustworthiness evaluation;
2. define problem formulation;
3. determine evaluation model and its parameters;
4. apply evaluation model.

The details of the STEP are presented below.

2.1 Problem Situation and Problem Formulation

Problem Situation (PS) refers to intrinsic structure and external context of problem. Our PS for trustworthiness evaluation can be defined as a triple $< A_{PS}, O_{PS}, RS >$ where:

  A_{PS} is the set of actors involved, including:
  - the software suppliers;
  - the trustworthy resources manager;
  - the users(evaluating users and potential users);
  - the evaluator.
  O_{PS} is the set of objects introduced by each actor in A_{PS}, including:
  - the software itself;
  - the quantity and satisfaction of the users;
  - the competence and stability of the develop team;
  - the evidences for software trustworthiness.
  RS is the set of resources allocated by each actor in A_{PS} for each object in O_{PS}, including:
  - knowledge of trustworthiness;
  - time constraint, the available time was short after new evidence was arrived;
  - human resource constraint, less management was expected.

A Problem Formulation (PF) is a formal presentation of the concerns expressed in the above PS. Different PF can be defined for different actor in PS. Our PF for the evaluator can be defined as a triple $\Gamma =< A_\Gamma, V_\Gamma, \Pi_\Gamma >$ where:
  A_Γ is the set of software which will be evaluated;
  V_Γ is the set of the dimensions of trustworthiness (According to the definition in Trustie project [11], the dimensions are availability, reliability, security, real time, maintainability, and survivability);
  Π_Γ is a problem statement defining what form of the final result is expected. It is an assignment for software evaluated to some predefined trust levels in our case, in other words, it is $P.\beta$ in terms of Joy's problem classification.
  The set of trustworthiness dimensions may differ from one domain to another. Dimensions we used here coincide with the dimensions listed in Trustie. However, the evaluation methodology does not depend on a specific division of trustworthiness.

2.2 Evaluation Model

The evaluation model we build uses ELECTRE TRI method to evaluate trustworthiness, consisting of a 7-tuple $< A^*, D, M, E, G, U, R >$ where:
  - A^* are the alternatives selected from A_Γ, let $A^* = A_\Gamma$;
  - D is a set of evaluation attributes transformed from V_Γ, including: availability(d_1), reliability(d_2), security(d_3), real time(d_4), maintainability(d_5), survivability(d_6);
  - M is the set of measures associated to the attributes in D. Original measurement data can be obtained from software supplier using the methods

recommended in ISO9126 and can be provided as evidence for trustworthiness. Then users scored the sub-attributes according the user satisfaction on original data and use experience;

- E is the set of scales associated to D. we propose a scale inspired by the Analytic Hierarchy Process (AHP) [12] and associate it to each attribute in D. The scale for single user is given in Table 1.

Table 1. Score the sub-attribute of trustworthiness by single user

Scoring	Explanation
9	Very satisfy the expectation for mission-critical use
7	Basically meet the expectation for mission-critical use
5	Very satisfy the expectation for Routine use
3	Basically meet the expectation for Routine use
1	Satisfy the expectation for Occasional use
0	Not available

If the user hesitates between two adjacent scores of 1, 3, 5, 7, 9, then scores it one of 2, 4, 6, 8.

Let C be the set of users who scored the software, L_u be the level of user u (treated as user's weight, scale = 1, 2, 3), s_i be the score u given to attribute i. Then the multi-user evaluation on attribute i, e_i, can be defined as follow:

$$e_i = \frac{\sum_{u \in C} (L_u \times s_i)}{\sum_{u \in C} L_u} \quad ; \tag{1}$$

- G is the set of criteria. A criterion g_i is an attribute equipped with a preference relationship. Let $g_i(a) = e_i(a)$ where a is the software evaluated, g_i maps the attribute scale to real;

- R is the aggregation technique adopted in the evaluation model. Let $R =$ ELECTRE TRI.

The weight assignment plays a crucial role in the ELECTRE TRI method, as well as in other aggregation algorithms. we introduce a base weight vector and a weight expectation function to solve this problem in a way that combines the opinions from the experts and the users. The values of other ELECTRE TRI parameters are also assigned below.

Definition 1. *Base Weight Vector*
Let $D = \{d_i | i = 1, \dots, k\}$ be a set of attributes and w_b be a vector function from D to $[0, 1]^k$ representing non-informative a priori weight over D before any user scoring the attributes, satisfying:

$$w_b(d_i) \geq 0 \quad and \quad \sum_{d_i \in D} w_b(d_i) = 1 \quad . \tag{2}$$

Then w_b is called a base weight vector.

Definition 2. *Weight Expectation Function*
Let $D = \{d_i | i = 1, \ldots, k\}$ be a set of attributes and w_b be a base weight vector on D. Let C_b be the w_b priori constant. Let N_i be the number of the users who scored the attribute d_i. The vector function w_e from D to $[0, 1]^k$ representing the posteriori weight expectation over D expressed as:

$$w_e(d_i) = \frac{w_b(d_i) \times C_b + N_i}{C_b + \sum\limits_{d_j \in D} N_j} \tag{3}$$

is then called the weight expectation function.

It can be shown that w_e satisfies the additivity principle:

$$w_e(d_i) \geq 0 \quad \text{and} \quad \sum_{d_i \in D} w_e(d_i) = 1 \quad . \tag{4}$$

N_i reflects how many users concern about the attribute d_i, and it can be used as a factor of attribute weight. In case the number of the users is not big enough initially, the base weight vector can play a role in determining weight values over D. C_b reflects the importance of priori weight assignment.

The profiles setting also coincides with Trustie project standard, namely $b_h(h = 1, \ldots, 5)$. We set the default value of credibility index as proposed by ELECTRE TRI software($\lambda_{cutting} = 0.76$) [13]. Since the evaluation value of an attribute has been normalized, we simplify the other parameters' setting as follows and the settings for all attributes are the same:

Indifference threshold $q = 0.2$, preference threshold $p = 1$, veto threshold $v = 2$.

The values given above are priori. They vary according to the software's domain and other relevant concerns, and can be set by experts before an evaluation application being submitted.

2.3   A Case Study

A CASE tool TEvaluator to support evaluating software was evaluated using the model presented above. Let $w_b(d_i) = 1/6$ where $i = 1, \ldots, 6$ and $C_b = 60$. The number of users who scored the attributes and the w_e obtained by applying the formula 3 are shown in Table 2.

The parameters for ELECTRE TRI method are assigned in Table 3. The values of the attributes were obtained by applying the formula 1.

A more intuitive description of the model is shown in Fig.1.

Table 2. Weight vector for the attributes

	Availability	Reliability	Security	Real time	Maintainability	Survivability
w_b	1/6	1/6	1/6	1/6	1/6	1/6
N_i	35	30	15	30	20	10
w_e	0.225	0.2	0.125	0.2	0.15	0.1

Table 3. Parameters for ELECTRE TRI method

Criteria	Attribute	Value	Weight	q	p	v	b_1	b_2	b_3	b_4	b_5
g_1	availability	7.3	0.225	0.2	1	2	1	3	5	7	9
g_2	reliability	6.14	0.2	0.2	1	2	1	3	5	7	9
g_3	security	4.85	0.125	0.2	1	2	1	3	5	7	9
g_4	real time	7.1	0.2	0.2	1	2	1	3	5	7	9
g_5	maintainability	5.11	0.15	0.2	1	2	1	3	5	7	9
g_6	survivability	3.93	0.1	0.2	1	2	1	3	5	7	9

$\lambda_{\text{cutting}} = 0.76$

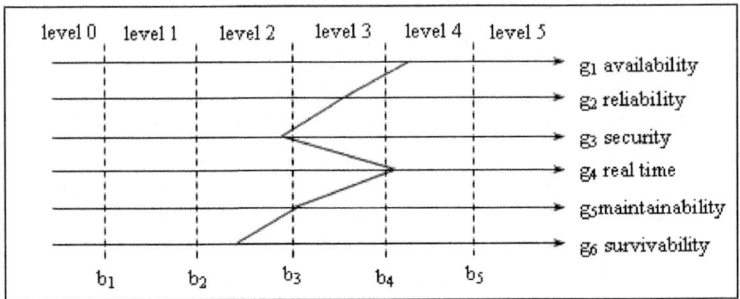

Fig. 1. Description of categories and profiles of the evaluation model

Applying the pessimistic rule, we compared TEvaluator, t for short, with the profiles. Let S be outranking (at least as good as) relationship. It is shown in Fig.1 that t S b_5 does not hold.

Next, we compared t with b_4, since $g_3(b_4) > g_3(t) + v$, then veto condition for t S h_4 is satisfied.

The outranking relationship between t and b_3 is inferred as follows:

According to the pseudo-criterion model defined by ELECTRE method:

$$a'\ S_i\ a \quad \text{iff } g_i(a') \geq g_i(a) - q_i\ , \quad \text{and} \quad a\ P_i\ a' \quad \text{iff } g_i(a) + p_i\ , \qquad (5)$$

Where S_i is the outranking relationship, P_i is the strict preference relationship, q_i is the indifferent threshold, and p_i is the strict preference threshold restricted to the criterion g_i.

$$\Longrightarrow t\ S_1\ b_3,\ t\ S_2\ b_3,\ t\ S_3\ b_3,\ t\ S_4\ b_3,\ t\ S_5\ b_3,\ b_3\ P_6\ t\ , \qquad (6)$$
$$\Longrightarrow \text{the concordance index } c(t, b_3) = w_e(d_1) + w_e(d_2) + w_e(d_3) +$$
$$w_e(d_4) + w_e(d_5) = 0.9\ , \qquad (7)$$

$$\text{the discordance index } d_i = \begin{cases} 0 \ , \ i = 1,2,3,4,5 \\ \frac{g_6(b_3)-g_6(t)-p_6}{v_6-p_6} = 0.07 < c(t,b_3), i = 6 \ , \end{cases} \quad (8)$$

$$\Longrightarrow \text{The credibility index } \rho(t \ S \ b_3) = c(t,b_3) = 0.9 > \lambda_{\text{cutting}} = 0.76 \ , \quad (9)$$

$$\Longrightarrow t \ S \ b_3 \ . \quad (10)$$

Then we assigned the software to level 3.

2.4   Discussion

To judge the trustworthiness of the software is a complex decision-making process. ELETRE methods provide a better way to solve such real-world problems. By adjusting the model parameters, the model can be adapted to different applications and domains. On the other hand, to set too many parameters for each trustworthiness dimension and aggregation technique also becomes a challenge for the model application. Expertise and skill will be needed to utilize the adaptability of the model. Our settings are based on prior experience and users' feedbacks. The prior values can be set at software category level and be taken as default settings for the software submitted to those categories. Using assignment examples and disaggregation approaches to infer parameters for ELECTRE TRI are also the practical methods [14][15].

Furthermore, since our evaluation model bases the result on a large number of users' feedbacks, in order to make the result more reliable, the evidences that users used to score the software can be taken into account. The considerations are as follows:

1. users are apt to rush to judge the software's trustworthiness regardless of whether the evidences are enough;
2. to assign software to higher level of trust should depend on more reliable cognitive evidences;
3. more requirements for evidence of software development process may guide to improve the software trustworthiness at development phase.

Our work aims at rating the software resources according their trustworthiness to meet the needs of potential users who want to choose more trustworthy software. However, different users have different trustworthiness models with different dimensions of trustworthiness, different weight assignment for the dimensions, and different aggregation methods. They always like to construct a specific model for their application and domain. This is not to say that the results produced by applying our evaluation model are useless, but to argue that they should be used as guidelines and as the basis for selecting trustworthy software. Hence we keep the dimensions at a coarse granularity (trustworthiness is only decomposed into one level) and without further sub-division. The evidences for two or more levels hierarchical model are still important for some users to get deeper understand of the software trustworthiness. But multi-level model may confuse others, and even make them refused to comment on software. It will also bring more arguments for sub-attributes weight assignment.

3   Conclusion

In this paper, we presented a method based on the MCDA approach to evaluate software trustworthiness. The method encompassed key activities performed during the STEP: define problem situation and formulation; design evaluation model based on ELECTRE TRI method; and apply the model. we especially presented a metric and a weight-inferring method for all trustworthiness dimensions. A case study was briefly reported for illustrating the model application. The process can produce evaluation result automatically after new feedback from users comes. The model parameters adjustment for different domains and the more evidence requirements for justifiable trust in software should be studied in our further work.

Acknowledgments. This work was supported by National High Technology Research and Development Program of China (863 Program) (No.2007AA 010301) and Key Program of National Natural Science Foundation of China (No.90818024).

References

1. Schneider, F.B.: Trust in cyberspace. National Academic Press, New York (1999)
2. Avizienis, A., Laprie, J.C., Randell, B., Landwehr, C.: Basic concepts and taxonomy of dependable and secure computing. IEEE Trans. on Dependable and Secure Computing 1(1), 11–33 (2004)
3. National Software Strategy Steering Group.: Software 2015: A National Software Strategy to Ensure U.S. Security and Competitiveness. Center for National Software Studies (2005)
4. Roy, B.: Multicriteria Methodology for Decision Aiding. Kluwer Academic, London (1996)
5. Mousseau, R., Slowinski, R., Zielniewicz, P.: A User-oriented Implementation of the ELECTRE TRI Method Integrating Preference Elicitation Support. Computers and Operations Research 27(7-8), 757–777 (2000)
6. Figueira, J., Greco, S., Ehrgott, M.: Multiple Criteria Decision Analysis: State of the art surveys. Springer, New York (2004)
7. Tian, J.: Quality-Evaluation Models and Measurements. IEEE Software 21(3), 84–91 (2004)
8. Sen, C.G., Baracli, H.: A Brief Literature Review of Enterprise Software Evaluation and Selection Methodologies: A Comparison in the Context of Decision-Making Methods. In: Proceedings of 5th International Symposium on Intelligent Manufacturing Systems, SaKarya, pp. 874–883 (2006)
9. Morisio, M., Tsoukias, A.: IusWare, A Methodology for the Evaluation and Selection of Software Products. IEEE Proceedings on Software Engineering 144, 162–174 (1997)
10. Stamelos, I., Tsoukias, A.: Software Evaluation Problem Situations. European Journal of Operations Research 145(2), 273–286 (2003)
11. Trustworthy software tools and integration environment, http://www.trustie.org
12. Saaty, T.L.: Decision Making with the Analytic Hierarchy Process. Int. J. Services Sciences 1(1), 83–98 (2008)

13. Mousseau, V., Slowinski, R., Zielniewicz, P.: ELECTRE TRI 2.0a Methodological Guide and user's Manual. In: Document du LAMSADE, vol. 111, Universite Paris-Dauphine (1999)
14. Mousseau, V., Figueira, J., Naux, J.P.: Using Assignment Examples to Infer Weights for ELECTRE TRI Method: Some Experimental Results. European Journal of Operational Research 130(2), 263–275 (2001)
15. Dias, L., Mousseau, V.: Inferring Electre's Veto-related Parameters from outranking Examples. European Journal of Operational Research 170(1), 172–191 (2006)

The Testing Method for Interface Customized Component[*]

Ying Jiang[1,2], Ying-Na Li[1], and Hai-Wang Zhang[1]

[1] Faculty of Information Engineering and Automation, Kunming University of Science and Technology, 650093 Kunming, China
[2] Key Laboratory of High Confidence Software Technologies (Peking University), Ministry of Education, 100871 Beijing, China
{jy_910,liyingna,2007zhanghaiwang}@163.com

Abstract. Recently, Component Based Software Development is used to develop large and complicated software application systems based on available and reusable components. After selecting components, reusers usually need to modify components to meet the new requirements. Through customization, components can be reused in specific application environment or interact with other components. The interfaces are the only point for the interaction among components. Customization of black-box or on-line component is often done by modifying the interface. In this paper, an extended component interface specification model is proposed to support the component customization and testing. Based on the four kinds of interface specifications and the relationship between the specification elements, the customization operators, testing process and testing reuse principles are proposed. Finally, some experiments are carried and the results have shown that the customization mechanism and testing reuse principles can support the testing of interface customized components.

Keywords: component, interface specification, customization operators, testing reuse principles.

1 Introduction

With the continual increase of software scale and complexity, it is more and more difficult to assure the reliability and quality of software products. Software quality will become the decisive factors to measure the success of software industry [1]. Software reuse is a key technology to improve software quality and software productivity, and Clement Szyperski presents the well-known definition of a software component [2]. Software components are the technical basis of software reuse. Component-based software development (CBSD) provides an approach to construct application system

---

[*] This research is sponsored by the National Science Foundation of China No. 60703116 and 61063006, and the Ministry of Education Research Foundation of Key Laboratory of High Confidence Software Technologies No. HCST200903.

B. Xie et al. (Eds.): ATC 2010, LNCS 6407, pp. 228–241, 2010.

with pre-packaged components. Its major objective is to reduce software development cost and time through reusing available components.

Being different from the traditional software development, component is the construction unit of system in CBSD. In order to reuse components in their system, the reusers' specifications need to be matched to those of the developers. If the developer's specification matches the reuser's requirement, components can be reused without modification. However, as the developer can hardly know all kinds of future reuse contexts of the component before hand, there are few components that meet new application fully. Hence, some reusers develop the new specified components, which will spend the plenty time and budget. For the sake of reducing the development cost, components can be reused after adaptable modification. The reusers usually need to customize the component to satisfy the specific application requirement.

According to Merriam-Webster's dictionary [3], to customize generally means "to build, fit, or alter according to individual specifications". Component customization is the process that involves 1) modifying the component for the specific requirement; 2) doing necessary changes to run the component on special platform; 3) upgrading the specific component to get a better performance or a higher quality [4]. Customization does not necessarily imply total adaptation of software to new needs, just partly modification [5]. The success of CBSD highly depends on the quality of reusable components used in the development process. In order to make the customized components reusable and reliable, new testing methods are needed as testing customized components may be quite different from testing traditional software [6]. Because of the differences between the specifications of customized and original components, the reusers need perform the component testing more efficiently through reuse the developers' testing.

In this paper, we propose an approach to test interface customized components. The rest of this paper is organized as follows. Section 2 discusses previous work related to ours. In Section 3, we present an extended component interface specification model for customization. The component customization mechanism is presented in Section 4. Section 5 describes the testing method for interface customized components. The description and analysis of our experimental study are presented in Section 6. We conclude this paper and present our future work in Section 7.

2   Related Works

There are some methods about component customization in recent years. Rashid et al. use Aspect-Oriented Programming to customize components [7]. Zewdie and Yuan customize components based on software architecture [8, 9]. Jarzabek et al. propose the method of component customization based on generative-programming [10, 11]. These researches use different levels to customize component, from programming to architecture. They discuss the problems of component customization, including the customization influence caused by component granularity, the customization time, the customization cost, and etc. According to the different focus of customization, Yau and Zhou present the method to customize the non-functional characteristics of component except the function customization [12, 13].

In order to assure the quality of software system, customized components must be tested again before reused. There are researches that aim at the testing of component reusers. However, the testing objects are components without being modified. Based on the specific definition of black-box class, white-box class and component, Yoon et al. either directly insert customization codes to white-box class or create a new class containing customization codes. They also discuss the testing approach for the three kinds of component customized pattern [14]. Gao et al. propose that the customization can be classified into three categories, including generalization customization, specialization customization and reconstruction customization. Then the effects of these customization activities along with each individual testing technique are discussed [6].

Based on the demand of component encapsulation and reuse, all component models must define the interface and implementation of a component. The interface describes the information to reuse component successfully. The implementation is the computational structure that be reused in new application. If source code of component is available, reusers can modify source code to meet the requirements while reusing components. Otherwise, the customization only can be done through component interface [15] or executable code instrumentation. Comparing with the source or executable code customization, the interface customization need not modify the internal logic and code of component. Then the customization implementation will be easy and the customization cost will be low [16]. Additionally, with the appearance of EJB, COM + and Web Services technologies, a large number of components provide services through the network directly. These on-line components usually do not provide the source codes, and the interface customization is the main method of component reuse.

Among the existed researches of component customization, the methods of customization and testing for components cannot deal with some modification through interface, such as semantic and protocol customization. Our customization and testing approach differs from these existing researches. In order to facilitate the hard issues in the testing of interface customized components, the additional information are defined and added into the component interface specification model. Moreover, we propose the customization operators and testing reuse principles based on our interface specification model.

3   Component Interface Specification Model

As to component-based software, interfaces are the only point of contact. The interactions among components have to go through interfaces [6]. Therefore, the interface specification is the basis of component customization and testing. Vallecillo et al. [17] point out that a comprehensive component interface model should include the syntactic specification, the semantic specification and the protocol specification. The syntactic specification describes the name, parameters and return type of the interface method. The semantic specification indicates the contracts of interactive data between the developer and the reuser, such as the value range of parameters. The protocol specification describes the behavior information of interactions among components, such as the manner of components interact.

There are various kinds of interface model definition language, such as IDL (Interface Definition Language) of CORBA, MIDL (Microsoft Interface Definition Language) of COM, and Web Services Definition Language. These interface specifications are limited to describe the syntactic specification. The lack of the semantic specification and the protocol specification will result in the ambiguous data and inaccurate description of the functionality and behavior of components. For the sake of the customization and testing of components, we extend the component interface specification model.

3.1 Elements and Hierarchy of Component Interface Specification

We propose a hierarchy component interface specification model, which depicted in Figure 1.

There are four parts specification in our extended model. Syntactic specification includes functional description and non-functional description. Semantic specification includes contract information, which can partially represent specifications of the software and is helpful to understand and compose the components. Protocol specification identifies the composite or single component and its URL address. Testing specification defines the testing information of component, includes test case, testing time and testing evaluation.

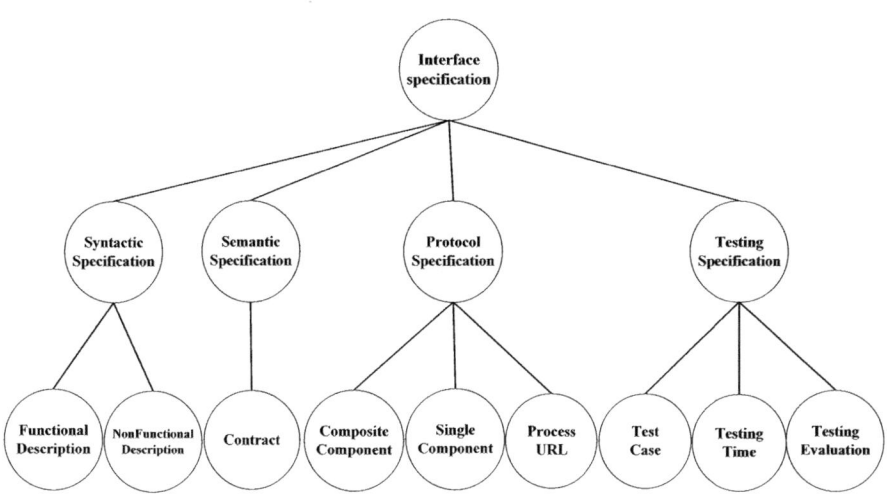

Fig. 1. Extended component interface specification model

In the following Figure 2, we present the detail grammar of extended component interface specification.

The extended component interface specification model can describe the functions, the interaction, and the testing result that component provides to the outside.

```
InterfaceSpecification ::= <SyntacticSpecification> [SemanticSpecification]
                           [ProtocolSpecification] [TestingSpecification]
SyntacticSpecification ::= <FunctionalDescription> [NonFunctionalDescription]
SemanticSpecification ::= <Contract>
ProtocolSpecification ::= (<CompositeComponent>| <SingleComponent>)
                           [ProcessURL]
TestingSpecification ::=  [TestCase][TestingTime] [TestingEvaluation]
FunctionalDescription ::= <FunctionalInformation> <ParameterInformation>
                           [TextDescription]
NonFunctionalDescription ::= [ReliabilityInformation] [AdditionalInformation]
Contract ::=    [Precondition][Invariant][Postcondition]
FunctionalInformation ::= <FunctionalName><ReturnType>
ParameterInformation ::= <ParamerterName><ParameterType>
ReliabilityInformation ::= [Cost][Time][Reputation]
AdditionalInformation ::= [Creator][Version][Domain][Deadline]
```

Fig. 2. The grammar of component interface specification

3.2   Relationships between Component Interface Specification Elements

There exist three kinds of relationships between component interface specification
elements. The relationships are listed as the following:

1) Hierarchy. This is a relationship between two elements at two adjacent abstraction levels. For example, Contract is a low hierarchy of Semantic Specification, and Functional Information is a high hierarchy of Functional Name.
   Hierarchy is a One-Many relationship.
2) Association. This is a relationship between testing specification elements and
   other three kinds of specification elements. For example, testing specification
   is associated with protocol specification. Association is a One-Many relationship, which means that testing information are produced based on syntax
   specification, semantic specification and protocol specification.
3) Dependency. This is a relationship between syntactic specification elements
   and semantic specification elements. For example, Contract is dependent on
   Functional Information. Dependency is a Many-Many relationship.

The relationship of Hierarchy and Dependency can be used to check the rationality
and validity when the developer and reuser define the specification. The relationship
of Association indicates the mappings between testing information and other component specification, which is the basis of testing reuse.

4   Customization Mechanism for Interface Specification

A software component can be customized in many different ways in a new context.
Customizations need to be performed on the component to adjust the component
specification to conform to the component reuser's specification. Without the regula-
tion of component customization, it is very difficult to find systematic solutions to

support the validation of customized components due to the lack of new testing methods and coverage criteria for customized components [6].

Based on the component interface specification model in Section 3, we analyze the possible customization type and propose three kinds of customization method for different component interface specification. For every kind of customization method, a set of customization operators are defined. Each customization operator represents the specified modification for the different kinds of interface specification of component.

4.1 Syntactic Specification Customization

For the syntactic specification of component interface, we define seven customization operators which are listed in Table 1.

Table 1. Syntactic Specification Customization Operators

Name	Meaning
COI	Cut Out Interface
MMR	Modify Method Return-type
MPN	Modify Parameter Name
MPT	Modify Parameter Type
APN	Add Parameter Number
DPN	Decrease Parameter Number
MQI	Modify QoS Information

4.2 Semantic Specification Customization

For the semantic specification of component interface, we define seven customization operators which are listed in Table 2.

Table 2. Semantic Specification Customization Operators

Name	Meaning
SPR	Strengthen PRecondition
WPR	Weaken PRecondition
SPO	Strengthen POstcondition
WPO	Weaken POstcondition
SIV	Strengthen InVariant
WIV	Weaken InVariant
SAC	Stuck-At Contract

4.3 Protocol Specification Customization

For the protocol specification of component interface, we define four customization operators which are listed in Table 3.

Table 3. Protocol Specification Customization Operators

Name	Meaning
CTS	Composite To Single
MCC	Modify Composite Configuration
STC	Single To Composite
MSC	Modify Single Configuration

According to the above three kinds of customization methods and related operators, the reusers can regularly customize component's interface specification to meet the application requirement.

5   Testing Method for Interface Customized Component

Usually, two specifications could exist for the same component, and they are very often not perfectly matched with each other. Customization will adopt a component into the application and reconcile the differences between the two specifications. When testing the component, the reusers have two choices: start from scratch or customize the component and make sure the customization will not adversely affect the software component. The former will spend more time and cost. For the latter, there are new challenges such as how to generate test data and assess the adequacy [6].

5.1   Testing Process for Interface Customized Component

In order to decrease the testing time and cost, we will reuse the testing information from component developers when testing the customized component. The researches of testing reuse mainly focus on the reuse of testing design and testing process [18]. In Section 3.2, we define the relationships between testing specification elements and other specification elements. Based on these relationships, we propose the method to test the interface customized component, whose process is shown in Figure 3.

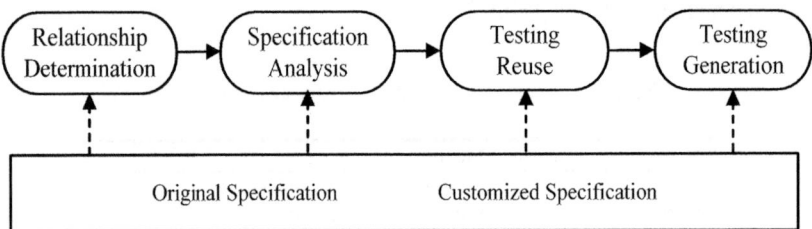

Fig. 3. The testing process for interface customized component

For each customized component, we use the following steps to reuse and generate the testing information.

1) Relationship Determination: obtain the relationships between the original specification and the testing information, and determine the corresponding testing information for the original specification;
2) Specification Analysis: analyze difference of the specification that customized before and after;
3) Testing Reuse: reuse the previous testing information for the unchanged specification;

4) Testing Generation: generate the new testing information for the changed specification.

For the different customization methods, there are differences in testing components. According to the modification modes defined by the customization operators, we define the reuse principles based on three kinds of specification customization.

5.2 Testing Reuse Principles for Syntactic Specification Customization

For the syntactic specification customization, we define the testing reuse principles as listed in Table 4.

Table 4. Testing Reuse Principles for Syntactic Specification Customization

Customization operators	Testing reuse principles
COI	Reuse the previous testing information for the remained interface
MMR	Reuse the previous testing information
MPN	Reuse the previous testing information for the unchanged parameters, generate the new testing information for the changed parameters
MPT	Reuse the previous testing information for the unchanged parameters, generate the new testing information for the changed parameters based on parameter type
APN	Reuse the previous testing information for the initial parameters, generate the new testing information for the added parameters
DPN	Reuse the previous testing information for the remained parameters
MQI	Generate the new testing information

5.3 Testing Reuse Principles for Semantic Specification Customization

For the semantic specification customization, we define the testing reuse principles as listed in Table 5.

Table 5. Testing Reuse Principles for Semantic Specification Customization

Customization operators	Testing reuse principles
SPR	Reuse the previous testing information selectively based on the new precondition
WPR	Reuse the previous testing information, generate the new testing information based on the new precondition
SPO	Reuse the previous testing information selectively based on the new postcondition
WPO	Reuse the previous testing information, generate the new testing information based on the new postcondition
SIV	Reuse the previous testing information selectively based on the new invariant
WIV	Reuse the previous testing information, generate the new testing information based on the new invariant
SAC	Reuse the previous testing information selectively based on the value of contract

5.4 Testing Reuse Principles for Protocol Specification Customization

For the protocol specification customization, we define the testing reuse principles as listed in Table 6.

Table 6. Testing Reuse Principles for Protocol Specification Customization

Customization operators	Testing reuse principles
CTS	Reuse the previous testing information for the start component of the composite component, generate the new testing information for the single component
MCC	Reuse the previous testing information for the unchanged components, generate the new testing information for the replaced components
STC	Reuse the previous testing information for the single component, generate the new testing information for the composite component
MSC	Generate the new testing information

In our previous research, we propose a component testing approach that combines the function-based and the error-based test-data generation [19], which will be used in the above testing reuse principles. For the changed specification, this approach can also be used to generate the new testing information.

6 Case Study

We developed a prototype tool of Customization and Testing for Web Services based on Microsoft .NET platform. Some experiments is performed on a 2.26G Hz Pentium4 system running Windows 2003 Server.

6.1 Experimented Components

The experiments use three testing objects listed in Table 7, including TriTyp, Deal and Permutation. Based on the original specification, the syntactic and semantic specification customizations are executed. Using six customization operators, the customized specification is also defined.

Table 7. Web Services Under Test

Web Services	Function	Original specification	Customization operators	Customized specification
TriTyp	determining the type of triangles based on the inputs of three sides	int a, int b, int c $0<a<100 \wedge$ $0<b<100 \wedge$ $0<c<100$	DPN	int a, int b
			SPR	$0<a<50 \wedge 0<b<50$ $\wedge 0<c<50$
Deal	transforming the Proper fraction to the sum of Egypt scores	int a, int b $a>0 \wedge b>0 \wedge$ $a<b$	APN	int a, int b, int c
			SAC	TRUE
Permutation	calculating the value of P_m^n	int m, int n $m>0 \wedge n>0$	MPN	int m, int b
			SIV	$m>1 \wedge n>1$

We use two kinds of method to generate test data for the customized component applied the customization operators in Table 7. Regeneration means that the test data of customized component will be generated again with the new specification. Reuse means that the test data of customized component will be generated using the reuse principles in Section 5.

6.2 Results and Analysis

Using the approach in [19], the number of test data in valid equivalence class and invalid equivalence class all are 3 for each Web Service under test. The experiment results of syntactic and semantic specification customization are listed in Table 8 and 9.

Table 8. Experimental results for syntactic customization

Web Services	TriTyp		Deal		Permutation	
Test data generation method	Regeneration	Reuse	Regeneration	Reuse	Regeneration	Reuse
Condition Coverage Score (%)	80	81.6	74.3	76	42	42
Branch Coverage Score (%)	92	92	88	88	22.5	24
Path Coverage Score (%)	100	100	100	100	36	31.3
Number of test case	2479	825	95	58	78	82
Time of generate test case (ms)	103	80	62	44	47	50
Time of execute test case (ms)	37	19	12	7	3	4

Table 9. Experimental results for semantic customization

Web Services	TriTyp		Deal		Permutation	
Test data generation method	Regeneration	Reuse	Regeneration	Reuse	Regeneration	Reuse
Condition Coverage Score (%)	83	83	85.7	87	37.5	34.4
Branch Coverage Score (%)	100	100	85.7	87	19	38.1
Path Coverage Score (%)	100	100	100	100	12.5	31.3
Number of test case	3375	729	49	63	81	72
Time of generate test case (ms)	126	74	53	60	59	57
Time of execute test case (ms)	42	16	2	3	5	3

From Figure 4 and Figure 5, we can see that the number of test case using the various test data generation method has difference. Both in syntactic customization and semantic customization, regeneration produce more test data than reuse in most cases. It also means that regeneration spends more time and cost than reuse during testing the customized components, which can be seen in Table 8 and 9.

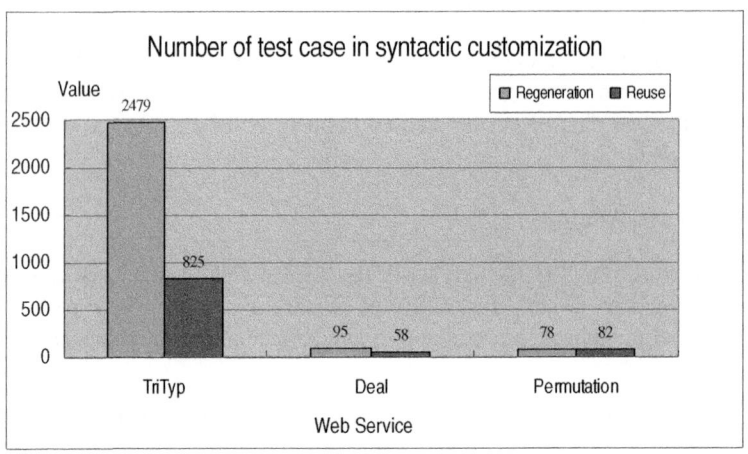

Fig. 4. The number of test case in syntactic customization

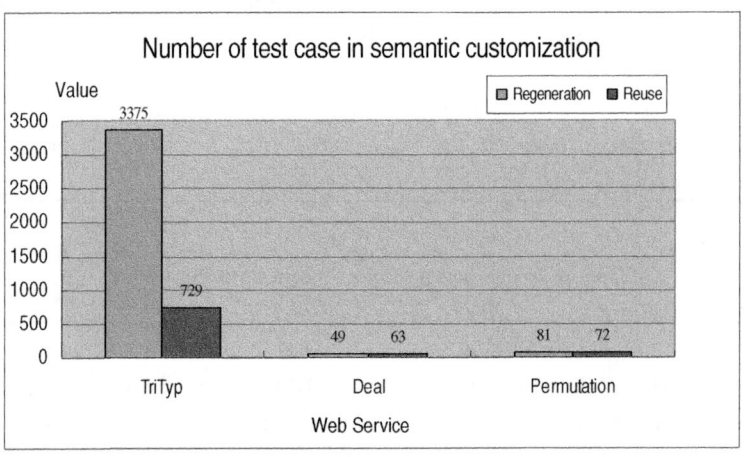

Fig. 5. The number of test case in semantic customization

Figure 6 and Figure 7 show the three kinds of coverage score (CCS: Condition Coverage Score; BCS: Branch Coverage Score; PCS: Path Coverage Score) of test case in syntactic customization and semantic customization. As shown in Figure 6 and 7, the three coverage scores of test data produced by reuse method are mostly equal to those produced by regeneration method. When testing the Permutation in semantic customization, the branch coverage score of reuse is higher than that of regeneration (38.1%: 19%), and the path coverage score of reuse is also higher than that of regeneration (31.3%:12.5%).

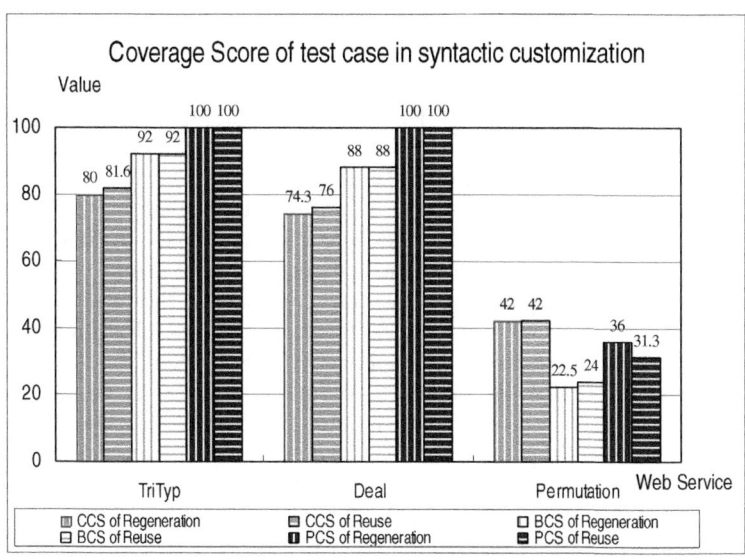

Fig. 6. The coverage score of test case in syntactic customization

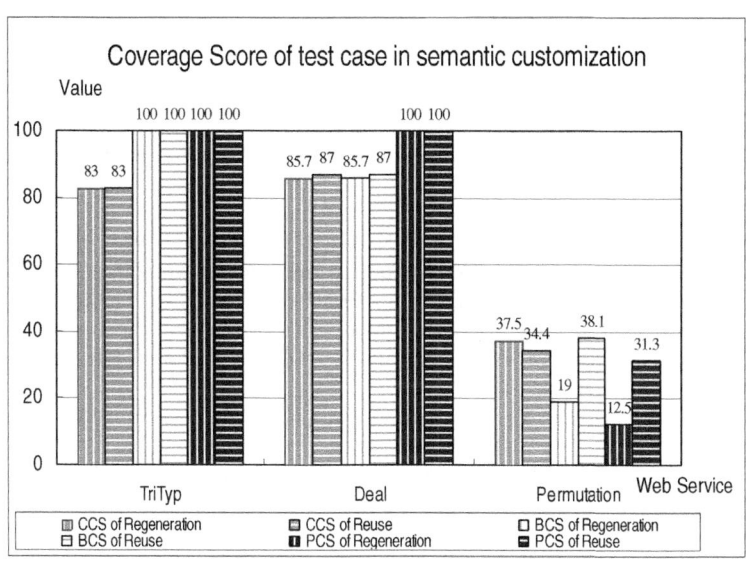

Fig. 7. The coverage score of test case in semantic customization

7 Conclusion and Future Work

In order to satisfy different requirements, component need customize before it can be reused in new application system. The method of customization will influence the time and cost of component reuse. So it is necessary to customize component regularly and assure the quality of customized component.

In this paper, we aim at the testing method for interface customized component. This paper defines an extended interface specification model for component, and proposes three kinds of customization methods based on the interface specifications. After defined eighteen customization operators, we propose the related testing reuse principles. The customization operators and testing reuse principles can help reuser to modify and test components under their application environment.

The experimental results can demonstrate the effectiveness of our customization mechanism testing reuse principles. We can also find that the efficiency of some test data is not always retained after reuse. The reason is related to the quality of the original test data and the process to determine useful test data. Furthermore, as the scale of the experimented components is not large enough, we plan to investigate the effectiveness of reuse method in the future. We will further perform more experiments using larger components. We will investigate whether there are other relationships between the different specification elements. Moreover, we will enhance the ability of specification definition and improve the efficiency of customization and testing.

References

1. Osterweil, L.: Strategic directions in software quality. ACM Computing Surveys 28(4), 738–750 (1996)
2. Szyperski, C.: Component Software—Beyond Object-Oriented Programming. Addison-Wesley, Reading (1999)
3. Merriam-Webster's collegiate dictionary. 10th ed. Merriam-Webster, Springfield (1996)
4. Xia, C., Lyu, M.R., Kam-Fai, W., Roy, K.: Component-based software engineering: technologies, development frameworks, and quality assurance schemes. In: Proceedings of the Seventh Asia-Pacific Software Engineering Conference, pp. 372–379 (2000)
5. Nordheim, S., Paivarinta, T.: Customization of enterprise content management systems: an exploratory case study. In: Proceedings of the 37th Annual Hawaii International Conference on System Sciences (2004)
6. Gao, J.Z., Tsao, H.-S.J., Wu, Y.: Testing and Quality Assurance for Component-Based Software. Artech House, Norwood (2003)
7. Rashid, A., Sawyer, P.: Aspect-orientation and database systems: an effective customisation approach. IEE Proceedings- Software 148(5), 156–164 (2001)
8. Zewdie, B., Carlson, C.R.: Adaptive Component Paradigm for Highly Configurable Business Components. In: IEEE International Conference on Electro/information Technology, pp. 185–190 (2006)
9. Yuan, L., Dong, J.S., Sun, J., Basit, H.A.: Generic Fault Tolerant Software Architecture Reasoning and Customization. IEEE Transactions on Reliability 55(3), 421–435 (2006)
10. Jarzabek, S., Knauber, P.: Synergy between component-based and generative approaches. ACM SIGSOFT Software Engineering Notes 24(6), 429–445 (1999)

11. Jarzabek, S., Seviora, R.: Engineering components for ease of customisation and evolution. IEE Proceedings- Software 147(6), 237–248 (2000)
12. Yau, S.S., Taweponsomkiat, C.: An approach to object-oriented component customization for real-time software development. In: Proceedings of the Fifth IEEE International Symposium on Object-Oriented Real-Time Distributed Computing, pp. 429–436 (2002)
13. Zhou, J., Cooper, K., Yen, I.-L.: A Rule-based Component Customization Technique for QoS Properties. In: Proceedings of the Eighth IEEE International Symposium on High Assurance Systems Engineering (2004)
14. Yoon, H., Choi, B.: Inter-class test technique between black-box-class and white-box-class for component customization failures. In: Proceedings of the Sixth Asia Pacific Software Engineering Conference, pp. 162–165 (1999)
15. Ferguson, F., et al.: SOA programming model for implementing Web Services, Part 6: The evolving component model,
    http://www-128.ibm.com/developerworks/webservices/library/ws-soa-progmodel6/
16. Ravichandran, T., Rothenberger, M.A.: Software reuse strategies and component markets. Communications of the ACM 46(8), 109–114 (2003)
17. Vallecillo, A., Hernandez, J., Troya, J.-M.: Component Interoperability. In: Guerraoui, R. (ed.) ECOOP 1999. LNCS, vol. 1628, Springer, Heidelberg (1999)
18. Ma, Y.-S., Oh, S.-U., Bae, D.-H., et al.: Framework for Third Party Teting of Component Software. In: Proceedings of the 8th Asia-Pacific Software Engineering Conference, Macau SAR, China, pp. 431–434 (2001)
19. Jiang, Y., Hou, Sh.-Sh., Shan, J.-H., Zhang, L., Xie, B.: An Approach to Testing Black-box Components Using Contract-Based Mutation. International Journal of Software Engineering and Knowledge Engineering 18(1), 93–117 (2008)

A New Monitor Model for Enhancing Trust-Based Systems

Lang Jia and Paddy Nixon

University College Dublin, UCD, Ireland
(lang.jia,paddy.nixon)@ucd.ie

Abstract. In recent years, with the rapid proliferation of new computing technologies, a variety of new computing environments have been introduced, such as decentralisation and mobility. The traditional security mechanisms are seen to be inadequate for these new environments. Trust is applied as a "soft security" to cope with new security concerns. Much research on trust systems has been carried out, it is important to identify the reliability of computational trust in different computing scenarios in order to make an enhancement. The reliability of trust systems for securing social interaction is demonstrated by showing the performance of the three trust-based systems under various scenarios in a pervasive computing environment. The focus of this paper is on enhancing trust-based systems and proposing a novel monitor model which supplements existing trust models.

Keywords: Security, Models.

1 Introduction

Trust is a social phenomenon, which has been defined by researchers in different academic fields, such as psychology, sociology, economics, philosophy.

Computational trust is built upon previous interaction experiences, which are used to reason about the outcome of future interactions. It is referred to as a "soft security" enabling autonomous collaboration between entities in decentralised computing environments. Therefore, it is important to identify how reliable is computational trust in different computing scenarios in order to make an enhancement.

The focus of this paper is on enhancing trust-based systems for social interaction. Current trust-based systems do not typically contain any revoke functionality, where once an entity is granted permissions the permissions remain granted until the interaction is complete. The previous interaction outcomes of an entity affects the decisions of the future requests. It is for this reason that trust models often fail to protect against unexpected behaviour and malicious attacks. This paper proposes a novel monitor model which supplements existing trust models. The proposed monitoring model attempts to facilitate trust models by making runtime decisions in order to minimise damages that are caused by the unexpected and malicious behaviours of entities.

B. Xie et al. (Eds.): ATC 2010, LNCS 6407, pp. 242–254, 2010.

The remainder of this paper is as follows. In section 2, three trust models are evaluated and analysed. Section 3 categorises the existing monitoring mechanisms, and introduces a new monitoring model for trust-based systems, and Section 4 analysises and discusses the existing monitoring models. Finally, Section 5 concludes this paper and discusses future work.

2 Performance Evaluation of Trust-Based Access Control Models

An evaluation was carried out using the scenario-based evaluation kit [4]. The aim of the evaluation was to identify the vulnerabilities of three trust models. A series of pervasive advertising scenarios were applied to each trust model, where each pervasive service provider attempts to advertise products of its assigned shops in a decentralised computing environment. Mobile users are able to receive the advertising services by uploading their shopping lists, preferences, etc. The three trust models evaluated were: TrustAC [5], Gray [6] and EnTrust [3]. The evaluation was divided into two parts, unexpected behaviour of entities and malicious attacks.

2.1 Unexpected Behaviours

The evaluated trust models are examined and analysed under a series of scenarios of unexpected behaviours that are carried out by pervasive service providers. The unexpected behaviours are considered as the behaviours that are carried out by the providers, which exceed the expectations of trust-based systems.

There were four cases of unexpected behaviours in the evaluation. The description of the cases and the according performances of the models are shown as the following,

- **Case 1:** The performance of the tested models were evaluated where unpredictable behaviours of unknown providers are involved. In order to build trust between previously unknown entities, the trust models grant the first requests from unknown providers. All three trust models failed to prevent from requests from the unknown malicious providers.
- **Case 2:** The models were tested to cope with the unexpected behaviour from the providers that were not completely unknown, where the entities have some previous positive experiences with the providers. As there was some previous positive experience with the providers, the trust models expected positive outcome of the following interactions with the provider. However, all of the tested models failed to prevent from malicious acts of the providers in this case.
- **Case 3:** In many circumstances, entities are also misled by incorrect actions that are carried out by the providers. These incorrect actions may also cause harmful damage to entities. For instance, if a genuine provider incorrectly recognises a malicious provider and then recommends the malicious provider to another entity, the entity may trust the malicious provider. All of the trust models in the evaluation granted requests to such providers.

- **Case 4:** Trust for an entity typically increases as positive previous experiences increase. Thus, if a malicious provider accomplishes a number of genuine interactions with an entity, it may have the intention of increasing trust to gain access to resources that have a high trust requirement. All of the tested trust models were unable to prevent from this type of unexpected behaviour.

As shown in the test cases, all of the models failed to prevent from the unexpected behaviours in the given scenarios. For trust models to establish trust in decentralised computing environments it is necessary for them to grant a basic level of trust with unknown entities. This approach enables once unknown entities to become known and trusted entities over time, but also introduces the risk that unknown malicious entities are granted a basic level of trust.

Trust value increases and decreases based on positive and negative experiences. This enables systems to reason about the outcome of future interactions. Yet, even entities that have many positive experiences can be incorrect or malicious at any point in the future, but trust models have no control over on the unexpected behaviours of the interactions.

Although, if an entity is malicious, the trust models can choose not to interact with it in the future, damage may already be caused by malicious unexpected behaviour.

2.2   Attacks

There are many attacks can affect trust decisions in pervasive computing environments. As trust-based systems take recommendations from third party entities, they are prone to many attacks, such as Sybil attacks [14], defamation and collusion attacks. The defamation and collusion attacks are also referred as bad-mouthing and ballot-stuffing attacks, where a group of entities have teamed up for the purpose of manipulating the reputation of other entities.

The goal of the second part of the evaluation was to test the performance of the trusted models with malicious attacks. The models were tested to measure their performance at preventing SPAM advertisements.

- **Case 1:** A number of Sybil attacks were carried out, where each Sybil attacker creates a different number of Sybil entities. Additionally, neither the Sybil attackers' group or their Sybil entities' group are previously known to the network. The evaluation examines the percentage of SPAM advertisements that each model receives under the Sybil attacks.

  As shown in figure 1, all of the tested models failed to prevent the Sybil attacks, where both Sybil attackers and Sybil entities groups are previously unknown. In this case, the reliability of recommendations that are received from the recommenders (Sybil entities) cannot be assessed, thus the attacks take place.

- **Case 2:** The same groups of Sybil attackers and their Sybil entities as in case 1 are involved in this case. Hence, there are previous experiences available from the victim entities (one victim entity for each recommendation process).

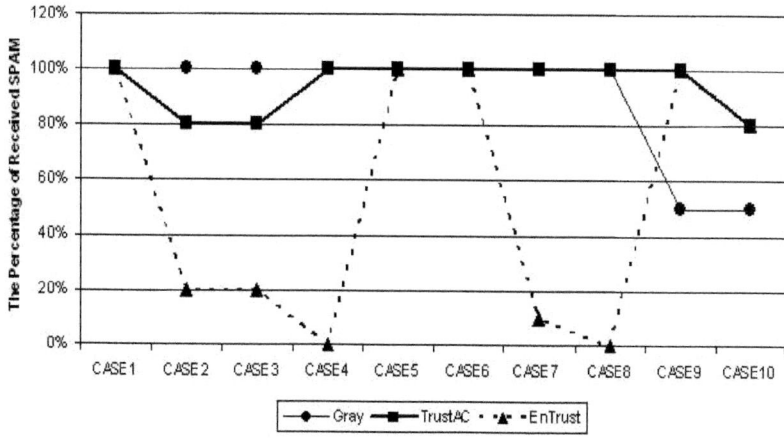

Fig. 1. The Attack Scenarios

Due to no previous interaction experiences being recorded, recommendations are not assessed by the Gray model, thus entities receive 100% SPAM advertisements under the Sybil attacks. Although the TrustAC model records the interaction history, it uses the direct trust to assess the recommendations, so the recommendations of the Sybil entities still significantly influence the trust decisions. EnTrust separates trust as direct trust and recommendation trust, and the recommendations that are received by EnTrust are analysed based on the recommendation trust of the recommenders. As the recommendations from the Sybil entities have less effect on the trust decisions, EnTrust is able to filter out 80% of SPAM advertisements.

- **Case 3:** In case three, the Sybil attackers keep the original identities, but demolish the old identities of their Sybil entities. The change of the new identities of the Sybil entities does not affect the performances of the tested models, hence the performances are shown to be identical as in the previous case.

- **Case 4:** The previous identities of the same Sybil attackers are abolished, but the previous identities of their Sybil entities are kept in this case. Due to both Gray and TrustAC having no mechanisms to punish the entities who provide malicious or wrong recommendations, both of the models receive 100% SPAM advertisements from the unknown Sybil providers that are recommended by the same group of the Sybil entities, whereas the performance of EnTrust is ideal.

- **Case 5:** The identities of the Sybil attackers and their Sybil entities are revoked after the attacks, and new identities are assigned to the Sybil attackers and Sybil entities. The new identities are unknown to the victim entities. All of the tested models failed to refuse advertising services from the malicious provider.

- **Case 6:** In this ballot-stuffing attack, a group of known entities decide to team up to boost the reputation of the unknown entities. All of the tested models accept the SPAM advertising services that are provided by the unknown entities who are recommended by the group of ballot-stuffing attackers.
- **Case 7:** This is another ballot-stuffing attack, the same group of entities attempt to boost the reputation for the same group of malicious service providers to other entities on the network. As there are previous negative experiences available with the victim entities from the previous case, the models are evaluated on the correctness of the trust decisions under the influence of both of the malicious and genuine recommendations.
- **Case 8:** In case 8, the same group of entities attempt to boost the reputation for different malicious providers. As seen in figure 1, EnTrust prevents entities from receiving services that are provided by the malicious entities, who are recommended by the same group of malicious recommenders. Nonetheless, as there is no mechanism to cope with the malicious recommender in Gray or TrustAC, the models are not able to prevent the victim entities from receiving SPAM advertisements.
- **Case 9:** The models are evaluated under the bad-mouthing attacks, where a group of entities in the network collaborate together for the defamation of the unknown genuine service providers. In this case, Gray shows a comparatively better performance, since the proportion of the malicious recommenders increases, the correctness of trust decisions decreases. Whereas the TrustAC and EnTrust models are prone to the bad-mouthing attacks.
- **Case 10:** In this scenario, the same group of entities attempt to bad-mouth a different group of genuine service providers. As the proportion of genuine recommenders increases, both TrustAC and EnTrust show an improved performance, whereas Gray performs in the same way as the previous bad-mouthing attack.

The models show different performances in the different attack scenarios. EnTrust separates divides trust into direct trust and recommendation trust, so when a entity is abused by a malicious entity, the recommendation trust of the recommenders is reduced for the future references. Though EnTrust has shown a dramatic improvement under the described attacks, overall, the models are shown to be inadequate to prevent the malicious attacks.

The models can choose not to interact with the malicious entities and/or not to consider any recommendations from the recommenders in the future, but damages may already be caused from the attacks. In addition, if there is no adequate authentication mechanisms applied for the trust models, the victim entities are likely to be attacked by the same attackers with different identities.

One solution for this problem is to continuously monitor the interactions taking place between entities, where if a provider is trusted, its trust level can change in real time based on what it is attempting to do.

3   Monitoring for Trust-Based Systems

To monitor is to observe or supervise the states of changes throughout processes. Monitoring is not a new research field. Many research works have been carried out in various areas in computing science. The monitoring approach observes the interactions while they take place, and makes run-time decisions at any critical points during the interactions, which is competent for the purpose of facilitating trust-based systems.

3.1   Categorisation of Existing Monitoring

Existing research on monitoring has been categorised as follows:

- **Network Monitoring** systems are applied to ensure the performance of networks, which it attempts to diagnosis and fix various network problems such as a server crashing.
- **Website Monitoring** is used to check the availability and the usability of web applications.
- **Grid/Distributed Monitoring** [11] systems are applied to provide information about grid resources for users by observing the status of the resources continuously in dynamic computing environments.
- **Run-time Software Monitoring** [7,8] attempts to check, analyse and recover from software failures throughout the system execution. Various existing run-time software monitors such as [9,10] are manual monitoring models. Moreover, many run-time software monitors are centralised, and require to be placed inline with monitored software. These features and requirements result in the monitors being inadequate and impractical for pervasive computing environments.
- **Run-time Interaction Monitoring** observes interactions between entities and makes run-time decisions based on the run-time analysis. Various run-time interaction monitoring approaches have been proposed for different monitoring purposes. The majority of run-time interaction monitors are proposed for service-based software. One of the first research works that applies interaction monitoring to a trust-based system was proposed by English et. al. [12].

The trust-based systems facilitate collaborating entities based on computational trust in decentralised computing environments. However, it was shown in the evaluation in section 2 that it cannot be solely relied on. A run-time interaction monitoring approach is one solution for supporting trust decisions at runtime. However the majority of existing monitoring mechanisms are unsuitable for trust perspectives due to the different monitoring purposes, the different domains required, etc.

Table 1. A Taxonomy and Catalogue of Run-time Interaction Monitoring

Model	Monitor Type	Placement	Decentralisation	Automation	Monitoring Objective	Monitoring Methods	Monitored Entity	Domain	Direct Monitoring	Indirect Monitoring
English	Trust	External	Y	Y	Ensure Trusted Interactions	Interaction Events	Provider	Ubiquitous System	Y	N
Uddin (ATM) [16]	Trust/Service	External	Y	Y	Ensure Trusted Interactions	Trust Rules	Requestor	Service-based Software	Y	N
Sandhu (TRM) [17]	Trust	External	Y	Y	Enable Security Policies in Trust Computing Environment	Policy Enforcement	Requestor	Trusted Computing	Y	N
Etalle [18]	Trust	3rd Party External	Y	Y	Integrity Constrains	3rd Party Observation on Policy Management	Provider	Trust-based Authorisation Systems	Y	N
Spanoudakis [19]	Service	3rd Party External	N	Y	Quality of Services based on the Requirements	Event Calculus and Observation on Service Requirements	Provider	Service-based Software (Web Services)	Y	N
Jurca [20]	Service	3rd Party External	N	N	Quality of Services	User Feedback	Provider	service-based Software (Web Services)	Y	N
Baresi [21]	Service	3rd Party External	N	Y	Assess the Correctness of Service Composition	1. Late-binding and Reflection 2. Standard Assertion	Provider	Service-based Software (Web Services)	Y	N
Skene [22]	Service	3rd Party External	N	Y	Quality of Services	3rd Party Observation for Events	Provider	Service-based Software	Y	N
Letla [23]	Service	3rd Party External	N	Y	Quality of Services	Z-specification	Provider	Service-based Software	Y	N
Yan [24]	Service	3rd Party External	N	Y	Errors in Service Execution	Model Based Diagnosis to Monitor Static and Dynamic Systems Using Partial Observations	Provider	Service-based Software (Web Services)	Y	N
Sahai [25]	Service	3rd Party External	N	Y	Management of E-services	Based on Common Information Model and Application Response Measurement	Provider	Web-based services	E-Y	N
Robinson (REQMON) [26]	Service	3rd Party External	N	Y	Exceptions in Aggregate Web Services	3rd Party Observation for System Actions	Provider	Service-based Software (Web Services)	Y	N
Zhang [27]	Service	3rd Party External	N	Y	Accountability in Service Composition	SLA-based Monitoring and Bayesian Network Reasoning for Diagnosing	Provider	Service-based Software (Web Services)	Y	N

The existing monitoring approaches are inadequate for securing trust inter-actions of pervasive computing applications, as they were proposed for different monitoring purposes. Most of the existing monitoring approaches are designed for different computing environments as shown in table 1. These approaches are insufficient for various pervasive computing environments. For instance, the centralised approach is impractical for decentralised computing applications and also it is expensive in terms of central management. Additionally, it can also cause a performance bottleneck or a single point of failure. The placement of the monitors is essential, where internal monitors (i.e. monitors that are embedded in the entities being monitored) are unreliable. In this case monitored entities are capable of altering the monitoring programs. Different types of monitors are pro-posed in different computing fields, e.g. network monitoring, website monitoring and grid run-time software monitoring, and it is impossible to have a universal monitoring model that is suitable for all fields. Given that the existing moni-toring approaches from the same category are proposed for diverse objectives, where they cannot be applied to all circumstances. Finally, as shown in table 1, English and Uddin are the only monitoring models that attempt to facilitate trust-based decisions by ensuring run-time trust-based interactions. However, Uddin focuses on monitoring requestors in services-based applications, where it checks whether requestors have the right access to the right resources. Likewise, both of the approaches trace events of monitored entities in order to analyse the interactions. Hence, both of the approaches require a rich set of clearly defined aspects of behaviour from monitored entities. The event observation approach requires that all events are predefined, where it can be impractical in many pervasive applications. In addition, neither of the monitors have mechanisms to prevent any of the malicious attacks.

A new run-time interaction monitor model requires the following: it must ob-serve the direct interactions while they take place and make run-time decisions at any critical points. Similarly, trust decisions for unknown entities are based on the indirect trust process, which takes recommendations from the third party entities. This results in the mechanism being prone to many malicious attacks, for example, Sybil attacks, as shown in Figure 1. As a result, the entities who have participated in the trust decisions by providing recommendations for the requestors should be monitored for the purpose of preventing any possible at-tacks. In addition, as the monitor is required to work in decentralised computing environments, it is impractical to have any third party entities for monitoring purposes. Finally, as it is unreliable to embed the monitor model within moni-tored entities, the monitoring model must be located on monitoring entities.

3.2   The Run-Time Trust-Based Interaction Monitoring Model

In order to deal with the issues described, the Run-time Trust-based Interaction Monitoring (RTIM) model is proposed. The objective of the RTIM model is to facilitate trust-based systems by making run-time decisions, where it identifies the occurrences of illegal use of resources and possible attacks from trust-based interactions.

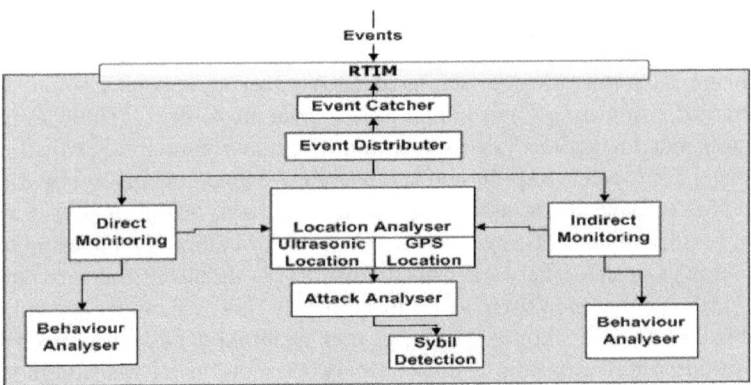

Fig. 2. RTIM

The *Event Catcher* is responsible for catching events taking place from both the direct interacting entities and the recommender entities who are involved in the indirect trust calculation process.

The *Event Distributer* process assigns events to the *Direct Monitoring* process and the *Indirect/Recommender Monitoring* process based on the event types. *Direct Monitoring* manages events that are issued by the direct interacting entities, where the events that are generated by the recommender entities are analysed by *Indirect Monitoring*. As discussed previously, it is important to not only observe the direct interacting entities, but also the indirect interacting entities. Thus, the *Indirect Monitoring* process is applied to observe the entities (recommender entities) that are involved in the indirect trust calculation process by providing recommendations.

The *Behaviour Analyser* continuously observes the states of the interactions and intervenes at critical points during run-time in an attempt to prevent trust-based systems from the unexpected behaviours of the interacting entities reducing the damage to a minimum cost. The English [12] model was selected to be applied to the monitoring task in the *Behaviour Analyser* process. English is a self-contained software component, and it is one of the first monitoring models that was proposed for observing the trust-based interactions in the ubiquitous computing environment. A trust-based interaction is represented as a set of trust events E_T and cost events E_C. The *Behaviour Analyser* process tracks the state of the interaction based on the result of the event notifications. The states of the trust and cost events of the interaction are used for calculating the current likelihood of outcome, along with the current risk-state of the interaction. Thus the interaction can be intervened if necessary. However, in order for *Behaviour Analyser* to perform effectively, a rich set of clearly defined aspects of behaviour from a monitored entity. Moreover, there are many possible interactions in different computing environments, and the observing events may not be predefined. As a result, the *Location Analyser* process is designed for the purpose of enhancing the monitoring model. Both the *Location Analyser* and the *Behaviour Analyser* are mutually exclusive, which means they do not depend on each other, and they observe entities in different approaches.

Since trust models involve getting recommendations for the unknown entities from third party entities, the trust decisions are easily influenced by many attacks as shown in the evaluation. For instance, one of the most common attacks, the Sybil attack, attempts to gain a large influence on reputation amongst recommender entities by impersonating many entities, all of its pseudonymous entities would physically bond together to the same device at a same physical location. Hence the physical location of an entity is essential information for identifying possible attacks (e.g. Sybil attacks) amongst the recommender entities.

The *Location Analyser* process monitors both the directly interacting entities and the recommender entities for any occurrences of "unusual locations" using the Ultrasonic Location System and the Global Positioning System. In this case, the "unusual locations" refer to when any sub-group of entities are located at the same physical location or within a close proximity due to the accuracy of the location systems.

If a group of entities are in an unusual location, the *Location Analyser* process divides the unusually located recommender entities into possible attack groups. Since in a mobile computing environment, there are possibilities where a group of genuine entities travelling in a close proximity or travelling to a same place, the *Attack Analyser* process is applied to choose a specific detection technique for the verification.

Sybil Detection uses an intrusion detection technique that is proposed by Newsome et. al. [15] for detecting Sybil attacks in sensor networks. The assumption is entities can only broadcast and receive on a same channel at a time, and there is only one radio available with each entity. The *Sybil Detection* validates entities using radio signals. It assigns each entity of a group of unusually located entities a different channel to broadcast on, and chooses a random channel to listen to. Only the messages of the entity who were assigned to the same channel for broadcasting should be received. Otherwise there is a possible Sybil attack, an alert should be sent to the monitor to provoke the access.

DOLPHIN [28] is an Ultrasonic Location System used by the *Location Analyser* for locating devices, where it is able to provide high precision 3-dimensional positioning within an indoor environment.

4   Conclusion

Computational trust enables collaborations between entities in decentralised computing environments. Much research has been carried out in many computing environments, such as ubiquitous computing, service-based computing.

In this paper, an evaluation is carried out to demonstrate the reliability of trust-based systems. The evaluation is divided into two parts. Three existing trust-based systems are evaluated under the scenarios when there are unexpected behaviours of entities involved, and the scenarios when there are malicious entities involved. All the tested models failed to prevent from the unexpected behaviours in the given four scenarios. In the second part of the evaluation, the models show different performances in the given scenarios due to the different trust mechanisms in the models. When malicious events occur, the trust models will change the trust of the relative entities, this is often too late as the damage has been done.

While computational trust allows the autonomous collaborations between entities attempting to cope with the new security concerns that are associated with the new computing environments, yet, the evaluation has shown that it is not enough to use computational trust solely to protect entities from being damaged from various cases. Hence, a prototype monitoring model is proposed for the purpose of facilitating trust-based systems by making runtime decision at critical points. The monitoring model was specifically designed to compensate for the weaknesses inherent in trust models, where granted access to resources may be revoked if an entities behaviour or location is deemed to be suspicious.

The proposed monitor model is currently being developed. For future work, the monitor model will be evaluated to examine the performance of enhancing trust-based systems in the given scenarios and further development will be based on the evaluation results.

Acknowledgments

The authors would like to acknowledge the support of Science Foundation Ireland (under the grant 07/CE/I1147).

References

1. Blaze, M., Feigenbaum, J., Lacy, J.: Decentralized Trust Management. In: Proceedings of the 1996 IEEE Symposium on Security and Privacy, p. 164. IEEE Computer Society, Washington (1996)
2. Abdul-Rahman, A., Hailes, S.: Supporting Trust in Virtual Communities. In: Proceedings of the 33rd Hawaii International Conference on System Sciences, vol, vol. 6, p. 6007. IEEE Computer Society, Washington (2000)
3. Jia, L., Nixon, P.: Trust-based SPAM Prevention for Pervasive Advertising. In: Proceedings of the Seventh International Conference on Pervasive Computing Pervasive 2009, Workshop on Pervasive Advertising (2009)
4. Jia, L., Collins, M., Nixon, P.: Evaluating Trust-Based Access Control for Social Interaction. In: Proceedings of the Third International Conference on Mobile Ubiquitous Computing, Systems, Services and Technologies, pp. 277–282. IEEE, Sliema (2009)
5. Almenarez, F., Marin, A., Campo, C., Garcia, R.C.: TrustAC: Trust-based Access Control for Pervasive Devices. In: Hutter, D., Ullmann, M. (eds.) SPC 2005. LNCS, vol. 3450, pp. 225–238. Springer, Heidelberg (2005)
6. Gray, E., O'Connell, P., Jensen, C., Weber, S., Seigneur, J.M., Yong, C.: Towards a Framework for Assessing Trust-Based Admission Control in Collaborative Ad Hoc Applications. Trinity College Dublin Technical Report, vol. 66. Dublin, Ireland (2002)

7. Plattner, B., Nievergelt, J.: Monitoring Program Execution: A Survey. Computer 14(1), 76–93 (1981)
8. Delgado, N., Gates, A.Q., Roach, S.: A Taxonomy and Catalog of Runtime Software-fault Monitoring Tools. IEEE Trans. Softw. Eng. 30(12), 859–872 (2004)
9. Gu, W., Eisenhauer, G., Kraemer, E., Schwan, K., Stasko, J., Vetter, J., Mallavarupu, N.: Falcon: On-line Monitoring and Steering of Large-Scale Parallel Programs. In: Proceedings of the Fifth Symposium on the Frontiers of Massively Parallel Computation, pp. 422–429. IEEE Computer Society Press, Washington (1995)
10. Bruegge, B., Gottschalk, T., Luo, B.: A Framework for Dynamic Program Analyzers. In: Proceedings of the Eighth Annual Conference on Object-oriented Programming Systems, Languages, and Applications, vol. 28, p. 82. ACM, Washington (1993)
11. Zanikolas, S., Sakellariou, R.: A Taxonomy of Grid Monitoring Systems. Future General Computer System 21(1), 163–188 (2005)
12. English, C., Terzis, S., Nixon, P.: Towards Self-protecting Ubiquitous Systems: Monitoring Trust-based Interactions. Personal and Ubiquitous Computing 10(1), 50–54 (2006)
13. Čapkun, S., Hubaux, J.P., Buttyán, L.: Mobility Helps Security in Ad Hoc Networks. In: Proceedings of the 4th ACM international symposium on Mobile ad hoc networking & computing, pp. 46–56. ACM, New York (2003)
14. Douceur, J.R.: The Sybil Attack. In: Druschel, P., Kaashoek, M.F., Rowstron, A. (eds.) IPTPS 2002. LNCS, vol. 2429, pp. 251–260. Springer, Heidelberg (2002)
15. Newsome, J., Shi, E., Song, D., Perrig, A.: The sybil attack in sensor networks: analysis & defenses. In: Proceedings of the 3rd international symposium on Information processing in sensor networks, pp. 259–268. ACM, New York (2004)
16. Uddin, M.G., Zulkernine, M.: ATM: an Automatic Trust Monitoring Algorithm for Service Software. In: Proceedings of the 2009 ACM symposium on Applied Computing, pp. 1040–1044. ACM Press, New York (2009)
17. Sandhu, R., Zhang, X.: Peer-to-peer access control architecture using trusted computing technology. In: Proceedings of the tenth ACM symposium on Access control models and technologies, p. 158. ACM, New York (2005)
18. Etalle, S., Winsborough, W.H.: Integrity constraints in trust management. In: Proceedings of the tenth ACM symposium on Access control models and technologies, p. 10. ACM, New York (2005)
19. Spanoudakis, G., Kloukinas, C., Androutsopoulos, K.: Towards Security Monitoring Patterns. In: Proceedings of the 2007 ACM symposium on Applied computing, p. 1525. ACM, New York (2007)
20. Jurca, R., Faltings, B., Binder, W.: Reliable QoS monitoring based on client feedback. In: Proceedings of the 16th international conference on World Wide Web, p. 1012. ACM, New York (2007)
21. Baresi, L., Ghezzi, C., Guinea, S.: Smart monitors for composed services. In: Proceedings of the 2nd international conference on Service oriented computing, pp. 193–202. ACM, New York (2004)
22. Skene, J., Skene, A., Crampton, J., Emmerich, W.: The monitorability of service-level agreements for application-service provision. In: Proceedings of the 6th international Workshop on Software and Performance, p. 14. ACM, New York (2007)
23. Letia, I.A., Marginean, A., Groza, A.: Z-Based Agents for Service Oriented Computing. In: Huang, J., Kowalczyk, R., Maamar, Z., Martin, D., Müller, I., Stoutenburg, S., Sycara, K. (eds.) SOCASE 2007. LNCS, vol. 4504, pp. 160–174. Springer, Heidelberg (2007)

24. Yan, Y., Cordier, M.O., Pencole, Y., Grastien, A.: MonitoringWeb Service Networks in a Model-based Approach. In: Proceedings of the Third European Conference on Web Services, p. 192. IEEE Computer Society, Los Alamitos (2005)

25. Sahai, A., Machiraju, V., Wursterl, K.: Monitoring and Controlling Internet Based E-Services. In: Proceedings of the Second IEEE Workshop on Internet Applications. IEEE Computer Society, Washington (2001)

26. Robinson, W.N.: Monitoring web service requirements. In: Proceedings of the 11th IEEE International Conference on Requirements Engineering, p. 65. IEEE, Los Alamitos (2003)

27. Zhang, Y., Lin, K.J., Hsu, J.Y.J.: Accountability monitoring and reasoning in service-oriented architectures. In: Proceedings of Service Oriented Computing and Applications, vol. 1, pp. 35–50. Springer, Heidelberg (2007)

28. Fukuju, Y., Minami, M., Morikawa, H., Aoyama, T.: DOLPHIN: An autonomous indoor positioning system in ubiquitous computing environment. In: Proceedings of IEEE Workshop on Software Technologies for Future Embedded Systems, vol. 53, p. 56. IEEE, Los Alamitos (2003)

Design and Analysis of "Flexible" k-out-of-n Signatures

Raylin Tso[1], Xun Yi[2], Tadahiko Ito[2], Takeshi Okamoto[3], and Eiji Okamoto[3]

[1] Department of Computer Science, National Chengchi University, Taiwan
[2] School of Computer Science and Mathematics,
Victoria University, Australia
Graduate School of Systems and Information Engineering,
University of Tsukuba, Japan
[3] Faculty of Health Sciences, Tsukuba University of Technology, Japan
raylin@cs.nccu.edu.tw,
Xun.Yi@vu.edu.au,
tada@cipher.risk.tsukuba.ac.jp,
ken@cs.k.tsukuba-tech.ac.jp,
okamoto@cipher.risk.tsukuba.ac.jp

Abstract. This paper presents a new kind of (k, n)-threshold ring signature ((k, n)-ring signature) which is just a combination of k $(1, n)$-ring signatures. Our construction guarantees that a single signer can close at most one ring so the result of the combination is the required (k, n)-ring signature. This construction is useful in, for example, electronic negotiations or games where gradual revelation on how many people signed a given document is required. It also provides flexibility of the threshold k. The threshold-flexibility means that, in our scheme, we can change a (k, n)-ring signature into a (k', n)-ring signature for any $k' \leq n$ *without revoking* the original (k, n)-ring signature. This is useful for signers to withdraw their signatures afterward and/or is useful for new signers to add their (partial of the ring) signatures into the original ring signature. In addition, when $k' < k$, this modification requires no extra computation. The security of the proposed scheme is proved in the random oracle model based on the hardness of the discrete logarithm problem and the intractability of inverting cryptographic one-way hash functions.

Keywords: DL problem, threshold-flexibility, hash functions, threshold ring signature.

1 Introduction

In many multi-user cryptographic applications, anonymity is required to ensure that information about the user is not revealed. Typical examples are electronic voting [8], whistle blowing [22], or anonymous membership authentication for ad hoc groups [5]. To provide the signer anonymity, there are two major paradigms: group signature [3,6,7,10] and ring signature [4,12,14,22]. These schemes specifies a set of possible signers and a proof that is intended to convince any verifier

B. Xie et al. (Eds.): ATC 2010, LNCS 6407, pp. 255–267, 2010.
© Springer-Verlag Berlin Heidelberg 2010

that the author of the signature belongs to this set, while hiding his identity. The difference between these two paradigms is that in a group signature, the anonymity of a signer can be revoked by an authority if necessary, while in a ring signature, it does not support anonymity revocation mechanism.

Ring signature scheme was first formalized by Rivest et al. [22]. After then, using the concept of partitioning, Bresson et al. [5] successfully extended the ring signature scheme into a k-out-of-n threshold ring signature ((k, n)-ring signature for short) scheme. A (k, n)-ring signature allows any group of k entities to spontaneously conscript arbitrarily $n - k$ entities and to generate a publicly verifiable k-out-of-n signature on behalf of the whole group while keeping the anonymity of the real signers. The anonymity of signers is preserved both inside (excluding the k signers) and outside the signing group. Following Bresson et.al.'s pioneer work, many researches have been done in an attempt to extend a ring signature into a (k, n)-ring signature. Most of them (eg., [9,16]) are based on the concept of secret sharing [24].

Motivation: In existing threshold ring signature schemes, the threshold k is fixed so the number of real signers is known to a verifier at beginning according to the protocol. It is nature to ask whether we can have a threshold scheme in which how many people signed a given document can be revealed gradually. This may be useful in applications such as the electronic negotiations or on-line games. On the other hand, in some applications, for example, in the case when a (k, n)-ring signature is used for whistle blowing, it is possible that, later on after signed the document, some signers changed their decisions and would like to withdraw the parts of their (anonymous) signatures. It is also possible that some entities (ie., non-signers) would like to join the signing group and sign the document afterward. To achieve this goal, the only way for secret sharing based (k, n)-ring signature schemes is to first revoke the original (k, n)-ring signature and then produce a new (k', n)-threshold ring signature. This would be very inefficient and is inconvenient for signers.

Our Contribution: In this paper, based on Abe et al.'s ($1, n$)-ring signature (AOS scheme) [1], we propose a new (k, n)-ring signature. Our scheme enables each signer to produce a AOS-like ($1, n$)-ring signature. In addition, by the trick of making good use of hash functions and the reuse of some short-term information in all rings, our scheme guarantees that each signer can form and close only one ring and the combination of these k signatures is the required (k, n)-ring signature. Since the result is the combination of k ($1, n$)-ring signatures, by revealing each ($1, n$)-ring signature one by one, our scheme is possible to gradually reveal how many people signed a given documents. In other words, verifiers may not now the threshold k until all the k signatures are revealed. This means that our scheme provides the flexibility of the threshold k.

In addition to reveal the number of signers gradually, flexibility of the threshold k is also useful in other purpose. That is, in our scheme, to revoke a signer's (partial) signature of a ring or to add a new entity into the signing group can be done very efficiently without the revocation of the original (k, n)-ring signature.

Moreover, if the new threshold $k' < k$, then the new signature can be done without any further computation. This can be achieved since our (k, n)-threshold ring signature is a combination of k individual $(1, n)$-ring signatures.

Related Work: Except the anonymity and unforgeability, there are some threshold ring signature schemes which provide other special properties. For example, a ring signature with a constant size, which is proposed by Dodies et al. [12]. An individual-linkability to threshold ring signature scheme proposed by Tsang et al. [25] which enables anyone to determine if two ring signatures are signed with the help of the same signer. A traceable ring signature proposed by Fujisaki and Suzuki [14] which can restrict excessive anonymity. A separable threshold ring signature proposed by Liu et al. [16] which enables the use of various flavours of public keys in a single threshold ring signature. A ring signature derived from a short signature proposed by Zhang et al. [27] and ring signature schemes with the property of identity-based (ID-based) which can be found in [2,9,15,26]. The first certificateless ring signature scheme which can avoid the public key validity checking is proposed by Chow and Yap [11]. On the other hand, there is no (k, n)-ring signature scheme that can provide the flexibility of the threshold k.

2   Preliminaries

2.1   Framework of Flexible (k, n)-Ring Signature Schemes

A flexible (k, n)-ring signature scheme is a triple of algorithms $(\mathcal{G}, \mathcal{S}, \mathcal{V})$.

- $(pk_j, sk_j) \leftarrow \mathcal{G}(1^{\lambda_j})$: A probabilistic polynomial-time algorithm $\mathcal{G}$ which takes a security parameter λ_j as input and the output is the public/private key pair (pk_j, sk_j) of an entity U_j.
- $\{\sigma_1, \cdots, \sigma_n\} \leftarrow \mathcal{S}^{k,n}(m, \widehat{SK}_k, L)$: A probabilistic polynomial-time algorithm $\mathcal{S}$ which takes as inputs a message m, a set of k private keys $\widehat{SK}_k$, and a set L of n public keys which includes the ones corresponding to $\widehat{SK}_k$, the output is a (k, n)-ring signature $\sigma = \{\sigma_1, \cdots, \sigma_n\}$ on m. In addition, each $\sigma_i, 1 \leq i \leq n$, is a $(1, n)$-ring signature on the same message m.
- $1/0 \leftarrow \mathcal{V}(m, \breve{\sigma}_t, L)$: A deterministic polynomial-time algorithm $\mathcal{V}$ which takes as inputs a message m, a subset $\breve{\sigma}_t \subseteq \sigma$ of t $(1, n)$-ring signatures where $t \leq k$ and a set L of n public keys, returns 1 or 0 for accept or reject the ring signature with threshold t, respectively.

2.2   Security Definitions

The security of a ring signature has two aspects: signer ambiguity and unforgeability. Following the definitions given in [1] and [16], the signer ambiguity is defined as follows:

Definition 1 (Signer Ambiguity). Let $L = \{pk_1, \cdots, pk_n\}$ be a set of n public keys where each key is generated as $(pk_i, sk_i) \leftarrow \mathcal{G}(1^{\lambda_i})$ for some $\lambda_i \in \mathbb{Z}$. A

(k, n)-ring signature scheme provides unconditionally signer ambiguous if, given $(\widehat{sk}_L, L, m, \sigma)$ where $\widehat{sk}_L$ and L are defined the same as those at Section 2.1. m is a message and σ is a valid signature generated by the signing algorithm (ie., $\sigma \leftarrow S^{k,n}(m, \widehat{SK}_k, L)$), any unbound adversary $\mathcal{A}$ outputs i such that $sk_i \in \widehat{SK}_k$ with probability k/n. Here $\widehat{SK}_k$ is a set of k private keys corresponding to the k public keys in L.

Signer ambiguity assures that even all the private keys are disclosed, it remains uncertain of which k signers out of n possible signers actually work jointly to generate a (k, n)-ring signature.

The unforgeability of a flexible (k, n)-ring signature scheme is defined in the following game between a simulator $\mathcal{S}im$ and an adversary $\mathcal{A}$.

Definition 2 (Simulation Game). Let $\mathcal{FRS} = (\mathcal{G}, \mathcal{S}, \mathcal{V})$ be a flexible (k, n)-ring signature scheme. Let $\mathcal{A}$ be a probabilistic polynomial-time (PPT) forging algorithm.

- At the beginning, $\mathcal{S}im$ generates a set of n public keys $L = \{pk_1, \cdots, pk_n\}$ and gives L to $\mathcal{A}$.
- at any time, $\mathcal{A}$ may query the following oracles according to any adaptive strategy.
  - $sk_i \leftarrow \mathcal{CO}(pk_i)$: The corruption oracle, on input a public key $pk_i \in L$, returns the corresponding secret key sk_i of pk_i.
  - $\{z_1, \cdots, z_n\} \leftarrow \mathcal{SGO}(L)$: The short-term public key generation oracle, on input the public key set L, returns the short-term public keys $Z = \{z_1, \cdots, z_n\}$ of $\{pk_1, \cdots, pk_n\}$ for each signing phase. Here each short-term public key set Z in one run of the protocol is independent of that generated in other runs of the protocol.
  - $r_i \leftarrow \mathcal{SCO}(z_i)$: The short-term private key corruption oracle, on input a short-term public key $z_i \in Z$, returns the corresponding short-term private key r_i of the user with public key pk_i.
  - $\sigma \leftarrow \mathcal{SO}(k, Z, \mathcal{K}, m)$: The signing oracle, on input a threshold $k \in \{1, \cdots, n\}$, a set Z of n short-term public keys which is generated from $\mathcal{SGO}$ and has not been used as part of the input to $\mathcal{SO}$ before, a set $\mathcal{K} \subseteq L$ s.t. $|\mathcal{K}| = k$ and a message $m \in \mathcal{M}$, returns a valid signature σ signed by the set of users whose public keys are in $\mathcal{K}$.
- $\mathcal{S}im$ is responsible for replying all the queries to the above mentioned oracles. In addition, $\mathcal{A}$ can also access to all the hash functions of the scheme which are treated as random oracles.
- The above steps can be executed in polynomially many number of times and $\mathcal{A}$ can decide in an adaptive fashion when to stop.
- At the end of the game, $\mathcal{A}$ outputs a forged (k, n)-ring signature σ^* along with a threshold $k \in \{1, \cdots, n\}$, a short-term public key set Z^* and a message $m \in \mathcal{M}$.

We say $\mathcal{A}$ wins the game if: (1) $\mathcal{V}(m, \sigma^*, L) = 1$, (2) the short-term public key set Z^* is fresh which is generated from $\mathcal{SGO}$ and has not been used as one of the input to $\mathcal{SO}$, (3)either at most $(k-1)$ of the public keys in L have been input to

$\mathcal{CO}$ or at most $(k-1)$ of the short-term public keys in Z^* corresponding to the forged signature σ^* have been input to $\mathcal{SGO}$, and (4) σ^* is not a query output of $\mathcal{SO}$ on any input containing the message m.

Definition 3 (Unforgeability). A flexible (k,n)-ring signature scheme is unforgeable if for any PPT attacking adversary $\mathcal{A}$, it wins the simulation game with only negligible probability in a security parameter λ.

3 Building Block: Abe et al.'s 1-out-of-n Signature Scheme

System Setting: For a user U_i in the system, define his public key to be $(p_i, q_i, g_i, y_i, H_i)$ and private key to be $x_i \in Z_{q_i}$. Here p_i, q_i are two large primes and $q_i | p_i - 1$, g_i is an element of $Z_{p_i}^*$ with order q_i and $y_i = g_i{}^{x_i} \bmod p$. In addition, $H_i : \{0,1\}^* \to Z_{q_i}$ is a collision resistant one-way hash function.

Signing: Let L be a list of n public keys. To generate a 1-out-of-n signature on a message $m \in \{0,1\}^*$, a signer U_k with a private key x_k do the following steps.

(1) **Initialization:** U_k chooses $\alpha_k \in_R Z_{q_k}$, then computes $a_k = g_k{}^{\alpha_k} \bmod p_k$, and $c_{k+1} = H_{k+1}(L||m||a_k)$.

(2) **Forward sequence:** For $j = k+1, \cdots, n-1, 0, \cdots, k-1$, U_k chooses $s_j \in_R Z_{q_j}$, then computes $a_j \leftarrow g_j{}^{s_j} y_j{}^{c_j} \bmod p_j$, and $c_{j+1} \leftarrow H_{j+1}(L||m||a_j)$.

(3) **Forming the ring:** U_k computes $s_k = \alpha_k - x_k c_k \bmod q_k$. The signature σ on m is $\sigma \leftarrow (c_1, s_1, \cdots, s_n)$.

Verifying: Any verifier checks the signature σ according to the following protocol:

- For j from 1 to n, computes $a_j = g_j{}^{s_j} y_j{}^{c_j} \bmod p_i$, and $c_{j+1} = H_{j+1}(L||m||a_j)$.
- Accept σ as a valid 1-out-of-n signature if and only if $c_1 = c_{n+1}$, otherwise, reject the signature.

Remark: It is obvious that running the above protocol k times does not guarantee generation of a (k,n)-ring signature, since the produced k signatures may be generated by less than k entities (or by even one entity in an extremely case). In the next section, by explicitly using hash functions, we show how to extend the $(1,n)$-ring signature into a (k,n)-ring signature.

4 From $(1,n)$-Ring Signatures to (k,n)-Ring Signatures

4.1 High-Level Overview

The general idea of our scheme is to provide each signer U_i an additional short-term private/public key-pair (r_i, z_i) where $z_i = g_i{}^{r_i} - H_i(l_i)$ for some public l_i. Each l_i is chosen by a singer U_i. The restriction is that l_i chosen by U_i is different from l_j chosen by U_j. For simplicity, each l_i, $1 \le i \le k$, will be chosen from 1 to k. Each l_i will stand for the index of the l_i-th ring (ie., the l_i-th 1-out-of-n signature) which will be closed (ie., signed) by the signer U_i. To sign a message, both the (long-term, short-term) private keys are required. However, although the short-term public key z_i of U_i remains the same in each ring, the corresponding (short-term) private key is different in each ring. To see this, assume there are k signers (ie., there are k rings signed by k different signers) and $l_i = i, 1 \leq i \leq k$, then for z_i of the signer U_i, $z_i = g_i^{r_{i1}} - H_i(1)$ in the first ring, $z_i = g_i^{r_{i2}} - H_i(2)$ in the second ring and so forth. Therefore, we have

$$z_i = g_i^{r_{i1}} - H_i(1) = \cdots = g_i^{r_{ij}} - H_i(j) = \cdots = g_i^{r_{ik}} - H_i(k).$$

Each r_i is the short-term private key in each ring corresponding to the short-term public key z_i which is "identical" in each ring. r_{i1} is required in order to close the first ring, r_{i2} is required in order to close the second ring, and so fourth. Because of the hardness of the DL problem, each singer U_i can only determine one secret r_i with regard to z_i as his short-term private key. Consequently, each signer can close only one ring. This means that our scheme ensures that each ring is closed by different signers and the combination of these rings is the required (k, n)-ring signature. Notice that the signature is verified using each U_i's public key pair (y_i, z_i) in all rings so no user can choose two different short-term public keys z_i and z'_i in two rings.

4.2   The Flexible (k, n)-Ring Signature Scheme

System Setting: The same as those in Section 3.

Signing: Let L be a list of n public keys. To generate a (k, n)-ring signature on a message $m \in \{0, 1\}^*$, a set S of k signers do the following steps. W.l.o.g., we assume $S = \{U_1, \cdots, U_k\}$.

(1) Each signer $U_i \in S$ picks a random number l_i where $1 \leq l_i \leq k$. In addition, l_i is picked in public to other signers in S in order to make sure that $l_i \neq l_{i'}$ if $U_i \neq U_{i'}$. For easy of description, in the rest of the paper, we will assume that for i from 1 to k, a signer U_i picks i.

(2) For the other members $U_j, k + 1 \leq j \leq n$, who are not real signers but their public keys $pk_{k+1}, \cdots, pk_n$ are in the set L, the signers in S collaborate in picking $z_j \in \mathbb{Z}_{p_j}$ at random for j from $k + 1$ to n.

(3) Each signer $U_i \in S$ computes a z_i of itself by first picking $r_i \in \mathbb{Z}_{q_i}$ at random and then computing $z_i = g_i^{r_i} - H_i(i) \bmod p_i$. U_i then opens z_i to all signers in S.

(4) With the common knowledge of $Z_L = \{z_1, \cdots, z_n\}$, where each z_j stands for the short term public key of U_j, each signer $U_i \in S$ does the following steps individually in order to form a ring (ie., to generate a $(1, n)$-ring signature).

- Pick $\alpha_{(i,i)} \in_R \mathbb{Z}_{q_i}$.
- Compute $a_{(i,i)} = g_i^{\alpha_{(i,i)}} \bmod p_i$.
- Compute $c_{(i,i+1)} = H_{i+1}(L||m||Z_L||a_{(i,i)})$.

Here a subscript of $\triangle_{(i,j)}$ means the j-th element of $\triangle$ of the i-th ring.

-(**Forward sequence**): for $j = i+1, \cdots, n, 1, \cdots$ to $i-1$, signer U_i computes the following parameters for U_j at the i-th ring.
- $s_{(i,j)} \in_R \mathbb{Z}_{q_j}$.
- $a_{(i,j)} \leftarrow ((z_j + H_j(i))g_j)^{s_{(i,j)}} y_j^{c_{(i,j)}} \bmod p_j$.
- $c_{(i,j+1)} \leftarrow H_{j+1}(L||m||Z_L||a_{(i,j)})$.

Remark: Note that at the i-th ring, in order to generate $a_{(i,j)}$, the input of each hash function $H_j, 1 \le j \le n$, is a fixed number i.

-(**Closing the ring**): the signer U_i closes the i-th ring by computing

$$s_{(i,i)} = (\alpha_{(i,i)} - x_i c_{(i,i)})/(r_i + 1) \bmod q_i$$

(5) Each U_i outputs the results of step (4) to signers in $\mathcal{S}$. That is, each $U_i, 1 \le i \le k$, outputs $(c_{(i,1)}, s_{(i,1)}, \cdots, s_{(i,n)})$.
(6) The signing group $\mathcal{S}$ outputs the results in step (5) together with the set of short-term public keys $Z_L = \{z_1, \cdots, z_n\}$, and forms the signature σ on m as

$$\sigma \leftarrow \left(Z_L, \bigcup_{1 \le i \le k} \left(c_{(i,1)}, s_{(i,1)}, \cdots, s_{(i,n)}\right)\right).$$

Verifying: Any verifier checks the signature σ according to the following protocol:

(1) For i from 1 to k, and for j from 1 to n, computes:
- $a_{(i,j)} = (z_j + H_j(i))g_j^{s_{(i,j)}} y_j^{c_{(i,j)}} \bmod p_j$.
- $c_{(i,j+1)} = H_{j+1}(L||m||Z_L||a_{(i,j)})$ if $j \ne n$.
(2) Accept σ as a (k,n)-ring signature if and only if $c_{(i,1)} = H_1(L||m||Z_L||a_{(i,n)})$ for all $i, 1 \le i \le k$. Otherwise, reject the signature.

5   Security Analysis

We first show the consistency of the scheme. The consistency of a scheme means that any properly generated signature via the signature generation protocol of the scheme should always be accepted by the signature verification protocol of the same scheme. In our scheme, to prove the consistency, it is sufficient to show that, for each i, $1 \le i \le k$, $((z_i + H_i(i))g_i)^{s_{(i,i)}} y_i^{c_{(i,i)}} \bmod p_i = g_i^{\alpha_{(i,i)}} \bmod p_i$. We show that this is always the case if the signature is properly generated.

$$
\begin{aligned}
((z_i + H_i(i))g_i)^{s_{(i,i)}} y_i^{c_{(i,i)}} &= ((z_i + H_i(i))g_i)^{(\alpha_{(i,i)} - x_i c_{(i,i)})/(r_i+1)} y_i^{c_{(i,i)}} \\
&= ((g_i^{r_i} - H_i(i) + H_i(i))g_i)^{(\alpha_{(i,i)} - x_i c_{(i,i)})/(r_i+1)} y_i^{c_{(i,i)}} \\
&= (g_i^{r_i} g_i)^{(\alpha_{(i,i)} - x_i c_{(i,i)})/(r_i+1)} y_i^{c_{(i,i)}} \\
&= g_i^{(r_i+1)(\alpha_{(i,i)} - x_i c_{(i,i)})/(r_i+1)} g_i^{x_i c_{(i,i)}} \\
&= g_i^{\alpha_{(i,i)} - x_i c_{(i,i)} + x_i c_{(i,i)}} \\
&= g_i^{\alpha_{(i,i)}} \qquad (\bmod p_i).
\end{aligned}
$$

To consider the signer ambiguity and unforgeability of the scheme, we first reduce the security of the propose scheme to the security of Abe et al.'s scheme [1] when $k = 1$.

Theorem 1. When $k = 1$, the proposed scheme is unconditionally signer ambiguous and provides existential unforgeability against adaptive chosen message attack (EUF-ACMA) if the Abe et al.'s scheme [1] is signer ambiguous and EUF-ACMA secure in the random oracle model.

Proof: Suppose an adversary $\mathcal{A}$ who can existentially forge a signature or break the signer ambiguous of the proposed scheme when $k = 1$. We construct a PPT algorithm/forger $\mathcal{B}$ which can break the EUF-ACMA security or the signer ambiguous of the scheme in [1] by running $\mathcal{A}$ and simulating the oracles that $\mathcal{A}$ can query.

Consider the game which is similar to that in Definition 4 with a little modification (since we assume $k = 1$ and consider the signer ambiguity in the same game) run by a simulator $\mathcal{S}$ and an algorithm $\mathcal{B}$. First, $\mathcal{S}$ runs the **System Setting** algorithm of Abe et al.'s scheme to generate a set L of public keys of users. Then $\mathcal{S}$ runs $\mathcal{B}$ by given the public keys of each user to $\mathcal{B}$. The purpose of $\mathcal{B}$ is either to forge a new signature or break the signer ambiguity of Abe et al.'s scheme. During the simulation, $\mathcal{B}$ can make queries onto three oracles: **random oracles** H_i, **sign oracle** $\mathcal{SO}$, and **reveal oracle** $\mathcal{RO}$. Each H_i is treated as a real oracle which output a random number from the domain Z_{q_i}. The **sign oracle** $\mathcal{SO}$ outputs a valid signature of Abe et al.'s scheme when given input a set of public key $L' \subseteq L$ and a message m. The **Reveal Oracle** $\mathcal{RO}$ reveal the real signer of a signature generated via the **sign oracle** $\mathcal{SO}$.

We now describe how $\mathcal{B}$ simulates our proposed scheme for $\mathcal{A}$ when $k = 1$. First, $\mathcal{B}$ sets L as the set of public keys of users of the proposed scheme. $\mathcal{B}$ then runs $\mathcal{A}$ on L. $\mathcal{A}$ can make queries onto five oracles: **random oracles** H_i^{new}, **short-term public key generation oracle** $\mathcal{SGO}^{new}$, **short-term private key corruption oracle** $\mathcal{SCO}^{new}$, **sign oracle** $\mathcal{SO}^{new}$, and **reveal oracle** $\mathcal{RO}^{new}$. Below are how the queries made by $\mathcal{A}$ are answered.

- **short-term public key generation oracle** $\mathcal{SGO}^{new}$: On input the public key set L, $\mathcal{B}$ picks $r_i \in Z_{q_i}$ and computes $z_i \leftarrow g_i^{r_i} - H_i(1) \bmod p_i$ for each $i, 1 \leq i \leq n$. Here $H_i(1)$ is the output of the real oracle H_i that $\mathcal{B}$ can access. $\mathcal{B}$ then returns $\{z_1, \cdots, z_n\}$ to $\mathcal{A}$. $\mathcal{B}$ also records $\{(r_1, z_1), \cdots, (r_n, z_n)\}$ in the $\mathcal{SGO}^{new} - List$ which is initially empty.

- **short-term private key corruption oracle** $\mathcal{SCO}^{new}$: On any input z_i, $\mathcal{B}$ output the corresponding r_i from the $\mathcal{SGO}^{new} - List$.

- **random oracles** H_i^{new}: On any input $(L'||m||Z_{L'}||a)$ of H_i^{new}, $\mathcal{B}$ set $m' = m||Z_{L'}$ and asks the random oracle H_i of itself on input $(L'||m'||a)$. The output of H_i is then forward to $\mathcal{A}$ as the output of H_i^{new}.

- **sign oracle** $\mathcal{SO}^{new}$: On input $(L', Z_{L'}, m)$ where $Z_{L'}$ is in the $\mathcal{SGO}^{new} - List$, $\mathcal{B}$ sets $m' = m||Z_{L'}$ and asks the sign oracle $\mathcal{SO}$ of itself on input L' and message m'. Assume the output from $\mathcal{SO}$ is $\sigma' = (c_1', s_1', \cdots, s_n')$. $\mathcal{B}$ then sets $s_i = s_i'/(r_i + 1)$ for each i from 1 to n. Here each r_i is found from $\mathcal{SGO}^{new} - List$ which is the corresponding short-term private key of z_i. $\mathcal{B}$ then sets the signature $\sigma = (Z_{L'}, c_1, s_1, \cdots, s_n)$ and returns σ to $\mathcal{A}$. (σ, σ') is then recorded in the $Sign - List$.

- **reveal oracle $\mathcal{RO}^{new}$:** On input a signature σ generated from **sign oracle** $\mathcal{SO}^{new}$, $\mathcal{B}$ finds the corresponding σ' from the $Sign - List$ and asks the **reveal oracle** $\mathcal{RO}$ of itself. The output, which is the public key of the real signer is then forwarded to $\mathcal{A}$ as the public key of the real signer of the signature σ.

Finally, $\mathcal{A}$ wins the game if

(1) $\mathcal{A}$ outputs a successful forgery $\sigma^* = (Z_{L^*}, c_1^*, s_1^*, \cdots, s_n^*)$ on the public key set L^* and a message m^* where Z_{L^*} is fresh and is generated from $\mathcal{SGO}^{new}$. The value of Z_{L^*} can then be found at $\mathcal{SGO}^{new} - List$.

(2) $\mathcal{A}$ outputs a public key pk^* of the real signer on a signature σ^* generated from $\mathcal{SGO}^{new} - List$.

If $\mathcal{A}$ wins the game via case (1), $\mathcal{B}$ then finds the corresponding r_i^* of each $z_i^* \in Z_{L^*}$, computes $s_i^{*'} = s_1^* \times (r_i + 1)$ for $1 \leq i \leq n$. Then $\sigma = (c_1^*, s_1^{*'}, \cdots, s_n^{*'})$ will be a successful forgery on the same public key set L^* and the message $m||Z_{L^*}$. On the other hand, if $\mathcal{A}$ wins the game via case (2), then $\mathcal{B}$ wins its game by outputting the same public key pk^* which belongs to the real signer who signed the signature $\sigma^{*'}$. The pair (σ^*, σ^*) is recorded in the $Sign - List$.

Consequently, when $k = 1$ if there exists an adversary $\mathcal{A}$ who can break the EUF-ACMA security or the signer ambiguity of the proposed scheme with non-negligible probability, then we can construct another adversary $\mathcal{B}$ who can break the EUF-ACMA security or the signer ambiguity of Abe et al.'s scheme [1] with non-negligible probability. This ends the proof. □

When $k \geq 2$ and assume a (k, n)-ring signature of our scheme is

$$\sigma = \left(\bigcup_{1 \leq i \leq n} z_i, \bigcup_{1 \leq i \leq k} \left(c_{(i,1)}, s_{(i,1)}, \cdots, s_{(i,n)} \right) \right).$$

then we first partition the signature σ into $\sigma_1, \cdots, \sigma_k$ where

$$\sigma_i = (c_{(i,1)}, z_1, \cdots, z_n, s_{(i,1)}, \cdots, s_{(i,n)}), 1 \leq i \leq k.$$

Note that all σ_i, $1 \leq i \leq k$, share the same values of $z_1, \cdots, z_n$.

From Theorem 1, we conclude that each $\sigma_i, 1 \leq i \leq k$, is unconditionally signer ambiguous and EUF-ACMA secure in the random oracle model. Consequently, to prove that the signature σ is a secure (k, n)-ring signature, it is sufficient to show that each signature σ_i is signed by different signers. In other words, the l-th ring (ie., the signature σ_l) is closed by the signer who picked l in Step (1) of our scheme.

We first prove that, given a fixed short-term public key z_i, a ring cannot be closed without the corresponding short-term private key r_i even though the long-term private key x_i is known. For easy to understand, assume that there is only 1 entity U_A in the ring so $L = pk_A$ and the $(1, 1)$-ring signature on a message m is (c, z, s). To verify the signature, anyone first computes $a = ((z + H(1))g)^s y^c$ then checks whether c is equal to $H(L||m||z||a)$ or not.

Let $z' = (z + H(1))g$ and convert the hash function H to another hash function H' by setting $H'(L||m||z'||a) = H(L||m||z||a)$, then the output of the signature scheme can be modified in the form of (c, z', s). To verify the correctness of the signature, anyone first computes $a = z'^s y^c$ and then checks whether c is equal to $H'(L||m||z'||a)$ or not. To compute s is equivalent to compute $\log_{z'} a/y^c$. Since the value a must be determined before c according to the one-way property of hash functions (ie., $c = H(L||m||z'||a)$) and the value of c is dependent on the value of a, $a/y^c \bmod p$ is a random value in $\mathbb{Z}_p$ which cannot be determined by U_A. So finding $\log_{z'} a/y^c$ is computationally infeasible and is as hard as fining $\log_g z'$. Using similar proof as that in [1], it can be prove that, if there exists an adversary who can forge a new signature without knowing $\log_g z'$, then given $(p, q, g, z' = (g^l \bmod p))$ to a simulator, the simulator can use the adversary as a black box and solve the DL problem $\log_g^{z'}$, which will be equal to $x(c_\pi - c'_\pi)/(s'_\pi - s_\pi) \bmod q$. Here x is a long-term private key which is determined by the simulator. We omitted this part due to the page limitation.

We have proved that a ring cannot be closed without a short-term private key r even though the long-term private key x is known. We now prove that no one knows two different short-term private keys r_i, r'_i corresponding to the same short-term public key z_i.

Since z_i is unique in each ring (ie. each signature) $\sigma_j, 1 \leq j \leq k$, if U_i wants to close j-th ring with subscript $j \neq i$, he must have the short-term private key r_j corresponding to z_i in j-th ring such that

$$g_i^{r_j} - H_i(j) = z_i = g_i^{r_i} - H_i(i) \pmod{p_i}.$$

Because of the hardness of the DL problem, we know that U_i is infeasible to find both r_i and r_j. Consequently, each signer U_i can close at most one ring and form one $(1, n)$ signature so the combination of the k signatures is the required (k, n)-ring signature scheme. We have the following theorem.

Theorem 2. Based on the hardness assumption of DL problem, the proposed (k, n)-ring signature scheme is unconditionally signer ambiguous and EUF-ACMA secure in the random oracle model.

6   Avoiding Insider Attacks

The signer ambiguity of the proposed scheme is only proved secure against adversaries from outside. When malicious signers exist who do not follow the protocol, the signer ambiguity will be vulnerable. However, anonymity of the signer must be remained, even if malicious signers exist.

If a malicious signer wants other signers to make a signature, he can persuade them to accept his short-term public key, say z_i, then after everyone else provides their 1-out-of-n signature, he can prove that his z_i can't be formed to $g_i^{r_i} - H_i(i)$, for example $z_i = H_i(d)$ where d is a random string. Therefore he can't be one of the signers.

In other words, malicious signer can control signer's ambiguity, and signer lose not only ambiguity, but also anonymity. To avoid this attack, each potential signer can prove the possession of the short-term private key to the other signers via a zero knowledge proof [20] before signing. A zero knowledge proof is a way that a prover can prove possession of a certain piece of information to a verifier without revealing it.

7   Flexibility of the Threshold k

In some applications, singners able to change their decisions after sign their (anonymous) signatures. On the contrary, it is also possible that some "non-signers" may hope to join the signing group and sign the same document afterward (before the signature being published). To do this, the way for secret sharing based ring signature schemes is to first revoke the original (k, n)-ring signature and then produce a new (k', n)-threshold ring signature. Our scheme solves this problem without revoking the original signature and does not require any further computation.

Since our (k, n)-ring signature is a combination of k individual $(1, n)$-ring signatures, in our scheme, assume the original (k, n)-ring signature σ on a message m is

$$\sigma = \left(\bigcup_{1 \leq i \leq n} z_i, \bigcup_{1 \leq i \leq k} \left(c_{(i,1)}, s_{(i,1)}, \cdots, s_{(i,n)} \right) \right)$$

and a signer, say U_k, who changed his decision and hopes to revoke his partial signature, what the signing group should do is to just withdraw U_k's signature σ_k and the new $(k-1, n)$-ring signature on m will become

$$\sigma' = \left(\bigcup_{1 \leq i \leq n} z_i, \bigcup_{1 \leq i \leq k-1} \left(c_{(i,1)}, s_{(i,1)}, \cdots, s_{(i,n)} \right) \right).$$

On the contrary, if U_k is hesitate in signing a document at the beginning, he can first participate in the signature generation at steps (1) to (3) of our protocol (in order to generate his short-term private key and publish his short-term public key). Then, he can individually form a ring signature of his part without opening the signature to other signers. In this case, the signature on m produced by other $k-1$ signers would be σ' and is actually a $(k-1, n)$-ring signature. Later on, when U_k decides to sign the document, he just appends his signature to σ' and the new signature would be σ, which is the desired (k, n)-ring signature. Note that U_k can do this since he knows both the short/long term private keys (r_k, x_k) of the corresponding public keys (z_k, y_k). In addition, Data size of signature is $n|p| + k(n+1)|q|$, and computation cost is $o(2kn^p)$ both for signature generation, and Verification.

8   Conclusion

In this paper, we propose a new (k, n)-ring signature scheme which is an extension of Abe's 1-out-of-n signature scheme[1]. Our scheme not only provides the flexibility of the threshold k but also the flexibility of public keys. The flexibility of public keys means that the key pair of each signer can be generated by different KGC and the domains of keys for all signers are not required to be identical.

Flexibility of the threshold k is useful in the applications when a signer wants to withdraw a ring signature of his part or wants to join the signing group and sign the same document later on. It also allows the value of the threshold to be revealed gradually.

References

1. Abe, M., Ohkubo, M., Suzuki, K.: 1-out-of-n signatures from a variety of keys. In: Zheng, Y. (ed.) ASIACRYPT 2002. LNCS, vol. 2501, pp. 415–432. Springer, Heidelberg (2002)
2. Awasthi, A.K., Lal, S.: ID-based ring signature and proxy ring signature schemes from bilinear pairings, Cryptology ePrint Archive, Report 2004/184 (2004), http://eprint.iacr.org/2004/184.pdf
3. Bellare, M., Micciancio, D., Warinschi, B.: Foundations of group signatures: Formal definitions, simplified requirements, and a construction based on general assumptions. In: Biham, E. (ed.) EUROCRYPT 2003. LNCS, vol. 2656, pp. 614–629. Springer, Heidelberg (2003)
4. Boneh, D., Gentry, C., Lynn, B., Shacham, H.: Aggregate and verifiably encrypted signatures from bilinear maps. In: Biham, E. (ed.) EUROCRYPT 2003. LNCS, vol. 2656, pp. 416–432. Springer, Heidelberg (2003)
5. Bresson, E., Stern, J., Szydlo, M.: Threshold ring signatures and applications to ad-hoc groups. In: Yung, M. (ed.) CRYPTO 2002. LNCS, vol. 2442, pp. 465–480. Springer, Heidelberg (2002)
6. Briefer, E., Aubin, T., Lehongre, K., Rybak, F.: How to identify dear enemies: the group signature in the complex song of skylark Alauda arvensis. Journal of Experimental Bilogy 211, 317–326 (2008)
7. Chaum, D., van Heijst, E.: Group signatures. In: Davies, D.W. (ed.) EUROCRYPT 1991. LNCS, vol. 547, pp. 257–265. Springer, Heidelberg (1991)
8. Cramer, R., Franklin, M., Schoenmakers, B., Yung, M.: Multi-authority secret-ballot elections with linear work. In: Maurer, U.M. (ed.) EUROCRYPT 1996. LNCS, vol. 1070, pp. 72–83. Springer, Heidelberg (1996)
9. Chow, S.S.M., Hui, L.C.K., Yiu, S.M.: Identity based threshold ring signature. In: Park, C.-s., Chee, S. (eds.) ICISC 2004. LNCS, vol. 3506, pp. 218–232. Springer, Heidelberg (2005)
10. Camenisch, J.: Efficient and generalized group signatures. In: Fumy, W. (ed.) EUROCRYPT 1997. LNCS, vol. 1233, pp. 465–479. Springer, Heidelberg (1997)
11. Chow, S.S.M., Yap, W.: Certificateless ring signatures, Cryptology ePrint Aechive, http://eprint.iacr.org/2007/236
12. Dodies, Y., Kiayias, A., Nicolosi, A., Shoup, V.: Anonymous identification in ad-hoc groups. In: Cachin, C., Camenisch, J.L. (eds.) EUROCRYPT 2004. LNCS, vol. 3027, pp. 609–626. Springer, Heidelberg (2004)
13. Fiat, A., Shamir, A.: how to prove yourself. In: Odlyzko, A.M. (ed.) CRYPTO 1986. LNCS, vol. 263, pp. 186–199. Springer, Heidelberg (1987)
14. Fujisaki, E., Suzuki, K.: Traceable ring signature. IEICE Transactions on Fundamentals of Electronics, Communications and Computer Sciences E91-A(1), 83–93 (2008)
15. Herranz, J.: Identity-based ring signatures from RSA. Theoretical Computer Science 389(1), 100–117 (2007)

16. Liu, J.K., Wei, V.K., Wong, D.S.: A separable threshold ring signature scheme. In: Lim, J.-I., Lee, D.-H. (eds.) ICISC 2003. LNCS, vol. 2971, pp. 12–26. Springer, Heidelberg (2004)

17. Liu, J.K., Wei, V.K., Wong, D.S.: Linkable spontaneous anonymous group signature for ad hoc groups. In: Wang, H., Pieprzyk, J., Varadharajan, V. (eds.) ACISP 2004. LNCS, vol. 3108, pp. 325–335. Springer, Heidelberg (2004)

18. Ohta, K., Okamoto, T.: On concrete security treatment of signatures derived from identification. In: Krawczyk, H. (ed.) CRYPTO 1998. LNCS, vol. 1462, pp. 354–369. Springer, Heidelberg (1998)

19. Pointcheval, D., Stern, J.: Security proofs for signature schemes. In: Maurer, U.M. (ed.) EUROCRYPT 1996. LNCS, vol. 1070, pp. 387–398. Springer, Heidelberg (1996)

20. Quisquater, J., Guillou, L., Berson, T.: How to explain zero-knowledge protocols to your children. In: Brassard, G. (ed.) CRYPTO 1989. LNCS, vol. 435, pp. 628–631. Springer, Heidelberg (1990)

21. Rivest, R.L., Shamir, A., Adleman, L.: A method for obtaining digital signatures and public key cryptosystems. Communications of the ACM 21, 120–126 (1978)

22. Rivest, R., Shamir, A., Tauman, Y.: How to lead a secret. In: Boyd, C. (ed.) ASIACRYPT 2001. LNCS, vol. 2248, pp. 552–565. Springer, Heidelberg (2001)

23. Schnorr, C.P.: Efficient signature generation by smart cards. Journal of Cryptology 4(3), 161–174 (1991)

24. Shamir, A.: How to share a secret. ACM Comm. 22, 612–613 (1979)

25. Tsang, P.P., Wei, V.K., Chan, T.K., Au, M.H., Liu, J.K., Wong, D.S.: Separable linkable threshold ring signatures. In: Canteaut, A., Viswanathan, K. (eds.) INDOCRYPT 2004. LNCS, vol. 3348, pp. 384–398. Springer, Heidelberg (2004)

26. Zhang, F., Kim, K.: ID-based blind signature and ring signature from pairings. In: Zheng, Y. (ed.) ASIACRYPT 2002. LNCS, vol. 2501, pp. 533–547. Springer, Heidelberg (2002)

27. Zhang, F., S-Naini, R., Susilo, W.: An efficient signature scheme from bilinear pairings and its application. In: Bao, F., Deng, R., Zhou, J. (eds.) PKC 2004. LNCS, vol. 2947, pp. 277–290. Springer, Heidelberg (2004)

A Formal Framework for Trust Policy Negotiation in Autonomic Systems: Abduction with Soft Constraints*

Stefano Bistarelli[1,2], Fabio Martinelli[2], and Francesco Santini[1,2]

[1] Dipartimento di Matematica e Informatica, Università di Perugia, Italy
{bista,francesco.santini}@dmi.unipg.it
[2] Istituto di Informatica e Telematica (CNR), Pisa, Italy
{stefano.bistarelli,fabio.martinelli,francesco.santini}@iit.cnr.it

Abstract. We show that soft constraints can be used to model logical reasoning, that is deduction and abduction (and induction). In particular, we focus on the abduction process and we show how it can be implemented with a (soft) constraint removal operator. As a running application example throughout the paper, we reason with access control policies and credentials. In this way, we can associate the level of preference defined by the "softness" of the constraint with a "level" of trust. The main benefit comes during the process of automated access authorization based on trust: soft constraint operations can be easily adopted to measure the level of trust required for each operation. Moreover, when the level is not sufficient, abduction can be used to compute the missing credentials and the levels that grant the access, making the request a (weighted) logical consequence. The proposed framework can be used to automate the deduction-abduction negotiation processes.

1 Introduction and Motivations

In this work we interpret *Logical Reasoning* [19,20] in the soft constraint field [2], in order to grant an authorization based on credentials and trust derivation. The classical operators as deduction and abduction are implemented by soft constraint operators, having in this way a powerful and expressive tool for the automated computation of these related problems, which also take a preference score into account.

Using logic programming languages for security policy is customary in computer security: in [5,6] the authors have presented a variant of RT language [16] (called it RT^W) that use soft constraints and is able to deal with weights on ground facts and to consequently compute a feedback result for the goal satisfaction. The proposed RT^W framework is able to represent policies: by querying

---

* This work has been partially supported by EU-FP7-ICT ANIKETOS, EU-FP7-ICT CONNECT projects and MIUR PRIN 20089M932N project: "Innovative and multi-disciplinary approaches for constraint and preference reasoning".

B. Xie et al. (Eds.): ATC 2010, LNCS 6407, pp. 268–282, 2010.
© Springer-Verlag Berlin Heidelberg 2010

such programs we can infer if the authorization, given a specific set of credentials, is allowed or not with a specific level of trust. For example, a credential can now state that the referred entity is a "student" with a probability of 80% because her/his identity of student is based on what an acquaintance asserts (thus, it is not as certain as declared in IDs). Therefore, also the final authorization decision can be taken according to a trust value related to the composition of all the used credentials, e.g. with a total probability greater than 90%. In literature there are many examples where trust or reputation are computed by aggregating some values together [5,6,13].

However, often the user simply wants to obtain a service or to access to a resource, and he does not know which credential is needed [15], or which level of trust is needed to obtain the access. Thus, often the user simply presents a very small set of credentials and expects the system to return enough information to guide him towards the missing credentials that grant him to access. When the user obtains such information, he can decide to present such credentials or, for instance, to buy the necessary credentials with "enough" trust level, in order to definitely access to the service. Two basic services can be used inside authorization systems. The first one is represented by deduction [15,19]: given a policy and a set of additional facts and events, the service finds out all consequences (actions or obligations) of the policy and the facts, i.e. whether granting the request can be deduced from the policy and the current facts. Abstracting away the details of the policy implementation, we can observe that only one reasoning service is actually used by policy based self-management: deduction. Given a policy, we find out all consequences (actions or obligations) of the policy, i.e. whether granting the request can be deduced from the policy and the current facts.

Access authorization usually needs another reasoning service: abduction [15,19]. Loosely speaking, abduction is deduction in reverse: given a policy and a request for access to (e.g.) services, it consists in finding the credentials/events that would grant access, i.e. a (possibly minimal) set of facts that added to the policy would make the request a logical consequence. The intuition behind an interactive (client-server) access control system is the following: i) initially a client submits a set of credentials and a service request then, ii) the server checks whether the request is granted by the access policy according to the client's set of credentials. If the check fails, iii) by using abductive reasoning the server finds a (minimal) solution set of (disclosable) missing credentials that unlocks the desired resource and iv) returns them to the client, so that v) he can provide them in the second round. At last we propose also how the third operator, i.e. induction, can be expressed with constraints.

These services provided by logical reasoning are important in autonomic networks of nodes [15], where partners offer services and lightly integrate their efforts into one (hopefully coherent) network. This cross enterprise scenario poses novel security challenges with aspects of trust management systems. Access to services is offered by autonomic nodes on their own and the decision to grant or deny access must rely on attribute credentials sent by the client [15]. Therefore, when speaking about autonomic authorization, the abduction process it is exactly what one node looks for. By using soft constraints, the user wishes to obtain a resource with a specific trust level, and the server answer has to provide not only the expected credential (that the user needs to present), but also the trust level of such credential. access to a generic student service, sometimes it could be enough to have an id-card, sometimes a personal badge for the student fitness activities, depending on the final trust level.

In Sec. 2 we summarize the fundamental notions about soft constraints, while Sec. 3 shows how classical deduction, abduction and induction operations can be implemented by using constraint composition and division, i.e. $\otimes$ and $\ominus$; to complete the presentation of logical reasoning. Section 4 shows an implementation of deduction/abduction operations by using *Constraint Handling Rules* [12]. At last, Sec. 5 discusses the related work and Sec. 6 draws the final conclusions.

2   Background on Soft Constraints

An absorptive semiring [4] S can be represented as a $\langle A, +, \times, \mathbf{0}, \mathbf{1} \rangle$ tuple such that: *i)* A is a set and $\mathbf{0}, \mathbf{1} \in A$; *ii)* $+$ is commutative, associative and $\mathbf{0}$ is its unit element; *iii)* $\times$ is associative, distributes over $+$, $\mathbf{1}$ is its unit element and $\mathbf{0}$ is its absorbing element. Moreover, $+$ is idempotent, $\mathbf{1}$ is its absorbing element and $\times$ is commutative. Let us consider the relation $\leq_S$ over A such that $a \leq_S b$ iff $a + b = b$. Then it is possible to prove that (see [7]): *i)* $\leq_S$ is a partial order; *ii)* $+$ and $\times$ are monotonic on $\leq_S$; *iii)* $\mathbf{0}$ is its minimum and $\mathbf{1}$ its maximum; *iv)* $\langle A, \leq_S \rangle$ is a complete lattice and, for all $a, b \in A$, $a + b = lub(a, b)$ (where lub is the *least upper bound*). Informally, the relation $\leq_S$ gives us a way to compare semiring values and constraints. In fact, when we have $a \leq_S b$ (or simply $a \leq b$ when the semiring will be clear from the context), we will say that b *is better than* a.

In [4] the authors extended the semiring structure by adding the notion of *division*, i.e. $\div$, as a weak inverse operation of $\times$. An absorptive semiring S is *invertible* if, for all the elements $a, b \in A$ such that $a \leq b$, there exists an element $c \in A$ such that $b \times c = a$ [4]. If S is absorptive and invertible, then, S is *invertible by residuation* if the set $\{x \in A \mid b \times x = a\}$ admits a maximum for all elements $a, b \in A$ such that $a \leq b$ [4]. Moreover, if S is absorptive, then it is *residuated* if the set $\{x \in A \mid b \times x \leq a\}$ admits a maximum for all elements $a, b \in A$, denoted $a \div b$. With an abuse of notation, the maximal element among solutions is denoted $a \div b$. This choice is not ambiguous: if an absorptive semiring is invertible and residuated, then it is also invertible by residuation, and the two definitions yield the same value.

To use these properties, in [4] it is stated that if we have an absorptive and complete semiring[1], then it is residuated. For this reason, since all classical soft constraint instances (i.e. *Classical, Fuzzy, Probabilistic* and *Weighted*) are complete and consequently residuated, the notion of semiring division can be applied

---

[1] If S is an absorptive semiring, then S is complete if it is closed with respect to infinite sums, and the distributivity law holds also for an infinite number of summands.

to all of them. Therefore, for all these semirings it is possible to use the $\div$ operation as a "particular" inverse of $\times$; its extension to soft constraints, defined as $\ominus$, can be used to remove soft constraints from the store.

A *soft constraint* [7,2] may be seen as a constraint where each instantiation of its variables has an associated preference. Given $S = \langle A, +, \times, \mathbf{0}, \mathbf{1} \rangle$ and an ordered set of variables V over a (finite) domain D, a soft constraint is a function which, given an assignment $\eta : V \to D$ of the variables, returns a value of the semiring. Using this notation $\mathcal{C} = \eta \to A$ is the set of all possible constraints that can be built starting from S, D and V.

Any function in $\mathcal{C}$ involves all the variables in V, but we impose that it depends on the assignment of only a finite subset of them. So, for instance, a binary constraint $c_{x,y}$ over variables x and y, is a function $c_{x,y} : (V \to D) \to A$, but it depends only on the assignment of variables $\{x, y\} \subseteq V$ (the *support*, or *scope*, of the constraint). Note that $c\eta[v := d_1]$ means $c\eta'$ where η' is η modified with the assignment $v := d_1$. Notice also that, with $c\eta$, the result we obtain is a semiring value, i.e. $c\eta = a$ with $a \in A$.

Given the set $\mathcal{C}$, the combination function of constraints $\otimes : \mathcal{C} \times \mathcal{C} \to \mathcal{C}$ is defined as $(c_1 \otimes c_2)\eta = c_1\eta \times c_2\eta$ (see also [7,2]). Having defined the operation $\div$ on semirings, the constraint division function $\ominus : \mathcal{C} \times \mathcal{C} \to \mathcal{C}$ (which subtracts the second constraint from the first one) is instead defined as $(c_1 \ominus c_2)\eta = c_1\eta \div c_2\eta$ [4]. Basing ourselves on the definition of $\div$ and given $S = \langle A, +, \times, \mathbf{0}, \mathbf{1} \rangle$, $a \div b$ is defined as the m maximal element of the set $\{x \in A \mid b \times x \leq a\}$. Therefore, $n \leq_S m$ for every other element n in the set and, extended to constraints, $c_n \sqsubseteq_S c_m \iff c_n(x = n) \leq_S c_m(x = m)$, i.e. the other possible constraints obtained by choosing a different x in $\{x \in A \mid b \times x \leq_S a\}$ imply the one obtained by choosing the m maximal element. For this reason, the $\ominus$ operator is able to find the minimal explanation (see Sec. 3). Given a constraint $c \in \mathcal{C}$ and a variable $v \in V$, the *projection* [7,2] of c over $V - \{v\}$, written $c \Downarrow_{(V \setminus \{v\})}$ is the constraint c' such that $c'\eta = \sum_{d \in D} c\eta[v := d]$. Informally, projecting means eliminating some variables from the support.

Informally, performing the $\otimes$ or the $\ominus$ between two constraints means building a new constraint whose support involves all the variables of the original ones, and which associates with each tuple of domain values for such variables a semiring element which is obtained by multiplying or, respectively, dividing the elements associated by the original constraints to the appropriate sub-tuples. The partial order $\leq_S$ over $\mathcal{C}$ can be easily extended among constraints by defining $c_1 \sqsubseteq c_2 \iff c_1\eta \leq c_2\eta$. Consider the set $\mathcal{C}$ and the partial order $\sqsubseteq$. Then, an entailment relation $\vdash \subseteq \wp(\mathcal{C}) \times \mathcal{C}$ is defined s.t. for each $C \in \wp(\mathcal{C})$ and $c \in \mathcal{C}$, we have $C \vdash c \iff \bigotimes C \sqsubseteq c$ (see also [2]). Therefore we can say that if, given a constraint store σ, $\sigma \sqsubseteq c$ (or $\sigma \vdash c$), then c is a *logical consequence* of σ.

Considering a semiring $S = \langle A, +, \times, \mathbf{0}, \mathbf{1} \rangle$, a domain of the variables D, an ordered set of variables V and the corresponding structure $\mathcal{C}$, then $S_\mathcal{C} = \langle \mathcal{C}, \otimes, \bar{\mathbf{0}}, \bar{\mathbf{1}}, \exists_x, d_{xy} \rangle$ is a cylindric constraint system ("a la Saraswat")[2].

---

[2] Notice that in SCCP, algebraicity is not required, since the algebraic nature of $\mathcal{C}$ strictly depends on the properties of the semiring [2].

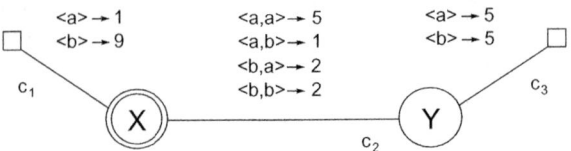

Fig. 1. A soft CSP based on a Weighted semiring

A SCSP Example. Figure 1 shows a weighted SCSP as a graph: the used semiring is the *Weighted* semiring, i.e. $\langle \mathbb{R}^+, \min, \hat{+}, \infty, 0 \rangle$ ($\hat{+}$ is the arithmetic plus operation). Variables and constraints are represented respectively by nodes and by arcs (unary for c_1 and c_3, and binary for c_2), and semiring values are written to the right of each tuple. $D = \{a, b\}$. The solution of the CSP in Fig. 1 associates a semiring element to every domain value of variables X and Y by combining all the constraints together, i.e. $Sol(P) = \bigotimes C$. For instance, for the tuple $\langle a, a \rangle$ (that is, $X = Y = a$), we have to compute the sum of 1 (which is the value assigned to $X = a$ in constraint c_1), 5 (which is the value assigned to $\langle X = a, Y = a \rangle$ in c_2) and 5 (which is the value for $Y = a$ in c_3). Hence, the resulting value for this tuple is 11. For the other tuples, $\langle a, b \rangle \to 7$, $\langle b, a \rangle \to 16$ and $\langle b, b \rangle \to 16$. The *blevel* for the example in Fig. 1 is 7, related to the solution $X = a, Y = b$.

3 Logical Reasoning with Soft Constraints

In this Section we redefine two basic logical reasoning processes [19], deduction and abduction, by using the framework based on soft constraints and presented in Sec. 2. To accomplish this, we adopt the $\otimes$, $\ominus$ and $\sqsubseteq$ operators as summarized in Sec. 2. We show that both deduction and abduction processes can be described them.

Deduction. Deduction means determining the conclusion, thus to use a rule and its precondition to make a conclusion [15,19]. An Example is "When a paper is poorly presented, it receives a bad review. The paper I am reviewing is poorly written, then I write a bad review". An argument is said to be deductive when the truth of the conclusion necessarily follows or is a logical consequence of the truth of the premises and (consequently) its corresponding conditional is a necessary truth. Deductive arguments are said to be valid or invalid, never true or false. A deductive argument is valid if and only if the truth of the conclusion actually does follow necessarily (or is indeed a logical consequence of) the premises and (consequently) its corresponding conditional is a necessary truth. In Def. 1 we define deduction through soft constraints:

Definition 1. [Deduction with soft constraints] *Given a soft constraint store σ which represents the current knowledge and a soft constraint c, if $\sigma \sqsubseteq c$ then the store entails (i.e. deduces) c.*

Therefore, w.r.t. Def. 1, the store σ represents the premise and c a logical consequence of σ. The $\vdash$ (or $\sqsubseteq$, see Sec. 2) consequently implements the deduction operator as for the crisp $\vdash$ entailment operator [10].

As introduced in Sec. 1, we use a running example based on Policy-based Access Control to show how "soft" deduction and abduction can be used. We suppose that the soft constraint store contains all the collected information, i.e. the access policy and the credentials presented by the requestor and other parties, that is, for example, external databases. A credential, in a general definition, is an attestation of qualification, competence, or authority issued to an individual by a third party with the authority or the competence to do so. A policy describes the rules that grant the authorization. With respect to Def. 1, the σ store represents the policy p and the collected credentials c, i.e. $\sigma = p \otimes c$, and the store entails (i.e. deduces) the access request r if $\sigma \sqsubseteq r$.

An example of policy and credentials is given in the program in Tab. 1: we adopt the RT_0^W language [5,6], a weighted extension of the well-known RT_0 language [16].

Table 1. An example in RT_0^W, with weights associated to the credentials

```
   EPub.disct  ⟵—  EPub.preferred ∩ EPub.brightStudent.
EPub.preferred  ⟵—  EOrg.highBudget ∩ EOrg.oldCustomer.
EPub.brightStudent  ⟵—  EPub.goodUniversity.highMarks.
EPub.goodUniversity  ⟵—  ABU.accredited.
      ABU.accredited  ⟵—  ⟨ StateU, 9 ⟩.
     StateU.highMarks  ⟵—  ⟨ Alice, 8 ⟩.
     EOrg.highBudget  ⟵—  ⟨ Alice, 6 ⟩.
    EOrg.oldCustomer  ⟵—  ⟨ Alice, 7 ⟩.
```

The example in Tab. 1 describes a fictitious Web publishing service, *EPub*, which offers a discount to anyone who is both a preferred customer and a bright student. *EPub* delegates the authority over the identification of preferred customers to its parent organization, *EOrg*. In order to be evaluated as a preferred customer, *EOrg* must issues two different types of credentials stating that the customer is not new (i.e. *EOrg.oldCustomer*) and has already spent some money in the past (i.e. *EOrg.highBudget*). *EOrg* assigns a cost value to both these two credentials to quantify its evaluation. *EPub* delegates the authority over the identification of bright students to the entities that are accredited universities. To identify such universities, *EPub* accepts accrediting credentials issued by the fictitious *Accrediting Board for Universities (ABU)*. *ABU* evaluates a university with a fuzzy score and each university evaluates its enrolled students. A student is bright if she/he is both enrolled in a good university and has high marks. To solve the example in Tab. 1, we use a *Weighted* semiring $S_{Weighted} = \langle \mathbb{R}^+, min, \hat{+}, +\infty, 0 \rangle$, where $\hat{+}$ is the arithmetic sum and where the preference levels in $\mathbb{R}^+$ represents the money cost that is needed to buy or retrieve a given credential (e.g. the cost to pay the office supplies and the clerk service): for example, `StateU.highMarks` $\longleftarrow$ $\langle$ Alice, 8 $\rangle$ in Tab. 1 certifies that Alice has obtained a good number of high marks for the exams completed at the StateU university (the credential is issued by StateU), and the cost associated with this credential is 8 euro.

The last four rules represent the weighted credentials presented to the authorization entity, while the other rules consist in the access policy. The example, together with the deduction process, is described in the next paragraph. The final money cost, obtained by composing together all the values of the used credentials, can be compared with a threshold to authorize the discount: e.g. only entities whose set of credentials produced a score greater than 7 are authorized. The four credentials, which are all used by the policy rules, prove that Alice is eligible for the discount with a money cost of 30: $6\hat{+}7\hat{+}8\hat{+}9 = 30$ euro.

By considering Def. 1 and the example in Tab. 1, we can use the deduction operation in the following simple and crisp example (also classical crisp problems can be cast in the soft framework [7,2] by using the *Classical* semiring $\langle\{true, false\}, \vee, \wedge, false, true\rangle$): if $\sigma = Student(Alice) \otimes HighMarks(Alice) \otimes (Student(x) \wedge HighMarks(x) \sqsubseteq Access(x))$, then $\sigma \sqsubseteq Access(Alice)$, we can deduce that Alice can access. The policy in Tab. 1 has been also implemented in *CIAO Prolog* in [6].

Abduction. Abduction consists in using the conclusion and the rule to support that the precondition could explain the conclusion [15,19]. For example, "When a paper is poorly presented, it receives a bad review. I received a bad review for my paper, therefore it is poorly presented". Therefore, if the σ does not store enough information to satisfy c (i.e. the c conclusion cannot be obtained with deduction), it is interesting to automatically obtain the missing information that would allow to satisfy c. In Def. 2 we define abduction by using the $\ominus$ operation presented in Sec. 2:

Definition 2. [Abduction with soft constraints] *Given a soft constraint store σ and a constraint c, then the abduction process is aimed at finding a constraint d, such that $\sigma \otimes d \sqsubseteq c$, i.e. $d = c \ominus \sigma$.*

Notice that the division operator we are adopting is a deterministic operator (see Sec. 2) and provides a single solution d (which is also the minimal solution, as explained in the following of this section). Considering Def. 2, the trivial case is when $\sigma \sqsubseteq c$ since $c \ominus \sigma = \bar{1}$, that is nothing must be added to the store in order to satisfy c, which is already implied by it.

Access Control for autonomic communication needs the abduction reasoning service [22]. The key idea is that in an autonomic network a client may have the right credentials but may not know them and thus an autonomic communication server needs a way to avoid leaving the client stranded. If we consider our application example on policy-based access control, $\sigma = p \otimes c$ represent the policy p and a c credential, and the abducted d constraint is such that $\sigma \otimes d \sqsubseteq r$, i.e. $d = r \ominus \sigma$, where d is the abducting credential for the access request r.

An explanation is an input which can explain the result (via the given the inference rules). A minimal explanation, is one which makes just as many assumptions as needed to obtain an explanation [10]. The concept of minimal explanation is important because it consists in the minimal amount of information needed to obtain the desired consequence: disclosing more credentials could lead to privacy problems since more than enough information is revealed. The abduction operation in Def. 2 is able to find the minimal (in this case, soft) explanation as proposed in [10] for the crisp version, according to the definition of ÷, and consequently ⊖ shown in Sec. 2 and in [4]. Therefore, the d constraint in Def. 2 is the minimal explanation of c.

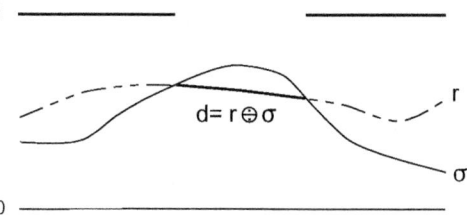

Fig. 2. The representation of σ, the request r and the abducted soft constraint d, represented with the thick line

A graphical intuition of the "soft" abduction definition is given in Fig. 2. There we consider the *Fuzzy* semiring $S_{Fuzzy} = \langle[0..1], max, min, 0, 1\rangle$, that is we analyze the truth degree connected to a credential and evaluated by the entity which signs and issues it, as proposed for the examples in [5,6]. Suppose that the soft constraints σ and r (and consequently $d = r \ominus \sigma$) have as their support only the variable x, which represents the entity that requests the authorization; these constraints are represented as functions in x in Fig. 2. Suppose that $\sigma = Student(Alice) \otimes (Student(x) \wedge HighMarks(x) \sqsubseteq Access(x))$, and that $r = Access(x)$, then $d = HighMarks(x)$. Moreover, if $\sigma(x= Alice) = 0.9$ and $r(x= Alice) = 0.7$, then $d(x= Alice) = 0.7$. Thus Alice needs to attest the fact that she has high marks with a trust score 0.7 or greater. Where $\sigma(x) \leq r(x)$, then $d(x) = 1$, otherwise $d(x) = r(x)$, according to the definition of ÷ given in [4]:

$$a \div b = max\{x \mid min\{b, x\} \leq a\} = \begin{cases} 1 & \text{if } b \leq a \\ a & \text{if } a < b \end{cases}$$

Now suppose to consider the *Weighted* semiring $S_{Weighted} = \langle\mathbb{R}^+, min, \hat{+}, +\infty, 0\rangle$. If $\sigma(x= Alice) = 7$ and $r(x= Alice) = 10$, then $d(x= Alice) = 3$ ($d = r \ominus \sigma$). Since $d = HighMarks(x)$, this operation suggests Alice to provide a credential attesting that she has *HighMarks* and to spend at least 3 euro, in order to be able to access. The definition of ÷ (i.e. the arithmetic subtraction $\hat{-}$) is:

$$a \div b = min\{x \mid b\hat{+}x \geq a\} = \begin{cases} 0 & \text{if } b \geq a \\ a\hat{-}b & \text{if } a > b \end{cases}$$

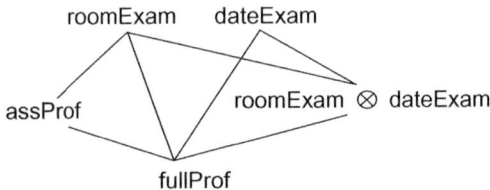

Fig. 3. A lattice representing the strength of roles: *fullProf* entails all the other roles

Notice that the credentials can be seen as partially ordered: *assistant profes-sor < associate professor < full professor*, that is the *full professor* credential provides higher access capabilities w.r.t. *assistant professor*. This partial order can be easily represented with semiring (see Sec 2). This role hierarchy, where higher the role in the hierarchy, more powerful it is, is adopted also in [15]. A role dominates another role if it is higher in the hierarchy and there is a direct path between them in the lattice representing the hierarchy of roles. For example, *fullProf(X)* ⊑ *dateExam(X)* ⊗ *roomExam(X)*, but *assProf(X)* ⊑ *roomExam(X)* only, i.e. the assistant professor has less rights. The complete lattice of roles is shown in Fig. 3.

It is worth to notice that our ⊕ operation can be considered as a "relaxation" of the store, and not only as a strict removal of the token representing the constraint, because in soft constraints we do not have the concept of token. Thus, if we perform $\sigma \ominus c$ during the abduction phase, c can be removed even if it is different from any other constraints previously added to σ; therefore, it is also possible to remove only a part of a piece of information (e.g. a part of a credential). For example, considering the five soft constraints reported in Fig. 4 and the *Weighted* semiring, $c_1 \otimes c_2 = c_3$, and at this point we can also remove c_4 from c_3, that is $c_3 \ominus c_4 = c_5$, even if c_4 has been not already added to the store before, but it is however implied by it. To show this concept with a crisp example, it is like if the constraint store is equivalent to *I have a car* and we could remove *A tire of my car is punctured* obtaining *I have a car with three not punctured tyres*.

Induction. Logical reasoning includes also a third kind of reasoning, i.e. *induc-tion*, also known as *inductive reasoning* or *inductive logic*, that is a type of rea-soning which involves moving from a set of specific facts to a general conclusion. In words, induction means determining the "rule" that leads to the conclusion

$$c_1 : (\{x\} \to \mathbb{N}) \to \mathbb{R}^+ \text{ s.t. } c_1(x) = x + 3 \qquad c_2 : (\{x\} \to \mathbb{N}) \to \mathbb{R}^+ \text{ s.t. } c_2(x) = x + 5$$
$$c_3 : (\{x\} \to \mathbb{N}) \to \mathbb{R}^+ \text{ s.t. } c_3(x) = 2x + 8 \qquad c_4 : (\{x\} \to \mathbb{N}) \to \mathbb{R}^+ \text{ s.t. } c_4(x) = x + 1$$
$$c_5 : (\{x\} \to \mathbb{N}) \to \mathbb{R}^+ \text{ s.t. } c_5(x) = x + 7$$

Fig. 4. Five weighted soft constraints; notice that $c_3 = c_1 \otimes c_2$ and $c_5 = c_3 \ominus c_4$

from precondition. An example of induction could start from the fact that "I have always received bad reviews when writing papers about bioinformatics", it is possible to learn the rule "If I write papers about bioinformatics, then I will receive a bad review" (because, for example, my interests cover only trust and security).

Induction is a valuable tool for autonomic nodes, because complete and consistent access policies may be difficult to write [15]. For example, if a node has only a partial policy and an additional set of examples of access, both permitted or forbidden. This node should be able, by generalizing from the examples, to derive a policy that matched the given examples and is also able to answer other similar queries.

Even if this paper is mainly focused on the abduction process, we can hint that constraint have been already used in literature to solve also this problem: in works as [8,23] the authors suggest learning algorithms that deduce (crisp or soft) constraints from assignments of values to sets of variables. This can be used when the formulation of the problem is not available, or also to find new constraints in order to fasten the search of the solution, by further reducing the allowed assignment of variables.

In [1] the authors simulate the task of learning an SCSP, given a fixed constraint graph and some examples of solution ratings. It is assumed that the level of preference for some solutions is known, and a suitable learning technique is defined to learn the values to be associated with each constraint tuple, in a way that is compatible with the level of preference.

4   Deduction and Abduction in CHR

In this section we implement the deduction and abduction operations presented in Sec. 3 by using the *Constraint Handling Rules* [12] (CHR) language.

CHR is a high-level language designed for writing user-defined constraint systems. It is essentially a committed-choice language consisting of guarded rules that rewrite constraints into simpler ones until they are solved. There are three kinds of CHR rules: *simplification, propagation* and *simpagation*. Simplification rules replace user-defined constraints by simpler ones. Propagation rules add new redundant constraints that may be necessary to do further simplifications. A simpagation rule is equivalent to a simplification rule with some of the heads repeated in the body. On a simpagation rule only the heads after the \ sign are removed. CHR libraries are available in most Prolog implementations: in particular, for the following examples we have used *SWI-Prolog* [24].

In Fig. 5 we implement the deduction process by translating the RT_0^W program in Tab. 1. Given the five simplification rules (i.e., *policy*1, ..., *policy*4), which represent the access policy, and the first query, (i.e. 1 ?-), that is *accredited(aBU, stateU, 9), highMarks(stateU, alice, 8), highBudget(eOrg, alice, 6), oldCustomer(eOrg, alice, 7), discount(alice, 25).*) which represents the set of presented credentials and the discount request (i.e. *discount(alice, 25)*), we are able to deduce that Alice can have discount. In fact the system answers with

```
:- use_module(library(chr)).

:- chr_constraint preferred/2, brightStudent/2, highBudget/3,
                  oldCustomer/3, highMarks/3, goodUniversity/2,
                  accredited/3, discount/2, access/1.

policyrule1    @ preferred(X, A), brightStudent(X, B), discount(X, T) <=>
                 (A+B)>= T | access(X).
policyrule2    @ highBudget(Z, X, A), oldCustomer(Z, X, B) <=>
                 preferred(X, C), C is (A+B).
policyrule3    @ goodUniversity(X, A), highMarks(X, Y, B) <=>
                 brightStudent(Y, C), C is (A+B).
policyrule4    @ accredited(X, Y, A) <=> goodUniversity(Y, A).

1 ?- accredited(aBU, stateU, 9), highMarks(stateU, alice, 8),
     highBudget(eOrg, alice, 6), oldCustomer(eOrg, alice, 7),
     discount(alice, 25).

access(alice)

2 ?- accredited(aBU, stateU, 9), highMarks(stateU, alice, 8),
     highBudget(eOrg, alice, 6), discount(alice, 25).

brightStudent(alice, 17)
highBudget(eOrg, alice, 6)
discount(alice, 25)
```

Fig. 5. Deduction with CHR rules: solving the example in Tab. 1

access(alice). The solver can fire the first rule (i.e. *policyrule1*) because the sum of the trust level of the credentials, which is $= 30$ is greater than the requested threshold in the discount request, which is 25. As a remind, in this example (as for the one in Tab. 1) we use the weighted semiring, that is the $\times$ operator of the semiring is modeled with the arithmetic addition.

The second query (i.e. 2 ?-) in Fig. 5 is presented to show what happens when any of the credentials is not presented to the authorization system: without the *oldCustomer(eOrg, alice, 7)* credential missing in the query, the CHR rules in Fig. 5 are not able to compute the consequences in *policyrule2* rule, that is Alice is *preferred* for *eOrg*.

In this case, that is when the *access* constraint is not added to the store and, therefore, the access is not granted, the rules in Fig. 6 can be used to abduce the missing credentials with the (minimum) required level of trust. The query is now represented by the store obtained at the end of the failed access in Fig. 5, i.e. *brightStudent(alice, 17), highBudget(eOrg, alice, 6), discount(alice, 25)*. The program answers that we need the *oldCustomer* credential with a level of trust equal or greater than 2: the sum of the weights of the other two credentials is 23 and the discount is required with 25. Notice that, w.r.t. the policy in Tab. 1, in Fig. 6 we show only a subset of the abduction rules for sakes of brevity, i.e. the subset concerning the branch under *EPub.preferred*. This subset represent only the rules needed to answer to the first abduction query, since the *brightStudent* has been already deduced by the program in Fig. 5: the other (not shown here) abduction rules are not used in this example.

```
:- use_module(library(chr)).

:- chr_constraint preferred/2, brightStudent/2, highBudget/3, oldCustomer/3,
                  discount/2, sum/1.

abdrule1  @   discount(X, A), brightStudent(X, B) <=> C is (A-B),
              preferred(X, C).
abdrule2  @   discount(X, A) <=> preferred(X, A).
abdrule3  @   preferred(X, A), highBudget(Z, X, B) <=> C is (A-B),
              oldCustomer(Z, X, C).
abdrule4  @   preferred(X, A), oldCustomer(Z, X, B) <=> C is (A-B),
              highBudget(Z, X, C).
abdrule5  @   preferred(X, A) <=> oldCustomer(Z, X, B),
              highBudget(Z, X, C) , sum(A).

1 ?- brightStudent(alice, 17), highBudget(eOrg, alice, 6), discount(alice, 25).

oldCustomer(eOrg, alice, 2)

2 ?- discount(alice, 25).

highBudget(_G88354, alice, _G88403)
oldCustomer(_G88354, alice, _G88356)
comb(25)
```

Fig. 6. Abduction with CHR rules

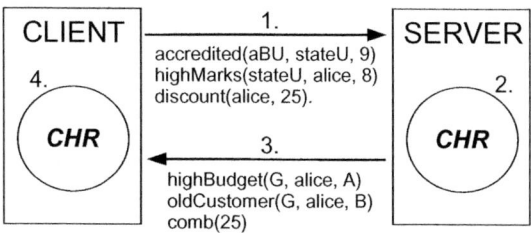

Fig. 7. Trust negotiation with CHR solvers

In the second query in Fig. 6 the program abduce both the missing credentials (i.e. *oldCustomer* and *highBudget*) needed to receive the discount. Moreover, it replays with a further constraint stating that the combination (i.e. the $\times$ semiring operator) of trust scores for these credentials must be 25 at least (i.e. *comb(25)*).

The deduction/abduction processes in CHR can be adopted to implement trust negotiation, as represented in the system architecture in Fig. 7: *1)* the client sends its credentials in order to be authorized, *2)* the server uses its CHR solver to deduce the authorization or to abduce the missing credentials, that *3)* are sent back to the client; *4)* the client then uses its solver to decide, for example, the appropriate level of trust to be assigned to each missing credential, in order to reach (by combining them) the required threshold (i.e. 25 for the example in Fig. 7). In this way, the negotiation process is interactive.

5   Related Work

The importance of the deduction and abduction operations for policy-based management of autonomic networks has been already highlighted in [15]. An Autonomic Network crosses organizational boundaries and is provided by entities that see each other just as business partners. Policy-based network management already requires a paradigm shift in the access control mechanism, from identity-based access control to trust management and negotiation. In [15] the authors present an algorithm whose operations are expressed with logic, and so the access authorization procedure is not directly implemented with a tool in the paper.

Among the most noticeable works concerning logical reasoning and (crisp) constraints, we need to cite Maher, e.g. [17] where he investigates abduction applied to fully-defined predicates, specifically linear arithmetic constraints over the real numbers. In [18], Maher and Huang address the problem of computing and representing answers of constraint abduction problems over the Herbrand domain. This problem is of interest when performing type inference involving generalized algebraic data types. Notice that in [21] the authors present a CHR-based tool for detecting security policy inconsistencies, where policy are represented by CHR rules.

In [11] the authors consider configuration problems with preferences rather than just hard constraints, and we analyze and discuss the features that such preference-based configurators should have. In particular, these configurators, should provide explanations for the current state, implications of a future choice. is done by keeping track of the inferences that are made during the constraint propagation enforcing phases.

Concerning instead systems to implement abduction and deduction processes, abduction reasoning has been already realized in *HYPROLOG* [9] (available also in SWI-Prolog), which is an extension of Prolog and CHR with abduction and assumptions. The system is basically implemented by a compiler that translates the HYPROLOG syntax in a rather direct way into Prolog and CHR. Another implementation of this kind of system is represented by ACLP [14]; ACLP is a system which combines abductive reasoning and constraint solving by integrating the frameworks of *Abductive Logic Programming* and *Constraint Logic Programming* (CLP). The ACLP system is currently implemented on top of the CLP language of ECLiPSe as a meta-interpreter exploiting its underlying constraint solver for finite domains.

6   Conclusions

In this paper we have proposed how two important logical reasoning processes, i.e. deduction and abduction can be modeled and solved with soft constraints [2]. We mainly focused on the abduction phase, since deduction was already available in the framework with the classical (soft) constraint entailment. Abduction can be implemented through the use of the $\oplus$ operator (see Sec. 2).

Deduction and abduction are presented with the help of a running example based on policy-based access control, in order to immediately describe a possible application of these operators and their importance to derive knowledge. We manage trust-based access authorization with weighted credentials, i.e. credentials where the associated level of trust can be used to enrich the authorization process. The proposed framework can be used to improve logical reasoning processes in autonomic networks of nodes [15], since these services (i.e. deduction and abduction) help the self-managing characteristics of distributed computing resources: a node sometimes needs to independently produce the missing information (through an abduction process).

As a future work, we plan to extend in SWI-Prolog the existent CHR module implementing soft constraints [3], by adding the $\div$ operator inside the soft module. In this way we could implement a stand-alone policy-based authorization system based on constraint programming. The distributed negotiation architecture shown in Fig. 7 can be enriched in order to model the mutual disclosure of credentials between strangers when credentials are sensitive.

References

1. Biso, A., Rossi, F., Sperduti, A.: Experimental results on learning soft constraints. In: KR, pp. 435–444 (2000)
2. Bistarelli, S.: Semirings for Soft Constraint Solving and Programming. LNCS, vol. 2962. Springer, Heidelberg (2004)
3. Bistarelli, S., Frühwirth, T., Marte, M.: Soft constraint propagation and solving in CHRs. In: SAC 2002: Proc. of the ACM Symposium on Applied Computing, pp. 1–5. ACM Press, New York (2002)
4. Bistarelli, S., Gadducci, F.: Enhancing constraints manipulation in semiring-based formalisms. In: ECAI 2006: European Conference on Artificial Intelligence, pp. 63–67 (2006)
5. Bistarelli, S., Martinelli, F., Santini, F.: A semantic foundation for trust management languages with weights: An application to the RT family. In: Rong, C., Jaatun, M.G., Sandnes, F.E., Yang, L.T., Ma, J. (eds.) ATC 2008. LNCS, vol. 5060, pp. 481–495. Springer, Heidelberg (2008)
6. Bistarelli, S., Martinelli, F., Santini, F.: Weighted datalog and levels of trust. In: ARES: Conference on Availability, Reliability and Security, pp. 1128–1134. IEEE Computer Society, Los Alamitos (2008)
7. Bistarelli, S., Montanari, U., Rossi, F.: Semiring-based constraint satisfaction and optimization. J. ACM 44(2), 201–236 (1997)
8. Bessière, C., Coletta, R., Petit, T.: Learning implied global constraints. In: IJCAI 2007: Proc. of the International Joint Conference on Artificial Intelligence, pp. 44–49 (2007)
9. Christiansen, H., Dahl, V.: Hyprolog: A new logic programming language with assumptions and abduction. In: Gabbrielli, M., Gupta, G. (eds.) ICLP 2005. LNCS, vol. 3668, pp. 159–173. Springer, Heidelberg (2005)
10. Codognet, C., Codognet, P.: Abduction and concurrent logic languages. In: ECAI 1994: European Conference on Artificial Intelligence, pp. 75–79. John Wiley and Sons, Chichester (1994)

11. Freuder, E.C., Likitvivatanavong, C., Moretti, M., Rossi, F., Wallace, R.J.: Computing explanations and implications in preference-based configurators. In: O'Sullivan, B. (ed.) CologNet 2002. LNCS (LNAI), vol. 2627, pp. 76–92. Springer, Heidelberg (2003)
12. Frühwirth, T.W.: Constraint handling rules. In: Selected Papers from Constraint Programming, London, UK, pp. 90–107. Springer, Heidelberg (1995)
13. Jøsang, A., Ismail, R., Boyd, C.: A survey of trust and reputation systems for online service provision. Decis. Support Syst. 43(2), 618–644 (2007)
14. Kakas, A.C.: ACLP: Integrating abduction and constraint solving. CoRR, cs.AI/0003020 (2000)
15. Koshutanski, H., Massacci, F.: A negotiation scheme for access rights establishment in autonomic communication. J. Network Syst. Manage. 15(1), 117–136 (2007)
16. Li, N., Mitchell, J.C., Winsborough, W.H.: Design of a role-based trust-management framework. In: SP 2002: Proc. of Security and Privacy, pp. 114–130. IEEE Computer Society, Los Alamitos (2002)
17. Maher, M.J.: Abduction of linear arithmetic constraints. In: Gabbrielli, M., Gupta, G. (eds.) ICLP 2005. LNCS, vol. 3668, pp. 174–188. Springer, Heidelberg (2005)
18. Maher, M.J., Huang, G.: On computing constraint abduction answers. In: Cervesato, I., Veith, H., Voronkov, A. (eds.) LPAR 2008. LNCS (LNAI), vol. 5330, pp. 421–435. Springer, Heidelberg (2008)
19. Menzies, T.: Applications of abduction: knowledge-level modelling. Int. J. Hum.Comput. Stud. 45(3), 305–335 (1996)
20. Pople, H.E.: On the mechanization of abductive logic. In: IJCAI 1973: Proc. of the International Joint Conference on Artificial Intelligence, pp. 147–152. Morgan Kaufmann, San Francisco (1973)
21. Ribeiro, C., Zuquete, A., Ferreira, P., Guedes, P.: Security policy consistency. CoRR, cs.LO/0006045 (2000)
22. Shanahan, M.: Prediction is deduction but explanation is abduction. In: IJCAI 1989: Proc. of the International Joint Conference on Artificial Intelligence, pp. 1055–1060 (1989)
23. Vu, X., O'Sullivan, B.: Semiring-based constraint acquisition. In: IEEE International Conference on Tools with Artificial Intelligence, vol. 1, pp. 251–258 (2007)
24. Wielemaker, J.: An overview of the SWI-Prolog programming environment. In: Proc. of the 13th International Workshop on Logic Programming Environments, pp. 1–16. Katholieke Universiteit Leuven, Heverlee (2003)

Towards Autonomic Mode Control of a Scalable Intrusion Tolerant Architecture

Tadashi Dohi and Toshikazu Uemura

Department of Information Engineering, Graduate School of Engineering
Hiroshima University, 1-4-1 Kagamiyama, Higashi-Hiroshima, 739-8527, Japan
dohi@rel.hiroshima-u.ac.jp

Abstract. In this article we consider an intrusion tolerant system with two detection modes; automatic detection mode and manual detection mode for intrusions, and describe the dynamic transition behavior by a continuous-time semi-Markov chain (CTSMC). Based on the embedded Markov chain (EMC) approach, we derive the steady-state probability of the CTSMC, the steady-state system availability and the mean time to security failure (MTTSF). Especially, we show necessary and sufficient conditions to exist the optimal switching time from an automatic detection mode to a manual detection mode, which maximizes the steady-state system availability. Next, we develop an autonomic mode control scheme to estimate the optimal switching time without specifying any probability distribution function in an adaptive way, where the basic idea comes from a statistically non-parametric algorithm by means of the total time on test concept. Numerical examples through a simulation study are presented for illustrating the optimal switching of detection mode, and investigating the asymptotic property of the resulting autonomic mode control scheme.

Keywords: autonomic control, intrusion tolerance, SITAR, system availability, MTTSF, CTSMC, EMC approach, statistical estimation, non-parametric algorithm, adaptive optimization.

1 Introduction

Although traditional security approaches which may be categorized into *intrusion detection approaches* establish proactive barriers such as a firewall, unfortunately, the efficiency of a single barrier is not still enough to prevent attack from sophisticated new skills by malicious attackers. As the result, the number of network attack incidents is tremendously increasing still now on. In contrast to pursue the nearly impossibility of a perfect barrier unit, the concept of *intrusion tolerance* is becoming much popular in recent years. An intrusion tolerant system can avoid severe security failures caused by intrusion and/or attack, and can provide intended services to users in a timely manner even under attack. This is inspired from traditional techniques commonly used for tolerating accidental faults in hardware and/or software systems, and can provide the system dependability which is defined as a property of a computer-based system, such that reliance can justifiably be placed on the service it delivers [1]. Most efforts in security have been focused on specification, design and implementation issues. In fact, several

B. Xie et al. (Eds.): ATC 2010, LNCS 6407, pp. 283–297, 2010.
© Springer-Verlag Berlin Heidelberg 2010

implementation techniques of intrusion tolerance at the architecture level have been developed for real computer-based systems. For an excellent survey on this research topic, see Deswarte and Powell [2].

Since the above methods can be categorized by a design diversity technique in secure systems and need much cost for the development, the effect on implementation has to be evaluated carefully and quantitatively. To assess quantitatively security effects of computer-based systems, reliability/performance evaluation with stochastic modeling is quite effective. Littlewood *et al.* [7] applied fundamental techniques in reliability theory to assess the security of operational software systems and proposed some quantitative security measures. Jonsson and Olovsson [5] also developed a quantitative method to study attacker's behavior with the empirical data observed in experiments. Ortalo, Deswarte and Kaaniche [10] used both privilege graph and continuous-time Markov chain (CTMC) to evaluate system vulnerability, and derived the mean effort to security failure. Uemura and Dohi [12],[16] focused on the typical DoS (Denial of Service) attacks for a server system and formulated an optimal patch management problem via continuous-time semi-Markov chains (CTSMCs). Later, the same authors [13] considered a secure design of an intrusion tolerant database system [21],[22] with a control parameter to switch an automatic detection mode to a manual detection mode after receiving an attack, and described its stochastic behavior by a CTSMC. Park *et al.* [11] considered an $M/G/1$ queueing model to descrive an intrusion tolerant server. Uemura *et al.* [18] describe the stochastic behavior of an IMS-based VoIP network system with intrusion tolerance. In this way considerable attentions have been paid to stochastic modeling in security evaluation of computer-based systems.

In this article we consider an existing system architecture with intrusion tolerance, called SITAR (Scalable Intrusion Tolerant Architecture). The SITAR was developed in MCNC Inc. and Duke University [19]. Madan *et al.* [8], [9] considered the security evaluation of SITAR and proposed a CTSMC model to describe the dynamic stochastic behavior. More precisely, they investigated effects of the intrusion tolerant architecture under some attack patterns such as DoS attacks. We consider the similar but somewhat different models from Madan *et al.* [8], [9]. Uemura *et al.* [15] introduced the preventive maintenance time such as a patch release time for the SITAR and showed that releasing a security patch at a suitable timing enables to increase the steady-state system availability effectively. Wang *et al.* [20] developed a stochastic reward nets model (SRNs) for the SITAR. Fujimoto *et al.* [4] also considered the similar model as [15] by means of Markov regenerare stochastic Peiri nets (MRSPNs) which belong to a wider class of stochastic process than CTSMCs. On the other hand, recently, the same authors [14],[17] introduced an additional control parameter, called the switching time from an automatic detection mode to a manual detection mode for intrusions, into the SITAR, and showed that the similar effect to increase the steady-state system availability can be obtained by controlling the switching time. However, it is worth noting that they assumed the discrete-time operation of the SITAR and developed a discrete-time semi-Markov chain (DTSMC) model. The basic idea on switching from an automatic detection mode to a manual detection mode of vulnerability is due to [13], [21] in the context of a intrusion tolerant database system.

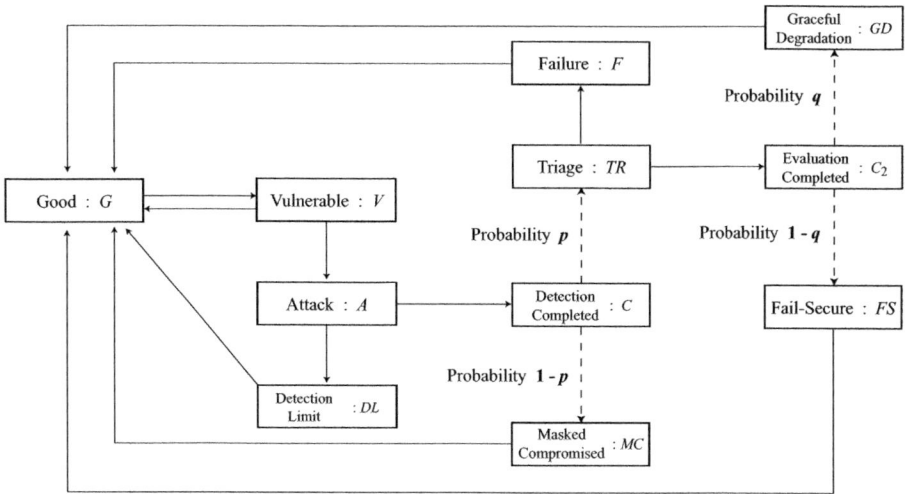

Fig. 1. Block diagram of SITAR behavior

The main purpose of this article is to describe the SITAR with two detection modes; automatic detection mode and manual detection mode by a CTSMC and derive the optimal switching time, which maximizes the steady-state system availability in a continuous time. Based on the embedded Markov chain (EMC) approach, we derive not only the steady-state probability of the CTSMC and the steady-state system availability but also the mean time to security failure (MTTSF). In addition to the difference between CTSMC and DTSMC, we develop a statistically non-parametric algorithm to estimate the optimal switching time without specifying any probability distribution function, based on the total time on test concept [3]. This algorithm would be quite useful because it is not so easy to identify the transition probability in the real-time operation of SITAR. In COTS (commercial-off-the-shelf) distributed servers like SITAR, the intrusion-detection function equipped for a proactive security management is not perfect and is often switched to a manual detection mode, in order to detect intrusions/vulnerable parts more speedy (see [13], [21]). The statistical estimation scheme proposed here can be used for scheduling of mode change under the incomplete knowledge of intrusion detection time under autonomic mode control [6]. In other words, it provides an adaptive control scheme of intrusion detection function within an intrusion tolerant system.

The article is organized as follows: In Section 2 we overview the SITAR and describe the fundamental stochastic behavior of it [8], [9]. Section 3 takes the EMC approach and obtains the representation of an embedded discrete-time Markov chain (DTMC) in the steady state for the CTSMC model. We derive the steady-state probability in the CTSMC by using the mean sojourn time and the steady-state probability in the embedded DTMC. Next we formulate the maximization problem of steady-state system availability in continuous time and show necessary and sufficient conditions to exist the optimal switching time from an automatic detection mode to a manual detection

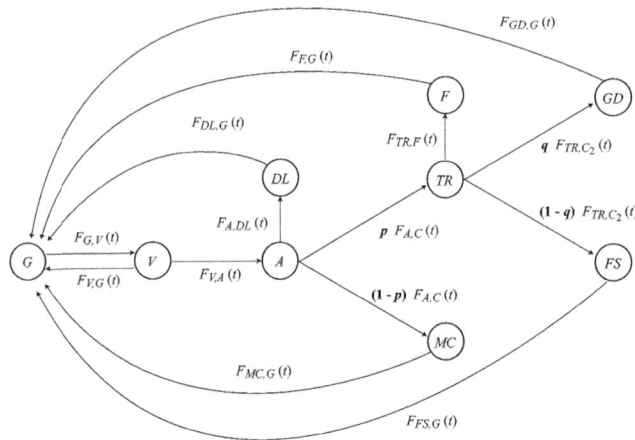

Fig. 2. Transition diagram of CTSMC

mode. In Section 4, we carry out the MTTSF analysis along with the EMC approach. In Section 5, we develop a statistically non-parametric algorithm to estimate the optimal switching time, where the total time on test concept is useful to obtain the resulting estimator. We translate the underlying optimization problem on analysis to a graphical one, and derive an estimator of the optimal switching time with the complete sample of the transition time data to an automatic detection mode. Numerical examples are presented in Section 6 for illustrating the optimal switching of detection mode and investigating the asymptotic property of the resulting estimator.

2   SITAR

The SITAR is a COTS distributed server with an intrusion tolerant function [19] and consists of five major components; proxy server, acceptance monitor, ballot monitor, adaptive reconfiguration module, and audit control module. Since the usual COTS server is vulnerable for an intrusion from outside, an additional intrusion tolerant structure is introduced in the SITAR. Madan *et al.* [8], [9] described the stochastic behavior of SITAR by means of CTSMC and gave its embedded DTMC representation. Figure 1 depicts the configuration of SITAR behavior under consideration. Let G be the normal state in which the COTS server can protect itself from adversaries. However, if a vulnerable part is detected by them, a state transition occurs from G to the vulnerable state V. Further if adversaries attack the vulnerable part, the state moves to the attack state A. On the other hand, if the vulnerable part is detected by vulnerability identifiers such as benign users, the vulnerable state V goes back to the normal state G again.

In the attack state A, two possible states can be taken. If the problem caused by the attack cannot be resolved and the containment of the damaged part fails, the corresponding event can be regarded as a security failure, and the initialization/reconfiguration of the system is performed as a corrective maintenance (repair) at DL. After completing it, the system state makes a transition to G again and becomes as good as new. While,

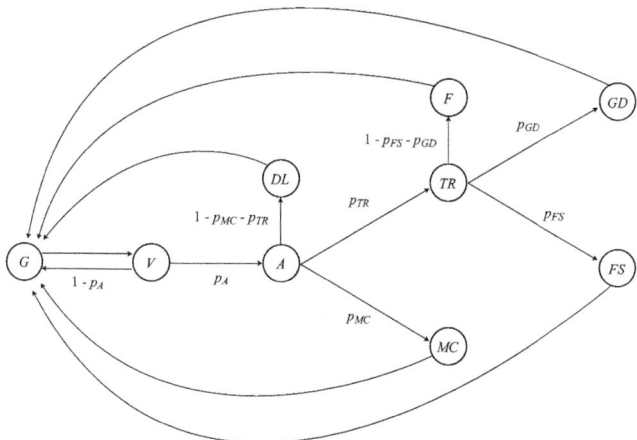

Fig. 3. EMC representation

if the intrusion/attack is detected, then the state goes to C. In the state C, one of two instantaneous transitions without time delay, which are denoted by dotted-lines in Fig. 1, can occur, *i.e.*, if the damaged part by attacking is not so significant and does not lead to a serious security failure directly, the system state makes a transition from C to MC with probability $1 - p$ $(0 \leq p \leq 1)$, and the damaged part can be contained by means of the fail safe function. After the containment, the system state moves back to G by masking the damaged part.

Otherwise, *i.e.* if the containment of the damaged part with serious effects to the system fails, the state goes to TR with probability p. We call this probability the *triage probability* in this article. In the triage state TR, several corrective inspections are tried in parallel with services. If the system is diagnosed as security failure, the state moves to F, the service operation is stopped, and the recovery operation starts immediately. After completing the recovery from the failure, the system becomes as good as new in G. Otherwise, it goes to the so-called non-failure state denoted by C_2. Here, two states can be taken; it may be switched to the gracefully service degradation in GD with probability q $(0 \leq q \leq 1)$, or the service operation is forced to stop and the corrective maintenance starts immediately.

The main differences from Madan *et al.* [8], [9] are (i) an automatic intrusion-detection can be switched to a manual detection mode at any timing in A, although Madan *et al.* [8], [9] did not take account of switching of automatic detection mode, (ii) In two states C and C_2 instantaneous transitions are allowed in the present model, although Madan *et al.* [8], [9] assumed random transitions with time delay. We define the time interval from G to G as one cycle and suppose that the same cycle repeats again and again over an infinite time horizon. For respective states, let $F_{i,j}(t)$ $(i, j \in \{G, V, A, DL, C, MC, TR, C_2, FS, GD, F\}$ denote the continuous transition probability distributions with probability density function (p.d.f.) $f_{i,j}(n)$ in CTSMC, where $f_{i,j}(0) = 0$ and mean $\mu_{i,j}$ (> 0).

In Fig. 2, we give the trandition diagram of CTSMC. It is assumed that the automatic detection function in SITAR is switched just after t_0 (≥ 0) time unit elapses in an active attack state A in CTSMC. More specifically, let $F_{A,DL}(t)$ be the transition probability from A to DL which denotes the manual detection mode. When it is given by the step function, i.e., $F_{A,DL}(t) = 1$ ($t \geq t_0$) and $F_{A,DL}(t) = 0$ ($t < t_0$), the switching time from an automatic detection mode to a manual detection model is given by the constant time t_0. From the preliminary above, we formulate the steady-state system availability as a function of the switching time t_0 in the following section.

3   Availability Analysis

3.1   EMC Approach

The embedded DTMC representation of CTSMC is illustrated in Fig.3. Let p_k, h_k and π_k denote the steady-state probability of CTSMC in Fig.2, the mean sojourn time and the steady-state probability of the embedded DTMC in Fig. 3, respectively, where $k \in \{G, V, A, DL, MC, TR, FS, GD, F\}$. From the definition, we can derive the the steady-state probability π_k of CTSMC by $\pi_G = h_G/\phi$, $\pi_V = h_V/\phi$, $\pi_A = p_A h_A/\phi$, $\pi_{DL} = p_A(1 - p_{MC} - p_{TR})h_{DL}/\phi$, $\pi_{MC} = p_A p_{MC} h_{MC}/\phi$, $\pi_{TR} = p_A p_{TR} h_{TR}/\phi$, $\pi_{FS} = p_A p_{TR} p_{FS} h_{FS}/\phi$, $\pi_{GD} = p_A p_{TR} p_{GD} h_{GD}/\phi$, $\pi_F = p_A p_{TR}(1 - p_{FS} - p_{GD})h_F/\phi$, where

$$\phi = h_G + h_V + p_A\Big[h_A + (1 - p_{MC} - p_{TR})h_{DL} + p_{MC}h_{MC}$$
$$+ p_{TR}\Big\{h_{TR} + p_{FS}h_{FS} + p_{GD}h_{GD} + (1 - p_{FS} - p_{GD})h_F\Big\}\Big]. \quad (1)$$

3.2   CTSMC Model

From the transition diagram of CTSMC in Fig. 2, we obtain

$$p_A = \int_0^\infty \overline{F}_{V,G}(t)dF_{V,A}(t), \quad (2)$$

$$p_{MC} = p_{MC}(t_0) = (1 - p)F_{A,C}(t_0), \quad (3)$$

$$p_{TR} = p_{TR}(t_0) = pF_{A,C}(t_0), \quad (4)$$

$$p_{FS} = (1 - q)\int_0^\infty \overline{F}_{TR,F}(t)dF_{TR,C_2}(t), \quad (5)$$

$$p_{GD} = q\int_0^\infty \overline{F}_{TR,F}(t)dF_{TR,C_2}(t), \quad (6)$$

where

$$h_G = \mu_{G,V}, \quad (7)$$

$$h_V = \int_0^\infty t\overline{F}_{V,G}(t)dF_{V,A}(t) + \int_0^\infty t\overline{F}_{V,A}(t)dF_{V,G}(t), \quad (8)$$

$$h_A = h_A(t_0) = \int_0^{t_0} \overline{F}_{A,C}(t)dt, \quad (9)$$

$$h_{DL} = \mu_{DL,G}, \tag{10}$$

$$h_{MC} = \mu_{MC,G}, \tag{11}$$

$$h_{TR} = \int_0^\infty t\overline{F}_{TR,F}(t)dF_{TR,C_2}(t) + \int_0^\infty t\overline{F}_{TR,C_2}(t)dF_{TR,F}(t), \tag{12}$$

$$h_{FS} = \mu_{FS,G}, \tag{13}$$

$$h_{GD} = \mu_{GD,G}, \tag{14}$$

$$h_F = \mu_{F,G} \tag{15}$$

and $\overline{F}_{A,C}(t) = 1 - F_{A,C}(t)$. The steady-state system availability is defined as a fraction of time when the service can be provided continuously. Hence, the formulation of the steady-state system availability is reduced to the derivation of the mean sojourn time at each state. It should be noted that the system down states correspond to states $DLCFS$ and F, so that the steady-state system availability is represented as a function of t_0 by

$$AV(t_0) = \pi_G + \pi_V + \pi_A + \pi_{MC} + \pi_{TR} + \pi_{GD} = U(t_0)/T(t_0), \tag{16}$$

where

$$
\begin{aligned}
U(t_0) &= h_G + h_V + p_A\Big\{h_A(t_0) + p_{MC}(t_0)h_{MC} + p_{TR}(t_0)(h_{TR} + p_{GD}h_{GD})\Big\} \\
&= H_{G,V} + \int_0^\infty \overline{F}_{V,G}(t)dF_{V,A}(t)\Big\{ \int_0^{t_0} \overline{F}_{A,C}(t) + \alpha F_{A,C}(t_0)\Big\}, \tag{17}
\end{aligned}
$$

$$
\begin{aligned}
T(t_0) &= U(t_0) + p_A\Big[\{1 - p_{MC}(t_0) - p_{TR}(t_0)\}h_{DL} \\
&\quad + p_{TR}(t_0)\Big\{p_{FS}h_{FS} + (1 - p_{FS} - p_{GD})h_F\Big\}\Big] \\
&= H_{G,V} + \int_0^\infty \overline{F}_{V,G}(t)dF_{V,A}(t)\Big\{ \int_0^{t_0} \overline{F}_{A,C}(t) + \mu_{DL,G}\overline{F}_{A,C}(t_0) + \beta F_{A,C}(t_0)\Big\},
\end{aligned}
$$

$$H_{G,V} = \mu_{G,V} + \int_0^\infty t\overline{F}_{V,G}(t)dF_{V,A}(t) + \int_0^\infty t\overline{F}_{V,A}(t)dF_{V,G}(t), \tag{18}$$

$$\alpha = (1-p)h_{MC} + p(h_{TR} + p_{GD}h_{GD}), \tag{19}$$

$$\beta = \alpha + p\Big\{p_{FS}h_{FS} + (1 - p_{FS} - p_{GD})h_F\Big\}. \tag{20}$$

In the above expressions, α and β mean that the mean up time and the total mean time from state C to G for one cycle, respectively.

3.3 Optimal Switching Time

Our next concern is to seek the optimal switching time, t_0^*, maximizing the steady-state system availability $AV(t_0)$. Taking the differentiation of $AV(t_0)$ with respect to t_0 and setting equal to 0 yield the non-linear equation $q(t_0) = 0$, where

$$q(t_0) = \Big\{1 + \alpha r_{A,C}(t_0)\Big\}T(t_0) - U(t_0)\Big\{1 + (\beta - \mu_{DL,G})r_{A,C}(t_0)\Big\} \tag{21}$$

and $r_{A,C}(t) = f_{A,C}(t)/\overline{F}_{A,C}(t)$ is the hazard rate. We make the following parametric assumptions:

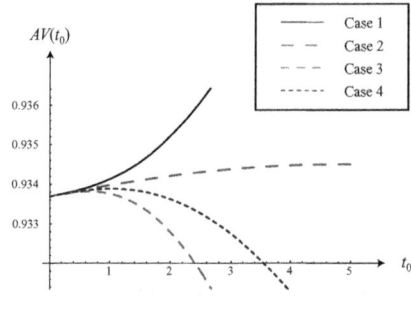

Fig. 4. Steady-state system availability   **Fig. 5.** MTTSF

(A-1) $\alpha + \mu_{DL,G} < \beta$,

(A-2) $\alpha\mu_{DL,G} < H_{G,V}(\beta - \alpha - \mu_{DL,G})$.

From the definition it is evident that $\alpha < \beta$. The assumption **(A-1)** implies that the sum of mean up time after state C and the mean corrective maintenance time is strictly smaller than the total mean time. On the other hand, the assumption **(A-2)** seems to be somewhat technical but is needed to guarantee a unique optimal switching time. These both assumptions were numerically checked and could be validated in many parametric cases. We characterize the optimal switching time maximizing the steady-state system availability as follows:

Proposition 1. (1) Suppose that $F_{A,C}(t)$ is strictly IHR (Increasing Hazard Rate) under the assumptions **(A-1)** and **(A-2)**, i.e., $dr_{A,C}(t)/dt > 0$.

(i) If $q(0) > 0$ and $q(\infty) < 0$, then there exists a unique optimal switching time t_0^* $(0 < t_0^* < \infty)$ satisfying $q(t_0^*) = 0$. The corresponding steady-state system availability $AV(t_0^*)$ is given by

$$AV(t_0^*) = \frac{1 + \alpha r_{A,C}(t_0^*)}{1 + (\beta - \mu_{DL,G})r_{A,C}(t_0^*)}. \tag{22}$$

(ii) If $q(0) \leq 0$, then the optimal switching time is $t_0^* = 0$ and the corresponding maximum steady-state system availability is given by

$$AV(0) = \frac{H_{G,V}}{H_{G,V} + \mu_{DL,G} \int_0^\infty \overline{F}_{V,G}(t)dF_{V,A}(t)}. \tag{23}$$

(iii) If $q(\infty) \geq 0$, then the optimal switching time is $t_0^* \to \infty$ and the corresponding maximum steady-state system availability is given by

$$AV(\infty) = \frac{H_{G,V} + (\mu_{A,C} + \alpha) \int_0^\infty \overline{F}_{V,G}(t)dF_{V,A}(t)}{H_{G,V} + (\mu_{A,C} + \beta) \int_0^\infty \overline{F}_{V,G}(t)dF_{V,A}(t)}. \tag{24}$$

(2) Suppose that $F_{A,C}(t)$ is DHR (Decreasing Hazard Rate) under the assumptions **(A-1)** and **(A-2)**, i.e., $dr_{A,C}(t) \leq 0$. If $AV(0) > AV(\infty)$ then $t_0^* = 0$ otherwise $t_0^* \to \infty$.

4   MTTSF Analysis

Next, we derive MTTSF [9],[15],[17]. Let X_a and X_t denote the absorbing states and the transient states in CTSMC. Let

$$P = \begin{bmatrix} Q & C \\ O & I \end{bmatrix} \tag{25}$$

be the whole transition probability matrix, where Q and C denote the transient and the absorbing probability matrices for $X_a = \{DL, FS, GD, F\}$ and $X_t = \{G, V, A, MC, TR\}$ in Fig.3:

$$Q = \begin{array}{c} \\ G \\ V \\ A \\ MC \\ TR \end{array} \begin{array}{c} G\ \ V\ \ A\ \ MC\ \ TR \\ \begin{bmatrix} 0 & 1 & 0 & 0 & 0 \\ \bar{p}_A & 0 & p_A & 0 & 0 \\ 0 & 0 & 0 & p_{MC} & p_{TR} \\ 1 & 0 & 0 & 0 & 0 \\ 0 & 0 & 0 & 0 & 0 \end{bmatrix} \end{array} \tag{26}$$

and

$$C = \begin{array}{c} \\ G \\ V \\ A \\ MC \\ TR \end{array} \begin{array}{c} DL\ \ \ \ \ \ FS\ \ GD\ \ \ \ \ \ F \\ \begin{bmatrix} 0 & 0 & 0 & 0 \\ 0 & 0 & 0 & 0 \\ p_{MC} + p_{TR} & 0 & 0 & 0 \\ 0 & 0 & 0 & 0 \\ 0 & p_{FS} & p_{GD} & \overline{p_{FS} + p_{GD}} \end{bmatrix} \end{array} \tag{27}$$

In Eq.(25), O and I are the zero matrix whose elements are 0 and the identity matrix, respectively. In Eqs.(26) and (27), it means that $\bar{p}_A = 1 - p_A$, $\overline{p_{MC} + p_{TR}} = 1 - p_{MC} - p_{TR}$, and $\overline{p_{FS} + p_{GD}} = 1 - p_{FS} - p_{GD}$. Using the mean visit number V_i and the mean sojourn time h_i in state i, MTTSF is defined by

$$\text{MTTSF} = \sum_{i \in X_t} V_i h_i, \tag{28}$$

where V_i is the solution of the following simultaneous equations:

$$V_i = q_i + \sum_j V_j q_{ji}, \qquad i, j \in X_t, \tag{29}$$

and q_{ji} denotes the elements of Q. For the initial probability vector in Eq.(29), we set:

$$q = [q_i] = [1\,0\,0\,0\,0\,0\,0\,0\,0]. \tag{30}$$

Finally, solving Eq.(29) yields the mean visit number:

$$V_G = \frac{1}{p_A \bar{p}_{MC}(t_0)}, \tag{31}$$

$$V_V = V_G, \tag{32}$$

$$V_A = p_A V_G, \tag{33}$$

$$V_{MC} = p_{MC}(t_0) V_A, \tag{34}$$

$$V_{TR} = p_{TR}(t_0) V_A \tag{35}$$

and leads to the analytical derivation of MTTSF.

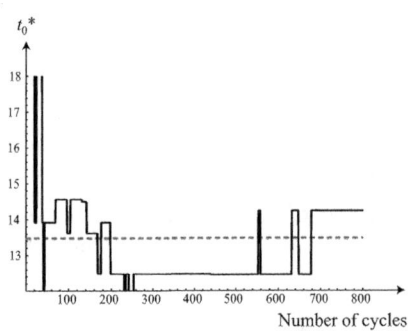
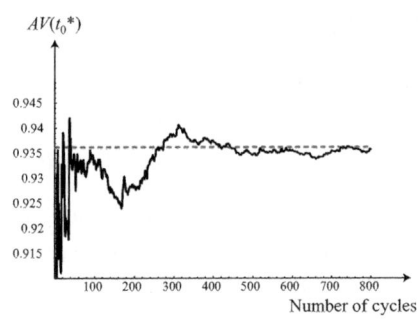

Fig. 6. Asymptotic berhavior of estimates for t_0 in Case 2

Fig. 7. Asymptotic behavior of estimates for $AV(t_0)$ in Case 2

5   Autonomic Mode Control Algorithm

Before developing a statistical estimation algorithm for the optimal switching time, we translate the underlying problem $\max_{0 < t_0 < \infty} AV(t_0)$ to a graphical one. We define the scaled total time on test (TTT) transform [3] of the probability distribution $F_{A,C}(t)$ by

$$\phi(p) = \frac{1}{\mu_{A,C}} \int_0^{F_{A,C}^{-1}(p)} \overline{F}_{A,C}(t) dt, \tag{36}$$

where

$$F_{A,C}^{-1}(p) = \inf\{t_0; F_{A,C}(t_0) \geq p\}, \quad 0 \leq p \leq 1. \tag{37}$$

It is well known that $F_{A,C}(t)$ is IHR (DHR) if and only if $\phi(p)$ is concave (convex) on $p \in [0, 1]$ [3]. After a few algebraic manipulations, we have the following result.

Proposition 2. Suppose that the assumptions **(A-1)** and **(A-2)** are satisfied. Obtaining the optimal switching time t_0^* maximizing the steady-state system availability $AV(t_0^*)$ is equivalent to obtaining p^* $(0 \leq p^* \leq 1)$ such as

$$\max_{0 \leq p \leq 1} \frac{\phi(p) + c_1}{p + c_2}, \tag{38}$$

where

$$c_1 = \frac{H_{G,V}}{p_A \mu_{A,C}} + \frac{\alpha \mu_{DL,G}}{\mu_{A,C}(\alpha - \beta + \mu_{DL,G})} \quad (> 0), \tag{39}$$

$$c_2 = \frac{\mu_{DL,G}}{\beta - \alpha - \mu_{DL,G}} \quad (< 0). \tag{40}$$

From the above result, it is seen that the optimal switching time $t_0^* = F_{A,C}^{-1}(p^*)$ is determined by calculating the optimal point p^* $(0 \leq p^* \leq 1)$ maximizing the tangent slope from the point $(-c_2, -c_1)$ to the curve $(p, \phi(p)) \in [0, 1] \times [0, 1]$ in the two-dimensional plane.

Next, suppose that the optimal switching time has to be estimated from an ordered complete (unsensored) observation $0 = x_0 \leq x_1 \leq x_2 \leq \ldots \leq x_n$ of the transition times from an absolutely continuous distribution $F_{A,C}(t)$, which is unknown. Then the scaled TTT statistics [3] based on this sample are defined by $\phi_{nj} = \psi_j / \psi_n$, where

$$\psi_j = \sum_{k=1}^{j} (n - k + 1)(x_k - x_{k-1}), \quad j = 1, 2, \ldots, n; \ \psi_0 = 0. \tag{41}$$

Since the empirical distribution function F_{nj} corresponding to the sample data x_j ($j = 0, 1, 2, \ldots, n$) is

$$F_{nj} = \begin{cases} j/n \text{ for } x_j \leq x < x_{j+1}, \\ 1 \quad \text{ for } \quad x_n \leq x, \end{cases} \tag{42}$$

the resulting polygon by plotting the points (F_{nj}, ϕ_{nj}) ($j = 0, 1, 2, \ldots, n$) and connecting them by line segments is called the *scaled TTT plot* [3]. In other words, the scaled TTT plot can be regarded as a numerical couter part of the scaled TTT transform.

The following result gives an autonomic mode control algorithm based on the non-parametric estimate for the optimal switching time.

Proposition 3. (i) Suppose that the optimal switching time has to be estimated from n ordered complete sample $0 = x_0 \leq x_1 \leq x_2 \leq \ldots \leq x_n$ from an absolutely continuous distribution $F_{A,C}(t)$, which is unknown. Then, a non-parametric estimator of the optimal switching time $\hat{t}_0^*$ which maximizes $AV(t_0)$ is given by x_{j^*}, where

$$j^* = \left\{ j \Big| \max_{0 \leq j \leq n} \frac{\phi_{nj} + c_1}{j/n + c_2} \right\} \tag{43}$$

and $\mu_{A,C}$ in Eq.(39) is replaced by $\sum_{k=1}^{n} x_k/n$.
(ii) The estimator given in (i) is strongly consistent, *i.e.* x_{j^*} converges to the optimal solution t_0^* uniformly with probability one as $n \to \infty$, if a unique optimal switching time exists.

6 Numerical Examples

6.1 Preliminary

In this section we derive the optimal switching time t_0^* characterized in Section 3 and quantify two security measures; steady-state system availability and MTTSF. Suppose the following parametric circumstance: $\mu_{G,V} = 72$, $\mu_{V,G} = 15$, $\mu_{V,A} = 24$, $\mu_{DL,G} = 15$, $\mu_{MC,G} = 12$, $\mu_{TR,F} = 6$, $\mu_{TR,C_2} = 8$, $\mu_{FS,G} = 30$, $\mu_{GD,G} = 40$ and $\mu_{F,G} = 48$. Especially we concern the following four cases:

(i) **Case 1:** $p = 0$, *i.e.*, the system state makes a transition from C to MC with probability one.

Table 1. Dependence of steady-state system availability on parameter k in continuous-time operation

k	Case 1			Case 2			Case 3			Case 4		
	t_0^*	$AV(t_0^*)$	$\Delta(\%)$	t_0^*	$AV(t_0^*)$	$\Delta(\%)$	t_0^*	$AV(t_0^*)$	$\Delta(\%)$	t_0^*	$AV(t_0^*)$	$\Delta(\%)$
1	∞	1	0	0	0.9337	0.3256	0	0.9337	10.5733	0	0.9337	4.2308
2	∞	1	0	1.4240	0.9339	0.2251	0.0459	0.9337	10.2650	0.1063	0.9337	4.0513
3	∞	1	0	5.0032	0.9345	0.1747	0.6529	0.9338	9.9807	1.0328	0.9339	3.8960
4	∞	1	0	9.1387	0.9353	0.1454	1.9098	0.9341	9.7255	2.6739	0.9342	3.7663
5	∞	1	0	13.4647	0.9361	0.1263	3.6058	0.9345	9.4938	4.7472	0.9347	3.6549

Table 2. Dependence of steady-state system availability on parameter d in continuous-time operation

d	Case 1			Case 2			Case 3			Case 4		
	t_0^*	$AV(t_0^*)$	$\Delta(\%)$	t_0^*	$AV(t_0^*)$	$\Delta(\%)$	t_0^*	$AV(t_0^*)$	$\Delta(\%)$	t_0^*	$AV(t_0^*)$	$\Delta(\%)$
1	∞	1	0	0.4524	0.9338	0.3652	0.0783	0.9337	10.6542	0.1209	0.9337	4.2797
4	∞	1	0	5.0032	0.9345	0.1747	0.6529	0.9338	9.9807	1.0328	0.9339	3.8960
20	∞	1	0	∞	0.9436	0	8.1195	0.9352	7.2335	13.8391	0.9361	2.4046
100	∞	1	0	∞	0.9687	0	0	0.9337	0.6777	∞	0.9510	0

(ii) Case 2: $p = 0.5$ and $q = 0.5$.

(iii) Case 3: $p = 1$ and $q = 0$, i.e., the service operation at C_2 is forced to stop with probability one.

(iv) Case 4: $p = 1$ and $q = 1$, i.e., the gracefully degradation can be observed with probability one.

6.2   Sensitivity Analysis

Suppose that $f_{A,C}(t)$ is the gamma p.d.f. with shape parameter k and scale parameter d:

$$f_{A,C}(t) = \frac{t^{k-1}\exp\{-t/d\}}{\Gamma(k)d^k}, \tag{44}$$

where $\Gamma(\cdot)$ denotes the standard gamma function. Tables 1 and 2 present the optimal switching time and its associated system availability for varying k and d for Case 1 $\sim$ Case 4, where $d = 4$ is fixed in Table 1, $k = 3$ is fixed in Table 2, and 'Δ' denotes the increment (%) from the non-switching time case ($t_0 \to \infty$). It can be shown that the steady-state system availability could be improved, especially, up to 10.6% in Case 3. The main reason why this observation could be obtained was the existence of services frequently stopped in Case 3. In Table 2, it can be seen that controlling the switching time is quite effective, especially, in Case 3. As the value of d increases more and more, i.e., the time to detection of intrusions is much longer, the steady-state system availability monotonically increases.

In Tables 3 and 4, we calculate the MTTSF with the optimal switching time maximizing system availability. Since DL is considered as the security failure state, MTTSF

Table 3. Dependence of MTTSF on parameter k in continuous-time operation

	Case 1			Case 2			Case 3			Case 4		
k	t_0^*	MTTSF(t_0^*)	Δ(%)	t_0^*	MTTSF(t_0^*)	Δ(%)	t_0^*	MTTSF(t_0^*)	Δ(%)	t_0^*	MTTSF(t_0^*)	Δ(%)
1	∞	∞	0	0	2.11E+02	-52.63	0	2.11E+02	-3.40	0	2.11E+02	-3.40
2	∞	∞	0	1.42	2.18E+02	-51.86	0.05	2.11E+02	-5.11	0.11	2.11E+02	-5.09
3	∞	∞	0	5.00	2.32E+02	-49.70	0.65	2.12E+02	-6.52	1.03	2.12E+02	-6.35
4	∞	∞	0	9.14	2.46E+02	-47.72	1.91	2.13E+02	-7.59	2.67	2.14E+02	-7.26
5	∞	∞	0	13.46	2.58E+02	-46.02	3.61	2.15E+02	-8.45	4.75	2.16E+02	-7.95

Table 4. Dependence of MTTSF on parameter d in continuous-time operation

	Case 1			Case 2			Case 3			Case 4		
d	t_0^*	MTTSF(t_0^*)	Δ(%)	t_0^*	MTTSF(t_0^*)	Δ(%)	t_0^*	MTTSF(t_0^*)	Δ(%)	t_0^*	MTTSF(t_0^*)	Δ(%)
1	∞	∞	0	0.45	2.13E+02	-52.03	0.08	2.11E+02	-2.92	0.12	2.11E+02	-2.90
4	∞	∞	0	5.00	2.32E+02	-49.70	0.65	2.12E+02	-6.52	1.03	2.12E+02	-6.35
20	∞	∞	0	∞	5.58E+02	0	8.12	2.19E+02	-20.14	13.84	2.25E+02	-18.06
100	∞	∞	0	∞	1.04E+03	0	0	2.11E+02	-58.96	∞	5.15E+02	0

decreases arbitrarily by controlling the switching time. Although we omit to show the detailed mathematical result, it is possible to consider the absorbing state and the transient state as $X_a = \{FS, GD, F\}$ and $X_t = \{G, V, A, DL.MC, TR\}$ in Fig.3. Then, the corresponding MTTSF could be improved, so that its effect was 5% at the minimum but it provided 1.29×10^4 times longer at the maximum, though we omit to show them for brevity.

Figures 4 and 5 illustrate the behavior of steady-state system availability and MTTSF, respectively. From these figures, we know that Case 3 with many service stops gave lower system availability and MTTSF, and that their decreasing rate was remarkable. Case 4 corresponds to the well-known DoS attack with G, V, A, DL, TR, GD and F, where the states MC and FS can be regarded as a security failure state under the DoS attack circumstance [8], [9]. The numerical results here suggest us that controlling the optimal switching time may be effective to keep the high level of system availability and to improve the system survivability.

6.3 Simulation Experiment

Next, we investigate the asymptotic property of an estimator of optimal switching time derived in Section 5. Throughout a Monte Carlo simulation, we examine the convergence property of the estimator x_{j*} as the operation time goes on. Based on the puseudo-random number with the gamma distribution, we generate and monitor the sample time from the probability distribution $F_{A,C}(t)$. For this sampling, we sequentially estimate the optimal switching time and calculate the steady-state system availability/MTTSF. For the brevity we focus on only Case 2. Figures 6 and 7 illustrate the asymptotic behavior of estimators of optimal switching time and its associated steady-state system availability, where $p = q = 0.5$. In these figures, the dotted line denotes the real (but unknown in advance) optimal solutions. We can find that as the operation time elapses the estimate of the optimal switching time fluctuates in early phase but the

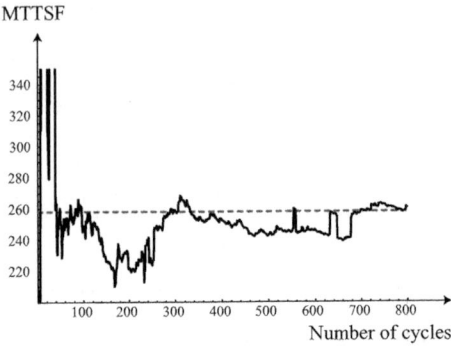

Fig. 8. Asymptotic behavior of estimates for MTTSF in Case 2

corresponding maximum system availability converges to the real value. In Fig. 8, we plot the asymptotic behavior of MTTSF when the optimal switching time is scheduled sequentially. It is seen that the resulting estimator of MTTSF also converges to a certain level in the steady state.

References

1. Avizienis, A., Laprie, J.C., Randell, B., Landwehr, C.: Basic concepts and taxonomy of dependable and secure computing. IEEE Transactions on Dependable and Secure Computing 1(1), 11–33 (2004)
2. Deswarte, Y., Powell, D.: Internet security: an intrusion-torelance approach. Proceedings of the IEEE 94(2), 432–441 (2006)
3. Dohi, T., Kaio, N., Osaki, S.: The total time on test processes and their application to maintenance problems. In: Hayakawa, Y., Irony, T., Xie, M. (eds.) System and Bayesian Reliability – Essays in Honor of Professor Richard E. Barlow on His 70th Birthday, pp. 123–143. World Scientific, Singapore (2001)
4. Fujimoto, R., Okamura, H., Dohi, T.: Security evaluation of an intrusion tolerant system with MRSPNs. In: Proceedings of 4th International Conference on Availability, Reliability and Security (ARES 2009), pp. 427–432. IEEE CSP, Los Alamitos (2009)
5. Jonsson, E., Olovsson, T.: A quantitative model of the security intrusion process based on attacker behavior. IEEE Transactions on Software Engineering 23(4), 235–245 (1997)
6. Kephart, J., Chess, D.: The vision of autonomic computing. IEEE Computer 36(2), 41–50 (2003)
7. Littlewood, B., Brocklehurst, S., Fenton, N., Mellor, P., Page, S., Wright, D., Doboson, J., McDermid, J., Gollmann, D.: Towards operational measures of computer security. Journal of Computer Security 2(2/3), 211–229 (1993)
8. Madan, B.B., Goseva-Popstojanova, K., Vaidyanathan, K., Trivedi, K.S.: Modeling and quantification of security attributes of software systems. In: Proceedings of 32nd Annual IEEE/IFIP International Conference on Dependable Systems and Networks (DSN 2002), pp. 505–514. IEEE CSP, Los Alamitos (2002)
9. Madan, B.B., Goseva-Popstojanova, K., Vaidyanathan, K., Trivedi, K.S.: A method for modeling and quantifying the security attributes of intrusion tolerant systems. Performance Evaluation 56(1/4), 167–186 (2004)

10. Ortalo, R., Deswarte, Y., Kaaniche, M.: Experimenting with quantitative evaluation tools for monitoring operational security. IEEE Transactions on Software Engineering 25(5), 633–650 (1999)
11. Park, B., Park, K., Kim, S.: A self-healing mechanism for an intrusion tolerance system. In: Katsikas, S.K., López, J., Pernul, G. (eds.) TrustBus 2005. LNCS, vol. 3592, pp. 41–49. Springer, Heidelberg (2005)
12. Uemura, T., Dohi, T.: Quantitative evaluation of intrusion tolerant systems subject to DoS attacks via semi-Markov cost models. In: Denko, M.K., Shih, C.-s., Li, K.-C., Tsao, S.-L., Zeng, Q.-A., Park, S.H., Ko, Y.-B., Hung, S.-H., Park, J.-H. (eds.) EUC-WS 2007. LNCS, vol. 4809, pp. 31–42. Springer, Heidelberg (2007)
13. Uemura, T., Dohi, T.: Optimizing security measures in an intrusion tolerant database system. In: Nanya, T., Maruyama, F., Pataricza, A., Malek, M. (eds.) ISAS 2008. LNCS, vol. 5017, pp. 26–42. Springer, Heidelberg (2008)
14. Uemura, T., Dohi, T., Kaio, N.: vailability analysis of a scalable intrusion tolerant architecture with two detection modes. In: Jaatun, M.G., Zhao, G., Rong, C. (eds.) CloudCom 2009. LNCS, vol. 5931, Springer, Heidelberg (2009)
15. Uemura, T., Dohi, T., Kaio, N.: Availability analysis of an intrusion tolerant distributed server system with preventive maintenance. IEEE Transactions on Reliability 59(1), 18–29 (2010)
16. Uemura, T., Dohi, T.: Optimal security patch management policies maximizing system availability. Journal of Communications 5(1), 71–80 (2010)
17. Uemura, T., Dohi, T., Kaio, N.: Dependability analysis of a scalable intrusion tolerant architecture with two detection modes. Journal of Internet Technology 11(2), 289–298 (2010)
18. Uemura, T., Dohi, T., Kaio, N.: Availability analysis of an IMS-based VoIP network system. In: Taniar, D., Gervasi, O., Murgante, B., Pardede, E., Apduhan, B.O. (eds.) Computational Science and Its Applications – ICCSA 2010. LNCS, vol. 6019, pp. 441–456. Springer, Heidelberg (2010)
19. Wang, F., Gong, F., Sargor, C., Goseva-Popstojanova, K., Trivedi, K.S., Jou, F.: SITAR: A scalable intrusion-tolerant architecture for distributed services. In: Proceedings of 2nd Annual IEEE Systems, Man and Cybernetics, Information Assurance Workshop, West Point, NY (June 2001)
20. Wang, D., Madan, B.B., Trivedi, K.S.: Security analysis of SITAR intrusion tolerance system. In: Proceedings of 2003 ACM Workshop on Survivable and Self-Regenerative Systems, pp. 23–32. ACM, New York (2003)
21. Wang, H., Liu, P.: Modeling and evaluating the survivability of an intrusion tolerant database system. In: Gollmann, D., Meier, J., Sabelfeld, A. (eds.) ESORICS 2006. LNCS, vol. 4189, pp. 207–224. Springer, Heidelberg (2006)
22. Wang, A.H., Yan, S., Liu, P.: A semi-Markovian survivability evaluation model for intrusion tolerant database systems. In: Proceedings of 5th International Conference on Availability, Reliability and Security (ARES 2010), pp. 427–432. IEEE CSP, Los Alamitos (2010)

Agent-Augmented Co-Space:
Toward Merging of Real World and Cyberspace

Ah-Hwee Tan and Yilin Kang

School of Computer Engineering
Nanyang Technological University, Nanyang Avenue, Singapore 639798
asahtan@ntu.edu.sg, kang0028@ntu.edu.sg

Abstract. Co-Space refers to interactive virtual environment modelled after the real world we are situated in. Through realistic 3D modelling and animation technologies, Co-Space simulates the real world in terms of look-and-feel of our physical surrounding. With the advancement in pervasive sensor network, Co-Space may also capture and mirror the happening in the physical world in real time. The development of Co-Space thus offers great opportunities for delivering innovative applications and services. Specifically, for enriching the experience of users in Co-Space, it is essential to incorporate knowledge facilities in the form of intelligent agents to enhance the interactivity and playability within. This paper will begin with a brief review of this emerging field of work related to agents in virtual worlds and integrated cognitive architectures. We then discuss the key requirement, issues and challenges in making Co-Space interactive and intelligent. Following the notion of embodied intelligence, we propose to develop cognitive agents, based on a family of self-organizing neural models, known as fusion Adaptive Resonance Theory (fusion ART). Our ultimate aim is to have such agents roaming freely in the landscape of Co-Space, developing an awareness of its surrounding and interacting with avatars of real human. As an illustration, a case study of our effort in building the Singapore Youth Olympic Village (YOV) Co-Space will be presented.

Keywords: Co-Space, Intelligent agents, virtual world.

1   Introduction

Virtual world has become a popular platform used in a variety of contexts, including education, business, and e-commerce [41]. Studies in South Korea have recently shown that users prefer virtual world to television [42]. Gartner even predicted that 80 percent of the Internet users will be actively participating in non-gaming virtual world by the end of 2011. To date, many popular virtual worlds exist, such as Second Life and Active Worlds, enabling users to create artificial content in virtual environment.

In our work, we are particularly interested in a special class of virtual world, called Co-Space, referring to interactive virtual environment modelled after a real physical world in terms of look-and-feel, functionalities and services. Through

B. Xie et al. (Eds.): ATC 2010, LNCS 6407, pp. 298–312, 2010.

realistic 3D modelling and animation technologies, Co-Space simulates the real world in terms of look-and-feel of our physical surrounding. With the advancement in pervasive sensor network, Co-Space may also capture and mirror the happening in the physical world in real time. Besides providing a much faster and easier access to information and services, the development of Co-Space has offered great opportunities for delivering innovative applications and services. Specifically, intelligent agents can be deployed in Co-Space enhancing its interactivity and playability.

Despite the appealing potential, deploying intelligent agents in a virtual world, just like in a real world, poses many challenges not addressed by traditional AI and machine learning algorithms. In particular, learning in virtual world is typically unsupervised, without an explicit teacher to guide the agent in learning. Furthermore, it requires an interplay of a myriad of learning paradigms. Due to such difficulties, most virtual worlds tend to constrain agents' actions to a very coarse level, dictated by hard coded rules [27,43,28].

In contrast to existing approaches, we take the view that a large part of an agent's intelligence is acquired through its interaction with the environment. This is in keeping with the view in modern cognitive science that cognition is a process deeply rooted in the body's interaction with the world [2]. Furthermore, we hypothesize that a cognitive autonomous system, with the appropriate architecture and the necessary adaptation mechanisms, is a sufficient self to learn and interact in a dynamic environment. Embodied cognition is also akin to the intensive study on reinforcement learning [31] in which an autonomous agent learns to adjust its behaviour according to evaluative feedback received from the environment.

Following the notion of embodied intelligence, we develop cognitive architectures, based on a family of self-organizing neural models, known as fusion Adaptive Resonance Theory (fusion ART) [35]. Fusion ART is a generalization of self-organizing neural models known as Adaptive Resonance Theory (ART) [5,8]. By extending the original ART model consisting of a single pattern field into a multi-channel architecture, fusion ART unifies a number of important neural models, developed over the past decades, including the original ART models, Adaptive Resonance Associative Map (ARAM) designed for supervised learning [32,39], and Fusion Architecture for Learning and Cognition (FALCON) [33,35], designed for reinforcement learning.

With the properties of self-adaptation, generalization, and fast yet stable real-time learning, fusion ART makes a suitable building block for designing learning agents in virtual world. By incorporating fusion ART, an agent will be able to learn from sensory and evaluative feedback signals received from the virtual environment largely without involving human supervision and intervention. In this way, the agent needs neither an explicit teacher nor a perfect model to learn from. Performing reinforcement learning in real time, it is able to adapt itself to the variations in the virtual environment and changes in the user behavior patterns.

In the next section, we shall review the related work on intelligent agents in virtual worlds and integrated cognitive architectures. We then discuss several issues and challenges in designing agents for an agent-augmented virtual environment.

We then present an embodied intelligence approach building upon the learning and adaptation capability of fusion ART and its extended architectures that integrate learning with higher level functions. Finally, we present a case study on a Co-Space known as Youth Olympic Village (YOV) Co-Space. The final section concludes and highlights possible future directions.

2   Related Work

2.1   Learning Agents in Virtual Worlds

Though intelligent agents have been popularly used for improving the interactivity and playability of virtual worlds, most such agents are based on scripts or predefined rules. For example, in the Virtual Theater project, synthetic actors portray fictive characters and provide improvising behaviors. The agents are based on a scripted social-psychological model with the defined personality traits which rely on the values of moods and attitudes [27]. Agents in Metaverse, built using Active Worlds, are capable of performing the tasks typically associated with human beings, such as taking tickets for rides and acting as shopkeepers. However, these agents are basically reactive agents which work in a hard-coded manner. Virtual psychotherapist ELIZA [43], designed to take care of the 'patients', is also achieved with rule-based, adeptly modeled small talk. A conversational virtual agent Max has been developed as a guide to the HNF computer museum, where he interacts with visitors and provides them with information daily [28]. However, the design remains rule-based.

In view of the limitations of static agents, some researchers have adopted learning methods into service agents in virtual world. For example, Yoon et.al. present a Creature Kernel framework to build interactive synthetic characters in the project Sydney K9.0 [44]. Their agents can reflect the characters' past experience and allow individual personalization. But all the capabilities of the agents rely on past knowledge and couldn't adapt to user gradually during run time. The co-present agents in a virtual gallery [12] utilize a knowledge base containing general input response knowledge, augmented with knowledge modules for special domains. More recently, an embodied conversational agent that serves as a virtual tour guide in Second Life has been implemented by Jan [15]. It uses NPCEditor [21] to learn the best output for any input from a training set of linked questions and answers. Again, it learns from past experience but does not adapt over time according to the habits of a particular player or the changes in the environment.

2.2   Integrated Cognitive Models

On the other hand, research in intelligent autonomous systems has been a key focus in the fields of cognitive science and artificial intelligence in the past decades [9]. Below we review six cognitive architectures, namely Soar, ACT-R, ICARUS, BDI, the subsumption architecture, and CLARION, roughly classified according to their roots and emphases.

Soar [18,20], based on the physical symbolic hypothesis [23], is one of the earliest and most extensively developed AI architectures in the history. ACT-R [1] (also with a long history) and ICARUS [19] (a relatively recent model) are cognitive systems developed with the primary aim of producing artificial intelligence mimicking human cognition. While the three architectures share many features of classical artificial intelligence, including symbolic representation, production rule based inference, and means-end analysis for problem solving, ACT-R and ICARUS are notably different from Soar by their strong emphasis of producing a psychologically motivated cognitive model.

Belief-Desire-Intention (BDI) architecture [3,26] is a popularly used framework, incorporating beliefs, desires and intentions, for designing intelligent autonomous agents. Based on the studies of folk psychology and intentional systems, BDI has a special focus on intentions, representing an agent's commitments to carry out certain plans of actions [11]. Coined as the new artificial intelligence, the subsumption architecture [4] is notably different from the other cognitive architectures in its approach and design. The subsumption architecture is behaviour based and thus does not contain any problem solving or learning module. The idea of higher layers subsuming lower layers in the subsumption architecture has its root from neurobiology. CLARION [30,29] is a hybrid model integrating both symbolic and connectionist information processing. The design of CLARION is based on neural networks as well as cognitive psychology. As a result, it is similar to ACT-R as both models are based on a combination of artificial intelligence, cognitive psychology and some favour of neurobiology.

All cognitive architectures contain certain features which make them unique. However, no single cognitive architecture has provided a solution that is within the level of human cognition. Reinforcement Learning is a field that has received intensive research effort, but has not been incorporated into cognitive architectures in a major and principled way. Among these hybrid systems, temporal difference learning using gradient descent based function approximator has been most commonly used. However, the gradient descent methods learn by making small error correction steps iteratively. In addition, there is the issue of instability as learning of new patterns may erode the previously learned knowledge. Consequently, the resultant systems may not be able to learn and operate in real time.

3   Issues and Challenges

3.1   How to Create Autonomy and Self-Awareness?

Autonomy is the ability of an agent to act and make decisions on its own independently of the programmer or user. It is required for an agent-based autonomous entities to be self-awareness so as to increase the dynamics of the virtual environment. For example, in a Co-Space populated with agent-based avatars, the non-player characters should be autonomous in initiating actions and interacting with users proactively. Autonomy is also necessary to enable an agent to explore the virtual environment in the absence of continuous instructions by the user.

3.2 How to Enhance Interactivity?

In the domain of computer games, researchers studied how to improve the game's playability, of which interactivity has been identified as one of the most important factors. For example, a player who is constantly engaged will find the place more interesting comparing to one who has been left alone to explore in a lifeless land. As such, when agents are augmented as enemies or fellows in a virtual world, those agents should have frequent and natural interaction with the players to enhance playability.

3.3 How to Enable Situatedness?

Situatedness is also a consideration for intelligent agents in virtual world as they tend to be used in a dynamic, unpredictable and unreliable environment. As the environment changes rapidly, the agent cannot assume that the situation will remain stationary while it figures how to achieve a goal. The environment can also be unpredictable sometime due to the limitations of the agent in obtaining accurate and complete information about the environment or that the environment is being modified in ways beyond the agent's knowledge and reasoning capability. Finally, the environment can be unreliable in that the actions that an agent can perform may fail for reasons beyond an agent's control.

3.4 How to Learn and Function in Real-Time?

The ability to learn is another important issue. A good agent needs to acquire new knowledge and skills and improve its performance in carrying out a particular task over time. For example, if a user signals to an agent that it performs poorly on a task, the agent should be able to learn from this experience and avoid making the same mistake in the future. The capability of learning can also be an issue of playability, as an agent should not struggle to learn the rules of how to behave in an appropriate manner. Furthermore, this issue of learning becomes much more complex and challenging in a real-time dynamic multi-agent environment.

3.5 How to Learn about Users for Personalization?

Especially in the domain of education and gaming, one important aspect of agents that has received a great deal of attention is user modelling and personalization. For example, teaching in many virtual worlds is achieved with pedagogical agents as virtual teachers to monitor and provide learners with personalized guidance. To achieve this goal, personalization becomes an important issue in agent technology, i.e., adapting the teaching to the needs of various learners.

4   An Embodied Intelligence Approach

Over the past decades, a family of neural models known as Adaptive Resonance Theory (ART) [7,8] has been steadily developed. With well-founded computational principles, ART has been applied successfully to many pattern analysis, recognition, and prediction applications [10,22]. These successful applications are of particular interest because the basic ART principles have been derived from an analysis of human and animal perceptual and cognitive information processing, and have led to behavioral and neurobiological predictions that have received significant experimental support during the last decade [13,25].

In this paper, we show that Adaptive Resonance Theory lays the foundation of a unified model that encompasses a myriad of learning paradigms, traditionally viewed as distinct. The proposed model is a natural extension of the original ART models from a single pattern field to multiple pattern channels. Whereas the original ART models perform unsupervised learning of recognition nodes in response to incoming input patterns, the proposed neural architecture, known as fusion ART, learns multi-channel mappings simultaneously across multi-modal pattern channels in an online and incremental manner.

4.1   Fusion ART

Fusion ART employs a multi-channel architecture (Figure 1), comprising a category field F_2 connected to a fixed number of (K) pattern channels or input fields through bidirectional conditionable pathways. The model unifies a number of network designs, most notably Adaptive Resonance Theory (ART) [7,8], Adaptive Resonance Associative Map (ARAM) [32] and Fusion Architecture for Learning, COgnition, and Navigation (FALCON) [33], developed over the past decades for a wide range of functions and applications. The generic network dynamics of fusion ART, based on fuzzy ART operations [6], is summarized as follows.

Input vectors: Let $\mathbf{I}^{ck} = (I_1^{ck}, I_2^{ck}, \ldots, I_n^{ck})$ denote the input vector, where $I_i^{ck} \in [0, 1]$ indicates the input i to channel ck. With complement coding, the input vector $\mathbf{I}^{ck}$ is augmented with a complement vector $\bar{\mathbf{I}}^{ck}$ such that $\bar{I}_i^{ck} = 1 - I_i^{ck}$.

Activity vectors: Let $\mathbf{x}^{ck}$ denote the F_1^{ck} activity vector for $k = 1, \ldots, K$. Let $\mathbf{y}$ denote the F_2 activity vector.

Weight vectors: Let $\mathbf{w}_j^{ck}$ denote the weight vector associated with the jth node in F_2 for learning the input patterns in F_1^{ck} for $k = 1, \ldots, K$. Initially, F_2 contains only one *uncommitted* node and its weight vectors contain all 1's.

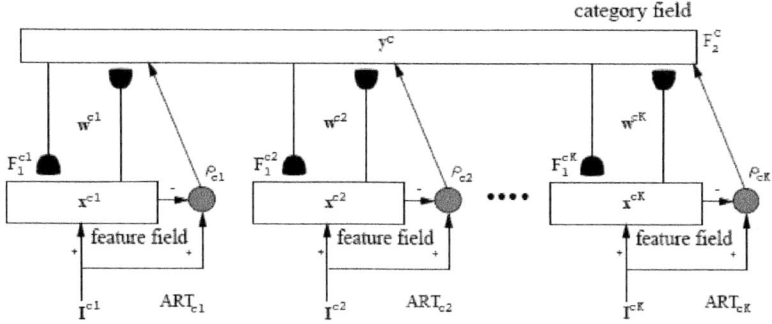

Fig. 1. The fusion ART architecture

Parameters: The fusion ART's dynamics is determined by choice parameters $\alpha^{ck} > 0$, learning rate parameters $\beta^{ck} \in [0,1]$, contribution parameters $\gamma^{ck} \in [0,1]$ and vigilance parameters $\rho^{ck} \in [0,1]$ for $k = 1, \ldots, K$.

As a natural extension of ART, fusion ART responds to incoming patterns in a continuous manner. It is important to note that at any point in time, fusion ART does not require input to be present in all the pattern channels. For those channels not receiving input, the input vectors are initialized to all 1s. The fusion ART pattern processing cycle comprises five key stages, namely code activation, code competition, activity readout, template matching, and template learning, as described below.

Code activation: Given the activity vectors $\mathbf{I}^{c1}, \ldots, \mathbf{I}^{cK}$, for each F_2 node j, the choice function T_j is computed as follows:

$$T_j = \sum_{k=1}^{K} \gamma^{ck} \frac{|\mathbf{I}^{ck} \wedge \mathbf{w}_j^{ck}|}{\alpha^{ck} + |\mathbf{w}_j^{ck}|}, \tag{1}$$

where the fuzzy AND operation $\wedge$ is defined by $(\mathbf{p} \wedge \mathbf{q})_i \equiv min(p_i, q_i)$, and the norm $|.|$ is defined by $|\mathbf{p}| \equiv \sum_i p_i$ for vectors $\mathbf{p}$ and $\mathbf{q}$.

Code competition: A code competition process follows under which the F_2 node with the highest choice function value is identified. The winner is indexed at J where

$$T_J = \max\{T_j : \text{for all } F_2 \text{ node } j\}. \tag{2}$$

When a category choice is made at node J, $y_J = 1$; and $y_j = 0$ for all $j \neq J$. This indicates a winner-take-all strategy.

Activity readout: The chosen F_2 node J performs a readout of its weight vectors to the input fields F_1^{ck} such that

$$\mathbf{x}^{ck} = \mathbf{I}^{ck} \wedge \mathbf{w}_J^{ck}. \tag{3}$$

Template matching: Before the activity readout is stabilized and node J can be used for learning, a template matching process checks that the weight templates of node J are sufficiently close to their respective input patterns. Specifically, resonance occurs if for each channel k, the *match function* m_J^{ck} of the chosen node J meets its vigilance criterion:

$$m_J^{ck} = \frac{|\mathbf{I}^{ck} \wedge \mathbf{w}_J^{ck}|}{|\mathbf{I}^{ck}|} \geq \rho^{ck}. \tag{4}$$

If any of the vigilance constraints is violated, mismatch reset occurs in which the value of the choice function T_J is set to 0 for the duration of the input presentation. Using a *match tracking* process, at the beginning of each input presentation, the vigilance parameter ρ^{ck} in each channel ck equals a baseline vigilance $\bar{\rho}^{ck}$. When a mismatch reset occurs, the ρ^{ck} of all pattern channels are increased simultaneously until one of them is slightly larger than its corresponding match function m_J^{ck}, causing a reset. The search process then selects another F_2 node J under the revised vigilance criterion until a resonance is achieved.

Template learning: Once a resonance occurs, for each channel ck, the weight vector $\mathbf{w}_J^{ck}$ is modified by the following learning rule:

$$\mathbf{w}_J^{ck(\text{new})} = (1 - \beta^{ck})\mathbf{w}_J^{ck(\text{old})} + \beta^{ck}(\mathbf{I}^{ck} \wedge \mathbf{w}_J^{ck(\text{old})}). \tag{5}$$

When an uncommitted node is selected for learning, it becomes *committed* and a new uncommitted node is added to the F_2 field. Fusion ART thus expands its network architecture dynamically in response to the input patterns.

4.2   Learning and Adaptation

The network dynamics described above can be used to support a myriad of learning operations. We show how fusion ART can be used for a variety of traditionally distinct learning tasks in the subsequent sections.

Learning by Similarity Matching. With a single pattern channel, the fusion ART architecture reduces to the original ART model. Using a selected vigilance value ρ, an ART model learns a set of recognition nodes in response to an incoming stream of input patterns in a continuous manner. Each recognition node in the F_2 field learns to encode a template pattern representing the key characteristics of a set of patterns. ART has been widely used in the context of unsupervised learning for discovering pattern groupings. Please refer to the selected ART literatures [7,8] for a review of ART's functionalities, interpretations, and applications.

Learning by Association. By synchronizing pattern coding across multiple pattern channels, fusion ART learns to encode associative mappings across distinct pattern spaces. A specific instance of fusion ART with two pattern channels is known as Adaptive Resonance Associative Map (ARAM), that learns multidimensional supervised mappings from one pattern space to another pattern space [32]. An ARAM system consists of an input field F_1^a, an output field F_1^b, and a category field F_2. Given a set of feature vectors presented at F_1^a with their corresponding class vectors presented at F_1^b, ARAM learns a predictive model (encoded by the recognition nodes in F_2) that associates combinations of key features to their respective classes.

Fuzzy ARAM, based on fuzzy ART operations, has been successfully applied to numerous machine learning tasks, including personal profiling [40], document classification [14], personalized content management [24,38], and DNA gene expression analysis [39]. In many benchmark experiments, ARAM has demonstrated predictive performance superior to those of many state-of-the-art machine learning systems.

Learning by Reinforcement. Reinforcement learning [31] is a paradigm wherein an autonomous system learns to adjust its behaviour based on reinforcement signals received from the environment. An instance of fusion ART, known as FALCON

(Fusion Architecture for Learning, COgnition, and Navigation), learns mappings simultaneously across multi-modal input patterns, involving states, actions, and rewards, in an online and incremental manner.

FALCON employs a three-channel architecture, comprising a category field F_2 and three pattern fields, namely a sensory field F_1^{c1} for representing current states, a motor field F_1^{c2} for representing actions, and a feedback field F_1^{c3} for representing reward values. A class of FALCON networks, known as TD-FALCON [34,37], incorporates Temporal Difference (TD) methods to estimate and learn value function $Q(s, a)$, that indicates the goodness to take a certain action a in a given state s.

The general sense-act-learn algorithm for TD-FALCON is summarized below. Given the current state s, the FALCON network is used to predict the value of performing each available action a in the action set $\mathcal{A}$ based on the corresponding state vector $\mathbf{S}$ and action vector $\mathbf{A}$. The value functions are then processed by an action selection strategy (also known as policy) to select an action. Upon receiving a feedback (if any) from the environment after performing the action, a TD formula is used to compute a new estimate of the Q-value for performing the chosen action in the current state. The new Q-value is then used as the teaching signal (represented as reward vector $\mathbf{R}$) for FALCON to learn the association of the current state and the chosen action to the estimated value.

4.3   Integrating Desire, Intention and Learning

To address the issue of autonomy and self-awareness, a hybrid architecture has been developed that integrates BDI components, including desire and intention, with a reinforcement learning system known as Temporal Difference - Fusion Architecture for Learning and Cognition (TD-FALCON). Following the Belief-Desire-Intention (BDI) framework, the proposed connectionist BDI-FALCON (cBDI-FALCON) architecture consists of three modules, namely the *desire* module, the *intention* module, and a *reactive* module, each of which is implemented as a fusion ART network. The three key modules and their relationships are exemplified in Figure 2. The detailed algorithms and processes are described in [36].

Reactive module: The low level reactive learning module is a TD-FALCON model that interacts with the environment through the sensory, motor, and feedback channels. Based on the goals defined in the desire module and the sensory inputs received from the environment, TD-FALCON performs reinforcement learning so as to acquire a set of action and value policies that enables the agent to achieve its goals.

Intention module: The intention module maintains the plan set and supports the key processes of plan learning, plan selection, plan execution and plan evaluation. Given a set of active goals and the current sensory inputs, the plan selection process identifies the most applicable plan to perform. During the plan execution, the action sequence of the adopted plan is extracted and performed through the motor channel of the reactive module. The execution of plans thus

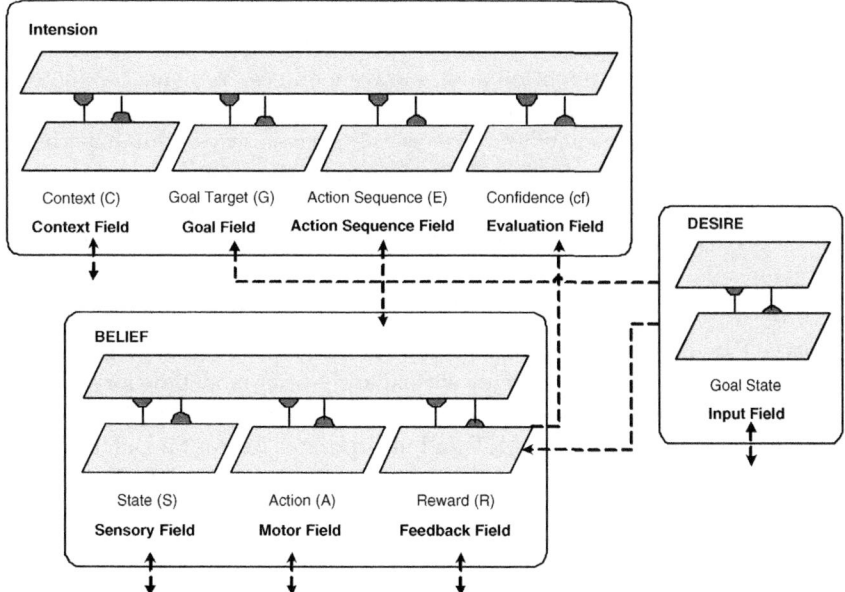

Fig. 2. A schematic architecture of cBDI-FALCON

enables an agent to perform a series of actions without the need of going through the typical sense-act-learn cycle for each action. This could potentially lead to saving in computation cost and enable the system to be more resilient in a challenging environment, wherein external signals may not be available all the time. Through a simple form of reinforcement learning, the plan evaluation process adjusts the confidence value of each adopted plan according to the outcome that it leads to. In contrast to other cognitive architectures, the intention module in the cBDI-FALCON is also modelled as a fusion ART neural network. Doing so enables plans to be learned and updated through reinforcement learning according to the outcomes of their use in a natural way.

Desire module: The desire module maintains an explicit representation of the agent's goals. Active goals are those that give direction to the agent's activities for it to achieve its objectives. By matching the defined goals with the corresponding current state attributes, the desire module computes how well the system has progressed towards the desired goals. The computed degrees of goal attainment in turn serve as reward signals to the feedback field of the reactive module and the evaluation field of the intention modules. Similar to the reactive and intention modules, the desire module in the architecture is also modelled as a one-channel fusion ART network. The overall design philosophy is thus aiming towards a unified framework by using a principled set of computational processes for supporting both intentional and reactive behaviour. In theory, all computations in the system can be operated in parallel on distributed neural networks, enabling the potential of speeding up.

To combine planned and reactive capabilities, we develop two strategies, known as the follow-through and the re-evaluation strategies to coordinate the output produced by the intention and reactive modules. We have conducted extensive experiments to analyze the behaviours of the integrated system, in terms of plan utilization, efficiency, and the overall success rates. Our experimental results on a minefield navigation task show that the integrated neural architecture is able to combine intentional and reactive action execution, leading to improvement both in terms of task completion performance and efficiency.

4.4   Learning Personal Agents with User Modelling

Adaptive Player Modelling.   To achieve real-time learning and personalization, we integrate learning personal agents with adaptive user modelling for service recommendation in Co-Space. Our personal agent is based on TD-FALCON [37] that employs a three-channel fusion ART and incorporates Temporal Difference (TD) methods to estimate and learn value functions of its recommendations. For player modelling, we adopt a two-channel fusion ART, that performs supervised learning through the pairing of the input patterns representing the recommendations and teaching signals representing the user's feedback received from the virtual environment. If an initial user profile is available, the model first initializes the player model by associating the attributes specified in the player's profile with positive reward signals. During play time, the player model learns the user's specific like's and dislike's by creating cognitive nodes associating the key attributes of the agent's recommendations to the user's feedbacks. Furthermore, the user's general interest could be inferred based on the frequency of the user's positive responses to recommendations given in a general interest category.

Integrating Player Model With Personal Agent.   The overall recommendation agent, incorporating the personal agent, the player model, and a search

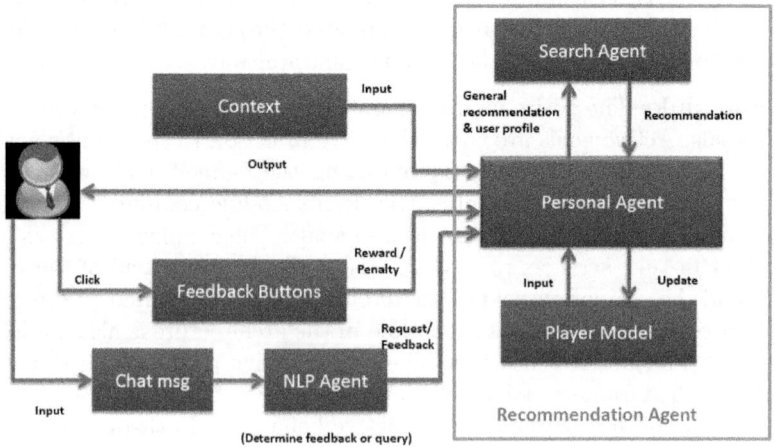

Fig. 3. Personal agent integrated with adaptive player model

agent, is shown in Figure 3. Specifically, the personal agent determines the appropriate class of services to recommend, such as accommodations, restaurants, YOV venues, shopping areas, and other general places of interest, according to the current situation and the user's context. Upon the user's feedback, the player model learns the player's specific preferences and updates the personal agent with the player's current general interests during the interplay. By incorporating the personal agent with the adaptive player model, the system would be more sensitive to the players' habits and eccentricity. Based on the recommendation output of the personal agent and the user preferences indicated by the player model, the search agent handles the retrieval of the requested information from the database.

5   The Youth Olympic Village Co-Space

The Youth Olympic Village (YOV) Co-Space is built to showcase the Youth Olympic Village (YOV) and the hosting country to visitors around the world in an interactive and playable manner. To achieve this objective, we are in the process of developing and populating human-like cognitive agents in the form of autonomous avatars that roam in the landscape of YOV Co-Space. The agents are designed to be aware of its surrounding and can interact with users through their human avatars. With the autonomous avatars befriending and providing personalized context-aware services to human avatars, we aim to make the content and services readily available to the users.

Figure 4 shows the architecture of the YOV Co-Space. As illustrated in this framework, the TD-FALCON based personal agent works in conjunction with the search agent in recommending functions and services to the users. Specifically,

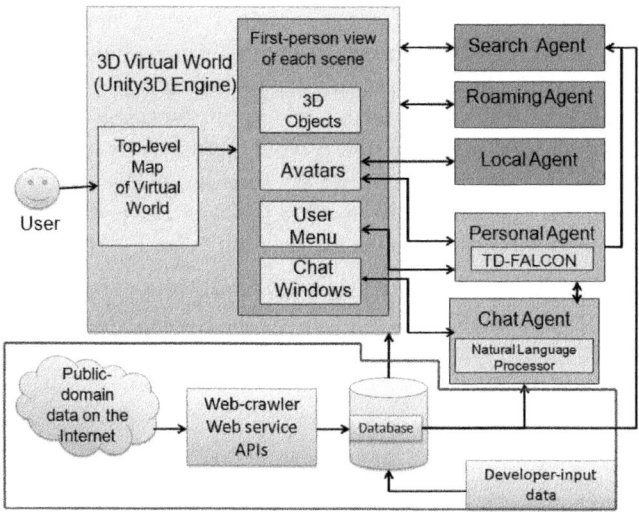

Fig. 4. The architecture of Co-Space

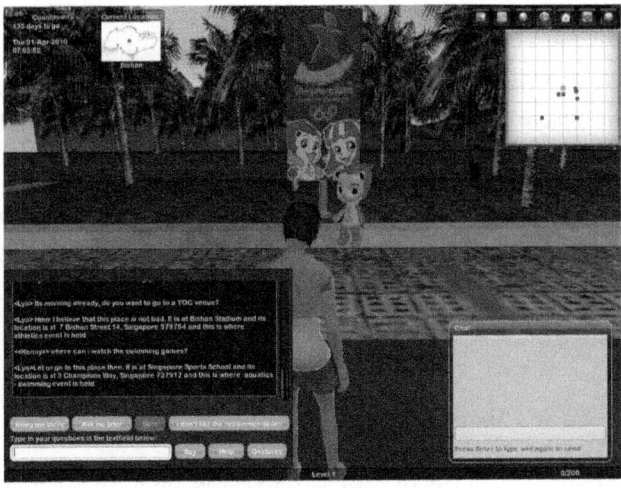

Fig. 5. A snapshot of TD-FALCON based personal agent in Co-Space

the personal agent determines the appropriate type of services to recommend whereas the search agent retrieves the specific services based on the environment situations as well as the users' context parameters. Figure 5 provides a snapshot of the virtual world, showing the personal agent Lyo serving the user. For a more detailed description of the YOV Co-Space and the experimental study, please refer to [16,17].

6   Conclusion

This paper has presented our ongoing work in developing and deploying intelligent agents for Co-Space based on a generalized neural model, known as fusion ART. Using a universal coding mechanism, the proposed model unifies a myriad of traditionally distinct learning paradigms, including unsupervised learning, supervised learning, and reinforcement learning. In fact, ART-style learning and matching mechanism seems to be operative in many levels of the cerebral cortex of the brain. The proposed framework may thus serve as a foundation model for developing high level cognitive information processing capabilities for intelligent agents, including awareness, reasoning, explaining, and surprise handling.

Acknowledgments. The reported work is supported by the Singapore National Research Foundation Interactive Digital Media R&D Program, under research Grant NRF2008IDM-IDM004-037.

References

1. Anderson, J.R., Bothell, D., Byrne, M.D., Douglass, S., Lebiere, C., Qin, Y.: An intergrated theory of the mind. Psychological Review 111, 1036–1060 (2004)
2. Anderson, M.L.: Embodied cognition: A field guide. Artificial Intelligence 149, 91–130 (2003)

3. Bratman, M.E., Israel, D.J., Pollack, M.E.: Plans and resource-bounded practical reasoning. Computational Intelligence 4(4), 349–355 (1988)
4. Brooks, R.A.: Cambrian Intelligence: The Early History of the New AI. MIT Press, Boston (1999)
5. Carpenter, G.A., Grossberg, S.: A massively parallel architecture for a self-organizing neural pattern recognition machine. Computer Vision, Graphics, and Image Processing 37, 54–115 (1987)
6. Carpenter, G.A., Grossberg, S., Rosen, D.B.: Fuzzy ART: Fast stable learning and categorization of analog patterns by an adaptive resonance system. Neural Networks 4, 759–771 (1991)
7. Carpenter, G.A., Grossberg, S. (eds.): Pattern Recognition by Self-Organizing Neural Networks. MIT Press, Cambridge (1991)
8. Carpenter, G.A., Grossberg, S.: Adaptive Rresonance Theory. In: Arbib, M.A. (ed.) The Handbook of Brain Theory and Neural Networks, pp. 87–90. MIT Press, Cambridge (2003)
9. Chong, H.-Q., Tan, A.-H., Ng, G.-W.: Integrated cognitive architectures: A survey. Artificial Intelligence Review 28(2), 103–130 (2007)
10. Duda, R.O., Hart, P.E., Stock, D.G. (eds.): Pattern Classification, 2nd edn. John Wiley, Chichester (2001) Section 10.11.2
11. Georgeff, M.P., Ingrand, F.F.: Decision-making in an embedded reasoning system. In: Proceedings of IJCAI, pp. 972–978 (1989)
12. Gerhard, M., Moore, D.J., Hobbs, D.J.: Embodiment and copresence in collaborative interfaces. Int. J. Hum.-Comput. Stud. 64(4), 453–480 (2004)
13. Grossberg, S.: How does the cerebral cortex work? development, learning, attention, and 3d vision by laminar circuits of visual cortex. Behavioral and Cognitive Neuroscience Reviews 2, 47–76 (2003)
14. He, J., Tan, A.-H., Tan, C.-L.: On machine learning methods for chinese documents classification. Applied Intelligence 18(3), 311–322 (2003)
15. Jan, D., Roque, A., Leuski, A., Morie, J., Traum, D.: A virtual tour guide for virtual worlds. In: Ruttkay, Z., Kipp, M., Nijholt, A., Vilhjálmsson, H.H. (eds.) IVA 2009. LNCS, vol. 5773, pp. 372–378. Springer, Heidelberg (2009)
16. Kang, Y., Tan, A.-H.: Learning personal agents with adaptive player modeling in virtual worlds. In: Proceedings, IEEE/WIC/ACM International Conference on Intelligent Agent Technology, Toronto, Canada (2010)
17. Kang, Y., Tan, A.-H.: Self-organizing agents for reinforcement learning in virtual worlds. In: Proceedings of IJCNN, Barcelona, Spain, pp. 3641–3648 (2010)
18. Laird, J.E., Rosenbloom, P.S., Newell, A.: Chunking in Soar: The anatomy of a general learning mechanism. Machine Learning 1, 11–46 (1986)
19. Langley, P., Choi, D.: A unified cognitive architecture for physical agents. In: Proceedings of AAAI, pp. 1469–1474 (2006)
20. Lehman, J.F., Laird, J.E., Rosenbloom, P.S.: A gentle introduction to soar, an architcture for human cognition (update 2006)
21. Leuski, A., Traum, D.: A statistical approach for text processing in virtual humans. In: 26th Army Science Conference (2008)
22. Levine, D.S.: Introduction to Neural and Cognitive Modeling, ch. 6. Lawrence Erlbaum Associates, New Jersey (2000)
23. Newell, A.: Unified Theories of Cognition. Harvard University Press, Cambridge (1990)
24. Ong, H.-L., Tan, A.-H., Ng, J., Pan, H., Li, Q.-X.: FOCI: Flexible organizer for competitive intelligence. In: Proceedings of CIKM, Atlanta, pp. 523–525 (2001)

25. Raizada, R., Grossberg, S.: Towards a theory of the laminar architecture of cerebral cortes: Computational clues from the visual system. Cerebral Cortex 13, 200–213 (2003)
26. Rao, A.S., Georgeff, M.P.: Modeling rational agents within a BDI architecture. In: Proceedings of Second International Conference on Principles of Knowledge Representation and Reasoning, pp. 473–484 (1991)
27. Rousseau, D., Roth, B.H.: A social-psychological model for synthetic actors. Stanford Knowledge Systems Laboratory Report KSL-97-07 (1997)
28. Kopp, S., Gesellensetter, L., Krämer, N.C., Wachsmuth, I.: A conversational agent as museum guide - design and evaluation of a real-world application. In: Panayiotopoulos, T., Gratch, J., Aylett, R.S., Ballin, D., Olivier, P., Rist, T. (eds.) IVA 2005. LNCS (LNAI), vol. 3661, pp. 329–343. Springer, Heidelberg (2005)
29. Sun, R., Merrill, E., Peterson, T.: From implicit skills to explicit knowledge: a bottom-up model of skill learning. Cognitive Science 25(2), 203–244 (2001)
30. Sun, R., Peterson, T.: Learning in reactive sequential decision tasks: The CLARION model. In: Proceedings of IEEE ICNN, pp. 1073–1078 (1996)
31. Sutton, R.S., Barto, A.G.: Reinforcement Learning: An Introduction. MIT Press, Cambridge (1998)
32. Tan, A.-H.: Adaptive Resonance Associative Map. Neural Networks 8(3), 437–446 (1995)
33. Tan, A.-H.: FALCON: A fusion architecture for learning, cognition, and navigation. In: Proceedings of IJCNN, Budapest, Hungary, pp. 3297–3302 (2004)
34. Tan, A.-H.: Self-organizing neural architecture for reinforcement learning. In: Wang, J., Yi, Z., Żurada, J.M., Lu, B.-L., Yin, H. (eds.) ISNN 2006. LNCS, vol. 3971, pp. 470–475. Springer, Heidelberg (2006)
35. Tan, A.-H.: Direct code access in self-organizing neural architectures for reinforcement learning. In: Proceedings of IJCAI, Hyderabad, India, pp. 1071–1076 (2007)
36. Tan, A.-H., Feng, Y.-H., Ong, Y.-S.: A self-organizing neural architecture integrating desire, intention and reinforcement learning. Neurocomputing 73(7-9), 1465–1477 (2010)
37. Tan, A.-H., Lu, N., Xiao, D.: Integrating temporal difference methods and self-organizing neural networks for reinforcement learning with delayed evaluative feedback. IEEE Transactions on Neural Networks 9(2), 230–244 (2008)
38. Tan, A.-H., Ong, H.-L., Pan, H., Ng, J., Li, Q.-X.: Towards personalized web intelligence. Knowledge and Information Systems 6(5), 595–616 (2004)
39. Tan, A.-H., Pan, H.: Predictive neural networks for gene expression data analysis. Neural Networks 18(3), 297–306 (2005)
40. Tan, A.-H., Soon, H.-S.: Predictive adaptive resonance theory and knowledge discovery in database. In: Terano, T., Chen, A.L.P. (eds.) PAKDD 2000. LNCS, vol. 1805, pp. 173–176. Springer, Heidelberg (2000)
41. Thomas, D., Brown, J.S.: Why virtual worlds can matter. International Journal of Media and Learning 1(1), 37–49 (2009)
42. Weinstein, J., Myers, J.: Same principles apply to virtual world expansion as to china and other new markets. Media Village 11 (2006)
43. Weizenbaum, J.: ELIZA: a computer program for the study of natural language communication between men and machines. Communications of the ACM 9 (1996)
44. Yoon, S., Burke, R.C., Blumberg, B.M., Schneider, G.E.: Interactive training for synthetic characters. In: Proceedings of AAAI, pp. 249–254 (2000)

On Alleviating Reader Collisions towards High Efficient RFID Systems

Ching-Hsien Hsu[1] and Chia-Hao Yu[2]

[1] Department of Computer Science and Information Engineering
[2] College of Engineering
Chung Hua University, Hsinchu, Taiwan 300, R.O.C.
{robert,yu}@grid.chu.edu.tw

Abstract. With the emergence of wireless technologies, RFID is increasingly used in many applications such as inventory management, object tracking, retail checkout etc. In an RFID system, readers are centered in a finite area within which they can communicate with tags. Because the same radio frequency is used for communication, readers may also interfere with the operations of other readers even if their interrogation zones do not overlap. Thus the problem of scheduling multiple readers to tags transmissions in dynamic systems has been arousing attention. This paper presents a priority based transaction method to coordinate simultaneous communications among multiple readers in order to increase the overall read rate in dynamic RFID systems. Through a contention-free scheduling, the reader-tag transmissions can be performed without collisions even the environment has hidden terminal. To evaluate the effectiveness of the proposed techniques, both network density and mobility of readers' join and leave are conducted in the tests. Experimental results show that the proposed techniques provide superior system throughput in both static and dynamic circumstances.

1 Introduction

The Radio Frequency Identification (RFID) system is an automatic technology that aids machines or computers in identifying, recording or controlling individual targets through radio waves. It is regarded as one of the leading technologies for realizing so-called ubiquitous computing and its services. Recently it has also starting to attract much attention from research communities and various industries.

An RFID system consists of three components, RFID reader, RFID tag and the back-end database. The electronics in the RFID reader use an outside power resource to generate a signal to drive the reader's antenna and turn it into a radio wave. The radio wave will be received by a RFID tag which will reflect the energy in the way of signaling its identification and other related information. To access the reflection, the RFID reader works as a receiver on sensing and decoding the signal to identify the tag. In simple RFID system, RFID tag is passive and powered by the energy of the reader's signals. In some matured systems, the reader's RF can also instruct the memory of tag to be read or write.

Since communications between the RFID tag and reader are executed on public RF channels, the systems could face many problems in accuracy, reliability, security and

B. Xie et al. (Eds.): ATC 2010, LNCS 6407, pp. 313–326, 2010.

communication collisions. As an RFID reader is designed to accept the tiny signal reflected from a tag, it will be particularly influenced by any relatively powerful transmissions from other readers that happen at the same time. Therefore, it will be necessary to install RFID readers at appropriated distances from each other. Otherwise the interference could be caused when the frequency band is shared by other potential users.

In order to prevent mutual interference among readers, there are possible reactions. With the distributed scheme, RFID readers switch the communication state with each other to avoid simultaneous transactions. The centralized control mode means that appropriate coordination is handled by a specific reader. In this paper, we combine the virtues of both centralized and distributed schemes and propose a Priority Based Transaction with Multiple Prime (*PBT-MP*) mechanism, aimed to efficiently perform reader-tag transmissions and to avoid communication collisions that are caused by hidden terminals[2, 3]. Employing dual channel scheme, in *PBT-MP*, communications among readers are established through control channel while the actual data transmission between reader and tag is carried out in the data channel[4]. The proposed *PBT-MP* scheduling mechanism is applicable in the arbitrary RFID network, in which readers may frequently join and leave, forming an ad-hoc network, and have unrestricted mobility. The *PBT-MP* is a simple mechanism for coordinating simultaneous transmission among multiple readers. A significant improvement of this approach is that *PBT-MP* can prevent reader collisions based on a contention free communication scheduling. The second advantage of the present technique is that *PBT-MP* is adaptive in both static and dynamic RFID environments.

To evaluate the performance of the proposed technique, we have implemented *PBT-MP* along with other previously proposed protocols. We study the impact of the density of RFID readers and the frequency of readers joining or leaving on system throughput and efficiency. The experimental results show that the *PBT-MP* can achieve better efficiency than the previously proposed *PBT* scheme. The easy-implementation is also advantage of the proposed scheme.

The paper is organized as follows. Section 2 briefly introduces hidden terminal problem. A Priority Based Transaction (*PBT*) method is introduced in Section 3, where we also define notations and terminologies used in this paper. An enhanced *PBT* scheme, term as *PBT-MP* will be explained in Section 4. The performance comparison is given in Section 5. Section 6 concludes this paper.

2 Hidden Terminal on RFID Network

To simplify the presentation of the following sections, we first explain some terminologies used in this paper. Figure 1 shows an example of hidden terminal problem in RFID network. In this example, Tag T_1 is surrounded by two readers. Each of the readers is located beyond the sensing range of the others in the RFID network. Therefore, these two readers are not able to communicate with each other and reader collision might happen. The situation is known as the hidden terminal problem, and has the following features:

● Reader doesn't reside in others' sensing range might interfere with tags and cause carrier sensing to become ineffective.

- When queries or transmissions from multiple readers collide on a tag, signals can be distorted and the queries might be incorrect.
- RFID tags can communicate only when they are activated by readers because it is a passive element. Therefore, RFID tags will not able to pro-actively communicate with readers for avoiding collisions.

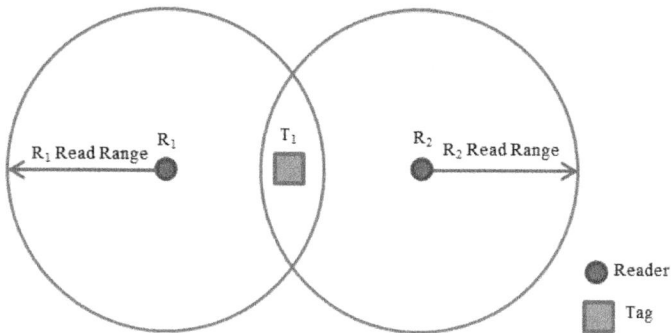

Fig. 1. Hidden terminal in RFID network

Interferences in RFID system are usually classified into reader to reader frequency interference and reader-to-tag interference [5, 6]. We further describe these two type in the following subsections.

2.1 Reader Frequency Interference

Reader to reader frequency interference is also called frequency interference, which occurs when readers interfere with others in communicating with tags. Figure 2 shows that RFID reader R_2 resides in the frequency interference range of reader R_1 which has a wider interference signal range (the dotted line). When tag T_1 responds to reader R_2, it might be influenced by the interference signal of reader R_1. Such hidden terminal problem occurs even when the range of the two readers do not overlap.

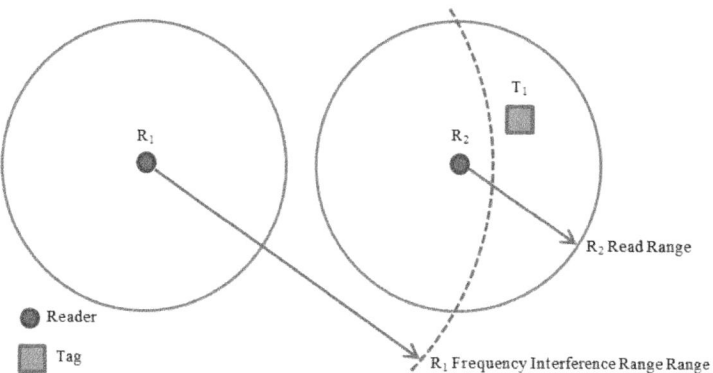

Fig. 2. Reader frequency interference

2.2 Multiple Readers to Tag Interference

Also referred as simply tag interference, it occurs when two or more readers in the transmission zone attempt to communicate with one tag simultaneously. In this situation, each reader performs a one to one communication with the tag. However, it is not known by the readers that the tag is responsible for multiple readers, simultaneously, as a result, reader collision might happen in this undesirable way. Figure 3 indicates an overlapping of three readers, R_1, R_2 and R_3 are not able to detect others when communicating with tag T_1. Such interference is also referred as part of the hidden terminal problem.

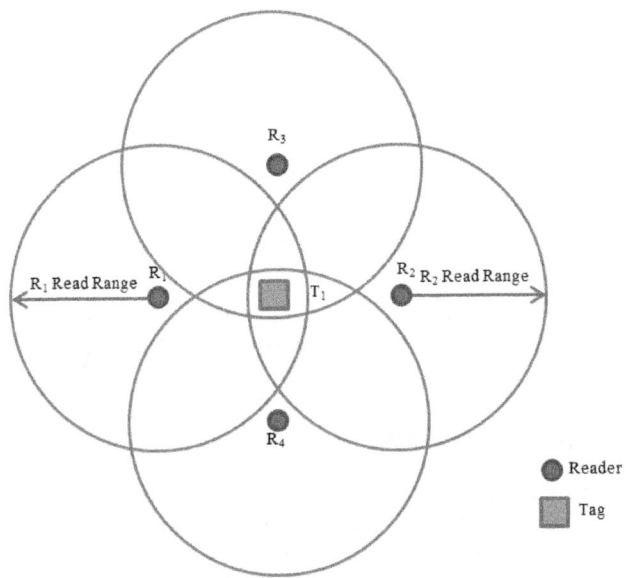

Fig. 3. Multiple readers to tag interference with read range overlapped

Many methods have been proposed to resolve the hidden terminal problem. Nan Li et al. [7] present *DCMA* (Dual Channel Multiple Access) protocol for active RFID systems with low power advantage. S Jain et al. [8] developed a CSMA-based MAC protocol to avoid reader-reader and reader-tag collisions in a dense RFID network. The network is implemented using mote-based RFID readers. Performance comparison was conducted with a Naive, a Random and the *CSMA* protocol. The evaluation shows much superior performance relative to a naive and a randomized protocol in dense deployment environments both in regards to accuracy and time per tag read. Xu Huang *et al.* [9] present an efficient dynamic framed slotted *ALOHA* protocol, which improves the performance of conventional *ALOHA* in high density environment. Choi *et al.* [10] presented performance comparison of another class of anti-collision protocol i.e. tree based protocols; bi-slotted query tree algorithm (*BSQTA*) and bi-slotted collision tracking tree algorithm (*BSCTTA*). Performance was measured on the basis of minimum time required to identify users accessing a common source. Maselli *et al.* [11]

proposed an optimized slotted *ALOHA* protocol for dynamic tag estimation in RFID networks. Muhammad U. Farooq *ey al.* [12] investigated the performance of multiple access protocols (*ALOHA* and *CSMA* protocols) used in RFID environments.

3 Priority Based Transaction Scheduling

To avoid reader collision in a high density environment, the nature of time division multiple access is employed to enforce reading RFID tags at different time slots and guarantee that readers do not interfere with each other. In addition, through registering the presence of new join/leave readers (in control channel) to a coordinating agent which is associated with the target RFID tag, all transactions between readers and tags can be performed in a contention-free manner. In this section, we introduce the *PBT* scheduling algorithm aimed at avoiding communication contention in a dynamic RFID system.

3.1 Motivating Example

Figure 4 shows an example of four readers R_1, R_2, R_3 and R_4 residing within the communication range reachable to the tag. However, each of them unable to communicate with others because it is beyond its sensing range. The hidden terminal problem, therefore, exists. It is expected that if the readers know existence of others, communications with tags will not be collided. Therefore, a coordinator reader (R_5) could be, on demand, associated with the target tag. Meanwhile, the coordinator can communicate with all of the readers who attempt to read the target tag. Namely, in this case the request readers ($R_1 \sim R_4$) can notify the coordinator (R_5) of their existence by sending beacon information. The coordinator keeps track of the total amount of readers and makes readers be informed in order to build their own transaction schedule locally.

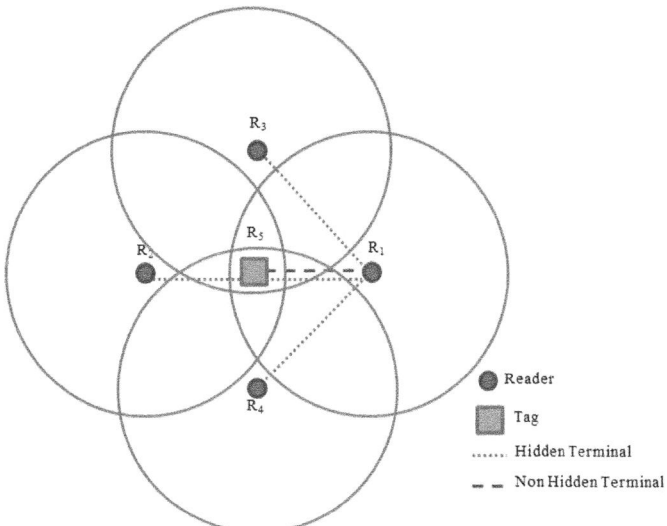

Fig. 4. An RFID network with coordinating reader (R_5)

The information of the RFID network is handled by a centralized coordinator while scheduling reader-tag transactions is distributed and self-determined locally, the proposed technique is classified as a semi-distributed algorithm, which has the following characteristics. Each request reader sends a beacon through the control channel to the corresponding coordinator, notifying its attempt to communicate with a tag before transmitting data. The coordinating reader learns the beacon's source address according to the received frame. Then, it informs existing readers of the fact that a new prime number (i.e., representing a priority factor) is assigned by sending a reply to the beacon. In this way, if two or more readers transmit data with a tag at the same time slot and cause communication conflict, the time slot with the larger prime number will have higher priority than small ones.

Time-slot	1	2	3	4	5	6	7	8	9	10
Reader		R_1	R_2	R_1		R_2		R_1	R_2	R_1
Time-slot	11	12	13	14	15	16	17	18	19	20
Reader		R_2		R_1	R_2	R_1		R_2		R_1

(a)

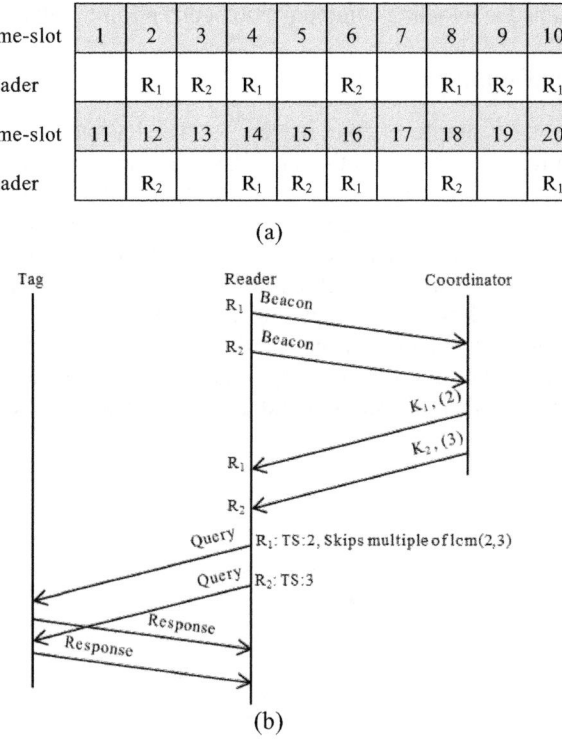

(b)

Fig. 5. Priority based transaction scheduling: (a) example of time slot allocation (b) interaction between reader and coordinator

Figure 5(a) gives an example showing that R_1 has been assigned time slots with multiples of prime number 2 for performing transactions, while R_2 uses multiples of prime number 3. Namely, R_1 transmits data with tag at time slots t_2, t_4, t_6 and t_8, etc. while R_2 transmits data with a tag every three time units (i.e., t_3, t_6, t_9, t_{12}, etc...). The complete interaction between RFID readers and coordinator is shown in Figure 5(b). It is obvious that readers joined the network earlier will be assigned a lower prime number, representing the use of a lower priority time slot. This strategy reflects the fact that the *PBT* design is based on a consideration of maintaining a fairness transaction and to prevent starvation that could have happened to RFID readers which joined late. Regarding the concept of larger prime number with higher priority, reader R_2 will have the ordinary transmission schedule based on prime number 3. For reader R_1, multiples of the $lcm(2, 3)$, e.g., t_6 and t_{12} are regarded as conflict slots and will be preempted by reader R_2 as it collided with higher priority slots. The complete interaction between RFID readers and coordinator is shown in Figure 5(b).

For readers dynamically join a network, following the circumstance of last example given in Figure 5, Figure 6(a) shows the distribution of time slots after reader R_3 joined the network. Because higher prime number are with higher priority, reader R_3 keeps an ordinary transaction schedule based on prime number 5 and preempts time slots that are multiples of $lcm(2, 5)$ and $lcm(3, 5)$ from readers R_1 and R_2, respectively.

For reader leave, given a snapshot of RFID system with n readers, $R1$, $R2$, ..., Rn residing in the network. Assume that the associated time slots for these readers are $k1$, $k2$, ..., kn, respectively, and $Rleave = Ri$, where $1 \leq i \leq n$. The dynamic adjustment of scheduling transactions will be performed with synchronization among the remaining readers. There are three different circumstances in dynamic scheduling. Firstly, for reader Rj whose id is smaller than i, i.e., $j < i$, it resets time slots that are multiples of $lcm(kj, kn)$ to 'valid'. Secondly, for reader Rj whose id is larger than i, i.e., $j > i$ and $j \neq n$, it switches its time slot from kj to $kj–1$ and sets all time slots that are in conflict with primes kj, $kj + 1$, ..., $kn – 1$ to 'invalid'. Thirdly, if $Rj = Rn$, the only change is to switch its transaction from kn-based time slots to $kn – 1$-based slots.

Time-slot	1	2	3	4	5	6	7	8	9	10
Reader		R_1	R_2	R_1	R_3	R_2	R_4	R_1	R_2	R_3
Time-slot	11	12	13	14	15	16	17	18	19	20
Reader		R_2		R_4	R_3	R_1		R_2		R_3

Fig. 6. Distribution of time slots after reader R_3 joined

Given an example, readers R_1, R_2, R_3 and R_4 are considered as prior existing readers in the RFID network as shown in Figure 7(a). Reader R_2 is assumed to be the one finished transaction with the tag and going to leave. Once R_2 leaves the network, reader R_1 enables time slots that are multiples of $lcm(2, 7)$ because prime number 7 will be reclaimed; reader R_3 switches its time slot from prime number 5 to prime number 3 and disables all time slots that conflict with prime 5. For reader R_4, it reset its time slot from prime number 7 to prime number 5 as shown in Figure 7(b).

Time-slot	1	2	3	4	5	6	7	8	9	10
Reader		R_1	R_2	R_1	R_3	R_2	R_4	R_1	R_2	R_3
Time-slot	11	12	13	14	15	16	17	18	19	20
Reader		R_2		R_4	R_3	R_1		R_2		R_3

(a)

Time-slot	1	2	3	4	5	6	7	8	9	10
Reader		R_1	R_3	R_1	R_4	R_3		R_1	R_3	R_4
Time-slot	11	12	13	14	15	16	17	18	19	20
Reader		R_3		R_1	R_4	R_1		R_3		R_4

(b)

Fig. 7. Distribution of time slots when reader leave (a) before R_2 leave (b) after R_2 leave

4   Priority Based Transaction with Multiple Primes

Owning the observations of low utilization of time slots in the *PBT* scheme, for ex-
ample, time slot t_1 is always idle; time slots t_5, t_7, t_{11}, t_{13}, t_{17}, t_{19}, remain idle in
low-density environment; an enhanced algorithm of the *PBT* scheme is proposed which
adds the following characteristics:

●   Time slot t_1 will be used by the one who was assigned to use prime number 2.
●   Multiple prime numbers could be assigned to one reader.

The idea of taking multiple primes is to fully utilize time slots in reader-tag communications. Given an example of RFID systems in which a reader needs to transmit data
m times with the desire tag to complete a transaction. To guarantee a 100% efficiency,
all time slots smaller than m could be taken by the same reader if only one exists in the
environment. As time slots of the *PBT* scheme is assigned based on prime numbers, that
means all primes smaller than m should be taken by the reader. Considering the environment with multiple reader, for example, n readers, all of the readers will need $n*m$
time slots to complete the n transactions. Thus all primes smaller than $n*m$ should be
applied among the n readers. In the *PBT-MP* scheme, a round-robin distribution of the
time slots is employed.

The algorithm of reader join in *PBT-MP* is given as follows:

//Coordinator procedure
seq = total numbers of readers in the network; //inital zero

if (new join beacon received) { //new reader join
    seq++; //increase total number of readers
   send *seq* to all readers; //notify presence readers
   }

//**Reader procedure**
//Activated upon new reader join, R_{seq} is the rank of one reader, initial zero
//Assume primes of reader $R_1,R_2,R_3,...$ are $k_1[],k_2[],k_3[],...$, respectively

if (R_{seq} == 0) { //the new join reader
  send "join" beacon to coordinator;
  receive beacon reply associated with the serial number seq;
  $R_{seq} = seq$;
} else { //presence readers
  receive beacon reply associated with the serial number seq;
}

$myrank = R_{seq}$;

while (tag transmission not complete) {
    if (ts == 1 && $myrank$ == 1) { //ts is current time slot
        receive data packet from tag;
    } else if ($myrank$ == seq) { //new reader join
        $flag = ts$ % $k_{myrank}[]$; //$k_{seq}[]$ are the prime of reader R_{myrank}
                        //flae == 0, ts is reader R_{myrank}'s time slot
        while ($flag > 0$); //skip lock
        receive data packet from tag;
    } else {
        $flag = ts$ % $k_{myrank}[]$; //flae == 0, ts is reader R_{myrank}'s time slot
        $suc\_slot = \prod_{j=myrank+1}^{seq} ts$ % $kj[]$;
        //suc_slot == 0, ts is time slot one of reader R_{id}'s successor readers
        while ($flag > 0$ || $suc\_slot == 0$); // skip lock
        receive data packet from tag;
    }
}

The algorithm of reader leave in *PBT-MP* is given as follows:

//**Coordinator procedure**
seq = total numbers of readers in the network;

if (receive leace beacon from reader R_i) { //reader R_i leave
    seq--; //decrease total number of readers
  send (seq,i) to all readers; //notify presence readers
  }

//**Reader procedure**
//Activated upon reader leave, *myrank* is the rank of one reader

receive beacon reply (seq,i);

if ($myrank > i$) { //successor readers of R_i
  $myrank$--; //upgrade its priority
}

sync(); //reset time slot = 1

```
if ( R_seq == 0 ) { //the new join reader
    send "join" beacon to coordinator;
    receive beacon reply associated with the serial number seq;
    R_seq = seq;
} else { //presence readers
    receive beacon reply associated with the serial number seq;
}
```

$myrank = R_{seq};$

```
while ( tag transmission not complete ) {
    if ( ts == 1 && myrank == 1) {
        receive data packet from tag;
    } else {
        flag = ts % k_myrank[];
        suc_slot = Π_{j=myrank+1}^{seq} ts % kj[];
        while ( flag > 0 || suc_slot == 0 ); // skip lock
        receive data packet from tag;
    }
}
```

5 Performance Evaluation

To evaluate the performance of proposed techniques, we have implemented the
PBT-MP method along with the *PBT* scheduling scheme. Both static and dynamic
circumstances were conducted in our simulations. Each test sample was executed 30
times to obtain a mean value.

5.1 Performance Metrics

To simplify the presentation, Table 1 summarizes notations and terminologies used in
our experiments.

5.2 Effect of R^{system} in Static Network

With the conditions of $\Delta = 9$ and $R^{system} = 1 \sim 80$, Figure 9 gives the performance
comparisons of the *PBT-MP(k)* and ordinary *PBT* scheme. The y-axis presents efficiency (%) and x-axis represents the number of readers in RFID network (R^{system}). The
value of k in *PBT-MP(k)* represents how many primes are assigned to each reader. In
low-density environment, the *PBT* achieves only 50%~80% efficiency. In high-density
environment, the *PBT* can reach 80%-90% efficiency. It is obvious that the *PBT-MP(3)*
and *PBT-MP(4)* present better efficiency than the ordinary *PBT* scheme. In most cases,
both *PBT-MP(3)* and *PBT-MP(4)* can achieve 100% efficiency due to the fully utilized
time slots with multiple primes.

Table 1. Definitions of notations and terminologies

R_{init}	Initially, the number of readers in a given RFID network
$R_{tm,\ tn}^{join}$	Numbers of readers which joined the network during time period tm ~ tn
$R_{tm,\ tn}^{system}$	$R_{tm,\ tn}^{system} = R_{init} + R_{tm,\ tn}^{system}$
N_{succ}	Number of time slots at which reader transmits data with tag successfully
N_{idle}	Number of time slots at which no reader performs transaction
$N_{collide}$	Number of time slots at which collision happened
N_{fail}	$N_{fail} = N_{idle} + N_{collide}$
$T_{complete}$	The completion time for all readers finished data transmission with tag
$T_{deadline}$	A given time limit for experiment
$\emptyset^3$	Number of time slots at which system is empty before $T_{complete}$
N_{free}	$N_{free} = T_{deadline} - (N_{succ} + N_{fail})$, i.e., number of time slots during time interval $(T_{complete},\ T_{deadline})$
N_{in_use}	The total number of time slots before $T_{complete}$
	$N_{in\_use} = T_{deadline} - T_{deadline}$
Δ	An integer value, representing the number of transactions should be performed by an RFID reader
K	Every RDIF reader can used the number of K smallest prime numbers
P	RFID reader have a P% probability to join the network at each time slot
Throughput	The value of N_{succ} before $T_{deadline}$
Efficiency	In static network,
	Efficiency $= R^{system} \times \Delta / T_{complete}$
	In dynamic network,
	Efficiency $= R^{system} \times \Delta / T_{complete} - \emptyset$

5.3   Effect of R^{system} in Dynamic Network

For dynamic circumstance, parameters of $\Delta = 9$, $R_{init} = 60$ and $P = 5$ are set in our experiments. Figure 10 show efficiency (%) of the *PBT* and *PBT-MP(k)* approaches. The x-axis represents 1000 time slots. The system read rate of the *PBT-MP(4)* maintains 100% efficiency at all time slot from 1 to 1000. Figures 11 and 12 are given to describe the stability of the *PBT-MP(k)* scheme in dynamic environments. The x-axis in both figures represent the order of RFID readers join the network. The y-axis in Figure 11 indicates the order a reader completes its work. From Figure 11 we can see that *PBT-MP(k)* presents more stable results reflecting a FCFS principle while the *PBT* method cannot guarantee the completion order of the readers. Figure 12 reports the waiting time of the two methods in dynamic RFID systems. It is also noticed that the *PBT-MP(k)* method has superior performance to the ordinary *PBT* scheme.

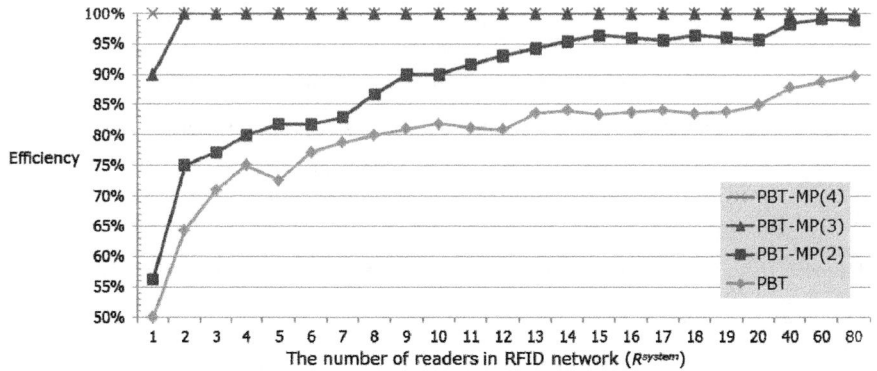

Fig. 9. Effect of R^{system} in static network

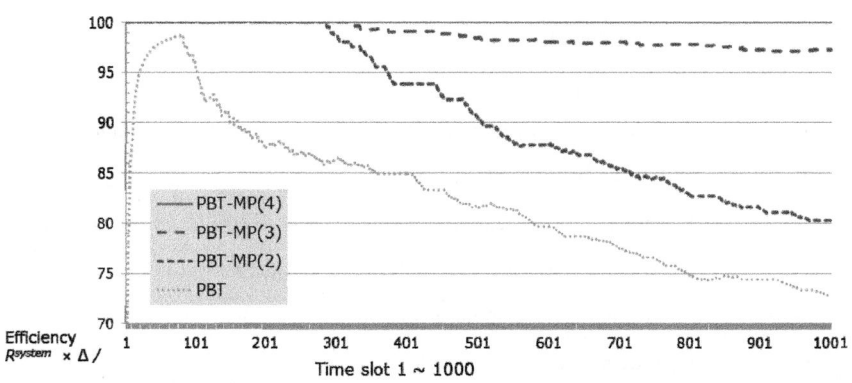

Fig. 10. Effect of R^{system} in dynamic network

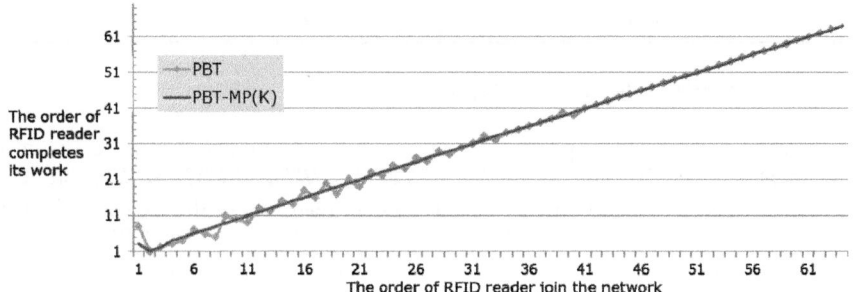

Fig. 11. Each RFID reader to complete the work order in dynamic network

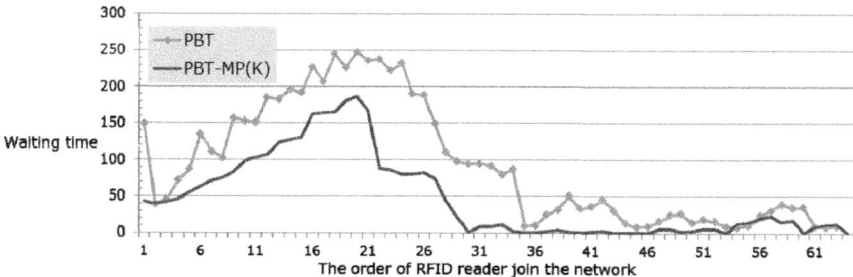

Fig. 12. RFID reader total waiting time before complete the work in dynamic network

Table 2 outlines the efficiency of the *PBT-MP* and *PBT* schemes in both low-density and high-density environments. From the above observation, both methods present its nature in avoiding reader collision. For read rate efficiency, the *PBT* achieves up to 80% efficiency in low density systems. In high density environments, the *PBT* performs at least 90% efficiency which is much better than that in low density environments. On the other hand, the *PBT-MP* can maintain a 100% efficiency in both low-and high-density environments.

Table 2. Comparisons of the *PBT-MP* and *PBT* in term of efficiency

Method	Low-density	High-density	Anti-collision
PBT-MP	100%	100%	Yes
PBT	< 80%	> 90%	Yes

6   Conclusions

RFID technologies help to advance next generation wireless communication. A RFID reader could be planted into a cell phone or PDA after compressing to use as sensor to RFID tag for information gathering. When a RFID tag is sensed, we can easily get the information required on a cell phone or PDA through the RFID tag at anytime and anywhere. With the increasing use of RFID applications, high reader density and mobility are two major features in future RFID systems. From this point of view, the condensed RFID network incurs reader collision problems, while the movement of readers brings out signal interference and prevents correct information reading in a dynamic environment.

In this paper, we have presented a *PBT–MP* scheduling technique for coordinating simultaneous transmissions among multiple readers and to increase the overall read rate in RFID system. The *PBT-MP* is a semi-distributed mechanism that employs a dual channel communication scheme. It overcomes the problem of hidden terminals in RFID systems and provides a contention-free communication method based on priority scheduling. The experimental results show that the proposed technique provides superior and stable performance in both static and dynamic environments. The *PBT* is shown to be effective in terms of system throughput and efficiency. In addition, the *PBT* scheduling technique is capable of scalability under high density and mobility networks.

References

[1] Hsu, C.-H., Chen, S.-C., Yu, C.-H.: A Priority Based Trans-action Mechanism towards High Reliable RFID Services. International Journal of Ad-Hoc and Ubiquitous Computing (IJAHUC), 323–333 (2009)

[2] Chen, W.-T., Ho, T.-W., Chen, Y.-C.: An MAC protocol for wireless ad-hoc networks using smart antennas. In: Proceedings of the 11th IEEE International Conference on Parallel and Distributed Systems (ICPADS 2005), pp. 446–452 (2005)

[3] You, T., Hassanein, H., Yeh, C.-H.: PIDC – towards an ideal mac protocol for multi-hop wireless LANs. In: Proceedings of the IEEE International Conference on Wireless Networks Communications and Mobile Computing, pp. 655–660 (2005)

[4] Jain, N., Das, S.R., Nasipuri, A.: A multichannel CSMA MAC protocol with receiver-based channel selection for multihop wireless networks. In: Proceedings of the 10th IEEE International Conference on Computer Communications and Networks, pp. 432–439.

[5] Engels, D.W., Sarma, S.E.: The reader collision problem. In: Proceedings of the 2002 IEEE International Conference on Systems, Man and Cybernetics, p. 6 (2002)

[6] Ho, J.J., Engels, D.W., Sarma, S.E.: HiQ: a hierarchical Q-learning algorithm to solve the reader collision problem. In: Proceedings of the International Symposium on Applications and the Internet Workshops (SAINTW 2006), pp. 88–91 (2006)

[7] Li, N., Duan, X., Wu, Y., Hua, S., Jiao, B.: An Anti-Collision Algorithm for Active RFID. In: Wireless Communications, Networking and Mobile Computing, pp. 1–4 (2006)

[8] Jain, S., Das, S.R.: Collision Avoidance in a Dense RFID Network, Stony Brook. In: International Conference on Mobile Computing and Networking, pp. 49–56 (2006)

[9] Hang, X., Le, S.: Efficient dynamic framed Slotted ALOHA for RFID Passive tags. In: The 9th International Conference on Advanced Communication Technology, pp. 94–97 (2007)

[10] Choi, J.H., Lee, D., Jeon, H., Cha, J., Lee, H.: Enhanced Binary Search with Time-Divided Responses for Efficient RFID Tag Anti-Collision. In: IEEE International Conference on Communications, ICC 2007, pp. 3853–3858 (2007)

[11] Maselli, G., Petrioli, C., Vicari, C.: Dynamic Tag Estimation for Optimizing Tree Slotted Aloha in RFID Networks. In: International Workshop on Modeling Analysis and Simulation of Wireless and Mobile Systems, pp. 315–322 (2008)

[12] Farooq, M.U., Asif, M., Azeemi, N.Z.: Performance Evaluation of Multiple Access Protocols for RFID Testbed Environment. In: Ultra Modern Telecommunications & Workshops, pp. 1–7 (2009)

Author Index